OFF SEASON

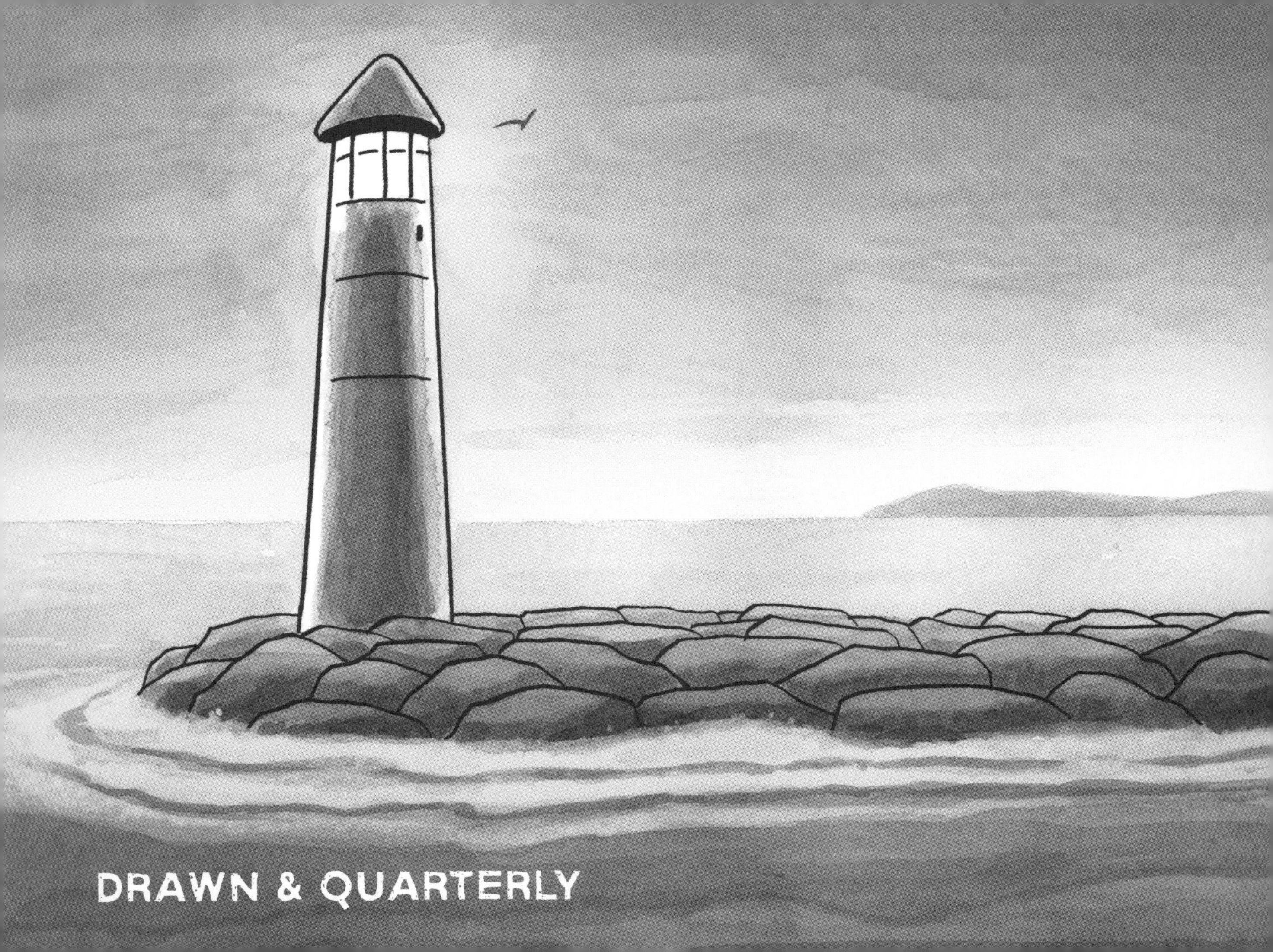
DRAWN & QUARTERLY

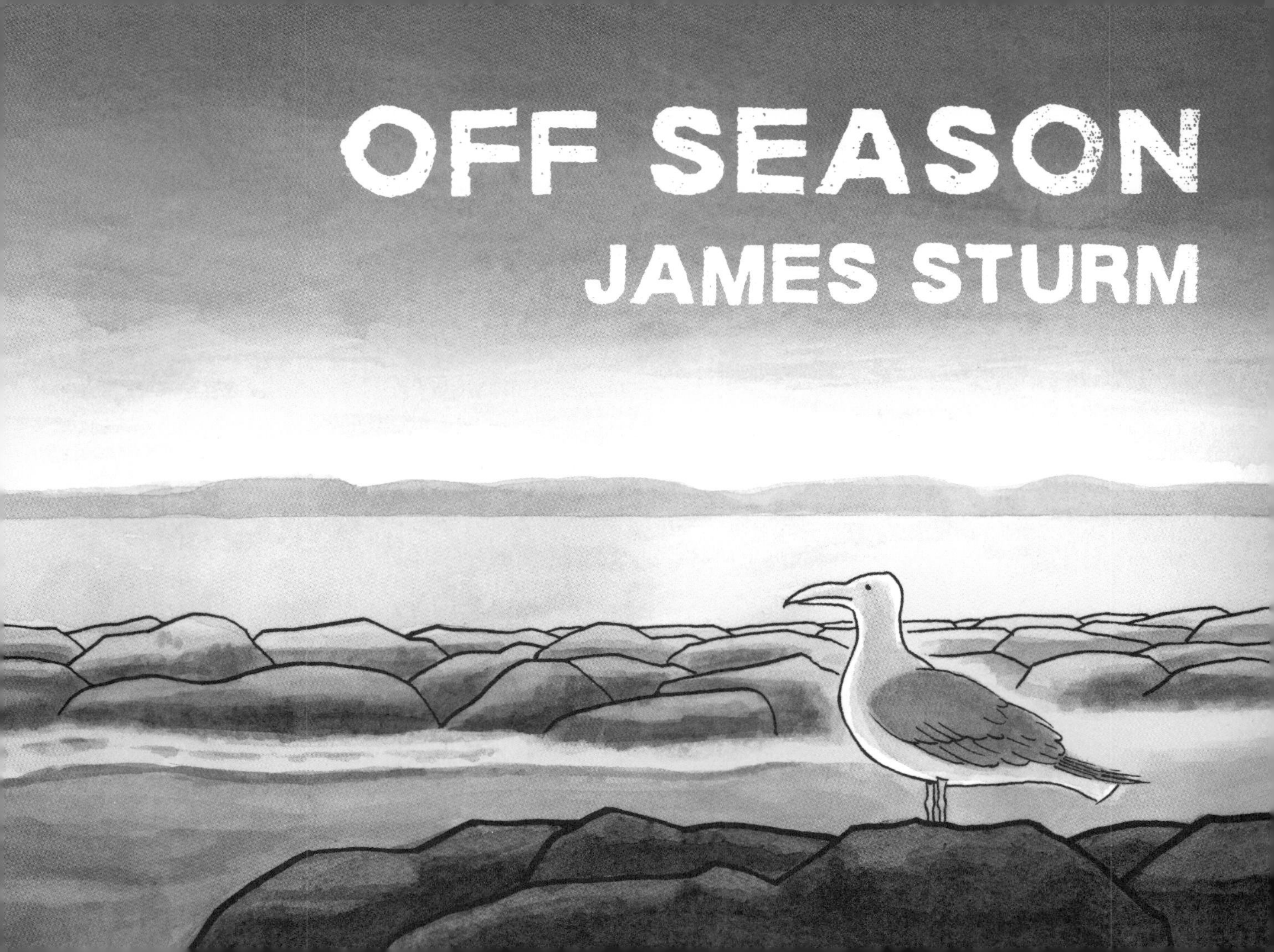
OFF SEASON
JAMES STURM

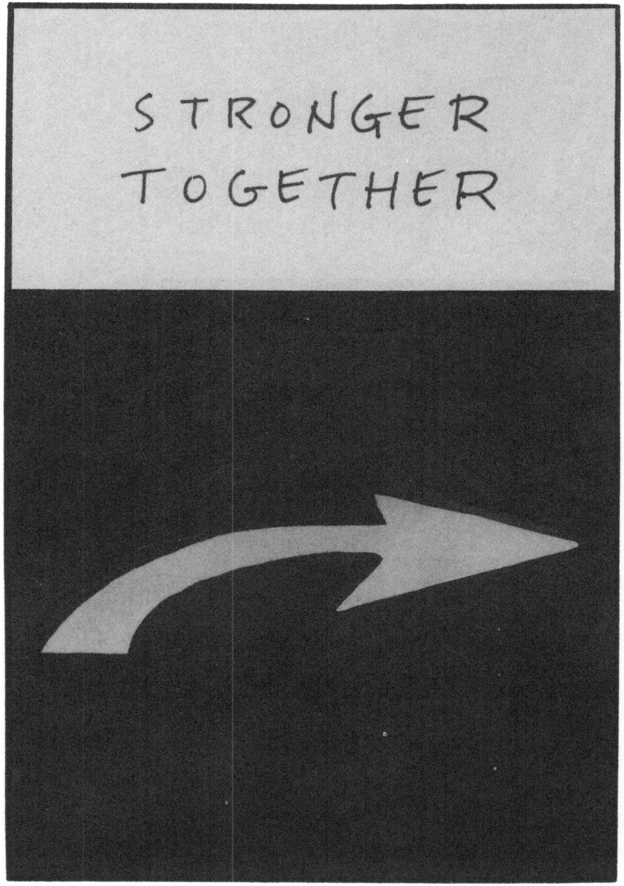
STRONGER
TOGETHER

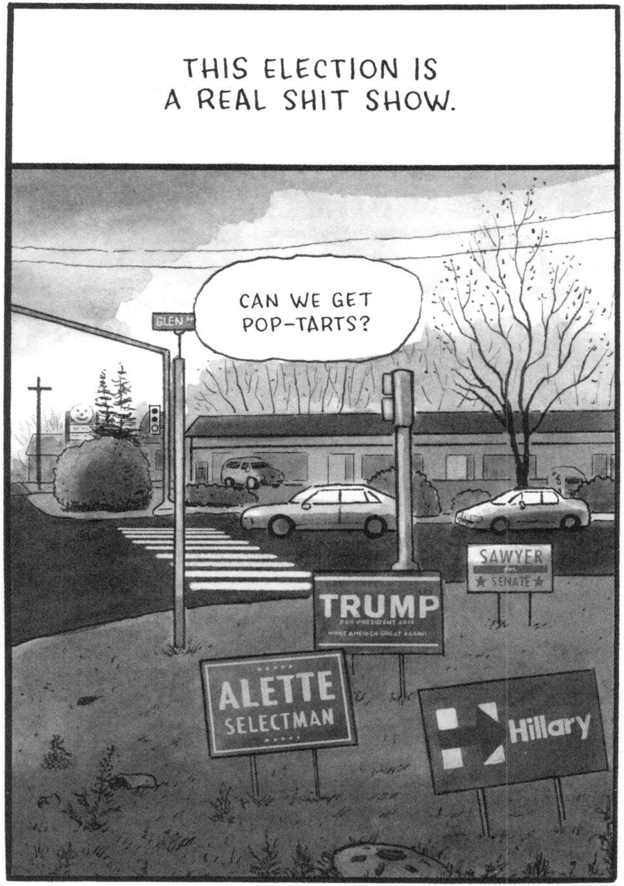
THIS ELECTION IS
A REAL SHIT SHOW.
CAN WE GET
POP-TARTS?
GLEN
SAWYER
SENATE
TRUMP
ALETTE
SELECTMAN
Hillary

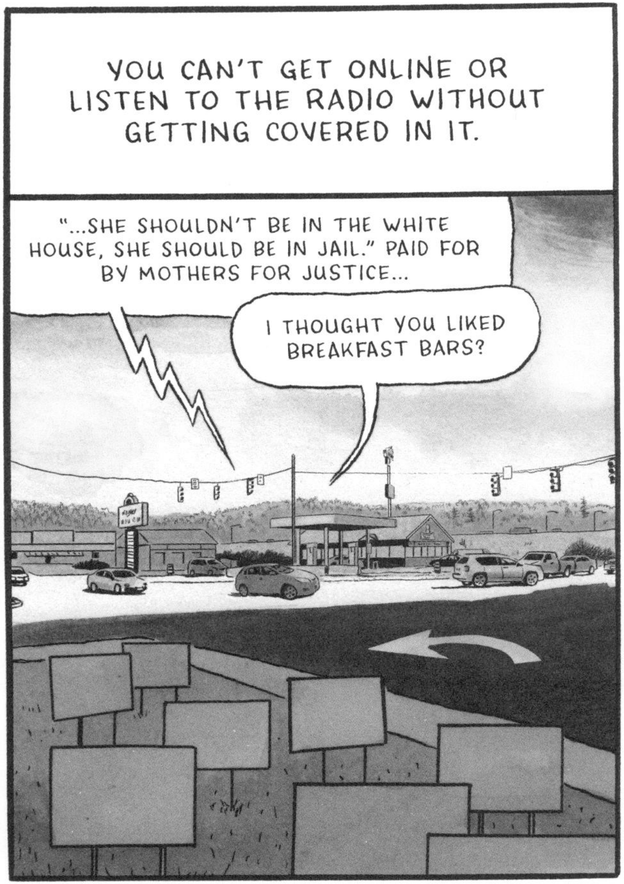
YOU CAN'T GET ONLINE OR LISTEN TO THE RADIO WITHOUT GETTING COVERED IN IT.
"...SHE SHOULDN'T BE IN THE WHITE HOUSE, SHE SHOULD BE IN JAIL." PAID FOR BY MOTHERS FOR JUSTICE...
I THOUGHT YOU LIKED BREAKFAST BARS?

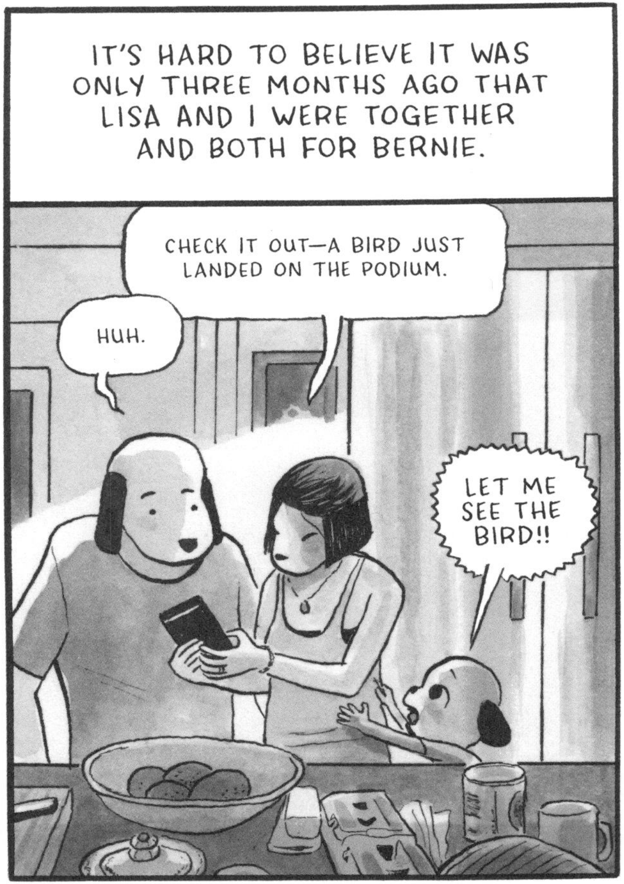
IT'S HARD TO BELIEVE IT WAS ONLY THREE MONTHS AGO THAT LISA AND I WERE TOGETHER AND BOTH FOR BERNIE.
CHECK IT OUT—A BIRD JUST LANDED ON THE PODIUM.
HUH.
LET ME SEE THE BIRD!!

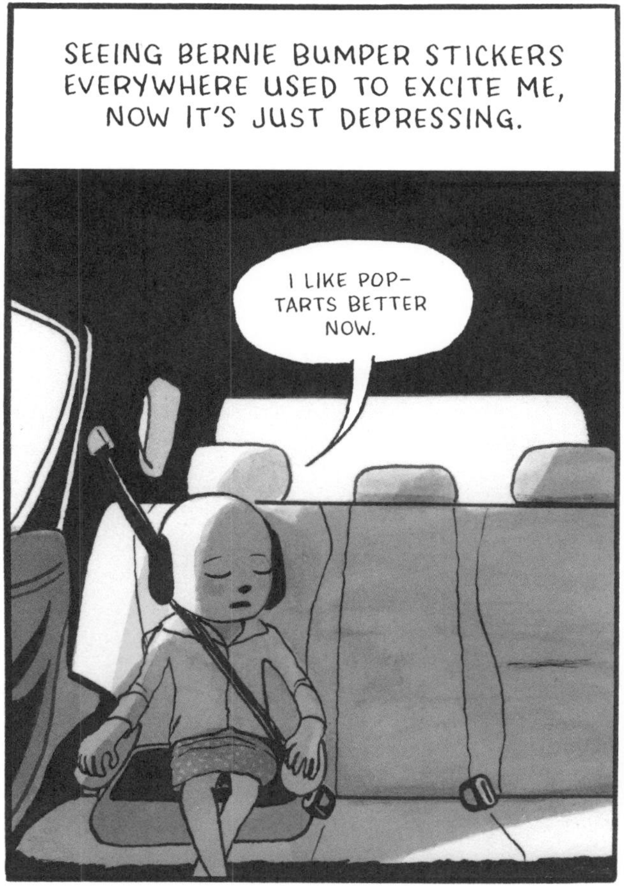
SEEING BERNIE BUMPER STICKERS EVERYWHERE USED TO EXCITE ME, NOW IT'S JUST DEPRESSING.
I LIKE POP-TARTS BETTER NOW.

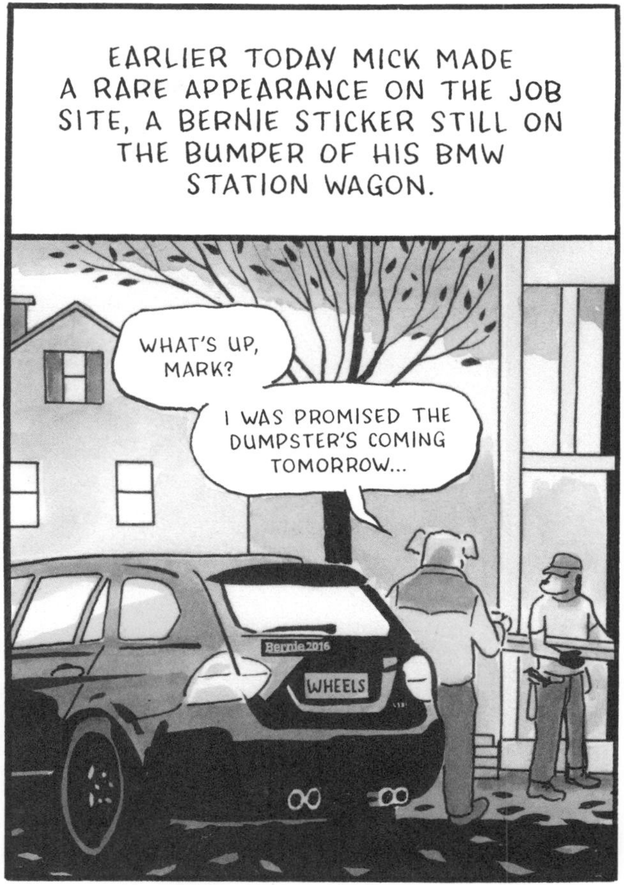
EARLIER TODAY MICK MADE A RARE APPEARANCE ON THE JOB SITE, A BERNIE STICKER STILL ON THE BUMPER OF HIS BMW STATION WAGON.
WHAT'S UP, MARK?
I WAS PROMISED THE DUMPSTER'S COMING TOMORROW...
Bernie 2016
WHEELS

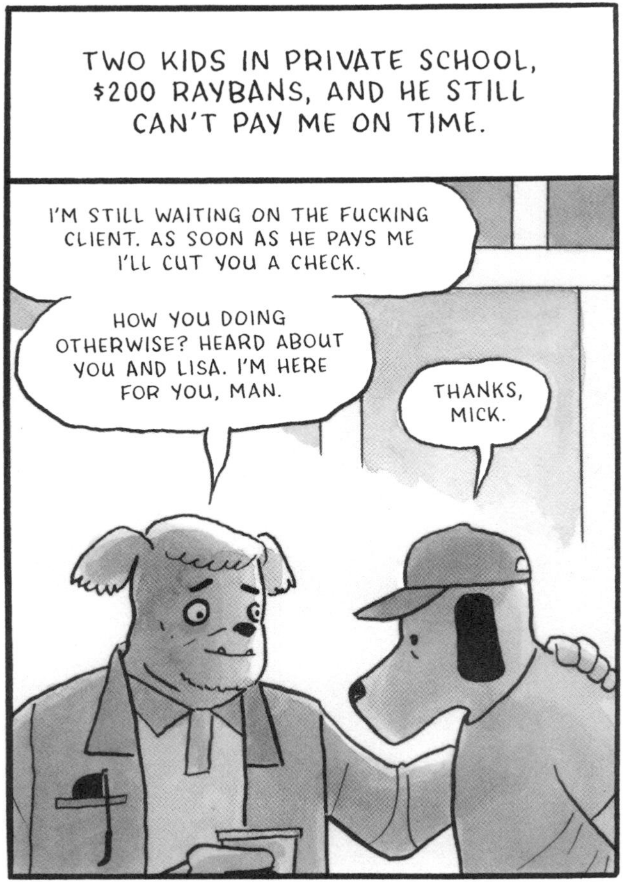
TWO KIDS IN PRIVATE SCHOOL, $200 RAYBANS, AND HE STILL CAN'T PAY ME ON TIME.
I'M STILL WAITING ON THE FUCKING CLIENT. AS SOON AS HE PAYS ME I'LL CUT YOU A CHECK.
HOW YOU DOING OTHERWISE? HEARD ABOUT YOU AND LISA. I'M HERE FOR YOU, MAN.
THANKS, MICK.

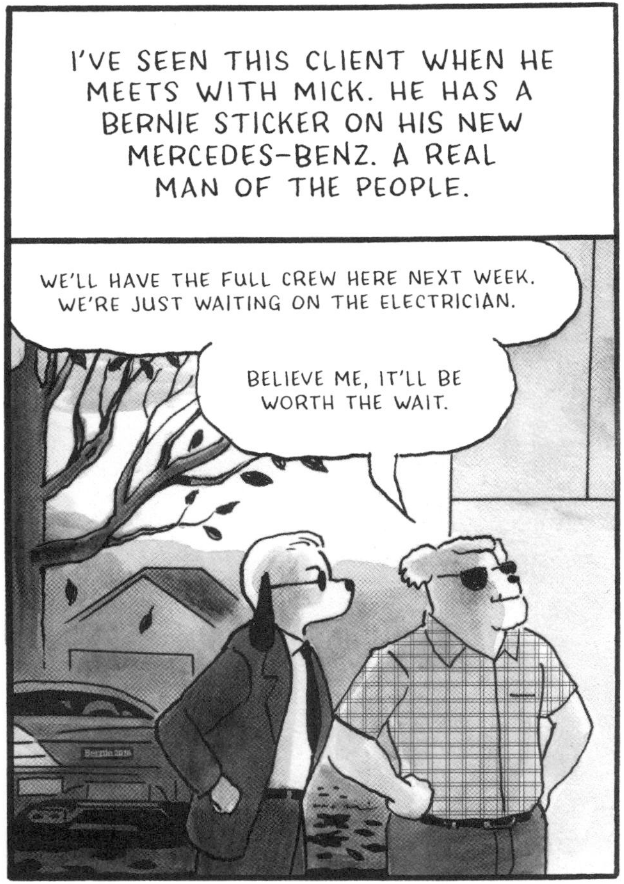
I'VE SEEN THIS CLIENT WHEN HE MEETS WITH MICK. HE HAS A BERNIE STICKER ON HIS NEW MERCEDES-BENZ. A REAL MAN OF THE PEOPLE.
WE'LL HAVE THE FULL CREW HERE NEXT WEEK. WE'RE JUST WAITING ON THE ELECTRICIAN.
BELIEVE ME, IT'LL BE WORTH THE WAIT.

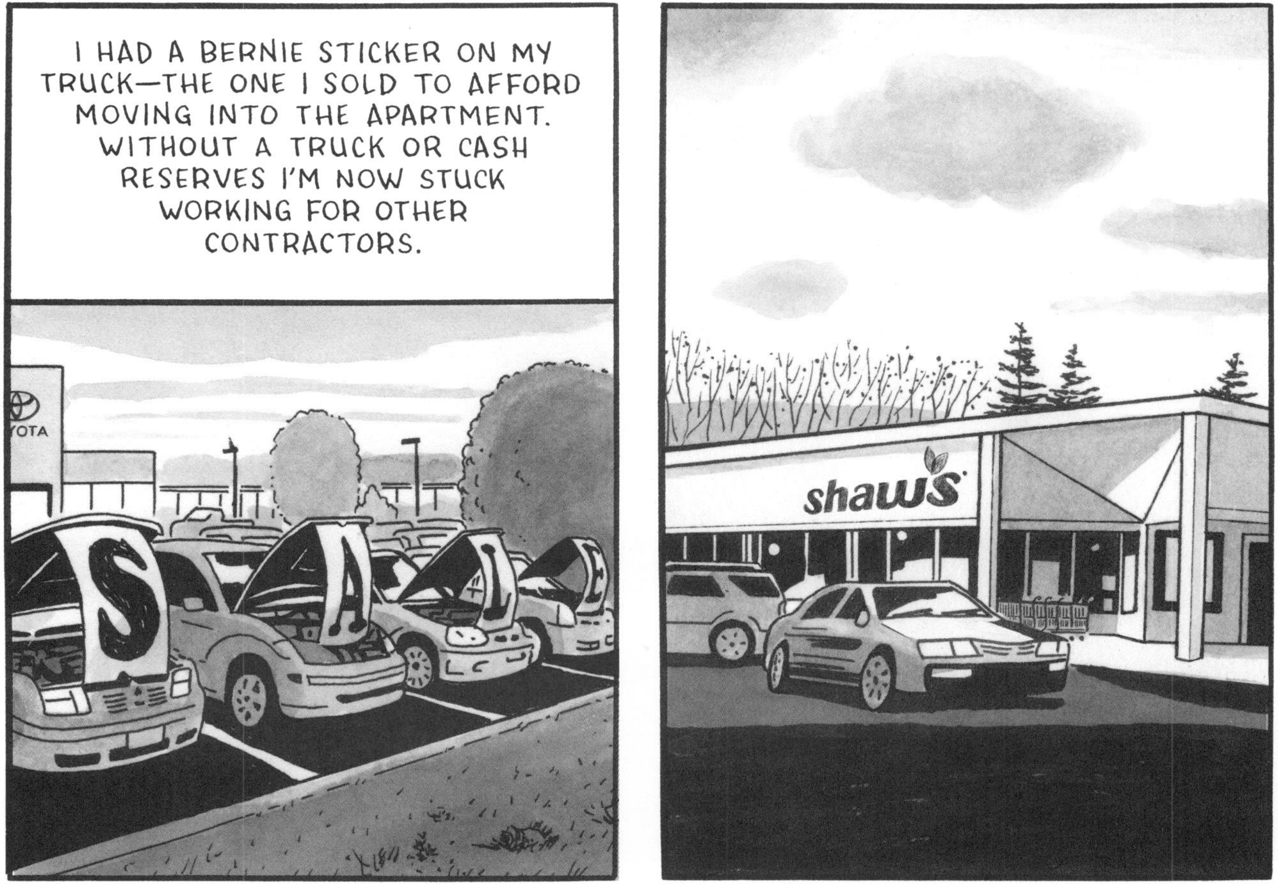
I HAD A BERNIE STICKER ON MY TRUCK—THE ONE I SOLD TO AFFORD MOVING INTO THE APARTMENT. WITHOUT A TRUCK OR CASH RESERVES I'M NOW STUCK WORKING FOR OTHER CONTRACTORS.
shaw's

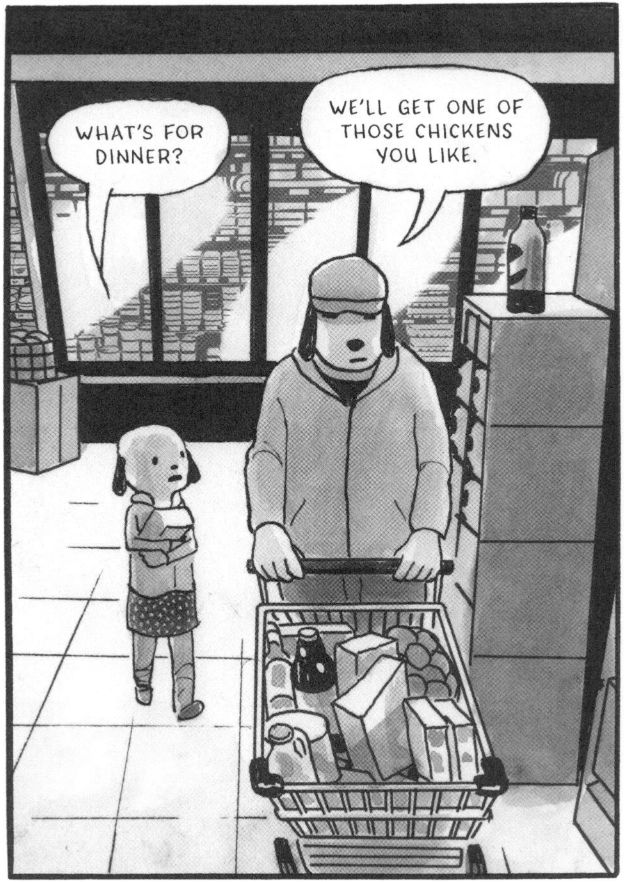
WHAT'S FOR DINNER?
WE'LL GET ONE OF THOSE CHICKENS YOU LIKE.

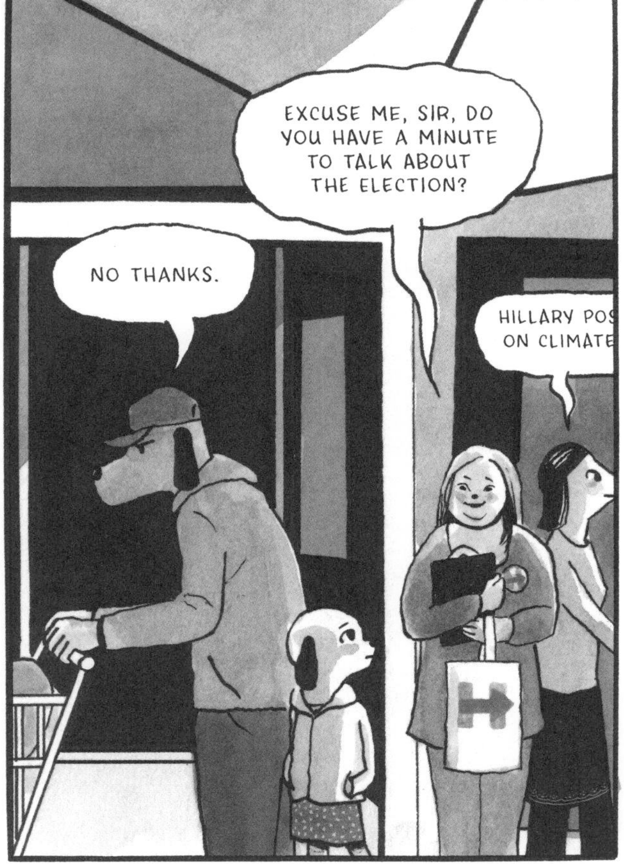
EXCUSE ME, SIR, DO YOU HAVE A MINUTE TO TALK ABOUT THE ELECTION?
NO THANKS.

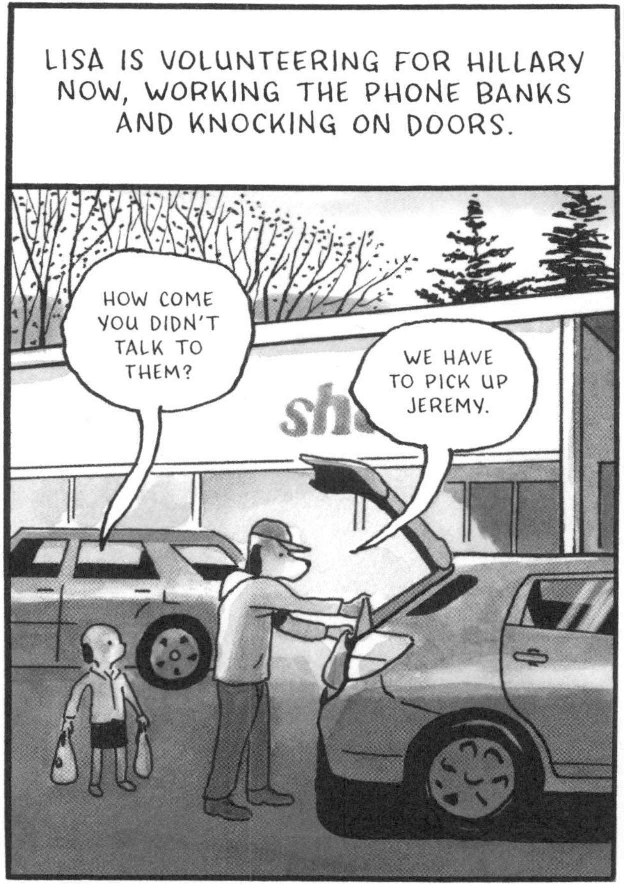
LISA IS VOLUNTEERING FOR HILLARY NOW, WORKING THE PHONE BANKS AND KNOCKING ON DOORS.
HOW COME YOU DIDN'T TALK TO THEM?
WE HAVE TO PICK UP JEREMY.

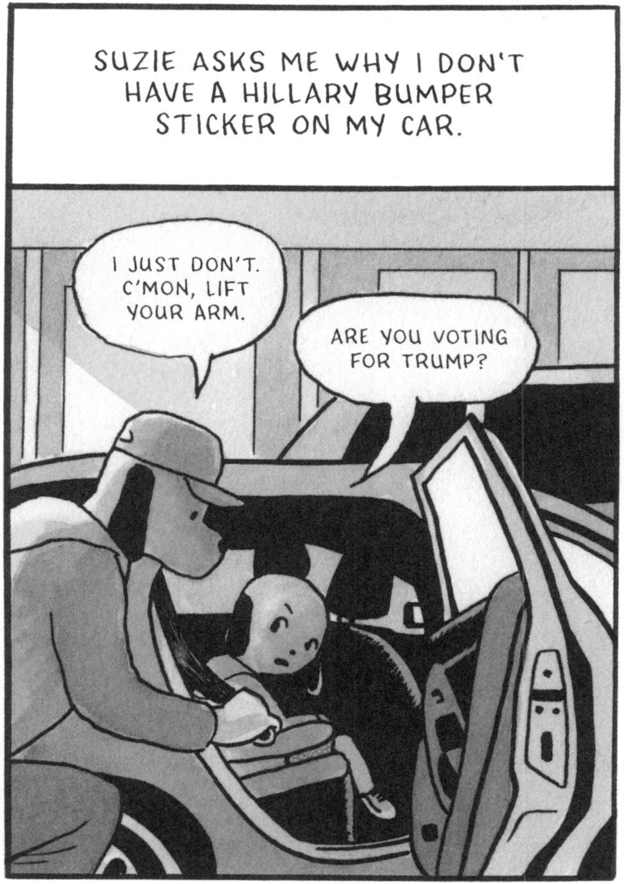
SUZIE ASKS ME WHY I DON'T HAVE A HILLARY BUMPER STICKER ON MY CAR.
I JUST DON'T. C'MON, LIFT YOUR ARM.
ARE YOU VOTING FOR TRUMP?

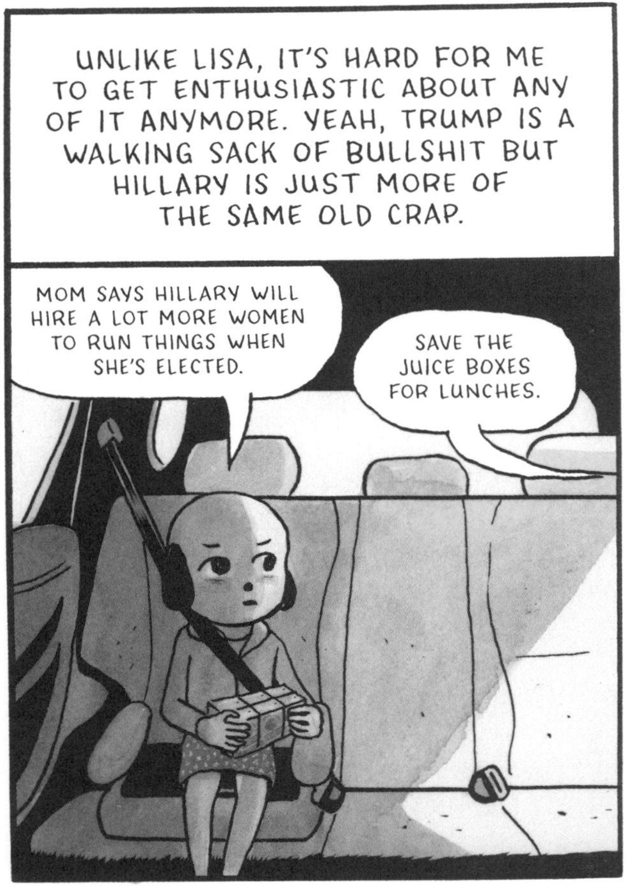
UNLIKE LISA, IT'S HARD FOR ME TO GET ENTHUSIASTIC ABOUT ANY OF IT ANYMORE. YEAH, TRUMP IS A WALKING SACK OF BULLSHIT BUT HILLARY IS JUST MORE OF THE SAME OLD CRAP.
MOM SAYS HILLARY WILL HIRE A LOT MORE WOMEN TO RUN THINGS WHEN SHE'S ELECTED.
SAVE THE JUICE BOXES FOR LUNCHES.

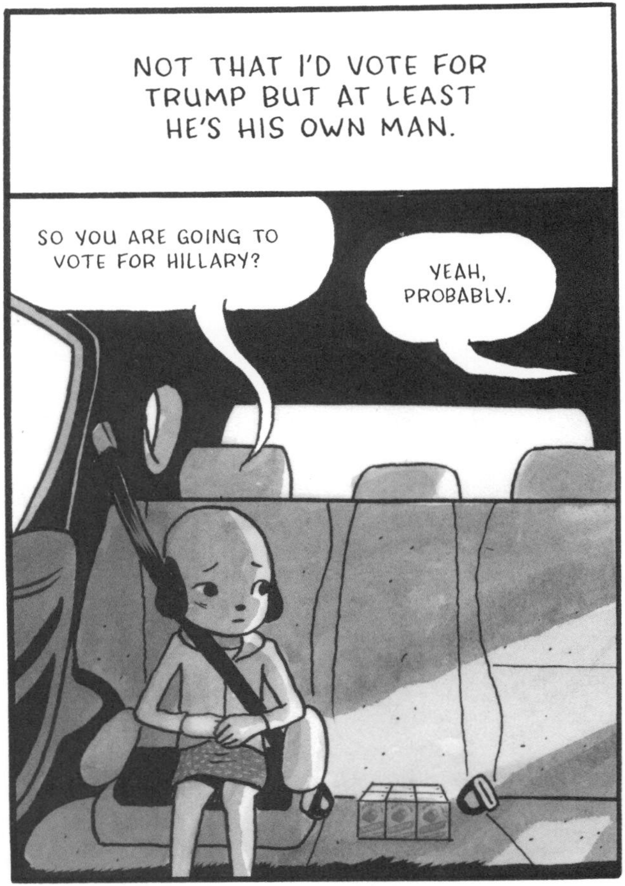
NOT THAT I'D VOTE FOR TRUMP BUT AT LEAST HE'S HIS OWN MAN.
SO YOU ARE GOING TO VOTE FOR HILLARY?
YEAH, PROBABLY.

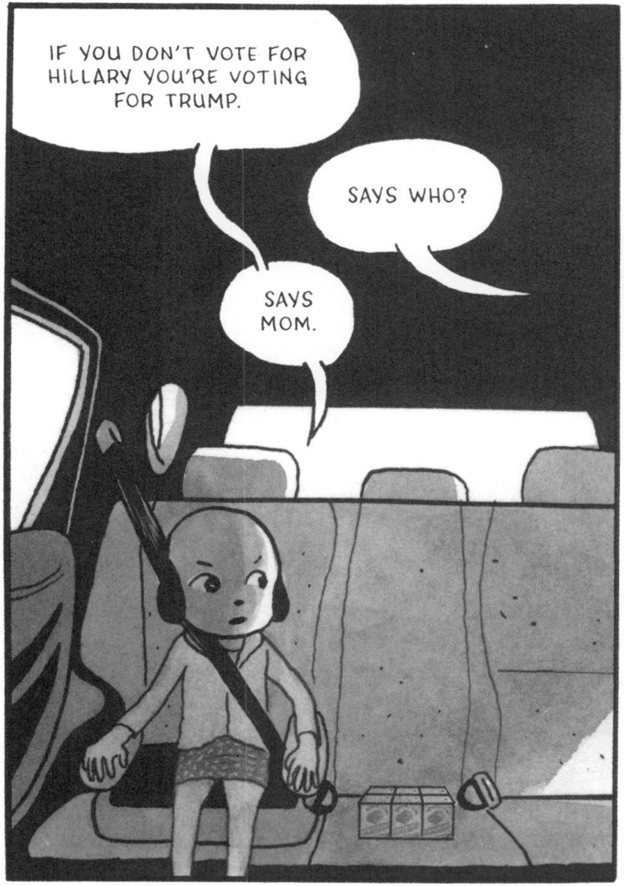
IF YOU DON'T VOTE FOR HILLARY YOU'RE VOTING FOR TRUMP.
SAYS WHO?
SAYS MOM.

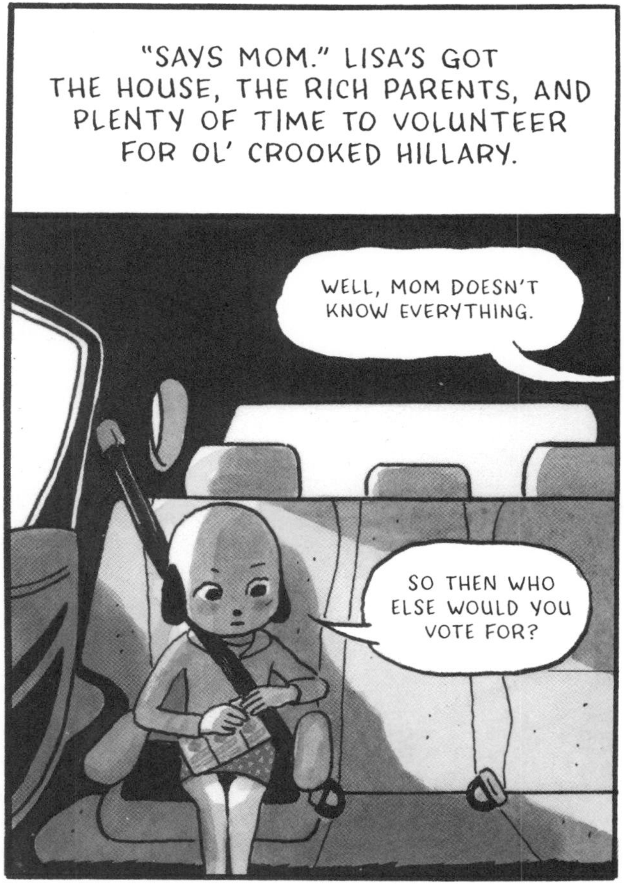
"SAYS MOM." LISA'S GOT THE HOUSE, THE RICH PARENTS, AND PLENTY OF TIME TO VOLUNTEER FOR OL' CROOKED HILLARY.
WELL, MOM DOESN'T KNOW EVERYTHING.
SO THEN WHO ELSE WOULD YOU VOTE FOR?

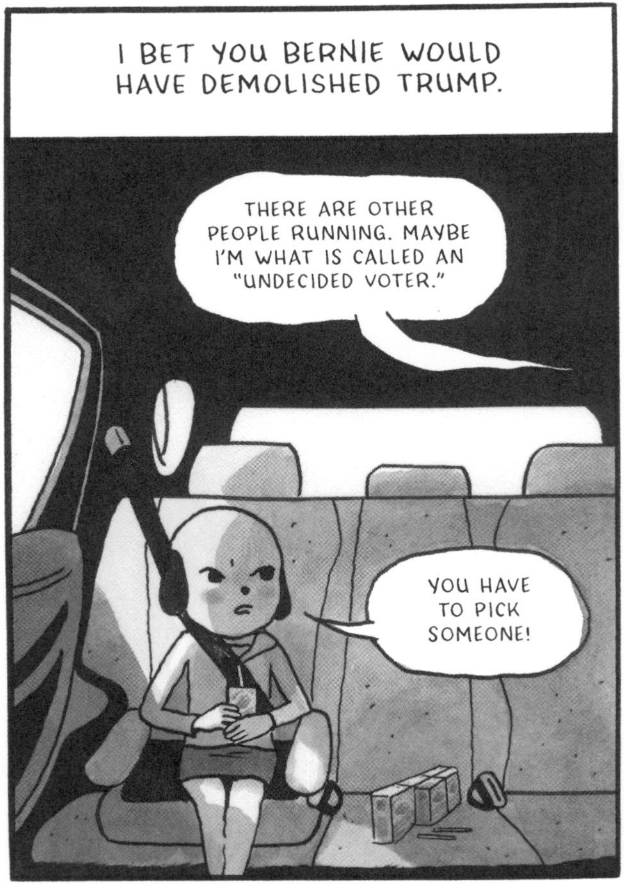
I BET YOU BERNIE WOULD HAVE DEMOLISHED TRUMP.
THERE ARE OTHER PEOPLE RUNNING. MAYBE I'M WHAT IS CALLED AN "UNDECIDED VOTER."
YOU HAVE TO PICK SOMEONE!

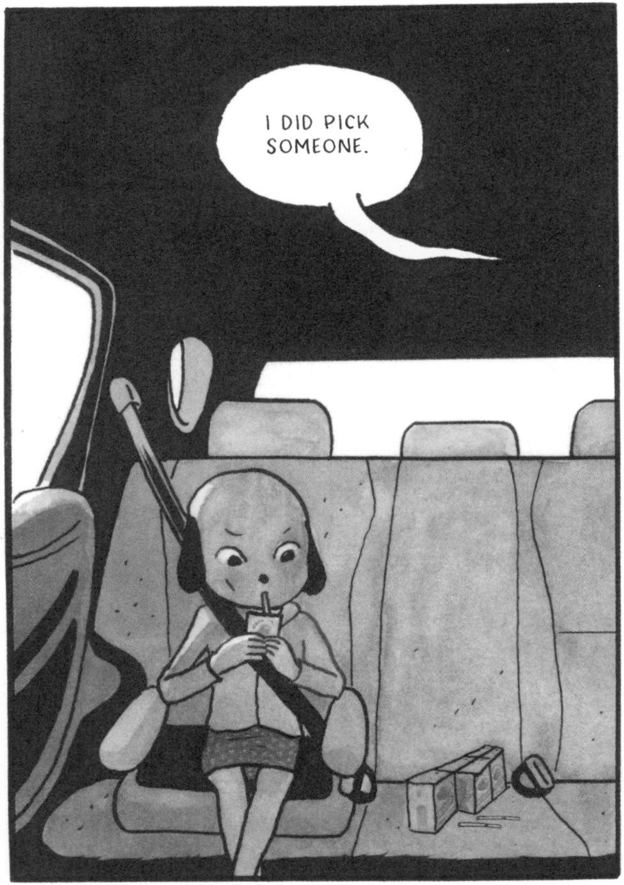
I DID PICK SOMEONE.

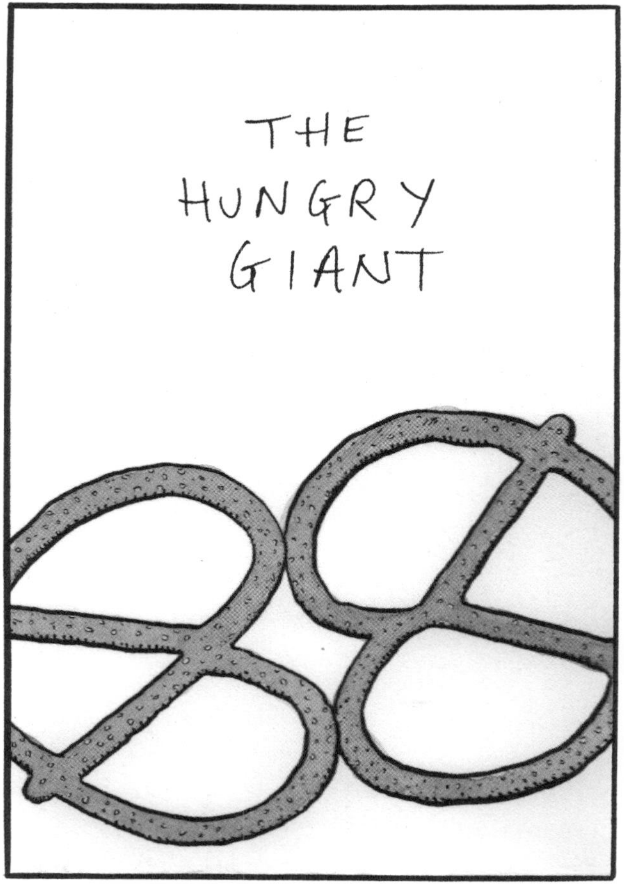
THE
HUNGRY
GIANT

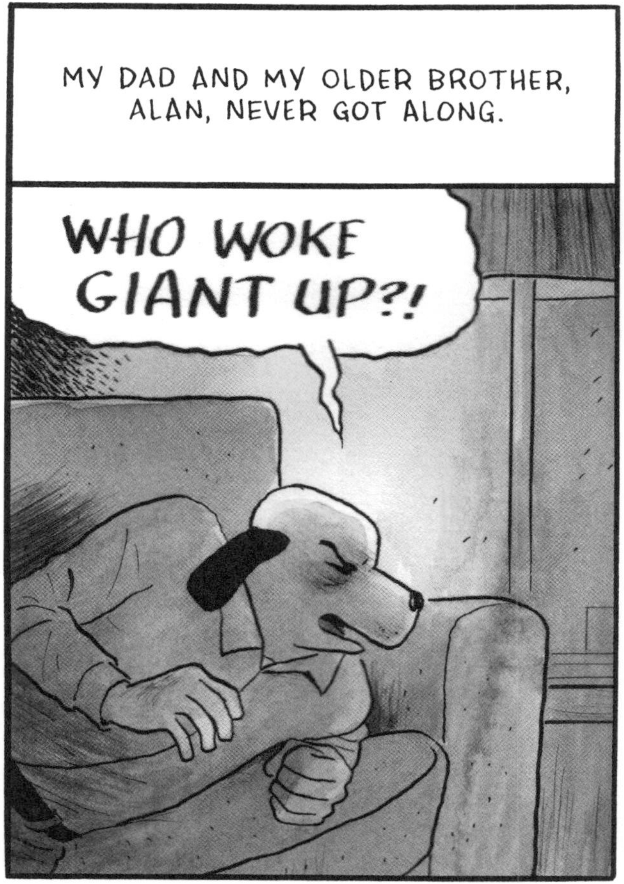
MY DAD AND MY OLDER BROTHER, ALAN, NEVER GOT ALONG.
WHO WOKE GIANT UP?!

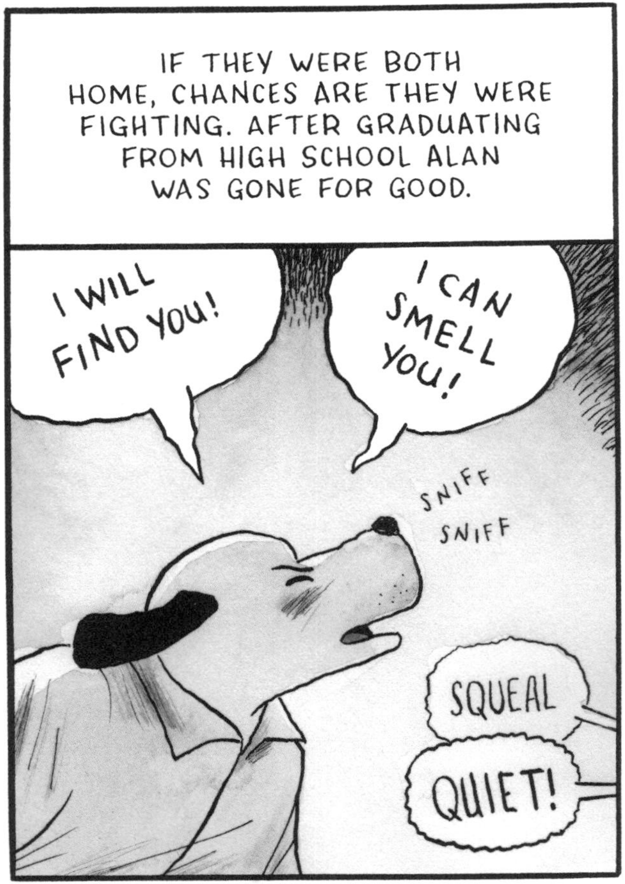
IF THEY WERE BOTH HOME, CHANCES ARE THEY WERE FIGHTING. AFTER GRADUATING FROM HIGH SCHOOL ALAN WAS GONE FOR GOOD.
I WILL FIND YOU!
I CAN SMELL YOU!
SNIFF SNIFF
SQUEAL
QUIET!

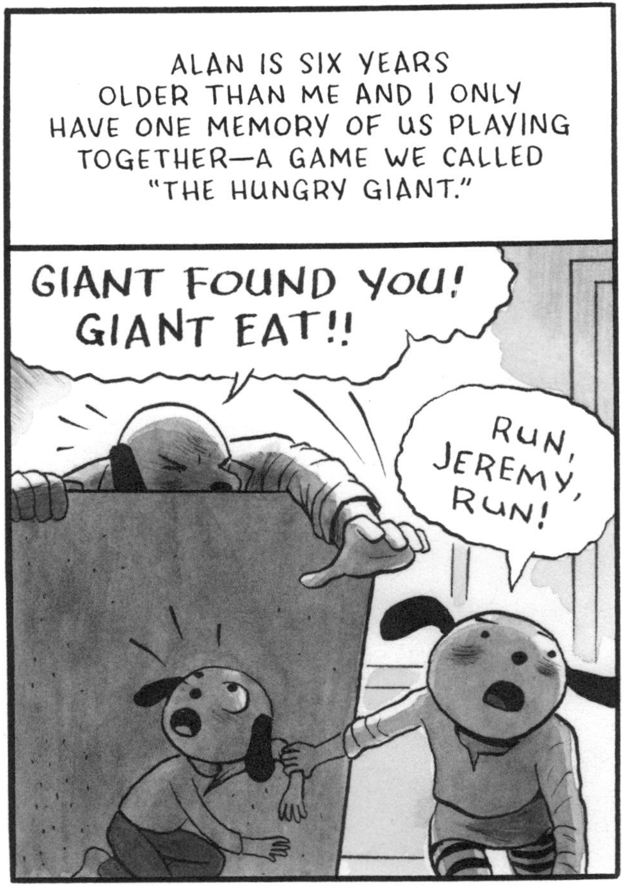
ALAN IS SIX YEARS OLDER THAN ME AND I ONLY HAVE ONE MEMORY OF US PLAYING TOGETHER—A GAME WE CALLED "THE HUNGRY GIANT."
GIANT FOUND YOU! GIANT EAT!!
RUN, JEREMY, RUN!

IT WAS EXHILARATING AND TERRIFYING AND GAVE ME NIGHTMARES FOR MONTHS. DESPITE THAT, I BEGGED ALAN TO KEEP PLAYING.

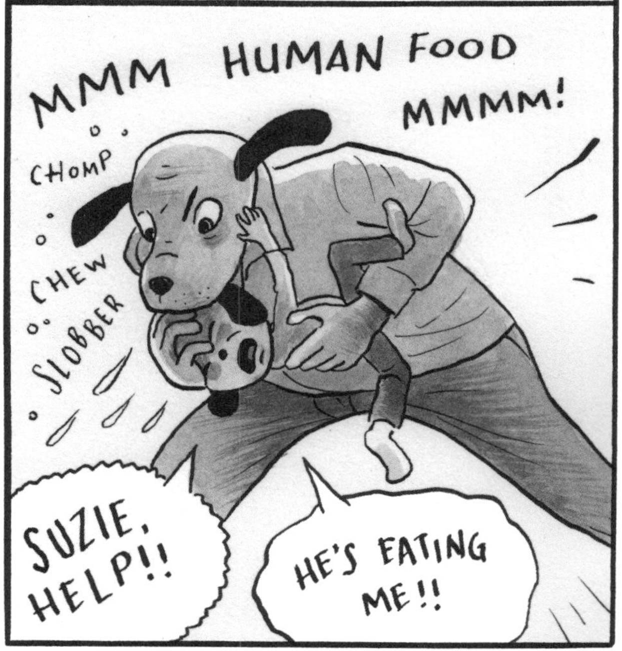
MMM HUMAN FOOD
MMMM!
CHOMP
CHEW
SLOBBER
SUZIE, HELP!!
HE'S EATING ME!!

ALAN EVENTUALLY SETTLED IN COLORADO. WE'D TALK ONCE OR TWICE A YEAR—ON A BIRTHDAY IF EITHER OF US REMEMBERED OR WHEN THE PATRIOTS WON A SUPER BOWL.

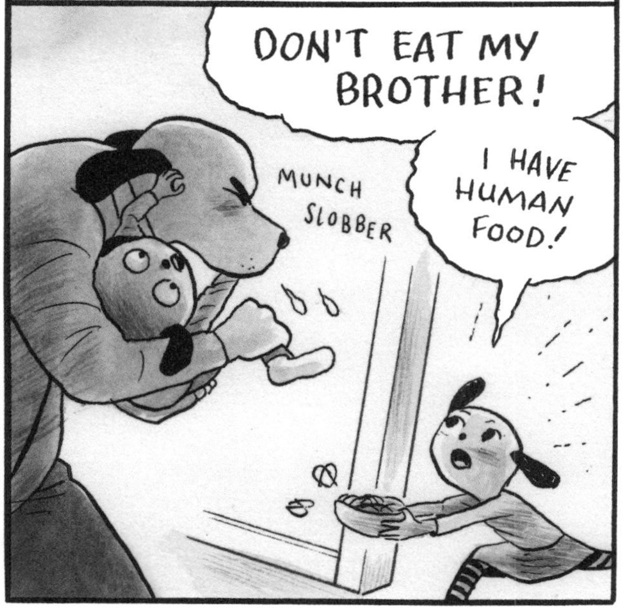
DON'T EAT MY BROTHER!
MUNCH
SLOBBER
I HAVE HUMAN FOOD!

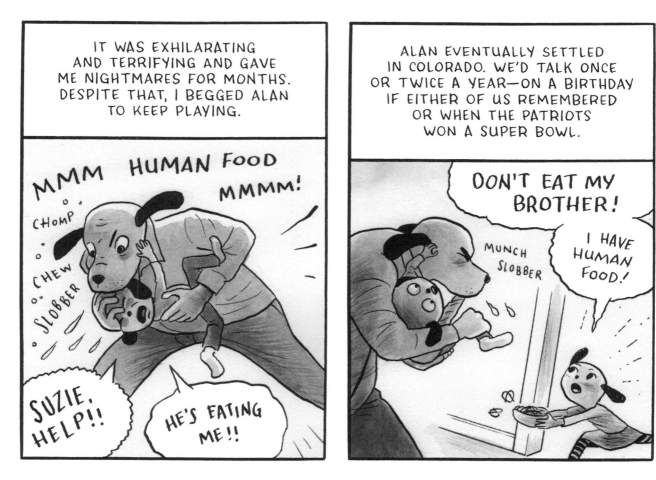

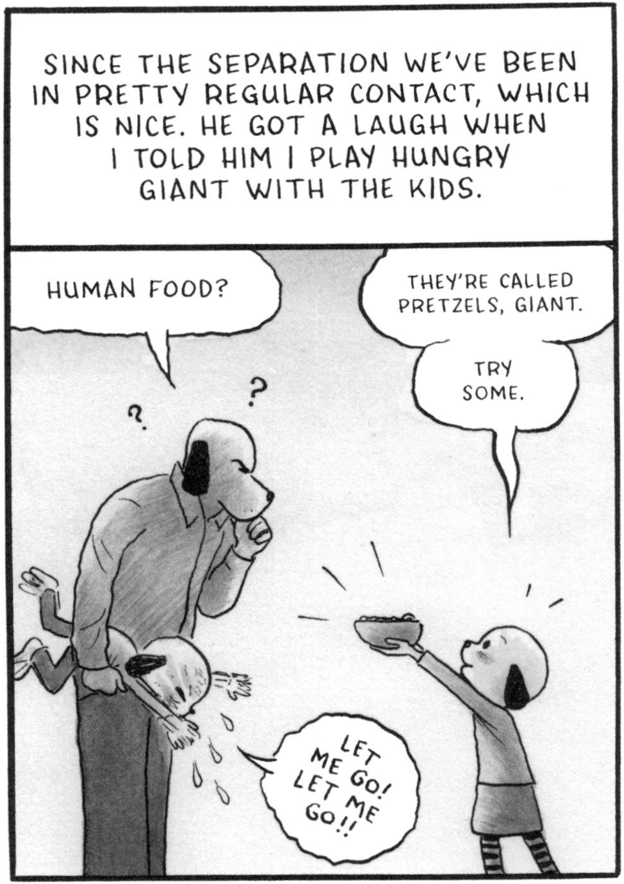
SINCE THE SEPARATION WE'VE BEEN IN PRETTY REGULAR CONTACT, WHICH IS NICE. HE GOT A LAUGH WHEN I TOLD HIM I PLAY HUNGRY GIANT WITH THE KIDS.
HUMAN FOOD?
THEY'RE CALLED PRETZELS, GIANT.
TRY SOME.
LET ME GO! LET ME GO!!

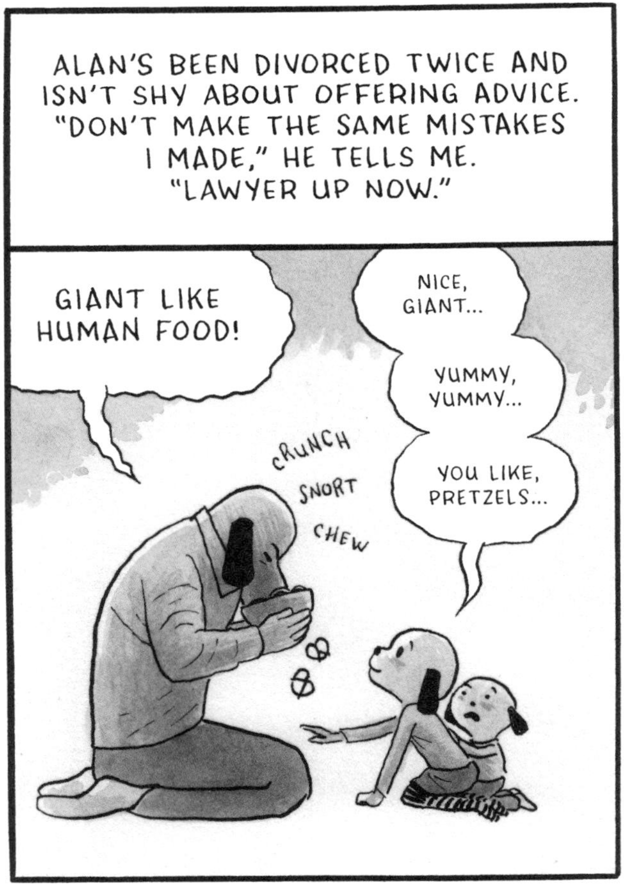
ALAN'S BEEN DIVORCED TWICE AND ISN'T SHY ABOUT OFFERING ADVICE. "DON'T MAKE THE SAME MISTAKES I MADE," HE TELLS ME. "LAWYER UP NOW."
GIANT LIKE HUMAN FOOD!
NICE, GIANT...
YUMMY, YUMMY...
YOU LIKE, PRETZELS...
CRUNCH
SNORT
CHEW

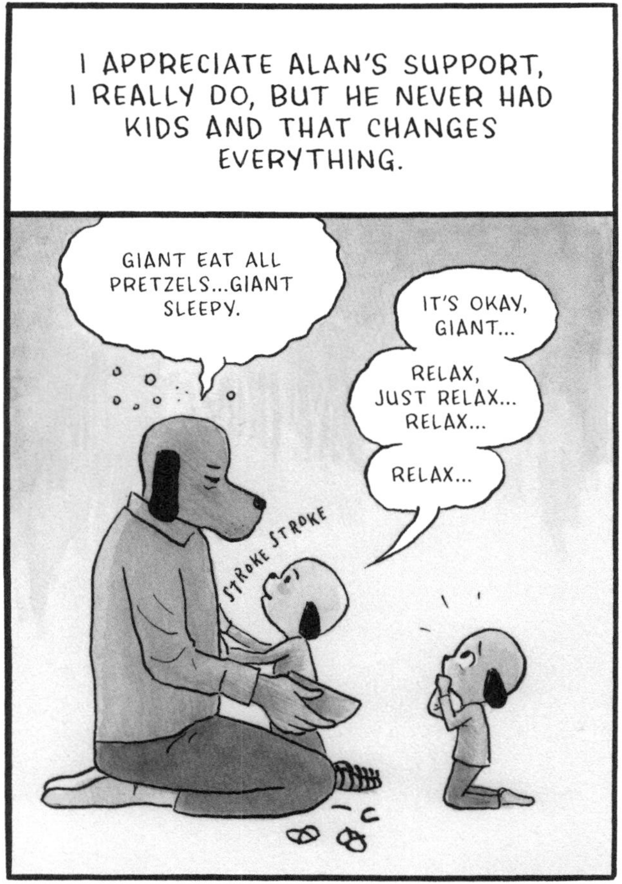
I APPRECIATE ALAN'S SUPPORT, I REALLY DO, BUT HE NEVER HAD KIDS AND THAT CHANGES EVERYTHING.
GIANT EAT ALL PRETZELS...GIANT SLEEPY.
IT'S OKAY, GIANT...
RELAX, JUST RELAX... RELAX...
RELAX...
STROKE STROKE

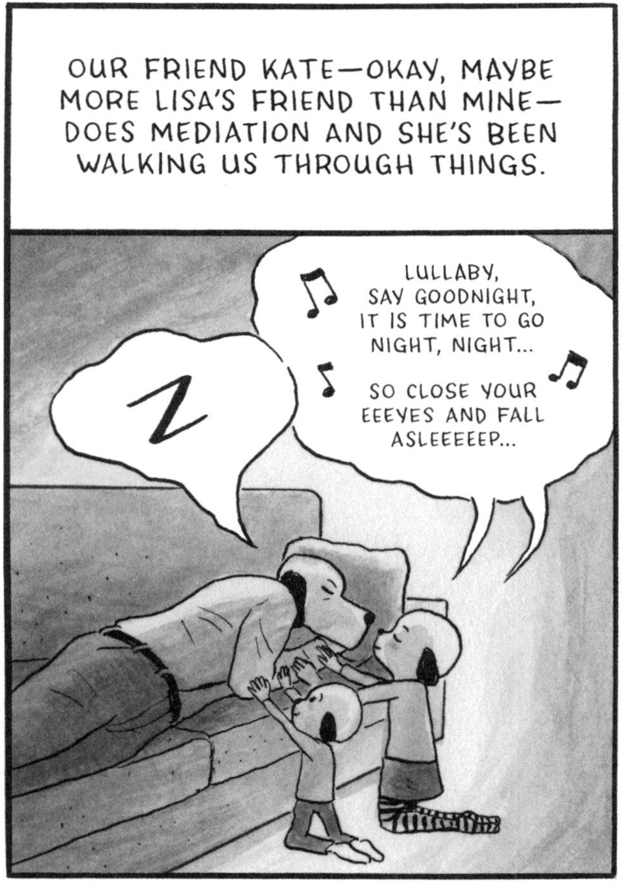
OUR FRIEND KATE—OKAY, MAYBE MORE LISA'S FRIEND THAN MINE—DOES MEDIATION AND SHE'S BEEN WALKING US THROUGH THINGS.
Z
LULLABY, SAY GOODNIGHT, IT IS TIME TO GO NIGHT, NIGHT...
SO CLOSE YOUR EEEYES AND FALL ASLEEEEEP...

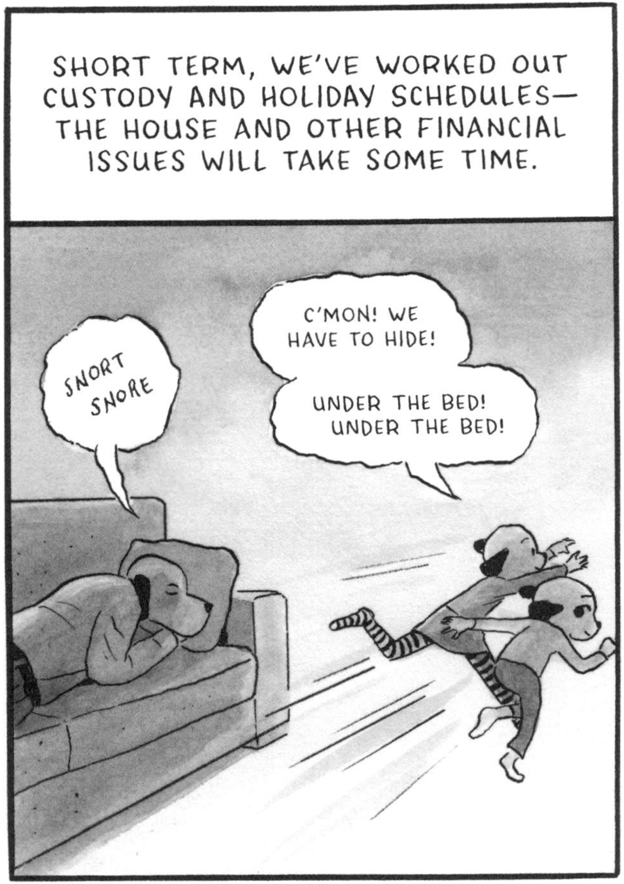
SHORT TERM, WE'VE WORKED OUT CUSTODY AND HOLIDAY SCHEDULES— THE HOUSE AND OTHER FINANCIAL ISSUES WILL TAKE SOME TIME.
SNORT SNORE
C'MON! WE HAVE TO HIDE!
UNDER THE BED! UNDER THE BED!

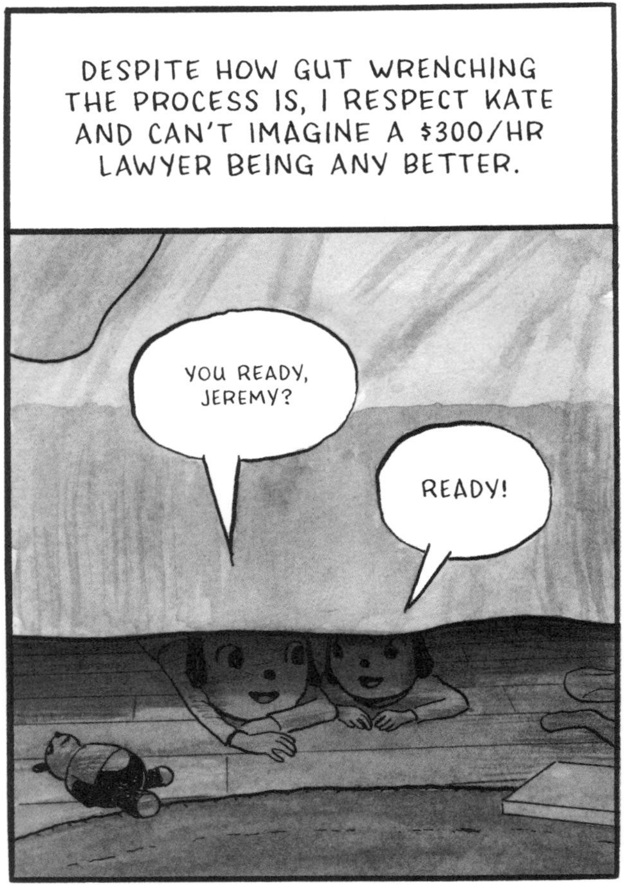
DESPITE HOW GUT WRENCHING THE PROCESS IS, I RESPECT KATE AND CAN'T IMAGINE A $300/HR LAWYER BEING ANY BETTER.
YOU READY, JEREMY?
READY!

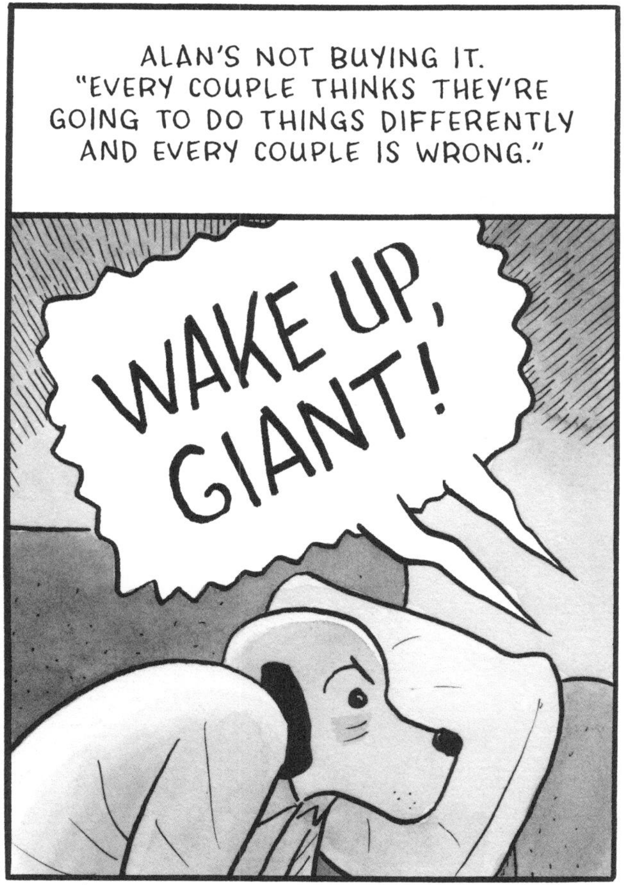
ALAN'S NOT BUYING IT. "EVERY COUPLE THINKS THEY'RE GOING TO DO THINGS DIFFERENTLY AND EVERY COUPLE IS WRONG."
WAKE UP, GIANT!

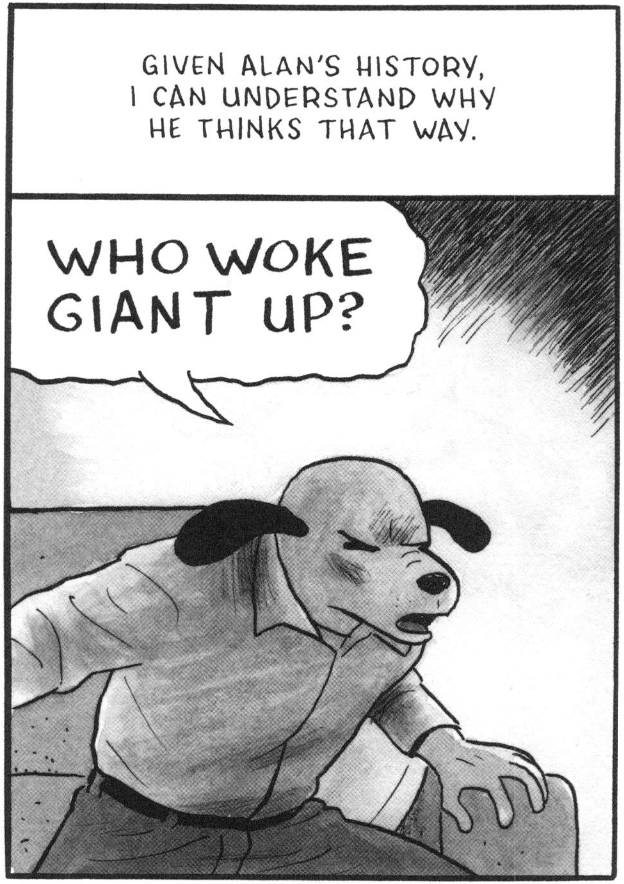
GIVEN ALAN'S HISTORY, I CAN UNDERSTAND WHY HE THINKS THAT WAY.
WHO WOKE GIANT UP?

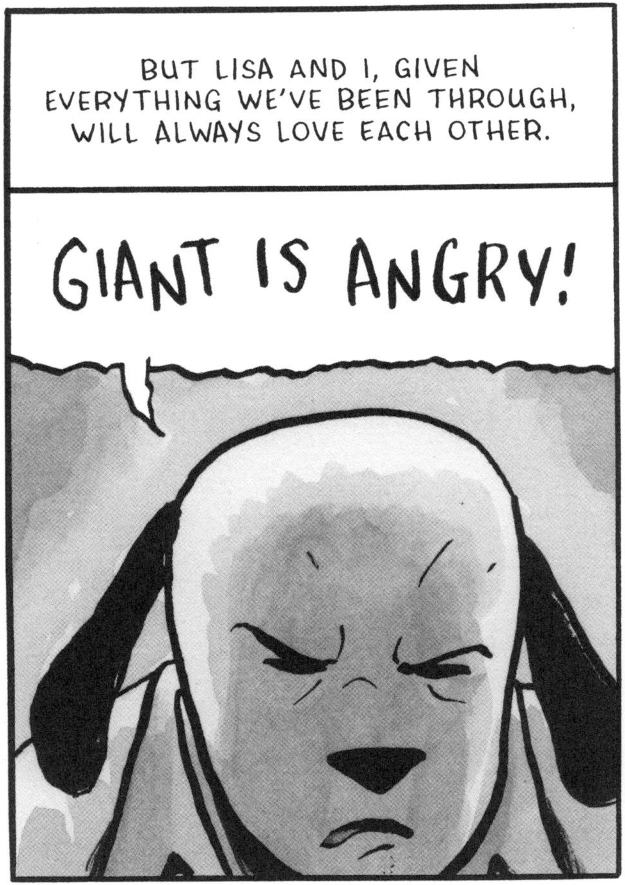
BUT LISA AND I, GIVEN EVERYTHING WE'VE BEEN THROUGH, WILL ALWAYS LOVE EACH OTHER.
GIANT IS ANGRY!

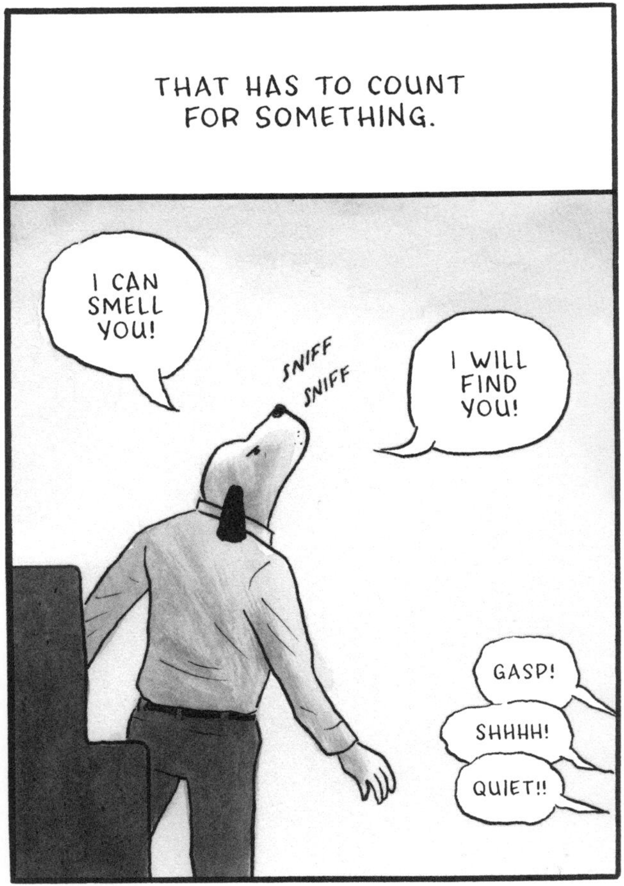
THAT HAS TO COUNT FOR SOMETHING.
I CAN SMELL YOU!
SNIFF
SNIFF
I WILL FIND YOU!
GASP!
SHHHH!
QUIET!!

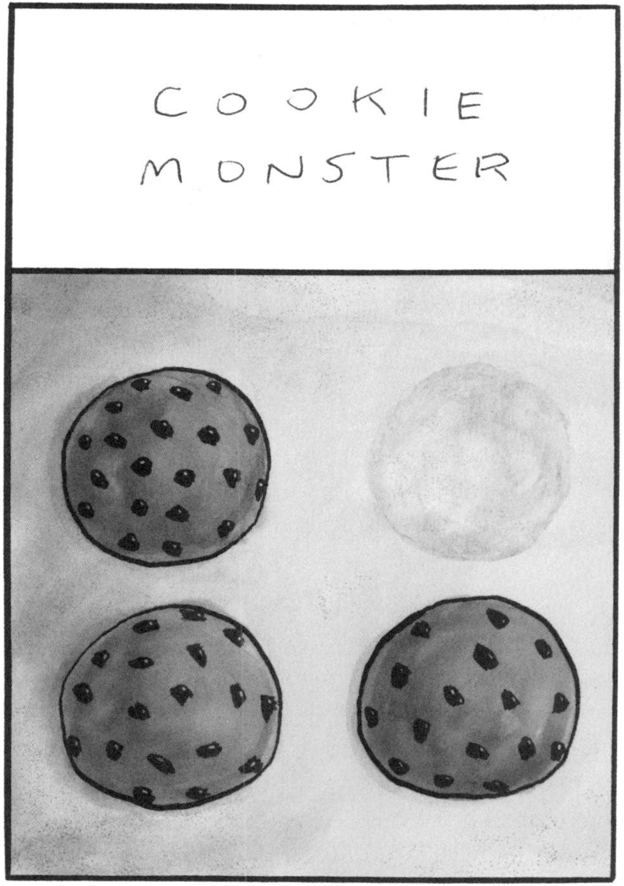
COOKIE
MONSTER

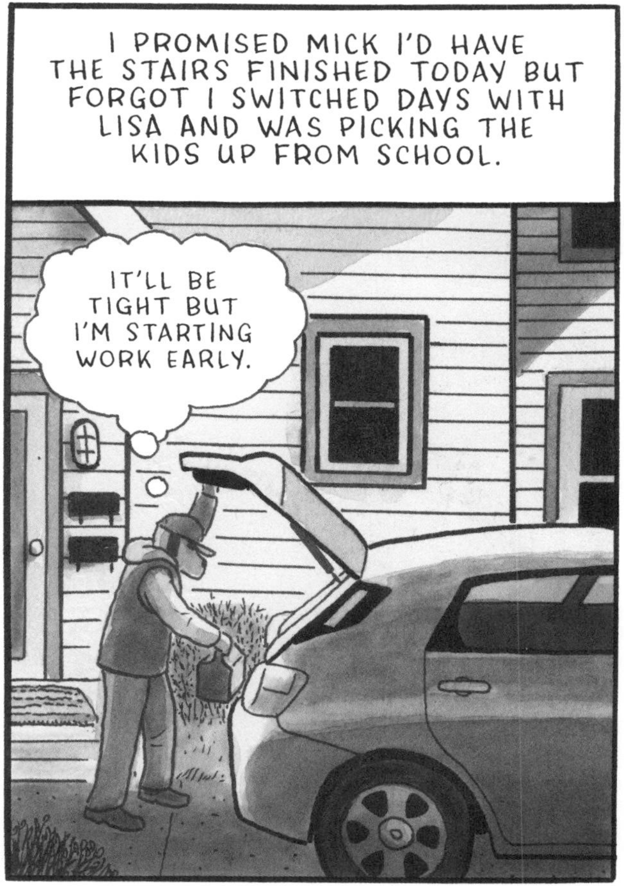
I PROMISED MICK I'D HAVE THE STAIRS FINISHED TODAY BUT FORGOT I SWITCHED DAYS WITH LISA AND WAS PICKING THE KIDS UP FROM SCHOOL.
IT'LL BE TIGHT BUT I'M STARTING WORK EARLY.

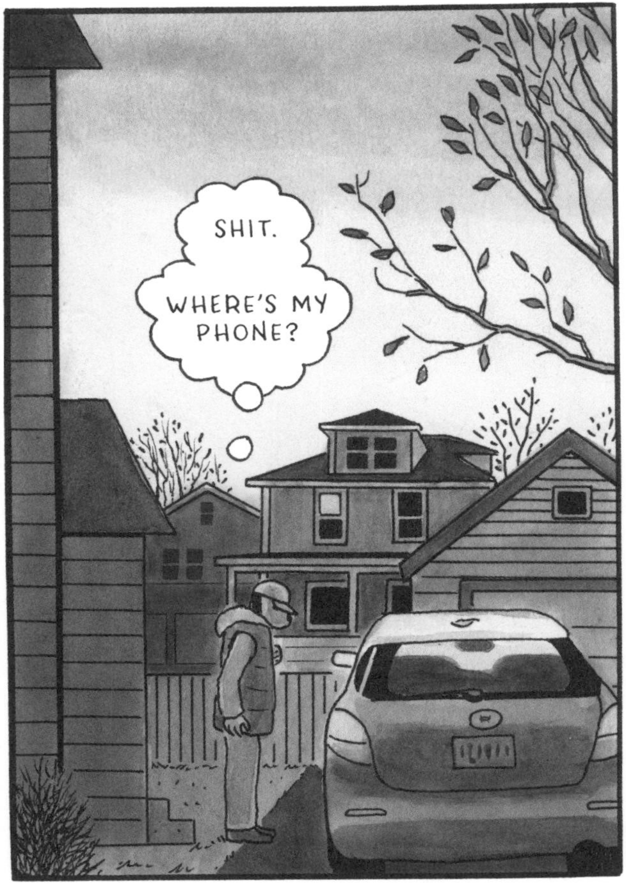
SHIT.
WHERE'S MY PHONE?

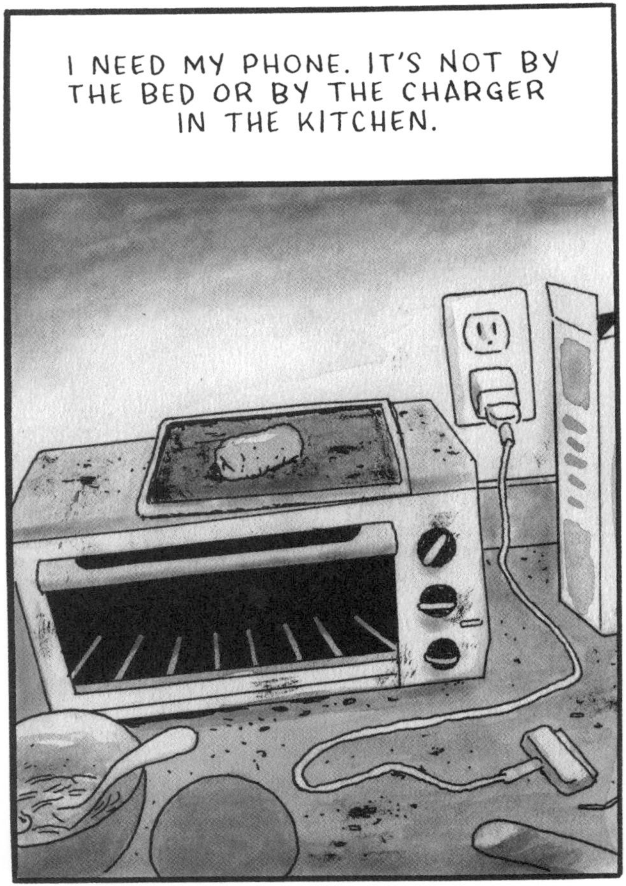
I NEED MY PHONE. IT'S NOT BY THE BED OR BY THE CHARGER IN THE KITCHEN.

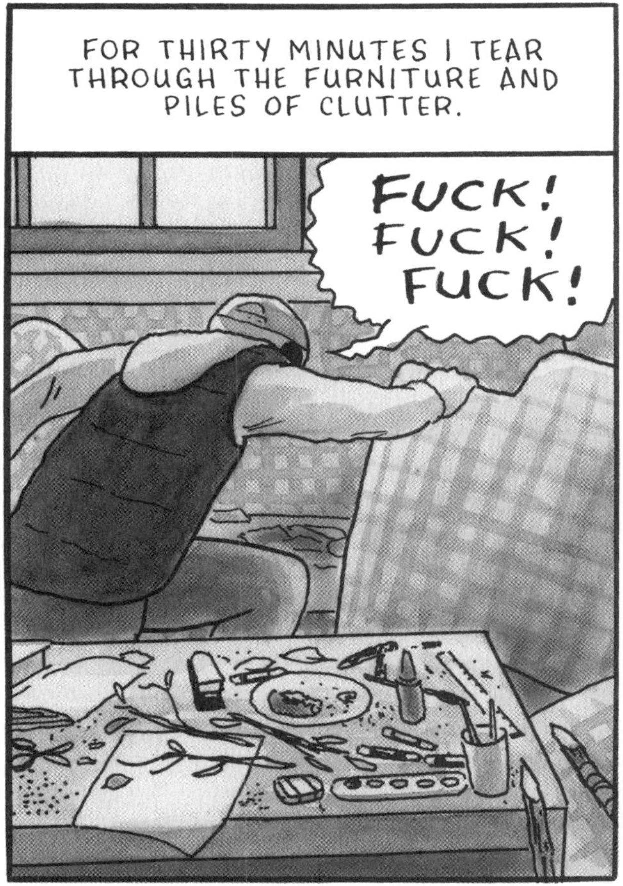
FOR THIRTY MINUTES I TEAR THROUGH THE FURNITURE AND PILES OF CLUTTER.
FUCK! FUCK! FUCK!

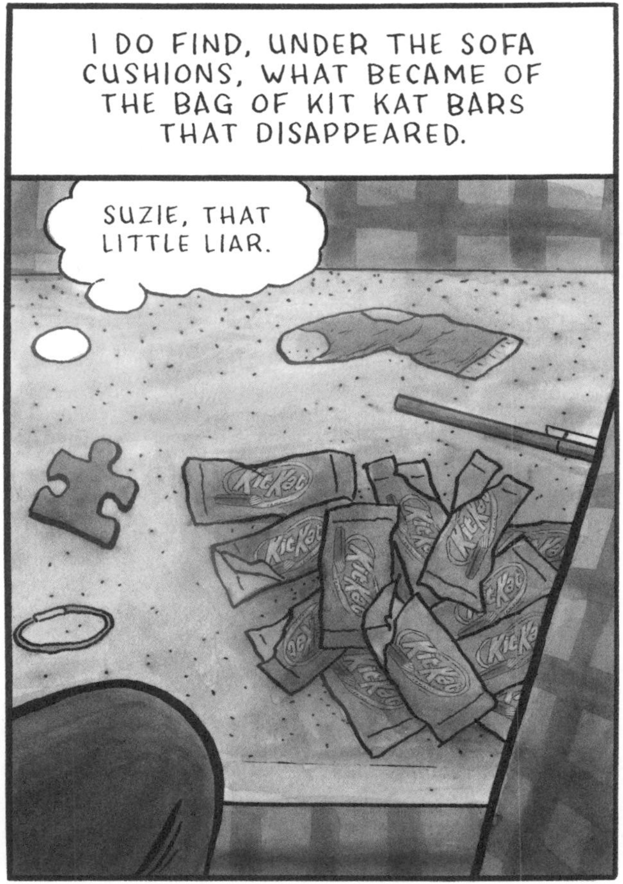
I DO FIND, UNDER THE SOFA CUSHIONS, WHAT BECAME OF THE BAG OF KIT KAT BARS THAT DISAPPEARED.
SUZIE, THAT LITTLE LIAR.

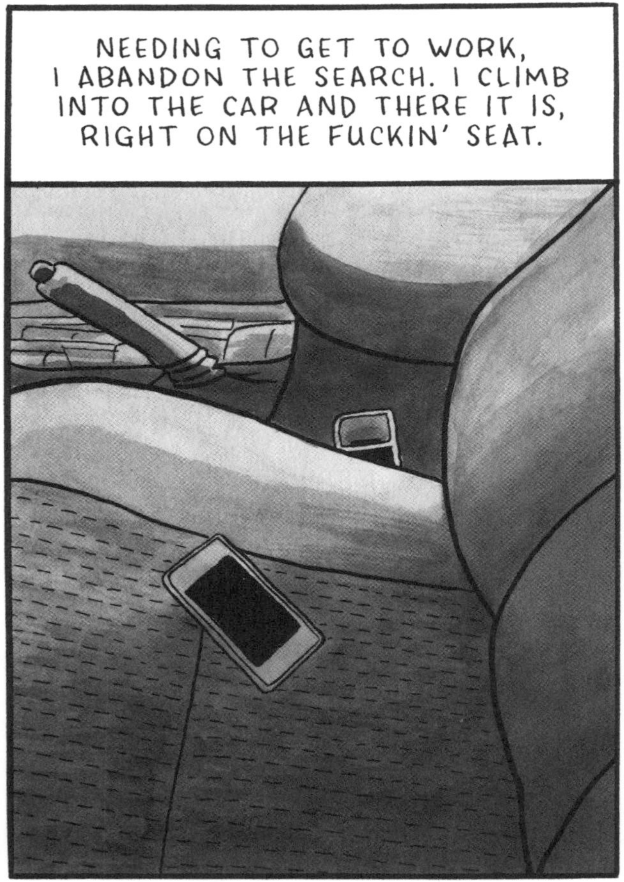
NEEDING TO GET TO WORK, I ABANDON THE SEARCH. I CLIMB INTO THE CAR AND THERE IT IS, RIGHT ON THE FUCKIN' SEAT.

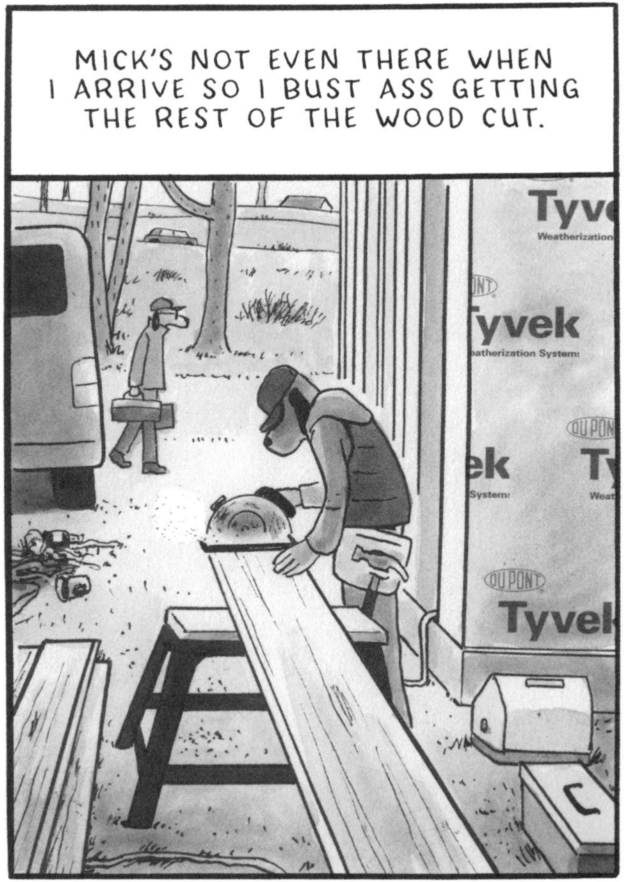
MICK'S NOT EVEN THERE WHEN I ARRIVE SO I BUST ASS GETTING THE REST OF THE WOOD CUT.
Tyvek
Weatherization System
DUPONT

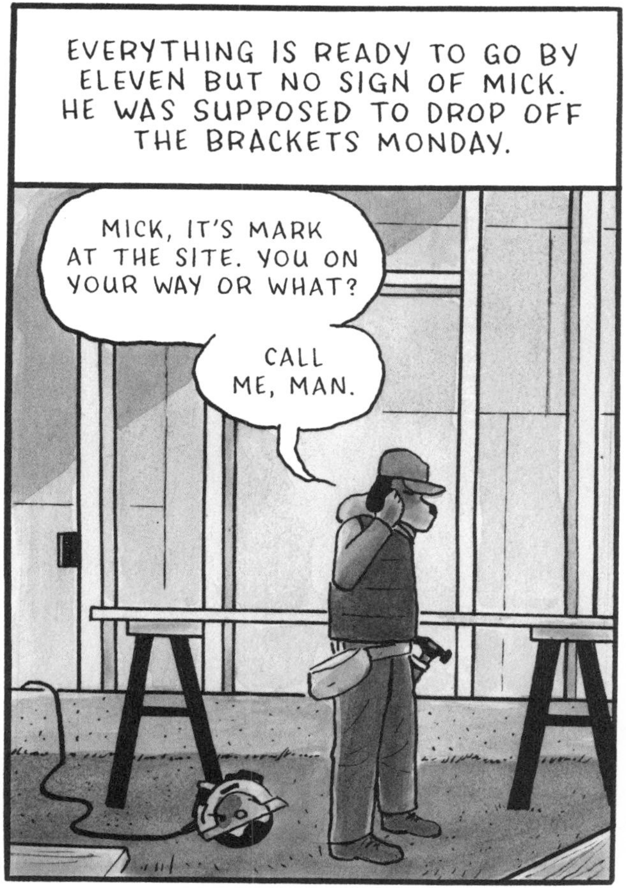
EVERYTHING IS READY TO GO BY ELEVEN BUT NO SIGN OF MICK. HE WAS SUPPOSED TO DROP OFF THE BRACKETS MONDAY.
MICK, IT'S MARK AT THE SITE. YOU ON YOUR WAY OR WHAT?
CALL ME, MAN.

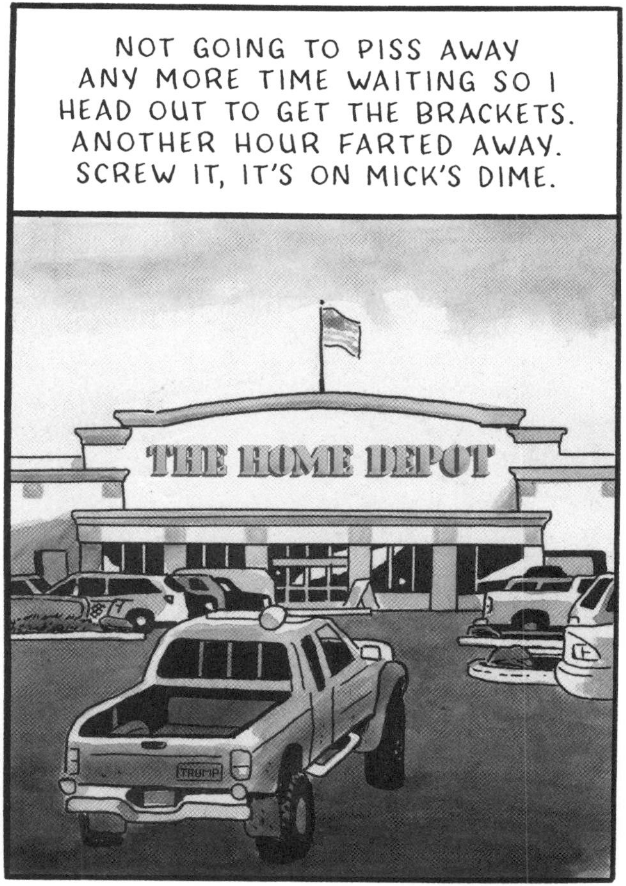
NOT GOING TO PISS AWAY ANY MORE TIME WAITING SO I HEAD OUT TO GET THE BRACKETS. ANOTHER HOUR FARTED AWAY. SCREW IT, IT'S ON MICK'S DIME.
THE HOME DEPOT
TRUMP

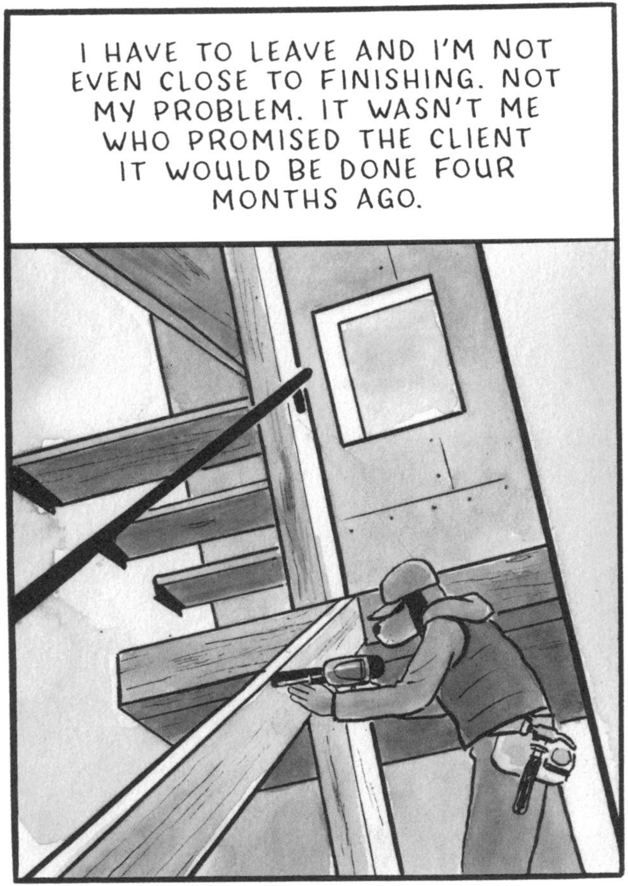
I HAVE TO LEAVE AND I'M NOT EVEN CLOSE TO FINISHING. NOT MY PROBLEM. IT WASN'T ME WHO PROMISED THE CLIENT IT WOULD BE DONE FOUR MONTHS AGO.

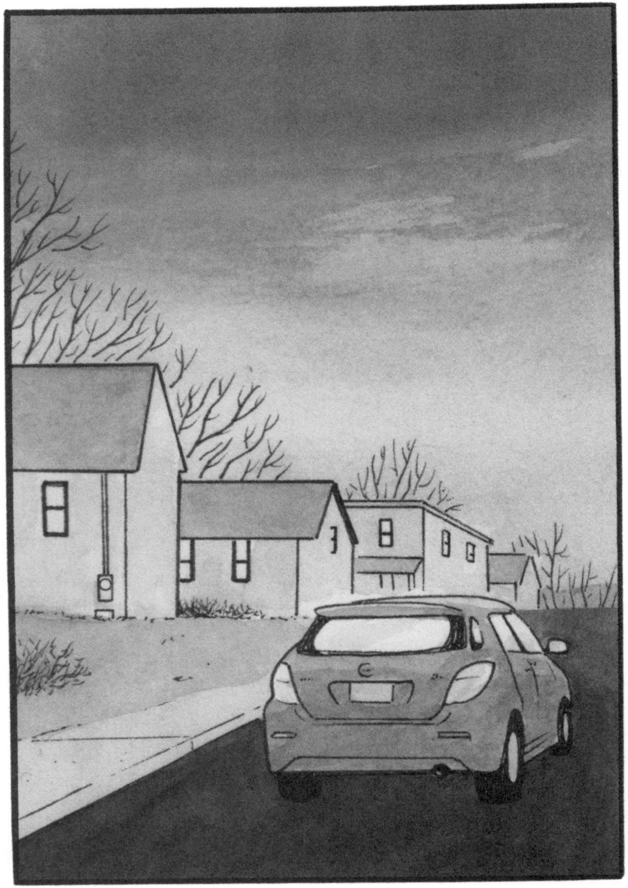

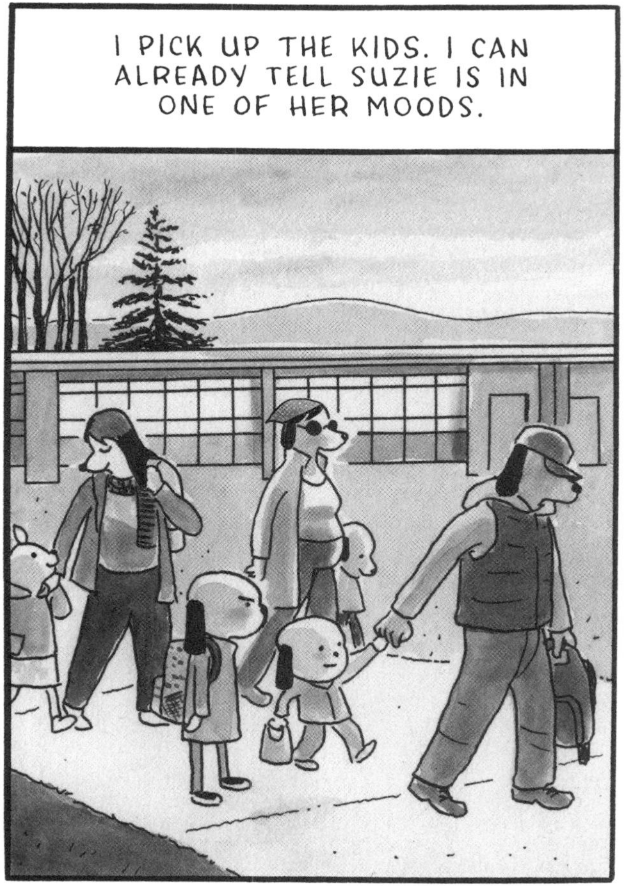
I PICK UP THE KIDS. I CAN ALREADY TELL SUZIE IS IN ONE OF HER MOODS.

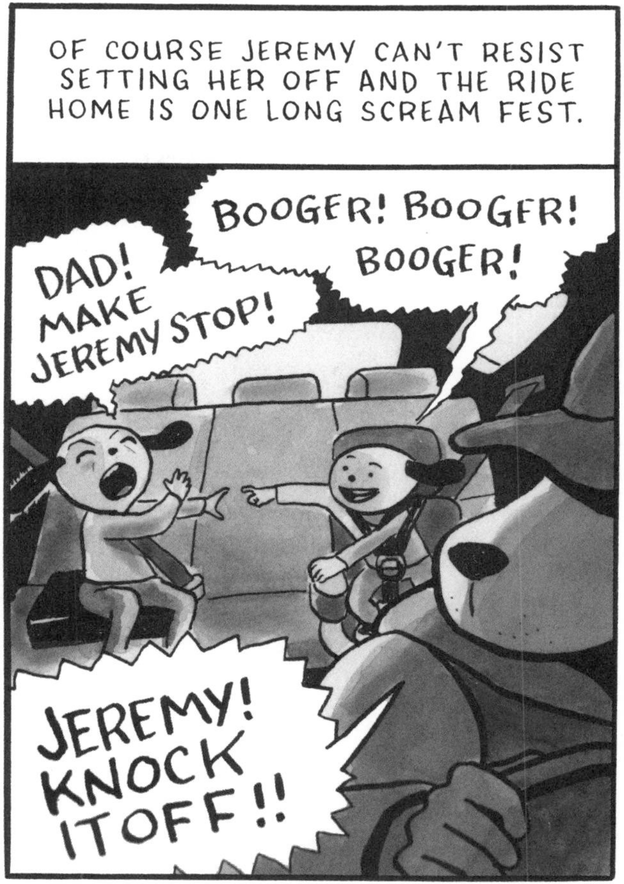
OF COURSE JEREMY CAN'T RESIST SETTING HER OFF AND THE RIDE HOME IS ONE LONG SCREAM FEST.
DAD! MAKE JEREMY STOP!
BOOGER! BOOGER! BOOGER!
JEREMY! KNOCK IT OFF!!

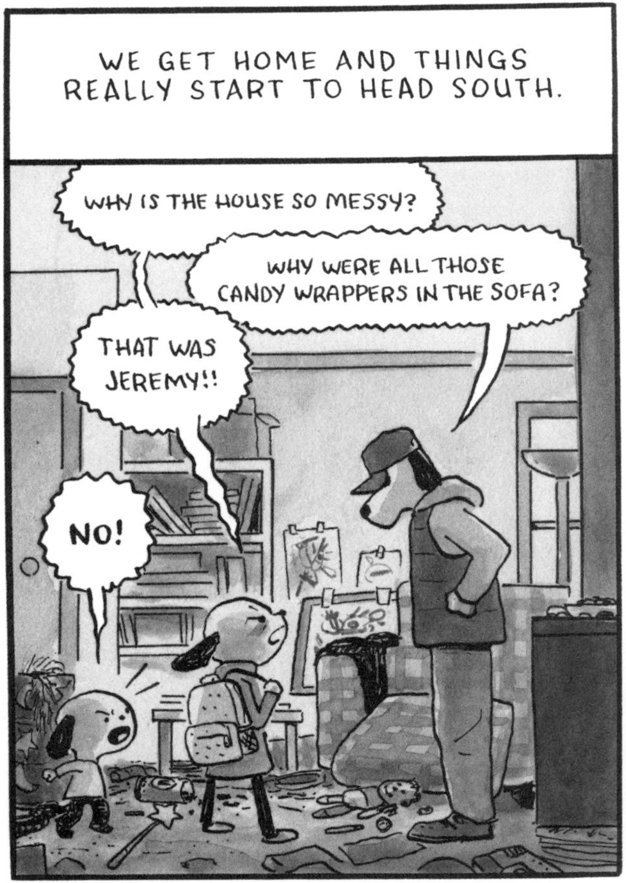
WE GET HOME AND THINGS REALLY START TO HEAD SOUTH.
WHY IS THE HOUSE SO MESSY?
WHY WERE ALL THOSE CANDY WRAPPERS IN THE SOFA?
THAT WAS JEREMY!!
NO!

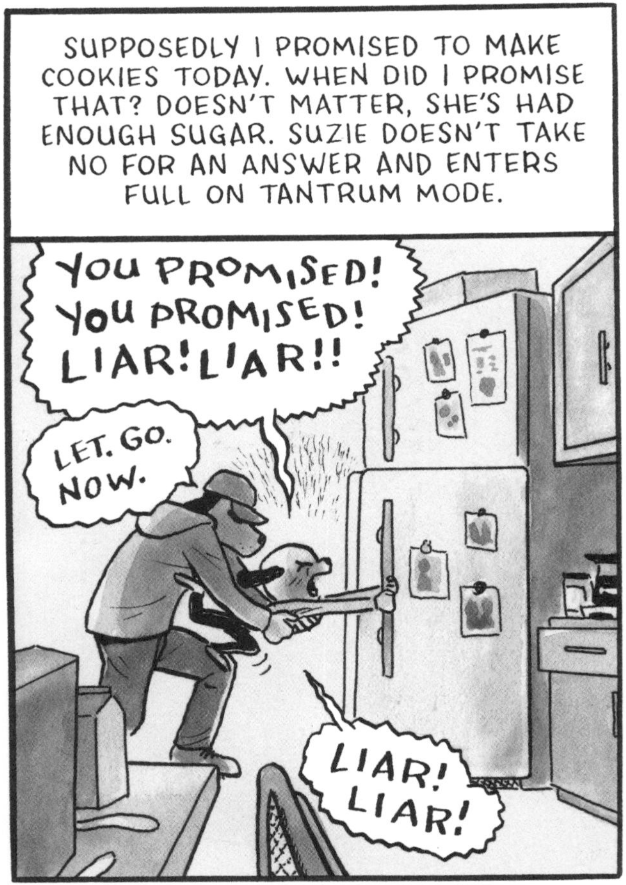
SUPPOSEDLY I PROMISED TO MAKE COOKIES TODAY. WHEN DID I PROMISE THAT? DOESN'T MATTER, SHE'S HAD ENOUGH SUGAR. SUZIE DOESN'T TAKE NO FOR AN ANSWER AND ENTERS FULL ON TANTRUM MODE.
YOU PROMISED! YOU PROMISED! LIAR! LIAR!!
LET. GO. NOW.
LIAR! LIAR!

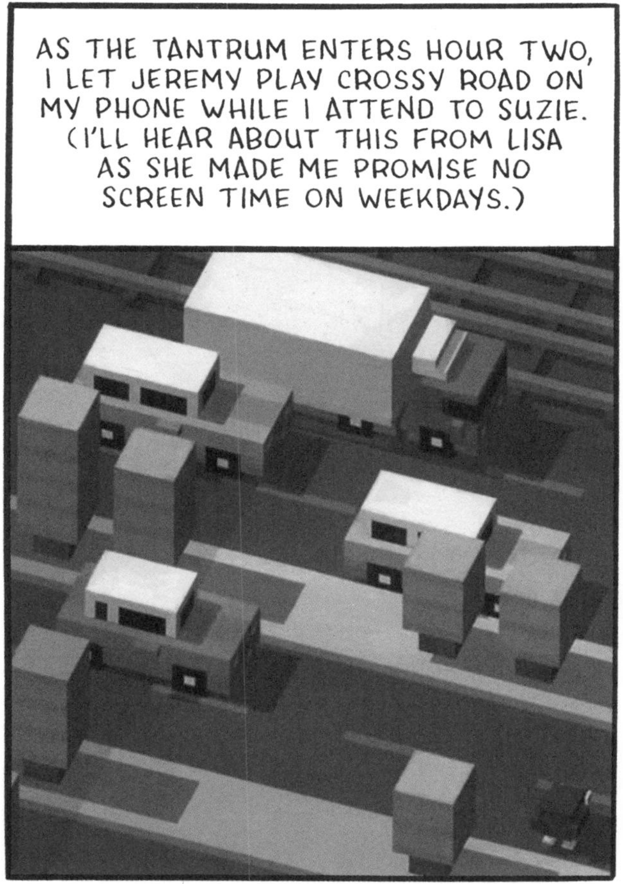
AS THE TANTRUM ENTERS HOUR TWO, I LET JEREMY PLAY CROSSY ROAD ON MY PHONE WHILE I ATTEND TO SUZIE. (I'LL HEAR ABOUT THIS FROM LISA AS SHE MADE ME PROMISE NO SCREEN TIME ON WEEKDAYS.)

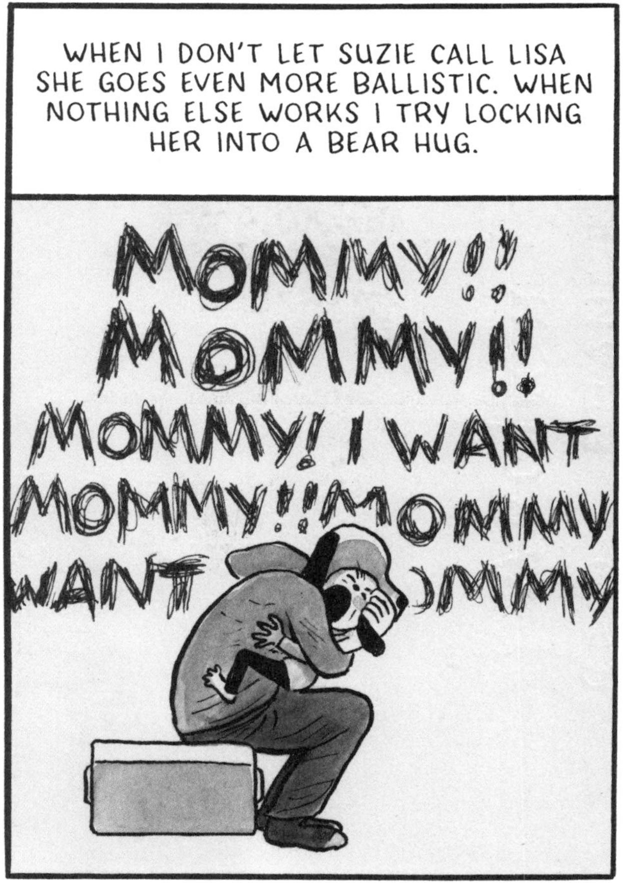
WHEN I DON'T LET SUZIE CALL LISA SHE GOES EVEN MORE BALLISTIC. WHEN NOTHING ELSE WORKS I TRY LOCKING HER INTO A BEAR HUG.
MOMMY!!
MOMMY!!
MOMMY! I WANT
MOMMY!! MOMMY
WANT

BY SEVEN, SUZIE, UTTERLY EXHAUSTED, ZONKS OUT ON THE FLOOR.

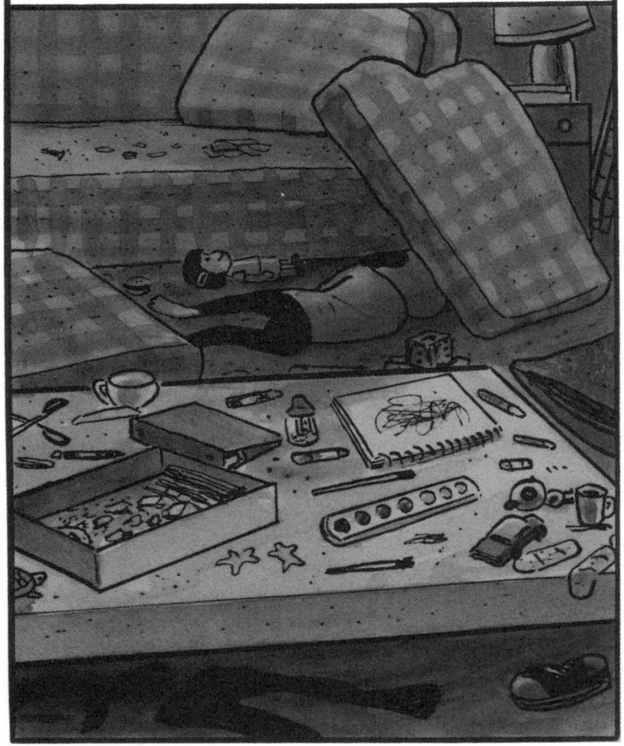

JEREMY AND I EAT FROZEN EGGROLLS FOR DINNER.

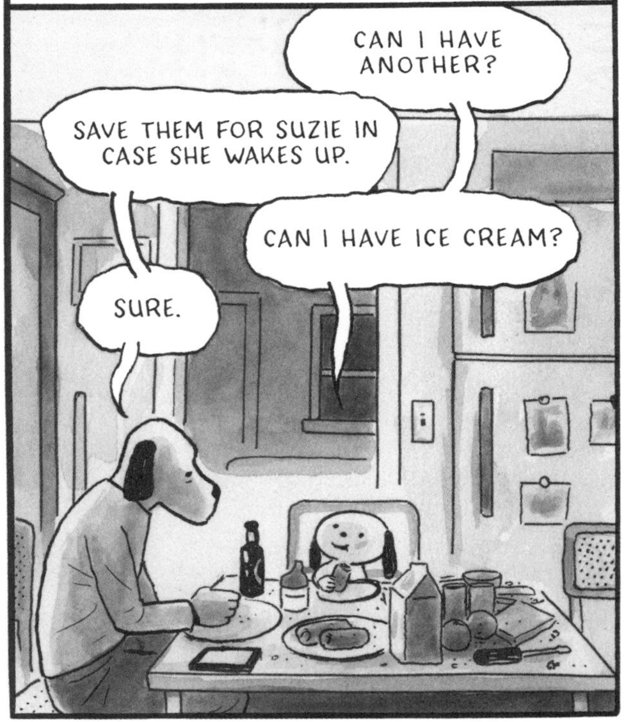
CAN I HAVE ANOTHER?
SAVE THEM FOR SUZIE IN CASE SHE WAKES UP.
CAN I HAVE ICE CREAM?
SURE.

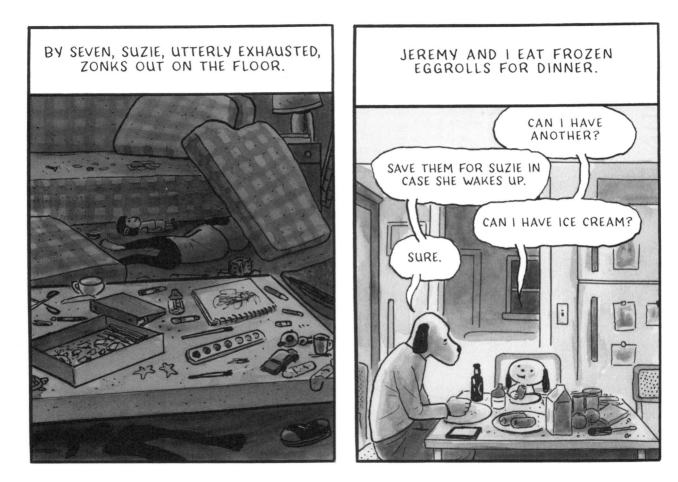

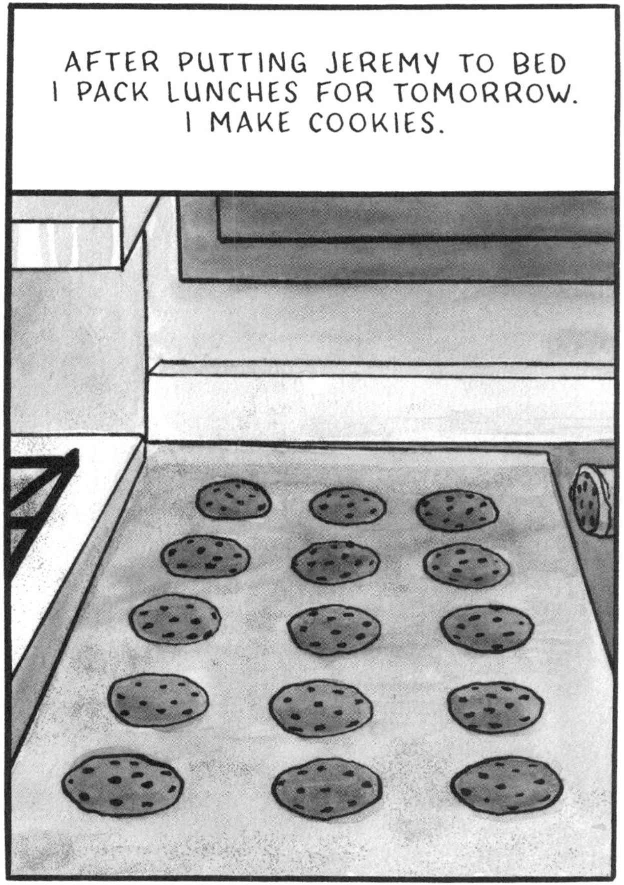
AFTER PUTTING JEREMY TO BED
I PACK LUNCHES FOR TOMORROW.
I MAKE COOKIES.

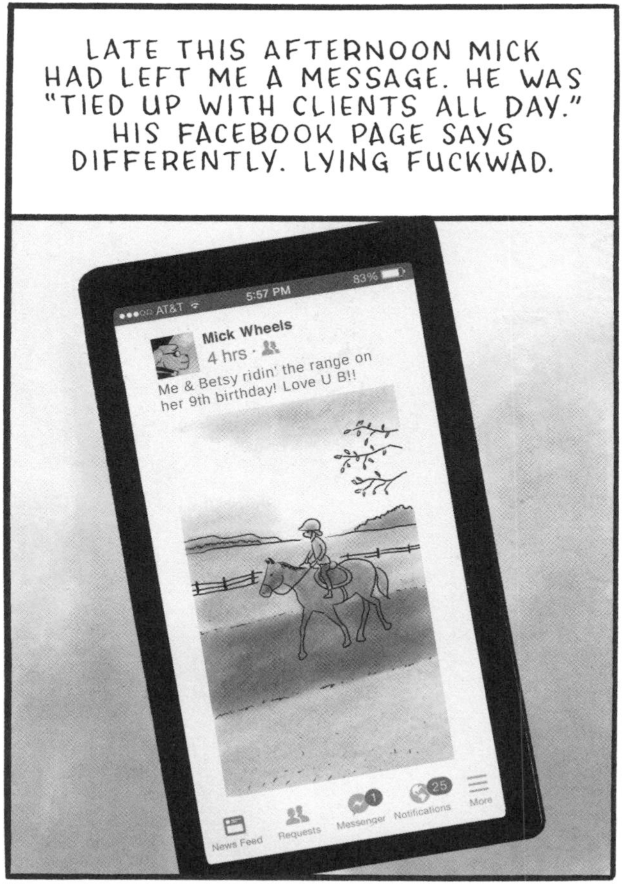
LATE THIS AFTERNOON MICK
HAD LEFT ME A MESSAGE. HE WAS
"TIED UP WITH CLIENTS ALL DAY."
HIS FACEBOOK PAGE SAYS
DIFFERENTLY. LYING FUCKWAD.
AT&T
5:57 PM
83%
Mick Wheels
4 hrs
Me & Betsy ridin' the range on
her 9th birthday! Love U B!!
News Feed
Requests
Messenger
Notifications
More

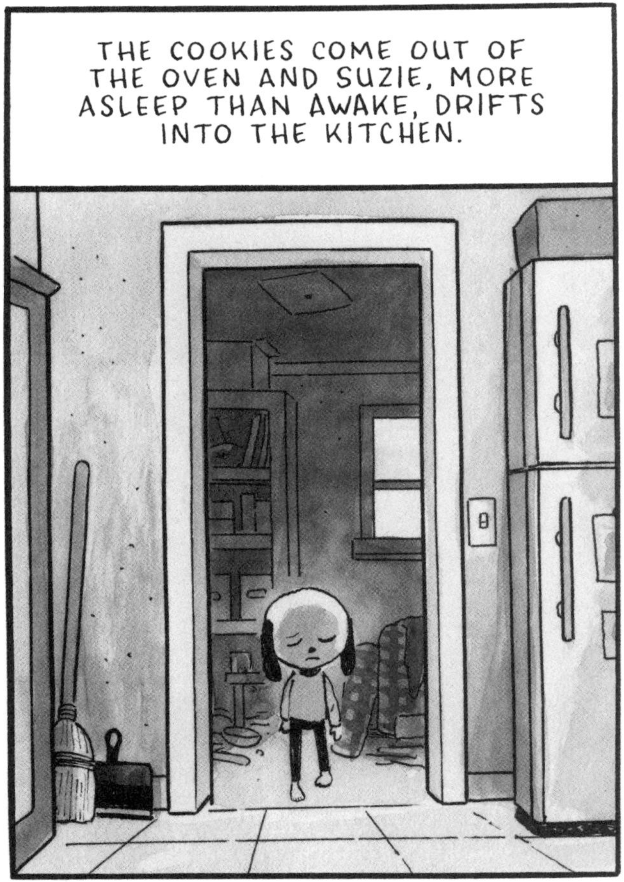
THE COOKIES COME OUT OF THE OVEN AND SUZIE, MORE ASLEEP THAN AWAKE, DRIFTS INTO THE KITCHEN.

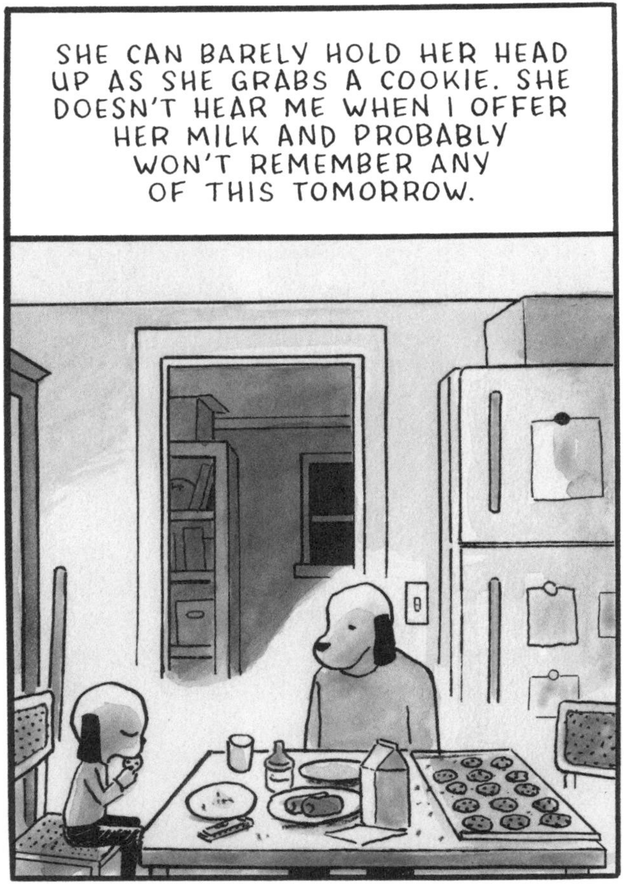
SHE CAN BARELY HOLD HER HEAD UP AS SHE GRABS A COOKIE. SHE DOESN'T HEAR ME WHEN I OFFER HER MILK AND PROBABLY WON'T REMEMBER ANY OF THIS TOMORROW.

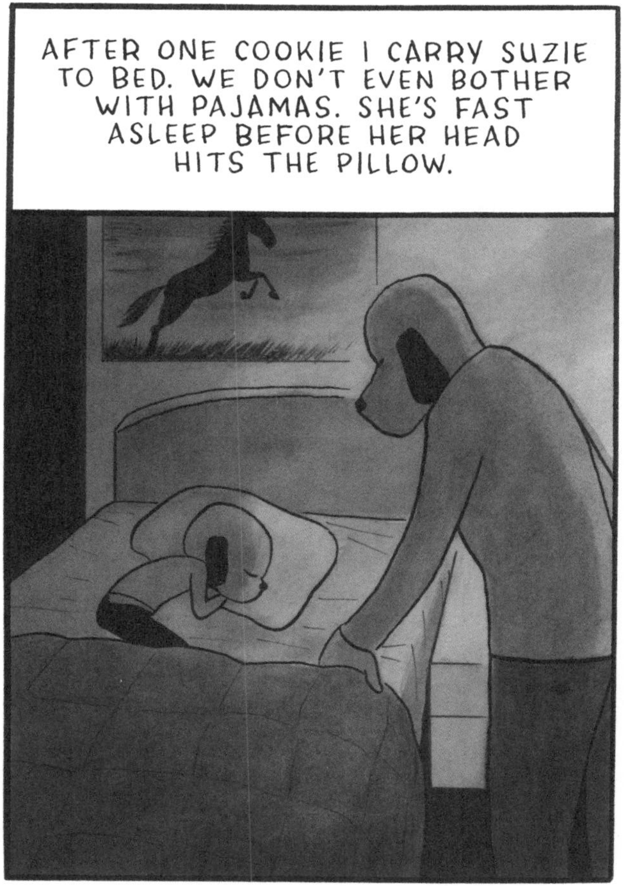
AFTER ONE COOKIE I CARRY SUZIE TO BED. WE DON'T EVEN BOTHER WITH PAJAMAS. SHE'S FAST ASLEEP BEFORE HER HEAD HITS THE PILLOW.

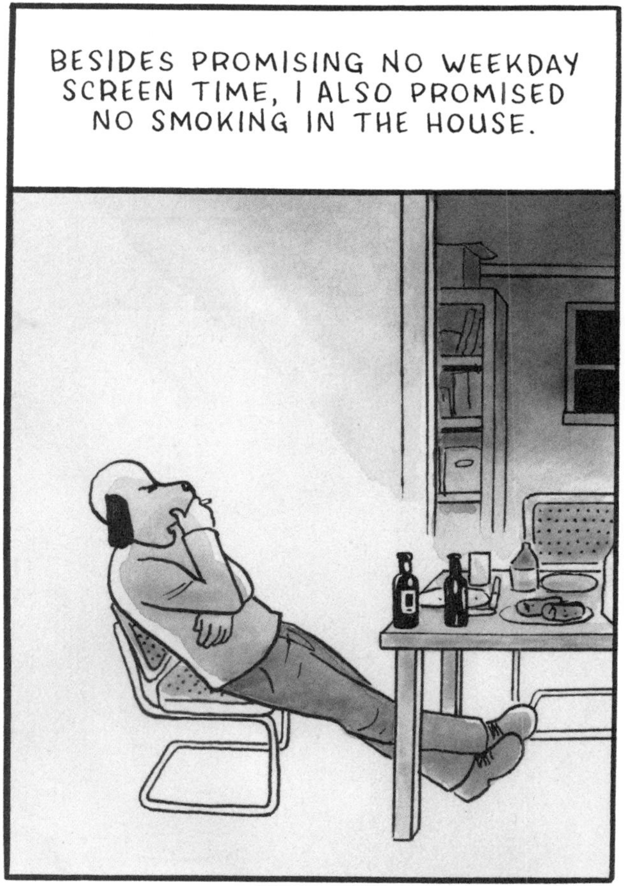
BESIDES PROMISING NO WEEKDAY SCREEN TIME, I ALSO PROMISED NO SMOKING IN THE HOUSE.

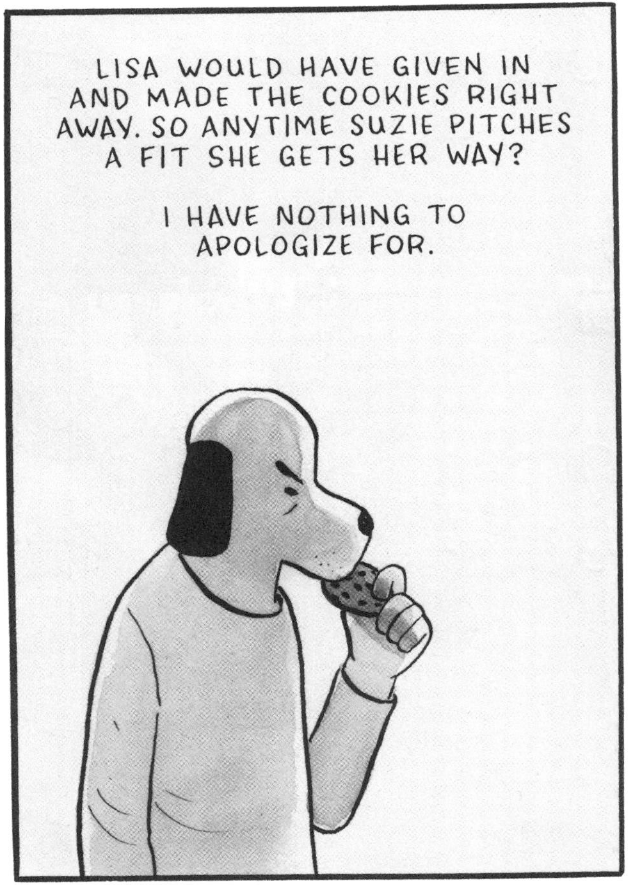
LISA WOULD HAVE GIVEN IN AND MADE THE COOKIES RIGHT AWAY. SO ANYTIME SUZIE PITCHES A FIT SHE GETS HER WAY?
I HAVE NOTHING TO APOLOGIZE FOR.

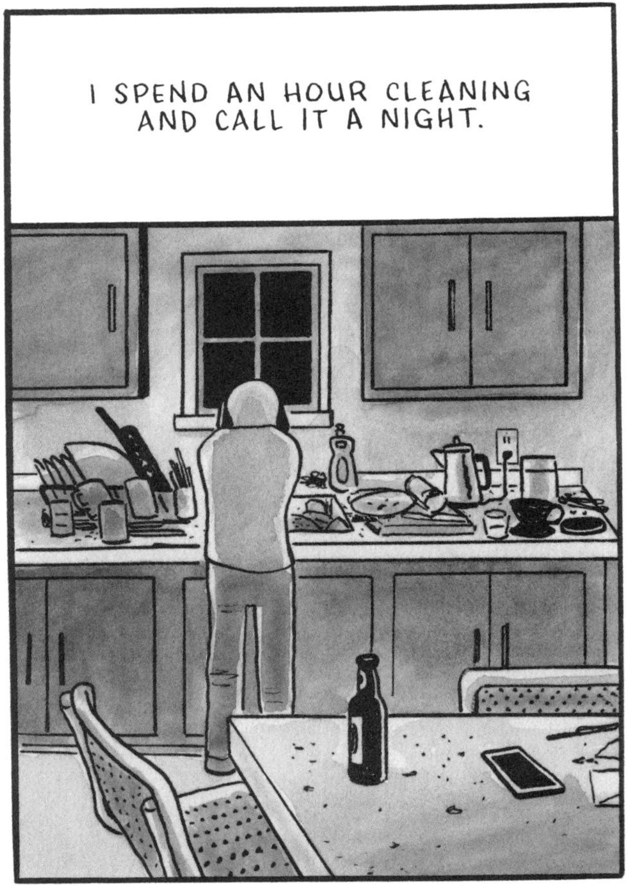
I SPEND AN HOUR CLEANING AND CALL IT A NIGHT.

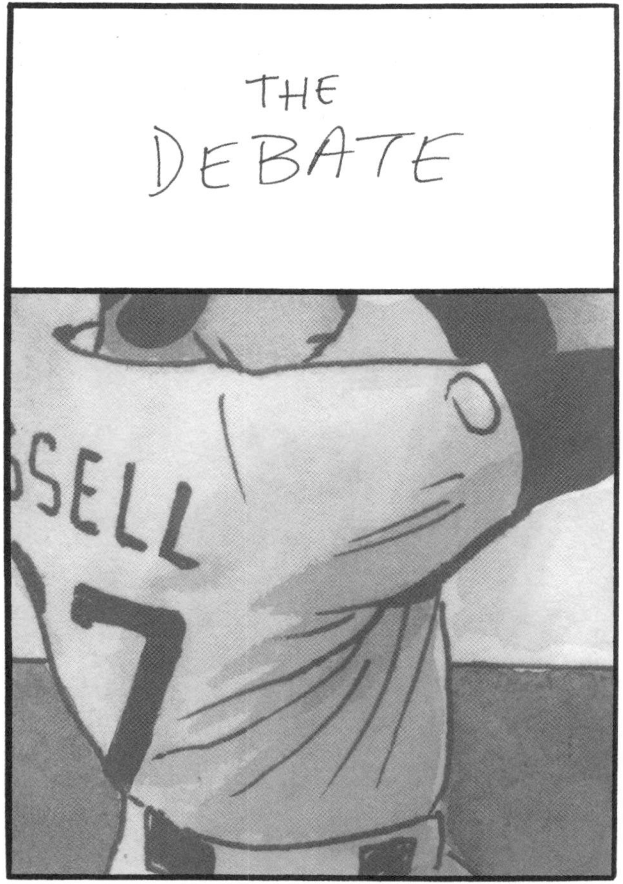
THE
DEBATE

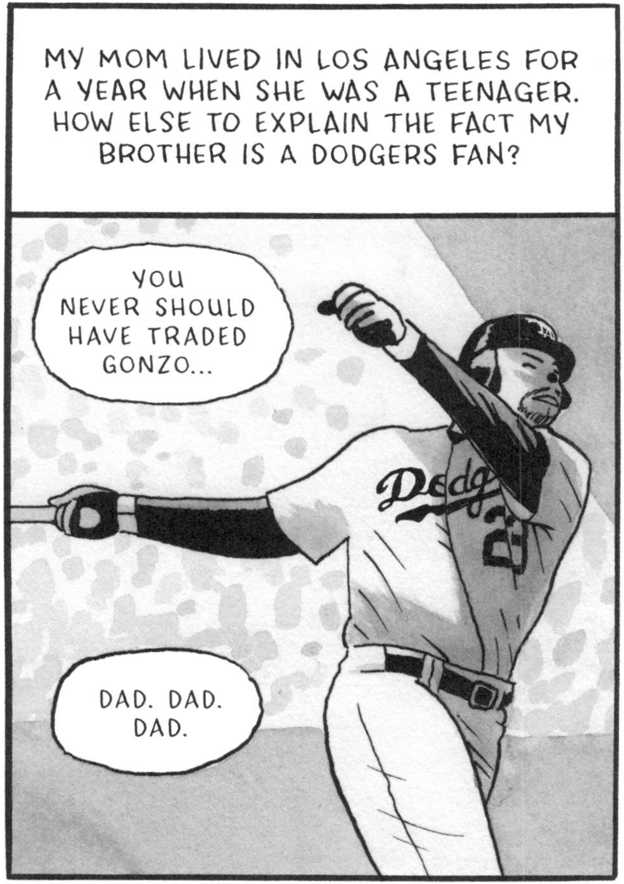
MY MOM LIVED IN LOS ANGELES FOR A YEAR WHEN SHE WAS A TEENAGER. HOW ELSE TO EXPLAIN THE FACT MY BROTHER IS A DODGERS FAN?
YOU NEVER SHOULD HAVE TRADED GONZO...
DAD. DAD. DAD.

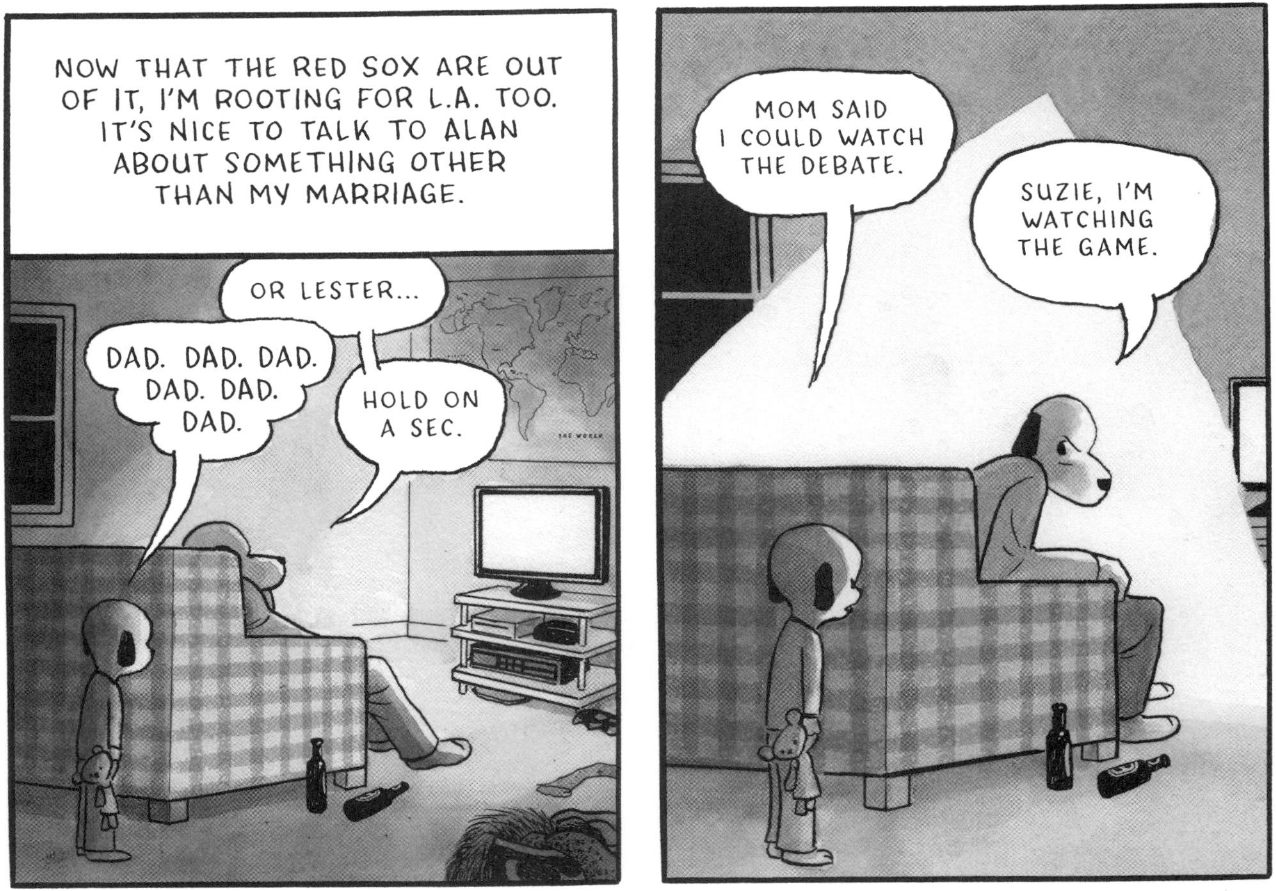
NOW THAT THE RED SOX ARE OUT OF IT, I'M ROOTING FOR L.A. TOO. IT'S NICE TO TALK TO ALAN ABOUT SOMETHING OTHER THAN MY MARRIAGE.
DAD. DAD. DAD. DAD. DAD. DAD.
HOLD ON A SEC.
OR LESTER...
MOM SAID I COULD WATCH THE DEBATE.
SUZIE, I'M WATCHING THE GAME.

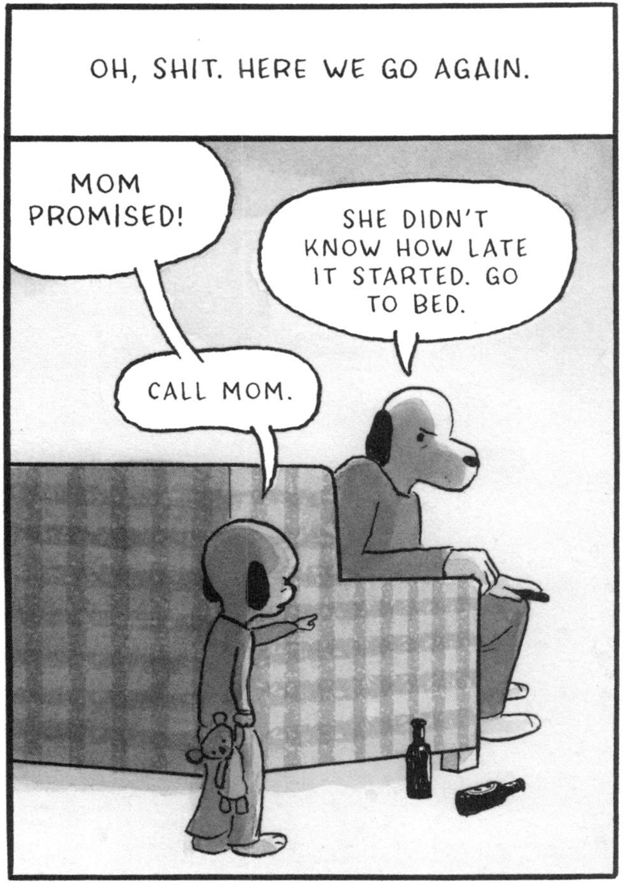
OH, SHIT. HERE WE GO AGAIN.
MOM PROMISED!
SHE DIDN'T KNOW HOW LATE IT STARTED. GO TO BED.
CALL MOM.

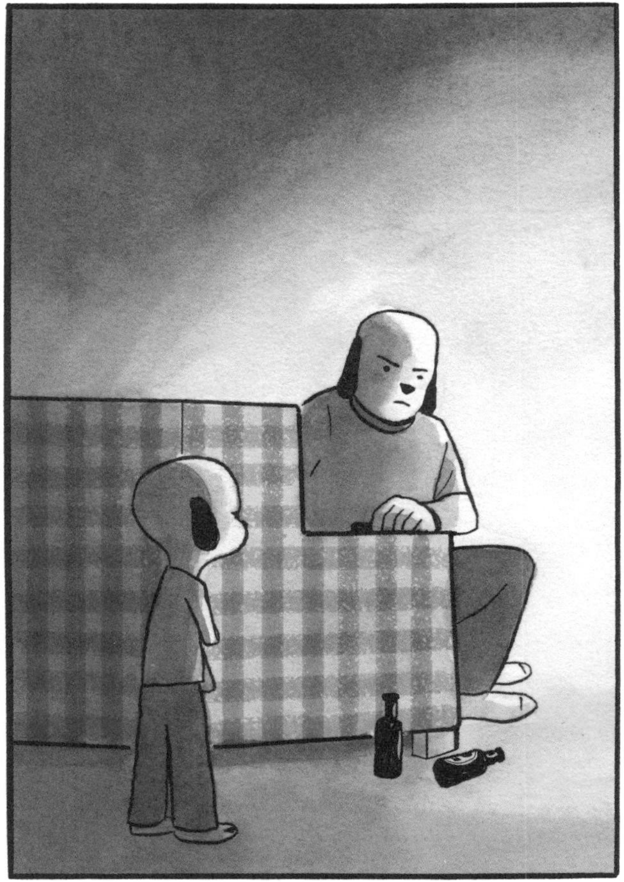

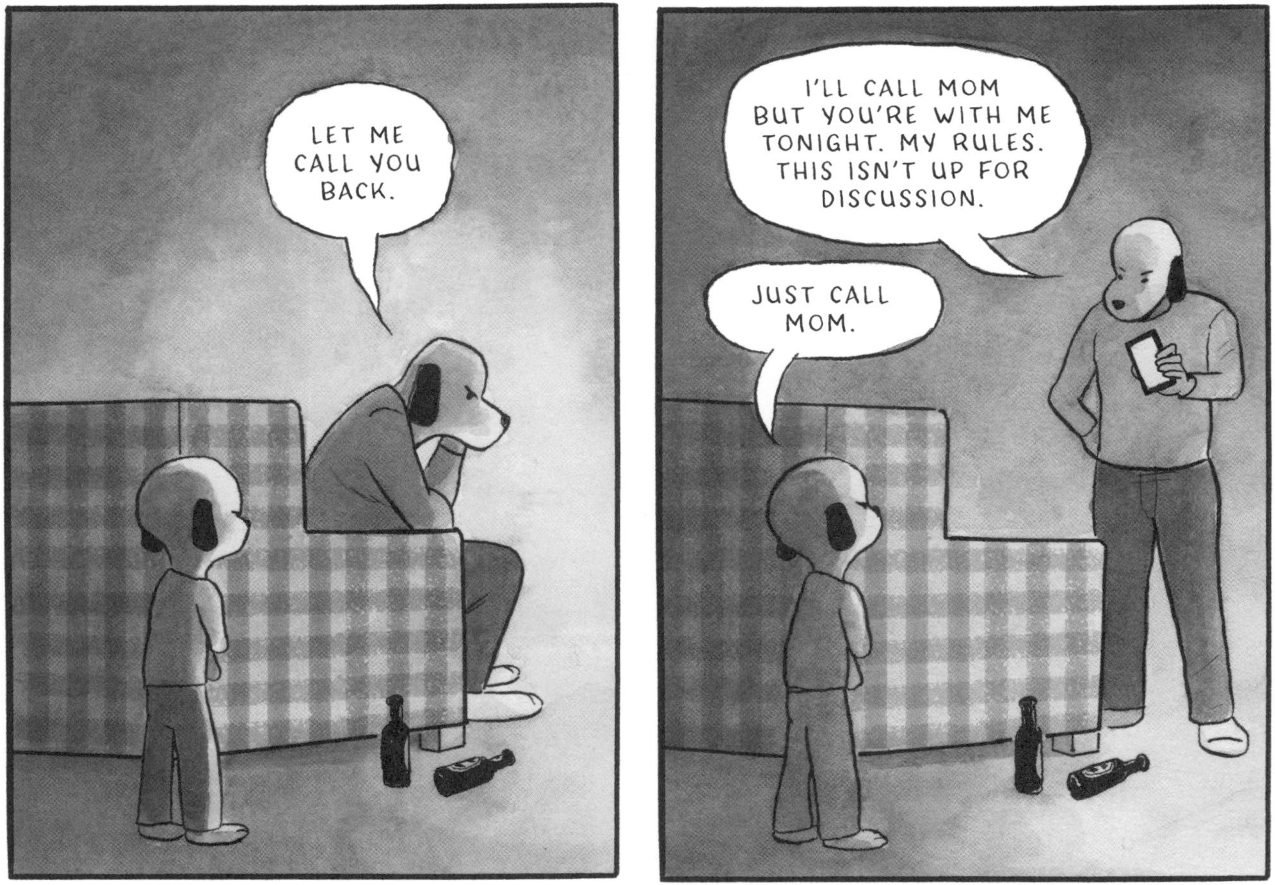
LET ME CALL YOU BACK.
I'LL CALL MOM BUT YOU'RE WITH ME TONIGHT. MY RULES. THIS ISN'T UP FOR DISCUSSION.
JUST CALL MOM.

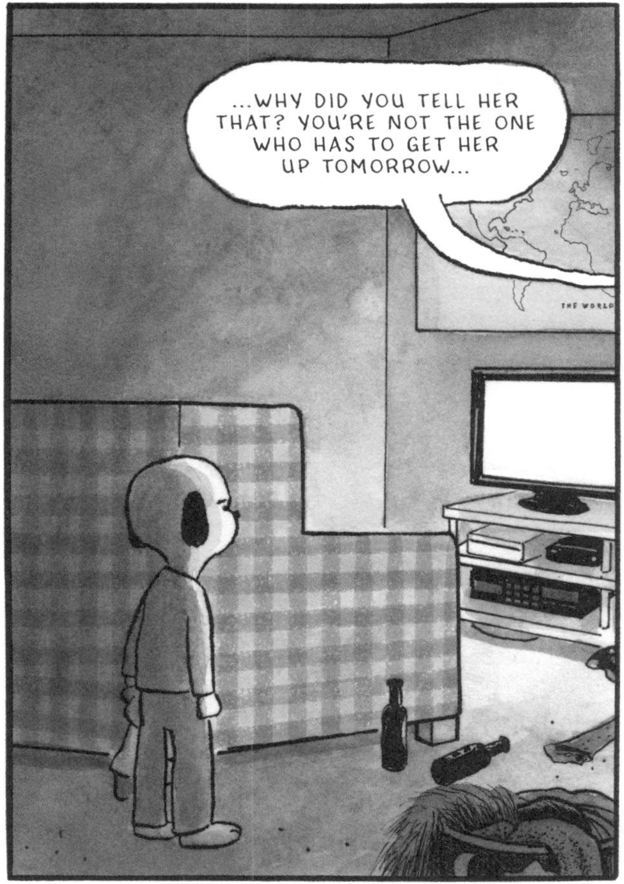
...WHY DID YOU TELL HER THAT? YOU'RE NOT THE ONE WHO HAS TO GET HER UP TOMORROW...
THE WORLD

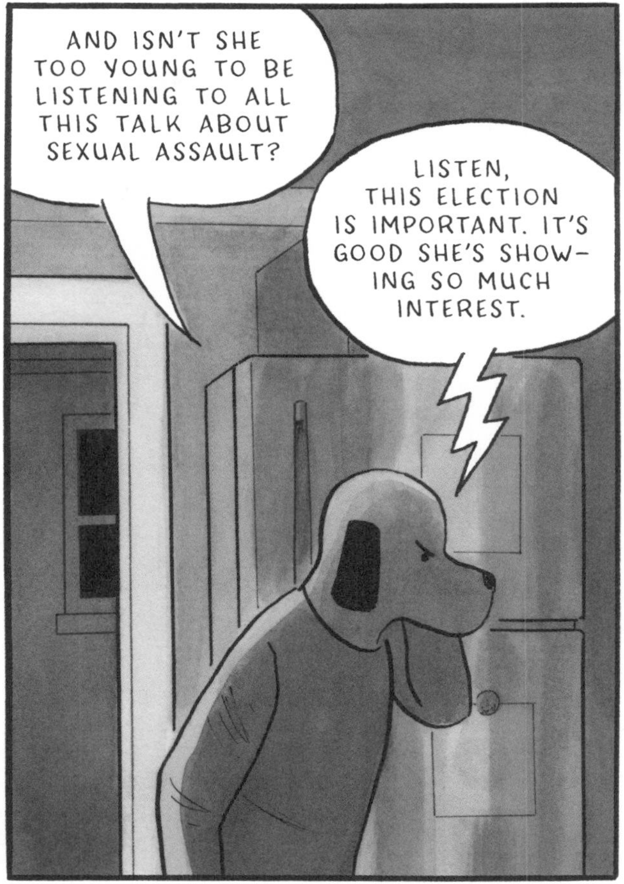
AND ISN'T SHE TOO YOUNG TO BE LISTENING TO ALL THIS TALK ABOUT SEXUAL ASSAULT?
LISTEN, THIS ELECTION IS IMPORTANT. IT'S GOOD SHE'S SHOW-ING SO MUCH INTEREST.

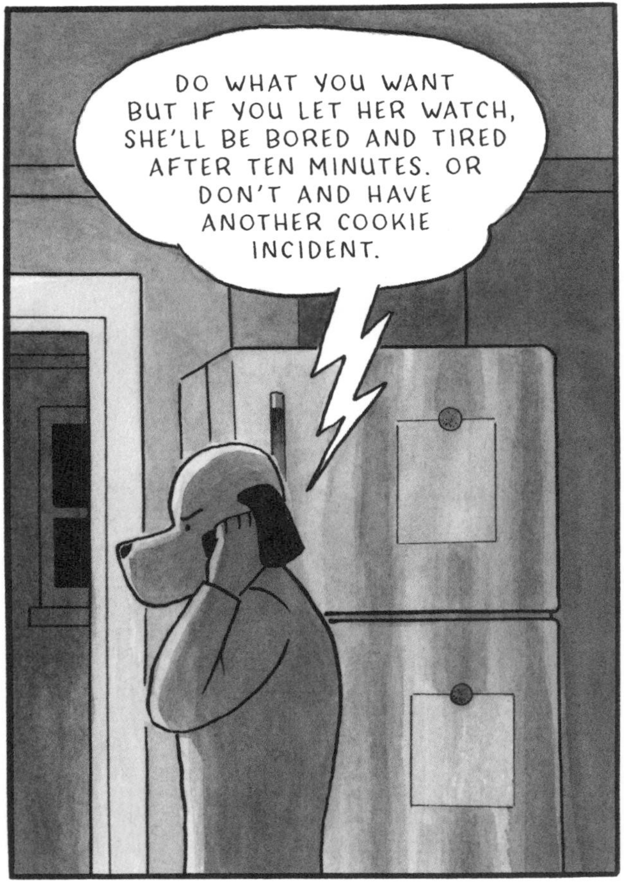
DO WHAT YOU WANT BUT IF YOU LET HER WATCH, SHE'LL BE BORED AND TIRED AFTER TEN MINUTES. OR DON'T AND HAVE ANOTHER COOKIE INCIDENT.

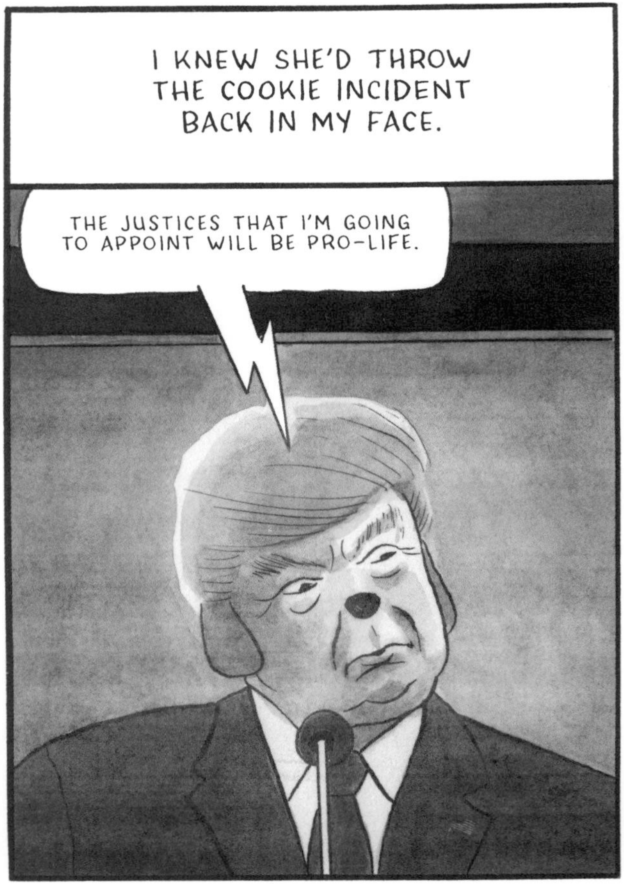
I KNEW SHE'D THROW THE COOKIE INCIDENT BACK IN MY FACE.
THE JUSTICES THAT I'M GOING TO APPOINT WILL BE PRO-LIFE.

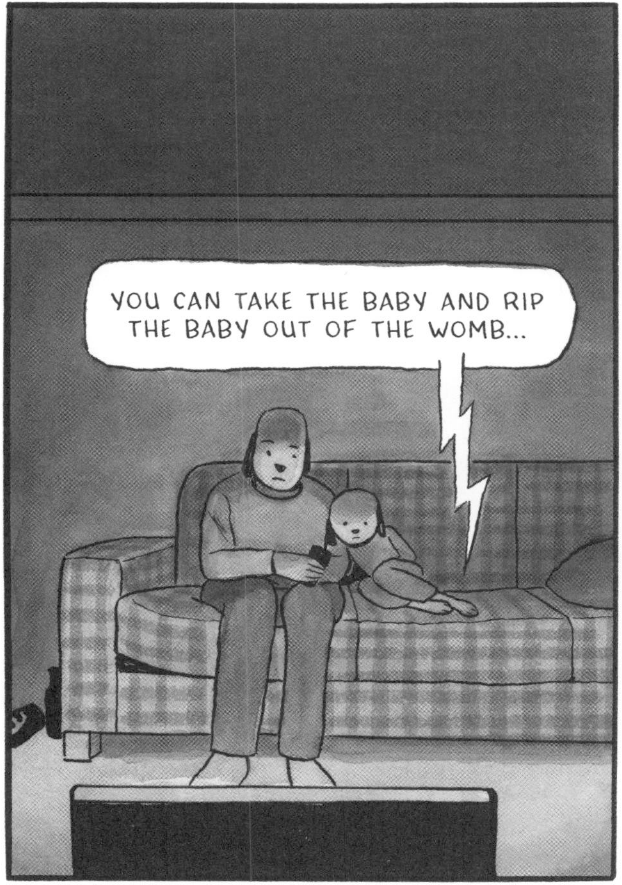
YOU CAN TAKE THE BABY AND RIP THE BABY OUT OF THE WOMB...

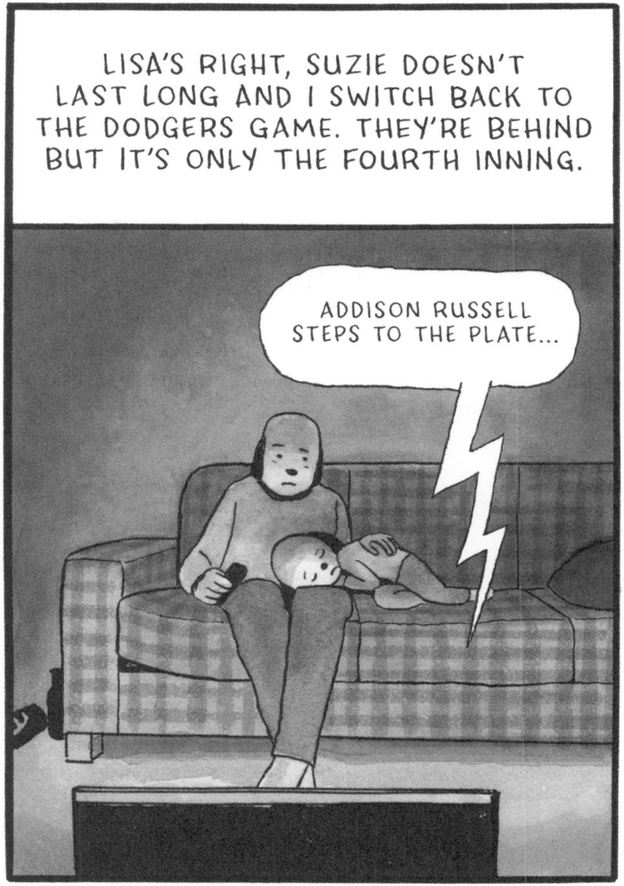
LISA'S RIGHT, SUZIE DOESN'T LAST LONG AND I SWITCH BACK TO THE DODGERS GAME. THEY'RE BEHIND BUT IT'S ONLY THE FOURTH INNING.
ADDISON RUSSELL STEPS TO THE PLATE...

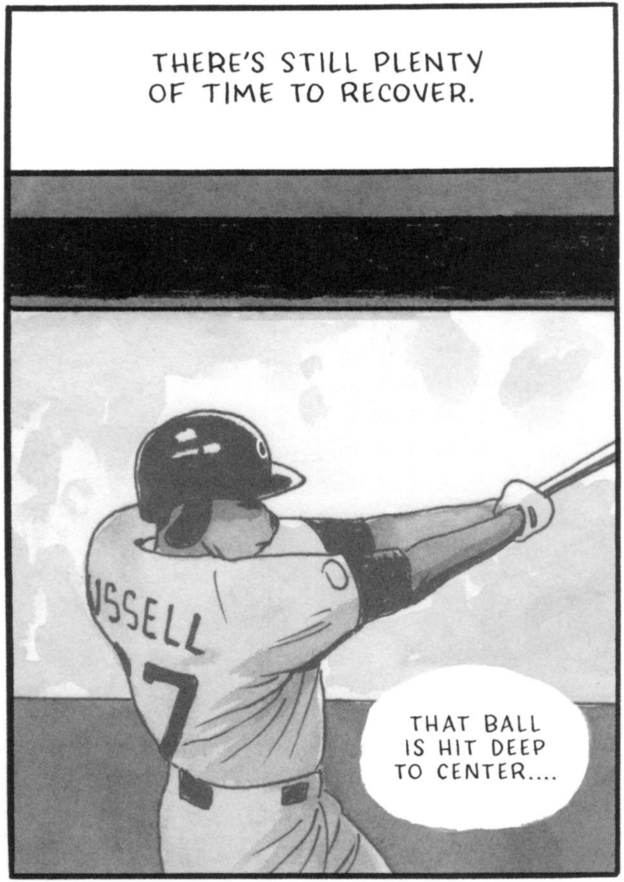
THERE'S STILL PLENTY OF TIME TO RECOVER.
USSELL
THAT BALL IS HIT DEEP TO CENTER....

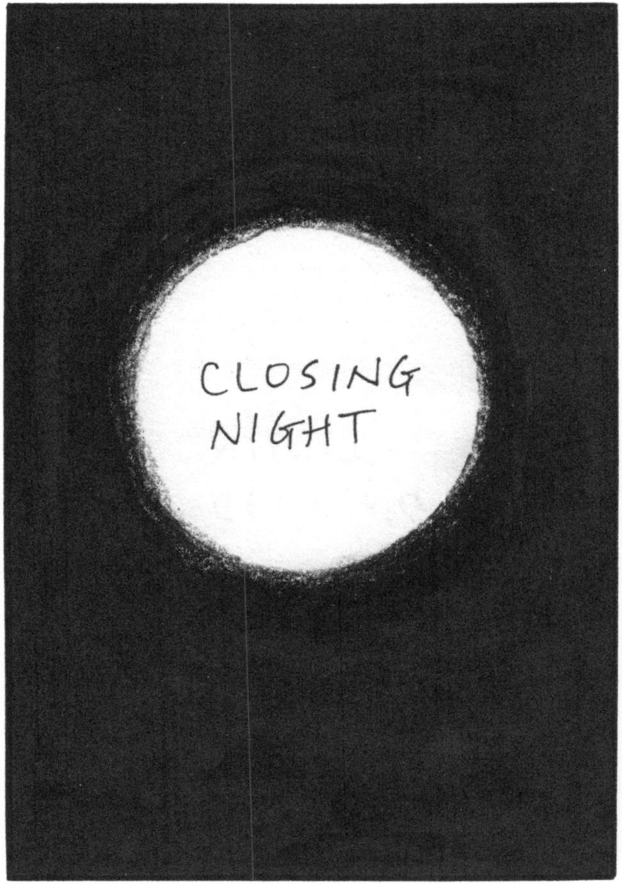
CLOSING NIGHT

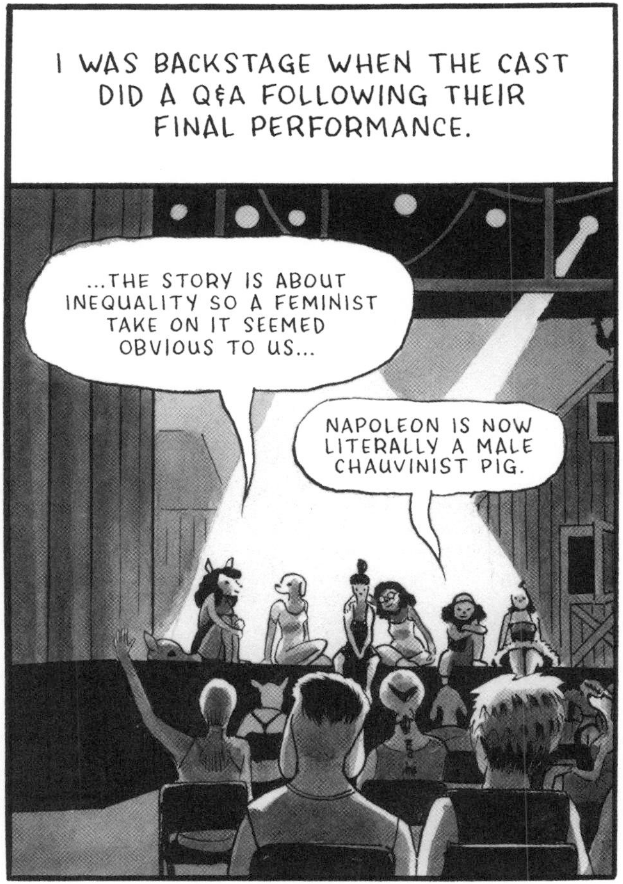
I WAS BACKSTAGE WHEN THE CAST DID A Q&A FOLLOWING THEIR FINAL PERFORMANCE.
...THE STORY IS ABOUT INEQUALITY SO A FEMINIST TAKE ON IT SEEMED OBVIOUS TO US...
NAPOLEON IS NOW LITERALLY A MALE CHAUVINIST PIG.

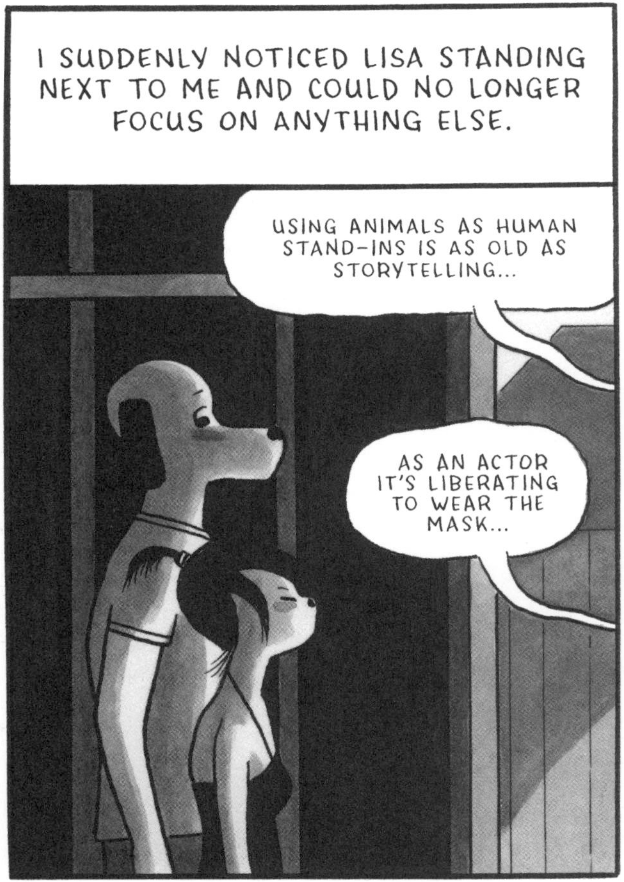
I SUDDENLY NOTICED LISA STANDING NEXT TO ME AND COULD NO LONGER FOCUS ON ANYTHING ELSE.
USING ANIMALS AS HUMAN STAND-INS IS AS OLD AS STORYTELLING...
AS AN ACTOR IT'S LIBERATING TO WEAR THE MASK...

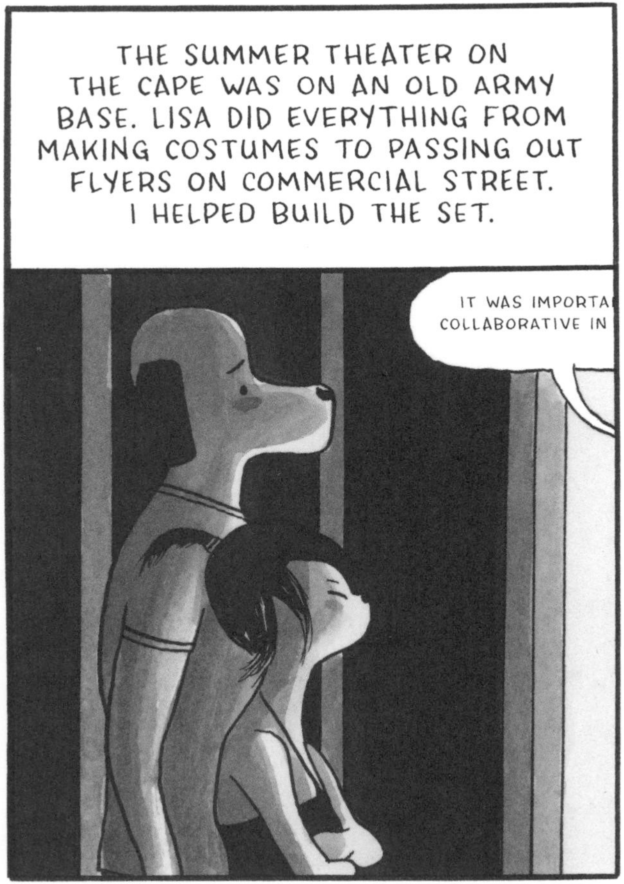
THE SUMMER THEATER ON THE CAPE WAS ON AN OLD ARMY BASE. LISA DID EVERYTHING FROM MAKING COSTUMES TO PASSING OUT FLYERS ON COMMERCIAL STREET. I HELPED BUILD THE SET.
IT WAS
COLLABORATIVE IN

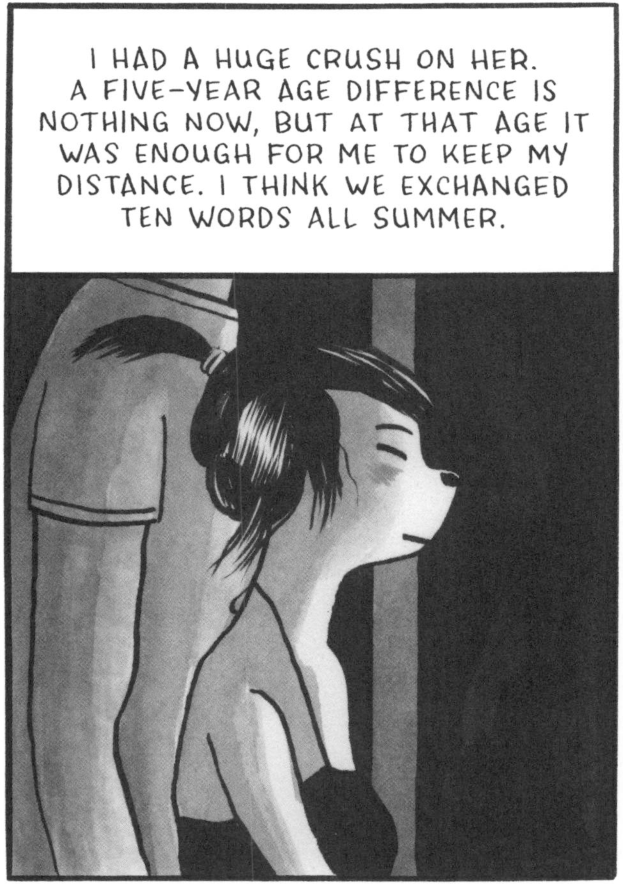
I HAD A HUGE CRUSH ON HER. A FIVE-YEAR AGE DIFFERENCE IS NOTHING NOW, BUT AT THAT AGE IT WAS ENOUGH FOR ME TO KEEP MY DISTANCE. I THINK WE EXCHANGED TEN WORDS ALL SUMMER.

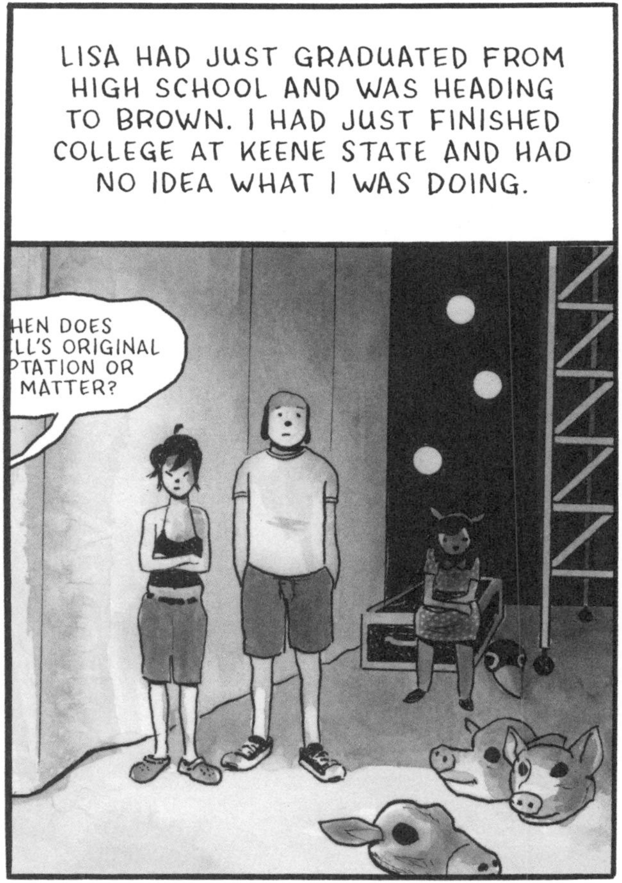
LISA HAD JUST GRADUATED FROM HIGH SCHOOL AND WAS HEADING TO BROWN. I HAD JUST FINISHED COLLEGE AT KEENE STATE AND HAD NO IDEA WHAT I WAS DOING.
HEN DOES LL'S ORIGINAL PTATION OR MATTER?

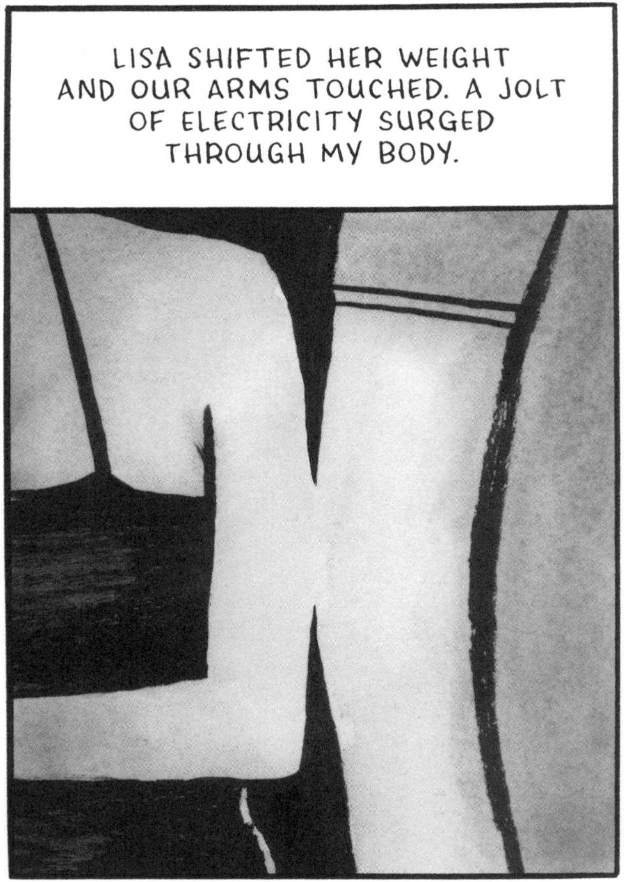
LISA SHIFTED HER WEIGHT AND OUR ARMS TOUCHED. A JOLT OF ELECTRICITY SURGED THROUGH MY BODY.

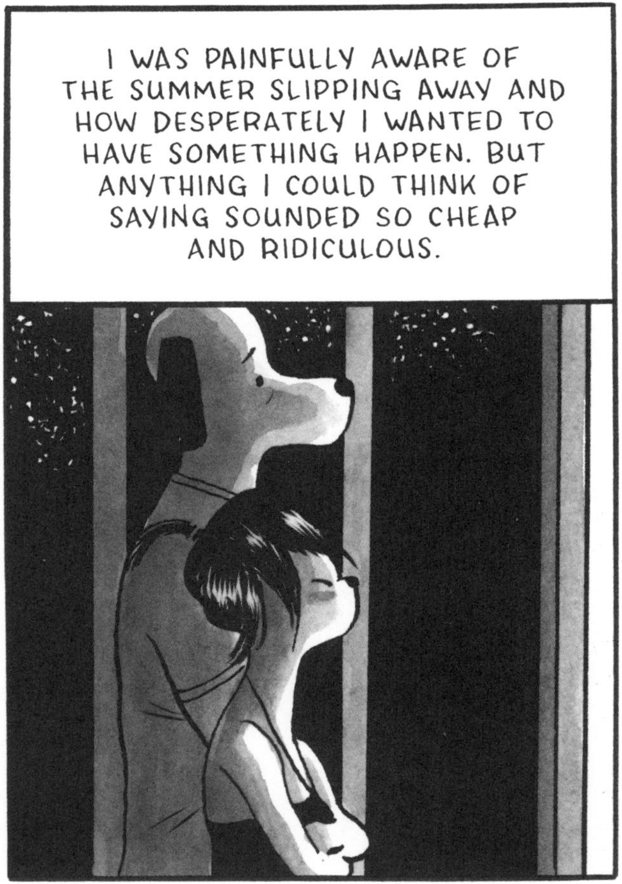
I WAS PAINFULLY AWARE OF THE SUMMER SLIPPING AWAY AND HOW DESPERATELY I WANTED TO HAVE SOMETHING HAPPEN. BUT ANYTHING I COULD THINK OF SAYING SOUNDED SO CHEAP AND RIDICULOUS.

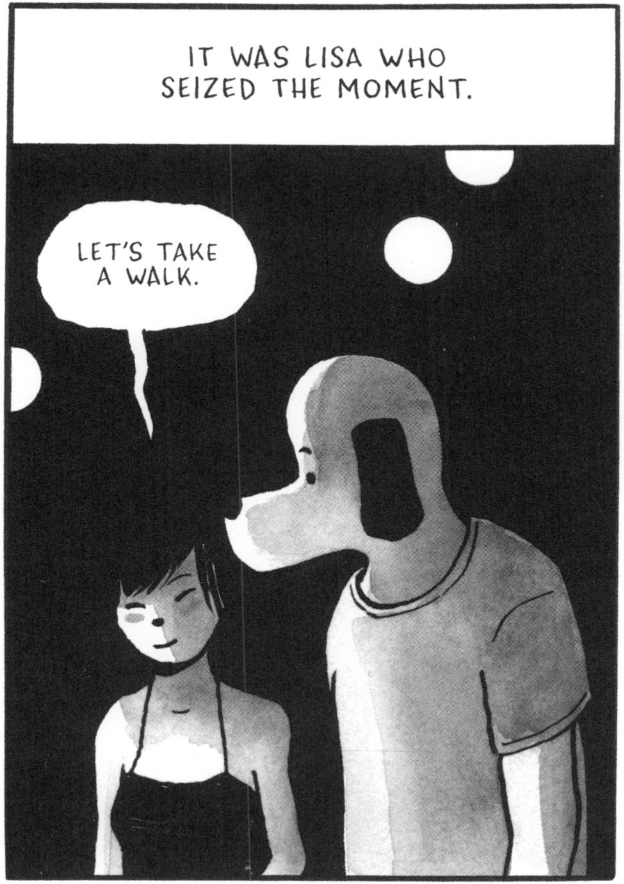
IT WAS LISA WHO SEIZED THE MOMENT.
LET'S TAKE A WALK.

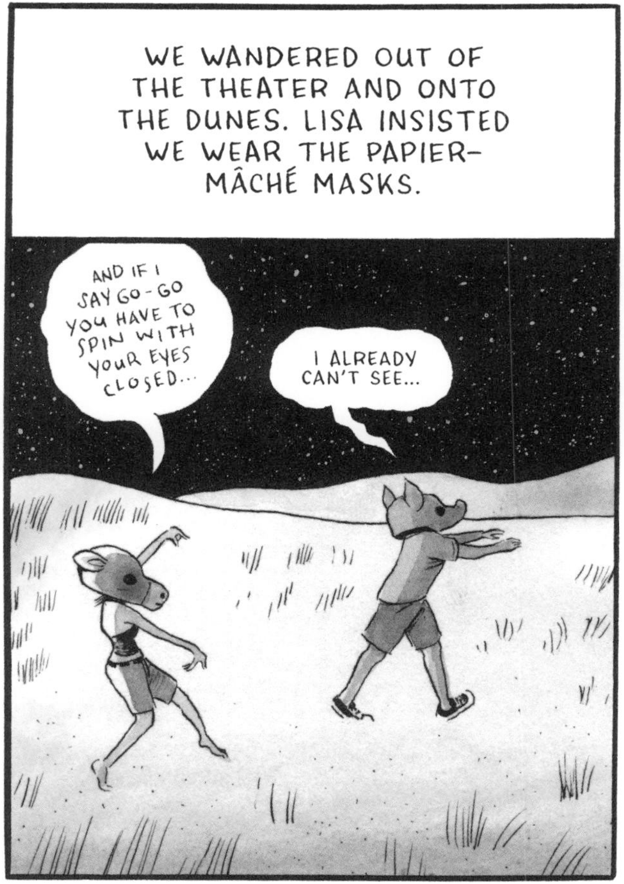
WE WANDERED OUT OF THE THEATER AND ONTO THE DUNES. LISA INSISTED WE WEAR THE PAPIER-MÂCHÉ MASKS.
AND IF I SAY GO-GO YOU HAVE TO SPIN WITH YOUR EYES CLOSED...
I ALREADY CAN'T SEE...

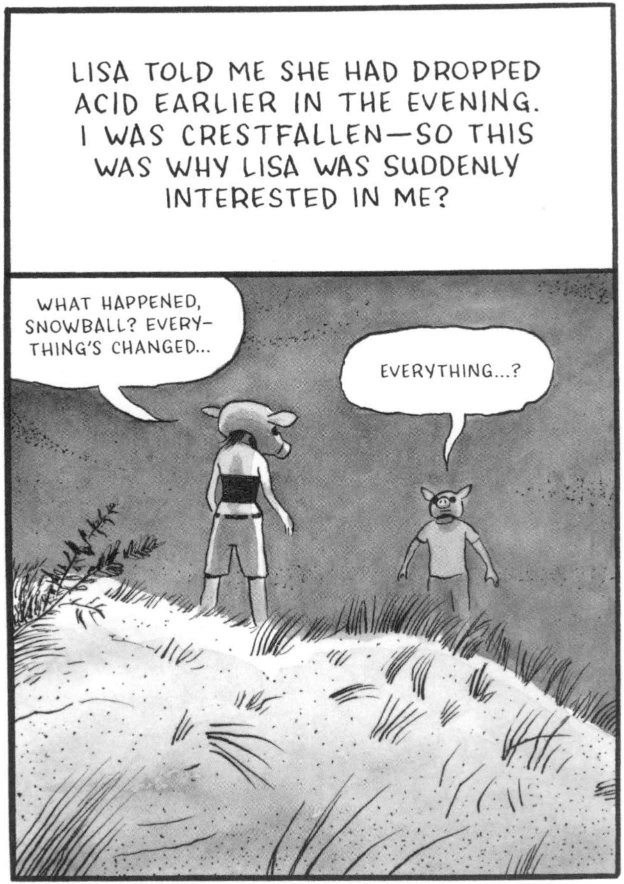
LISA TOLD ME SHE HAD DROPPED ACID EARLIER IN THE EVENING. I WAS CRESTFALLEN—SO THIS WAS WHY LISA WAS SUDDENLY INTERESTED IN ME?
WHAT HAPPENED, SNOWBALL? EVERY-THING'S CHANGED...
EVERYTHING...?

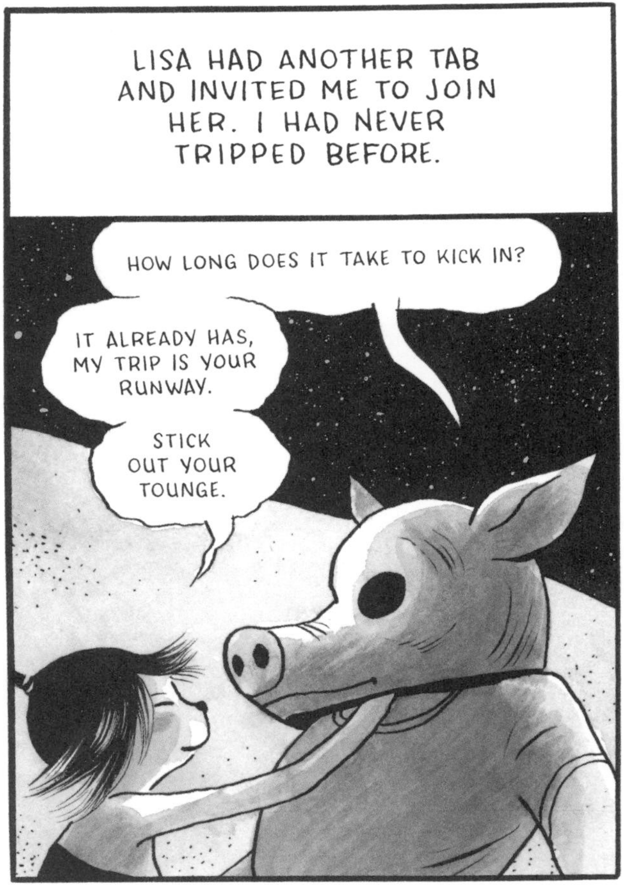
LISA HAD ANOTHER TAB AND INVITED ME TO JOIN HER. I HAD NEVER TRIPPED BEFORE.
HOW LONG DOES IT TAKE TO KICK IN?
IT ALREADY HAS, MY TRIP IS YOUR RUNWAY.
STICK OUT YOUR TOUNGE.

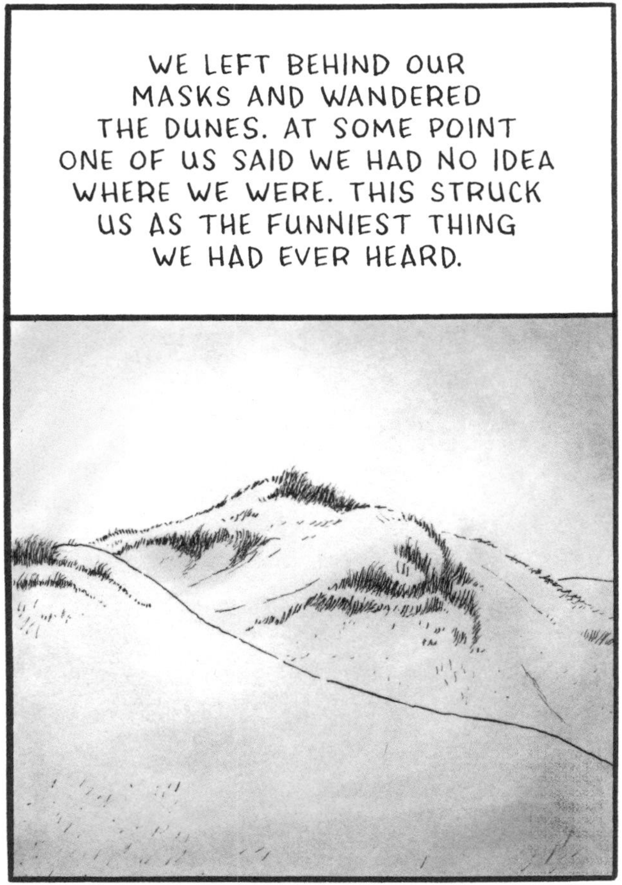
WE LEFT BEHIND OUR MASKS AND WANDERED THE DUNES. AT SOME POINT ONE OF US SAID WE HAD NO IDEA WHERE WE WERE. THIS STRUCK US AS THE FUNNIEST THING WE HAD EVER HEARD.

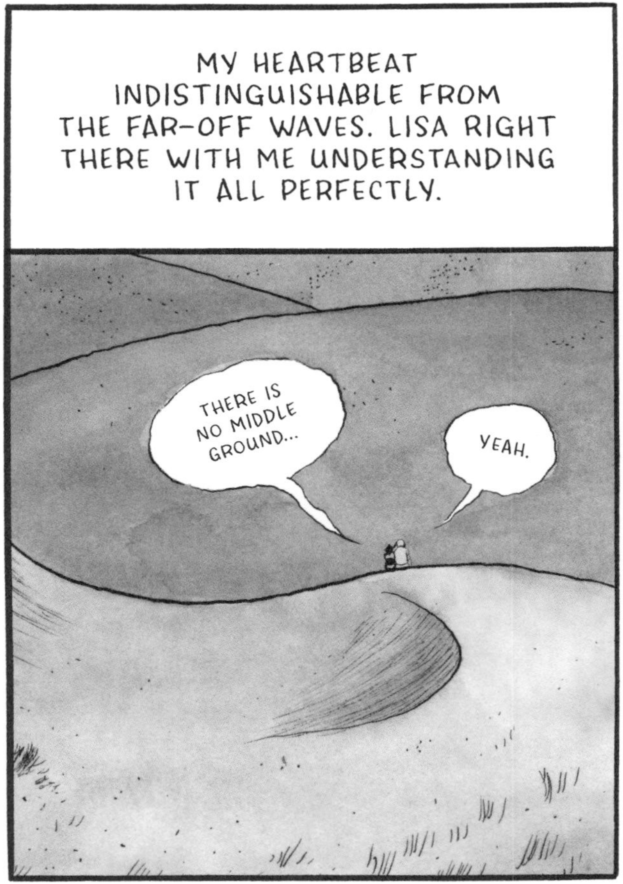
MY HEARTBEAT INDISTINGUISHABLE FROM THE FAR-OFF WAVES. LISA RIGHT THERE WITH ME UNDERSTANDING IT ALL PERFECTLY.
THERE IS NO MIDDLE GROUND...
YEAH.

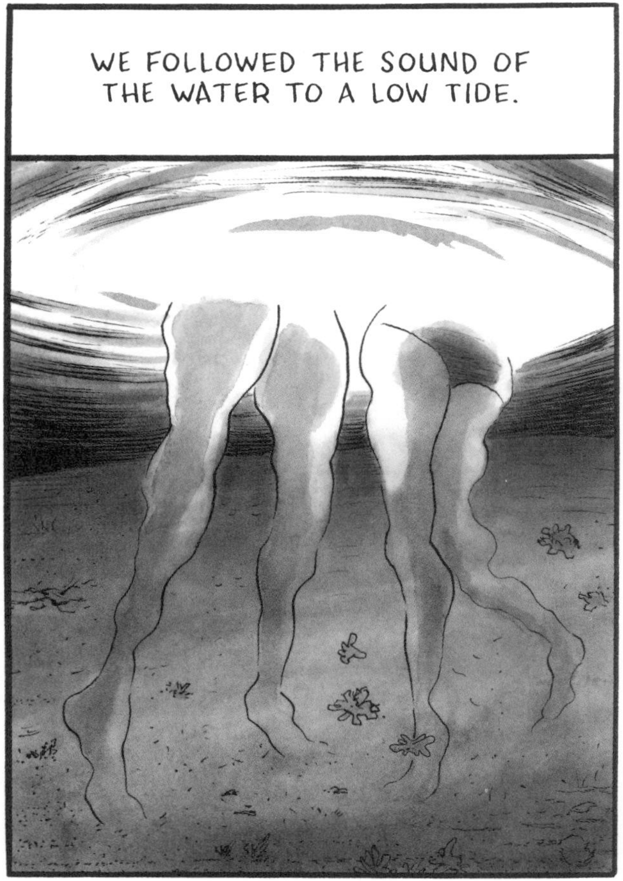
WE FOLLOWED THE SOUND OF THE WATER TO A LOW TIDE.

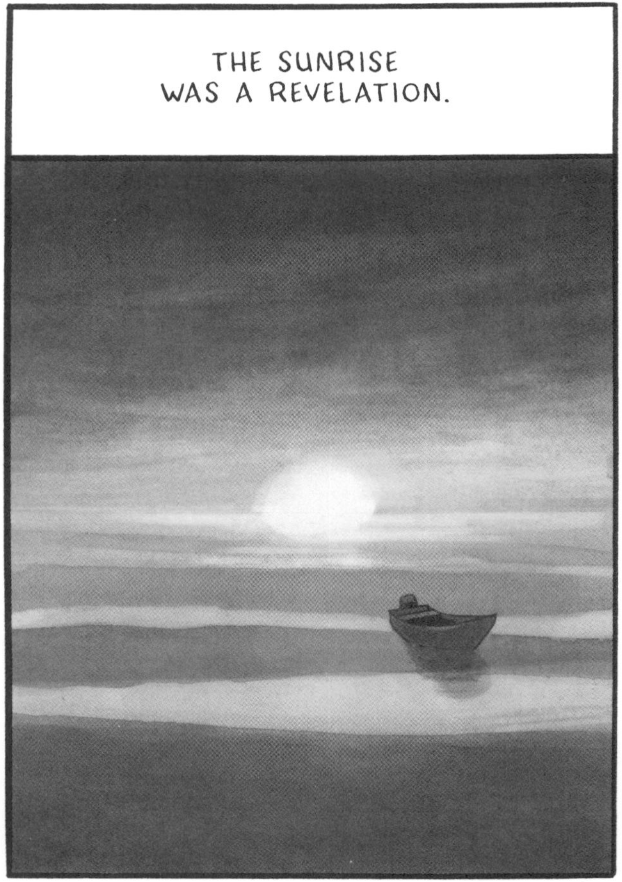
THE SUNRISE WAS A REVELATION.

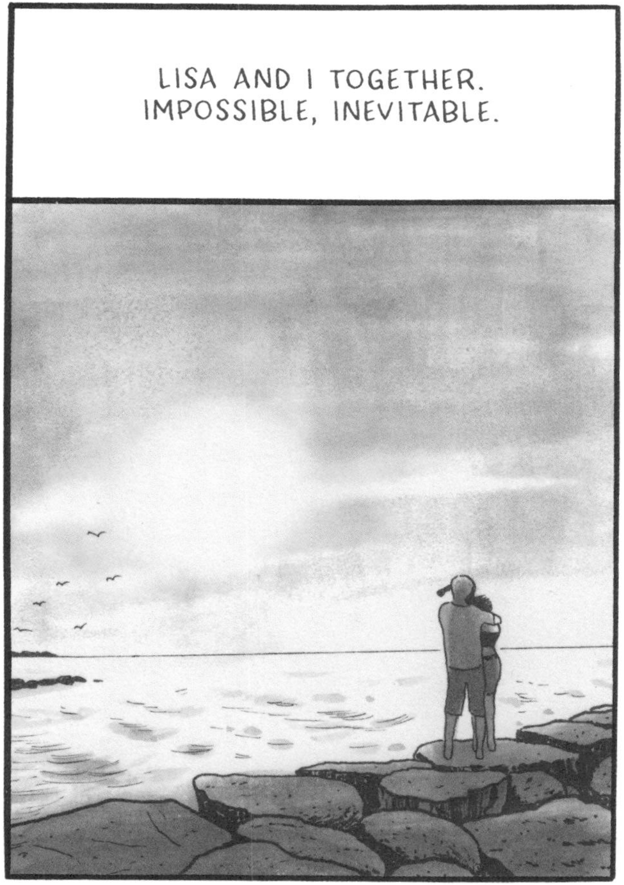
LISA AND I TOGETHER. IMPOSSIBLE, INEVITABLE.

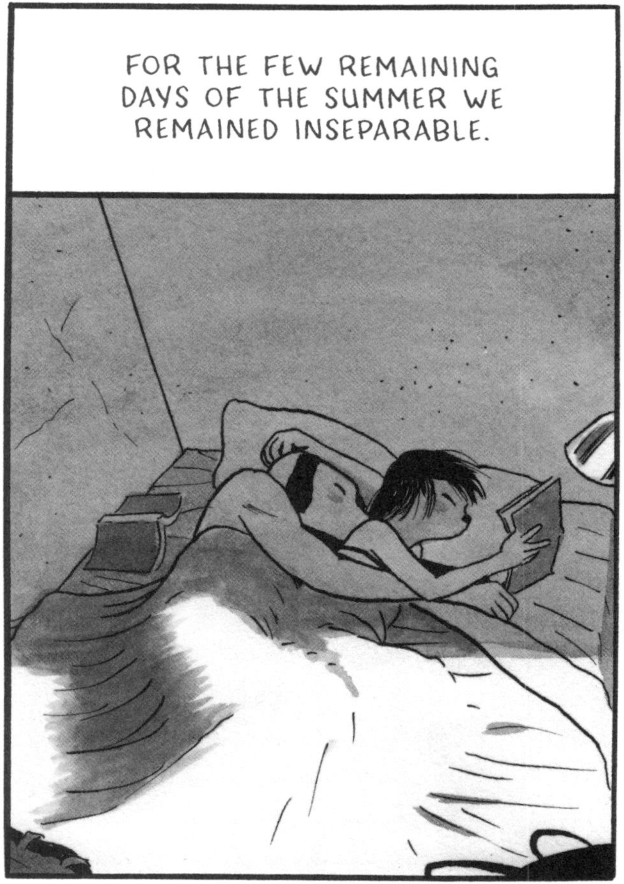
FOR THE FEW REMAINING DAYS OF THE SUMMER WE REMAINED INSEPARABLE.

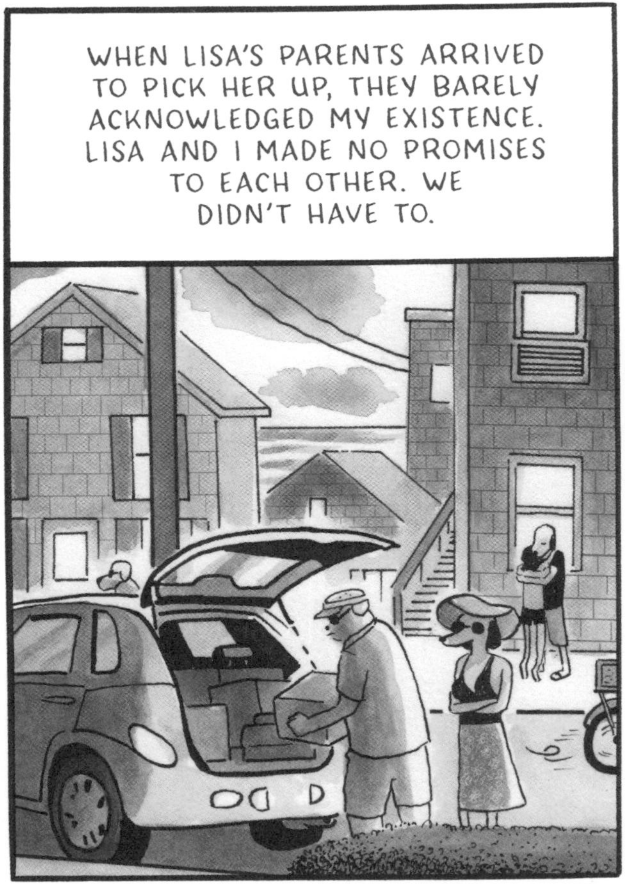
WHEN LISA'S PARENTS ARRIVED TO PICK HER UP, THEY BARELY ACKNOWLEDGED MY EXISTENCE. LISA AND I MADE NO PROMISES TO EACH OTHER. WE DIDN'T HAVE TO.

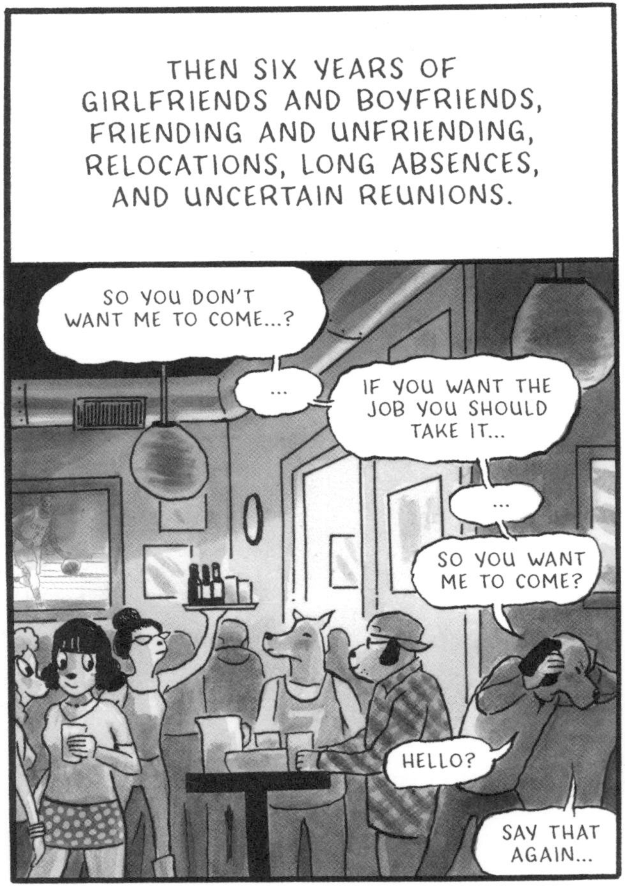
THEN SIX YEARS OF GIRLFRIENDS AND BOYFRIENDS, FRIENDING AND UNFRIENDING, RELOCATIONS, LONG ABSENCES, AND UNCERTAIN REUNIONS.
SO YOU DON'T WANT ME TO COME...?
...
IF YOU WANT THE JOB YOU SHOULD TAKE IT...
...
SO YOU WANT ME TO COME?
HELLO?
SAY THAT AGAIN...

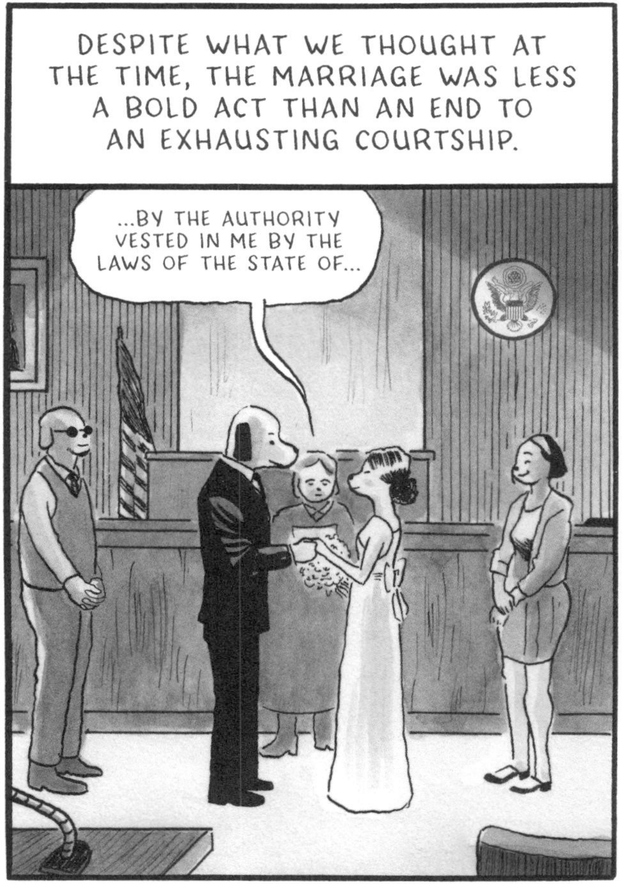
DESPITE WHAT WE THOUGHT AT THE TIME, THE MARRIAGE WAS LESS A BOLD ACT THAN AN END TO AN EXHAUSTING COURTSHIP.
...BY THE AUTHORITY VESTED IN ME BY THE LAWS OF THE STATE OF...

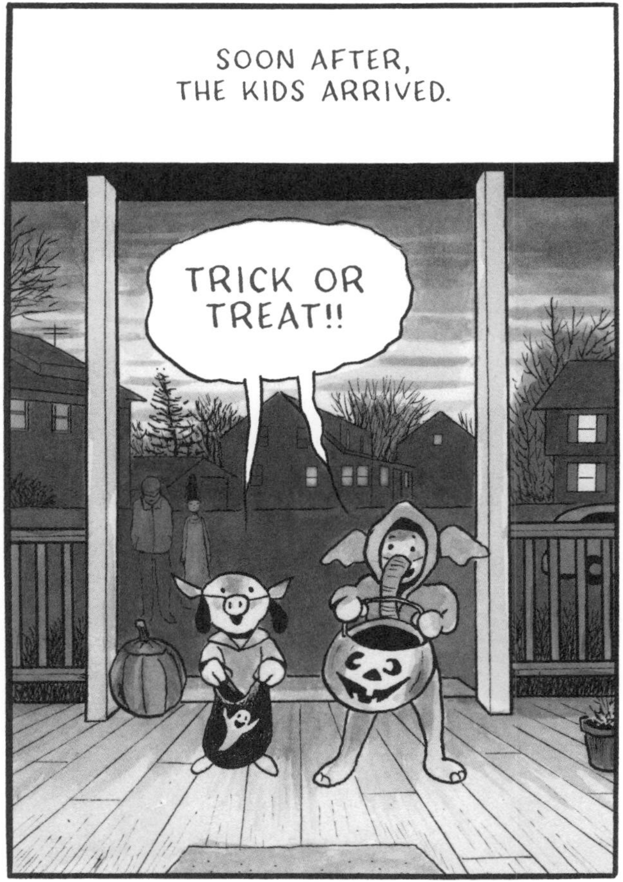
SOON AFTER, THE KIDS ARRIVED.
TRICK OR TREAT!!

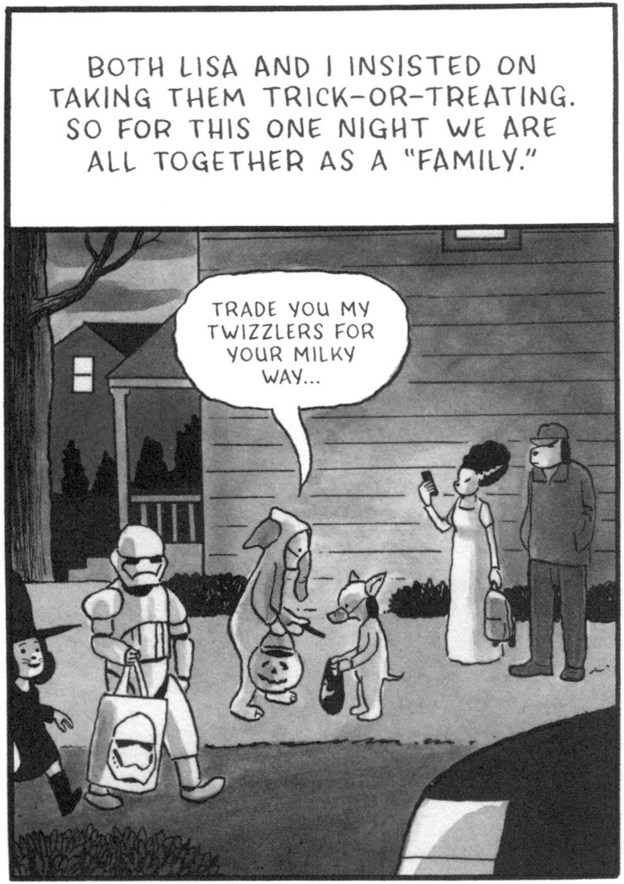
BOTH LISA AND I INSISTED ON TAKING THEM TRICK-OR-TREATING. SO FOR THIS ONE NIGHT WE ARE ALL TOGETHER AS A "FAMILY."
TRADE YOU MY TWIZZLERS FOR YOUR MILKY WAY...

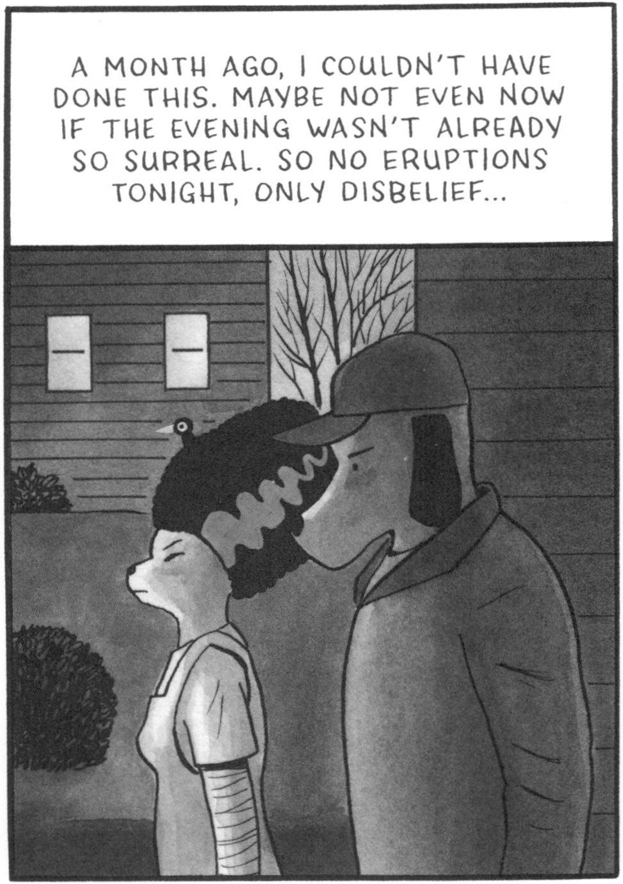
A MONTH AGO, I COULDN'T HAVE DONE THIS. MAYBE NOT EVEN NOW IF THE EVENING WASN'T ALREADY SO SURREAL. SO NO ERUPTIONS TONIGHT, ONLY DISBELIEF...

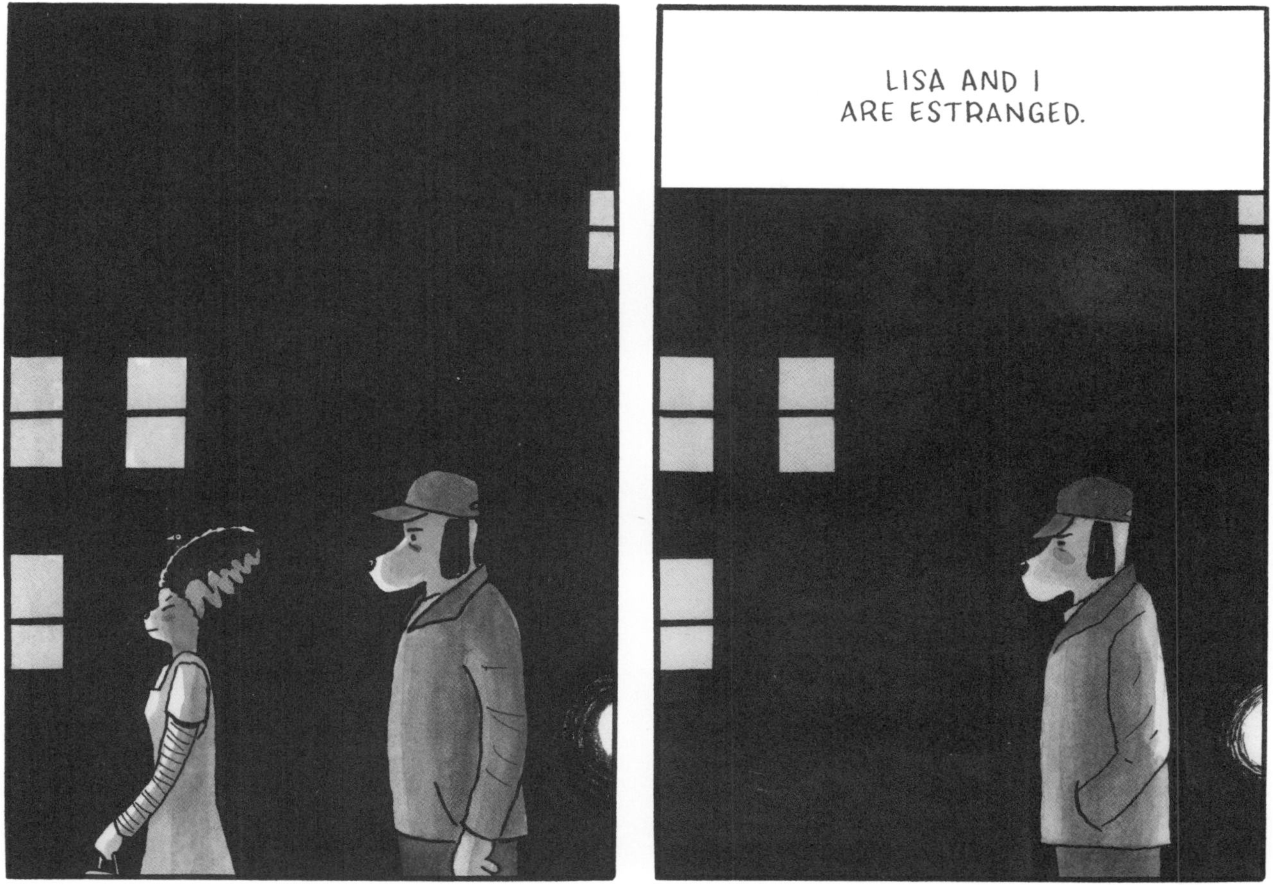
LISA AND I
ARE ESTRANGED.

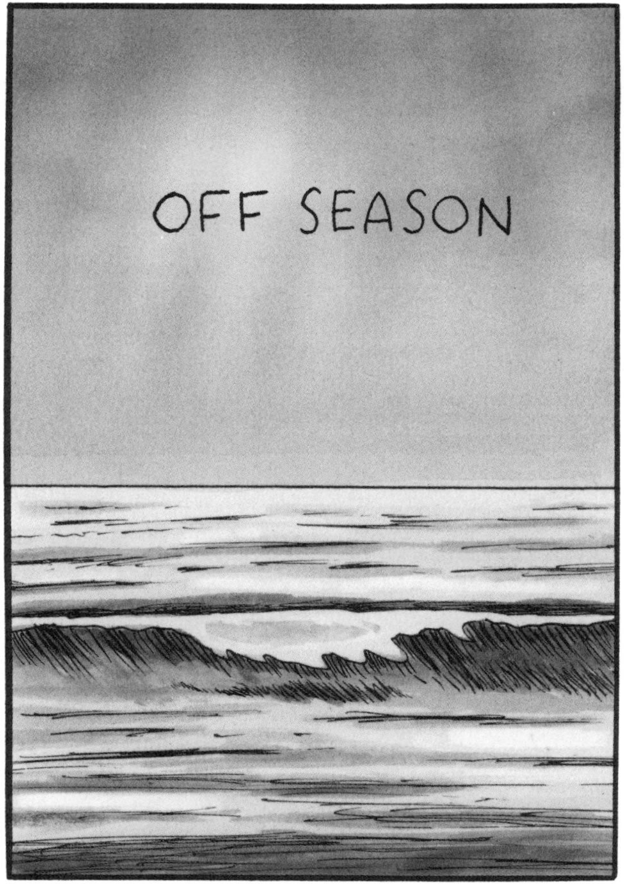
OFF SEASON

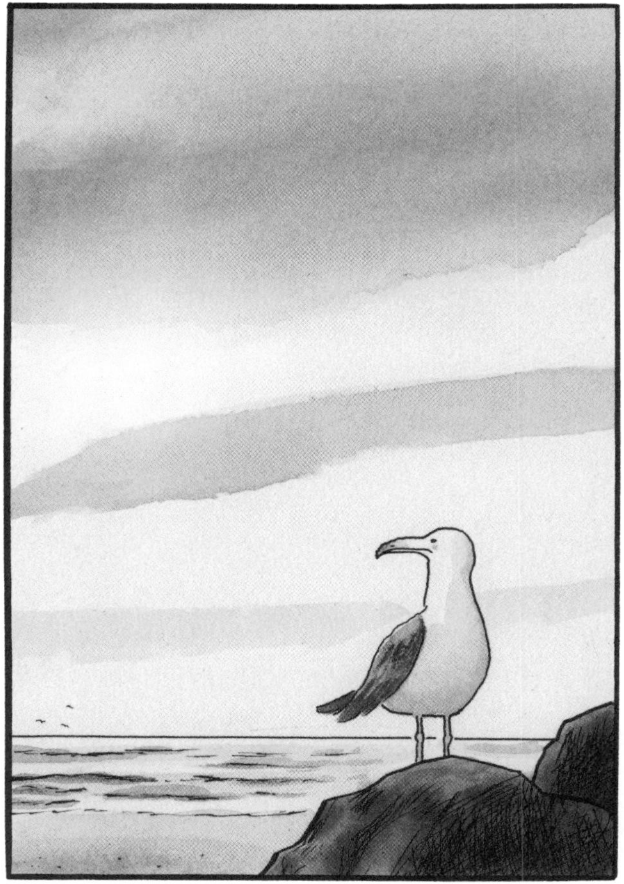

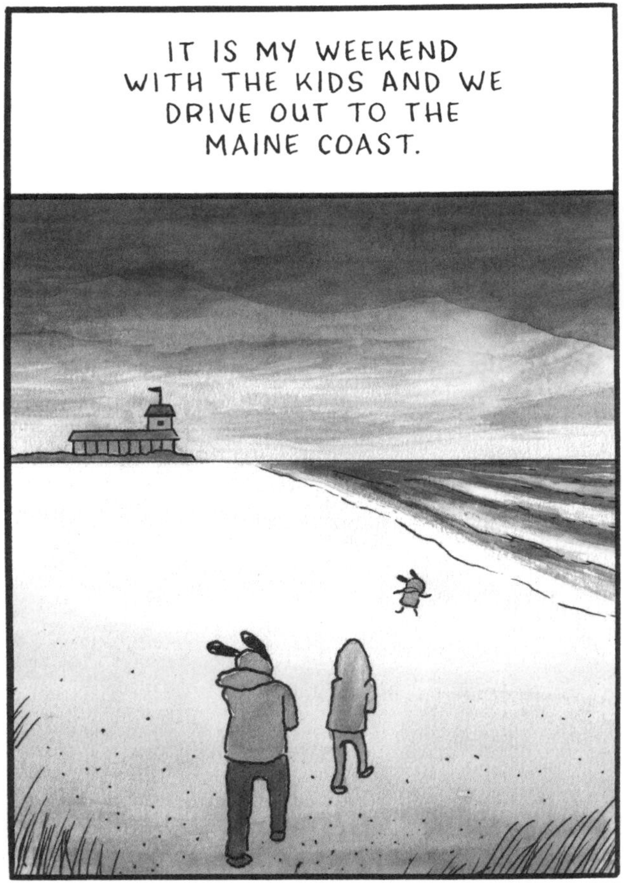
IT IS MY WEEKEND WITH THE KIDS AND WE DRIVE OUT TO THE MAINE COAST.

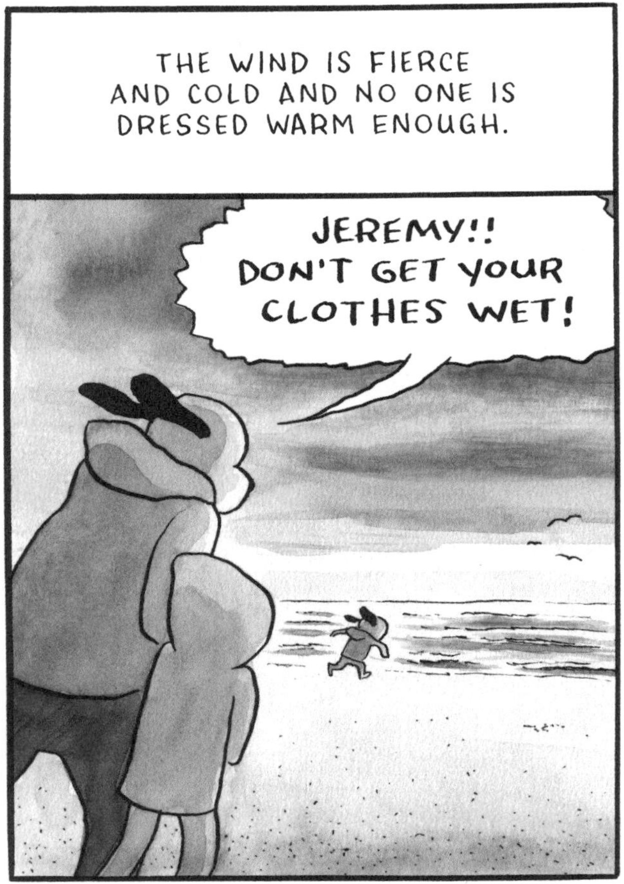
THE WIND IS FIERCE AND COLD AND NO ONE IS DRESSED WARM ENOUGH.
JEREMY!! DON'T GET YOUR CLOTHES WET!

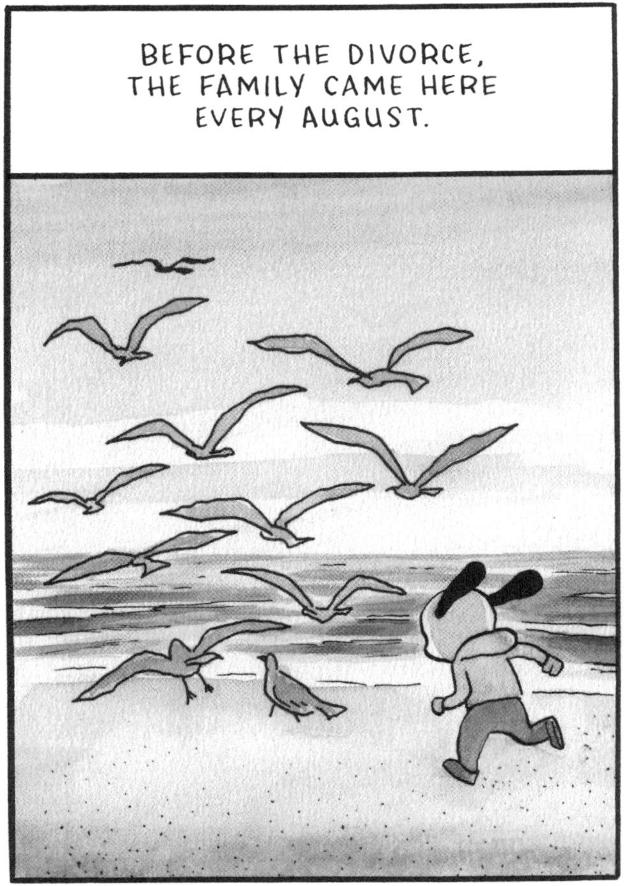
BEFORE THE DIVORCE, THE FAMILY CAME HERE EVERY AUGUST.

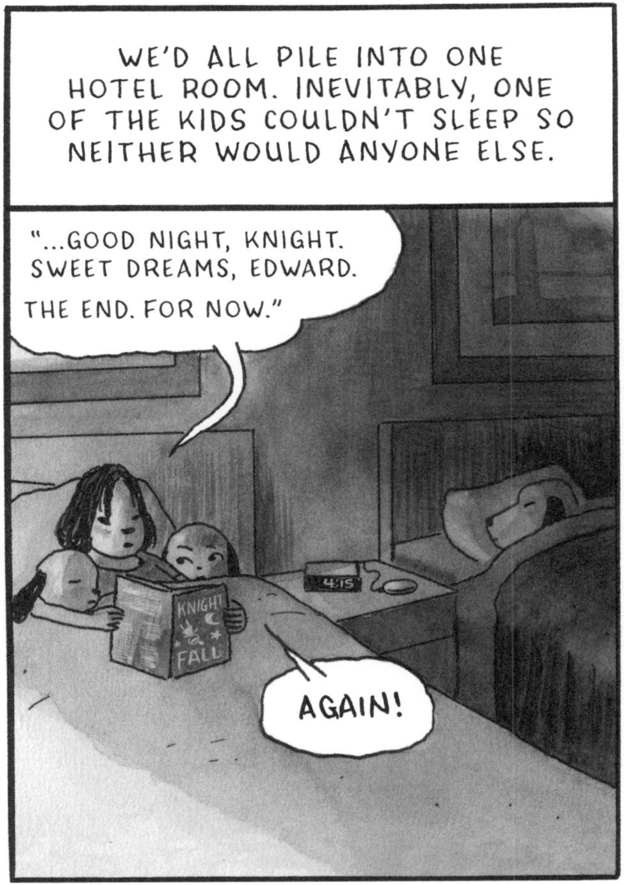
WE'D ALL PILE INTO ONE HOTEL ROOM. INEVITABLY, ONE OF THE KIDS COULDN'T SLEEP SO NEITHER WOULD ANYONE ELSE.
"...GOOD NIGHT, KNIGHT. SWEET DREAMS, EDWARD. THE END. FOR NOW."
KNIGHT FALL
4:15
AGAIN!

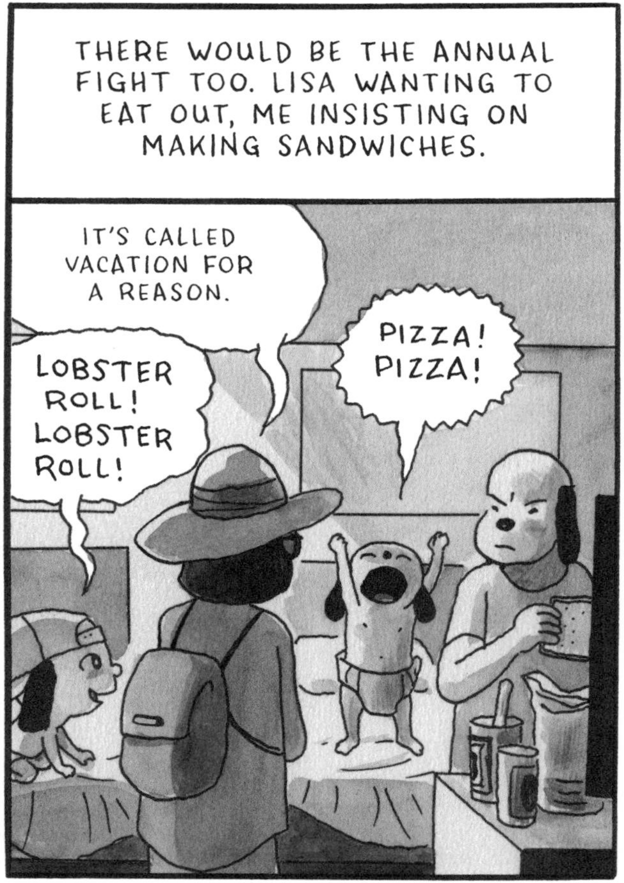
THERE WOULD BE THE ANNUAL FIGHT TOO. LISA WANTING TO EAT OUT, ME INSISTING ON MAKING SANDWICHES.
IT'S CALLED VACATION FOR A REASON.
LOBSTER ROLL! LOBSTER ROLL!
PIZZA! PIZZA!

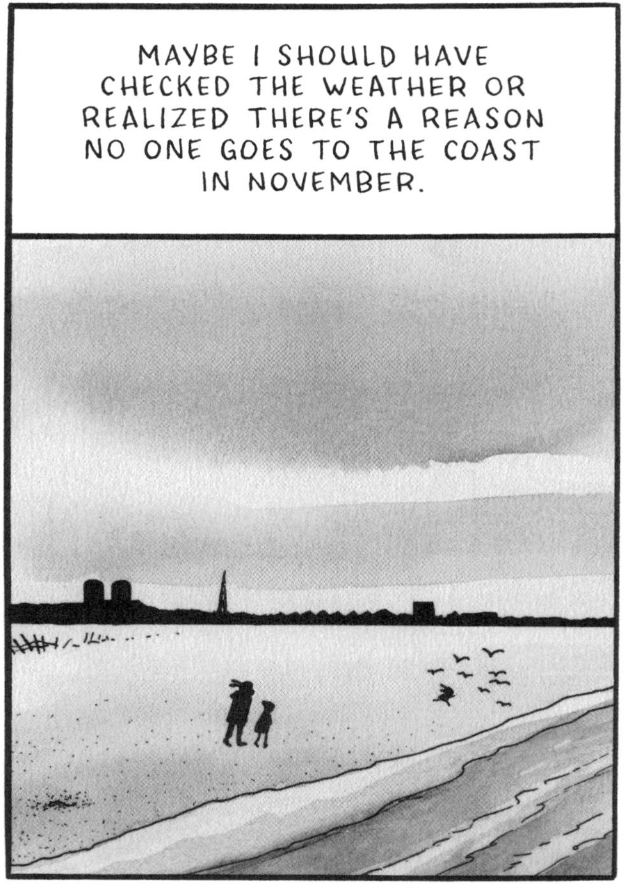
MAYBE I SHOULD HAVE CHECKED THE WEATHER OR REALIZED THERE'S A REASON NO ONE GOES TO THE COAST IN NOVEMBER.

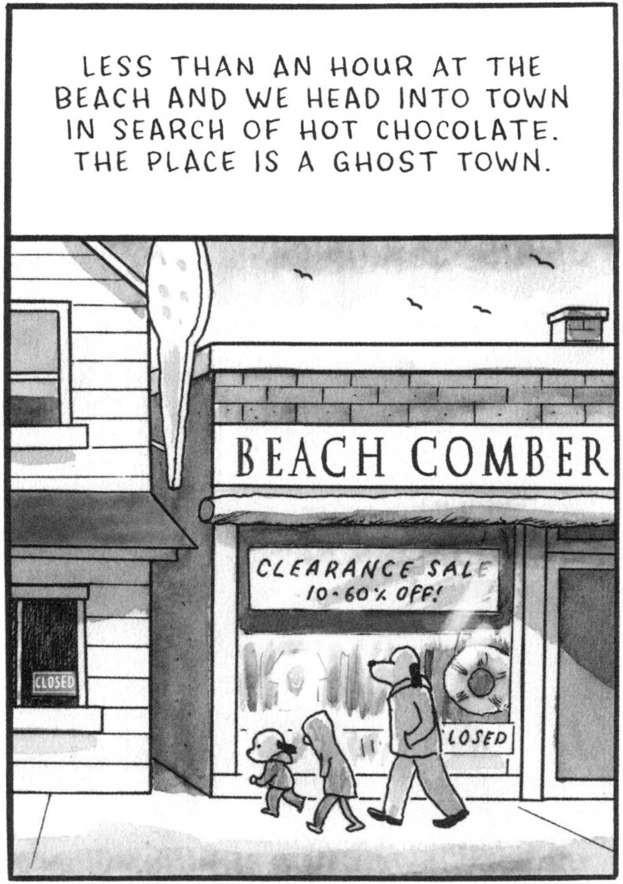
LESS THAN AN HOUR AT THE BEACH AND WE HEAD INTO TOWN IN SEARCH OF HOT CHOCOLATE. THE PLACE IS A GHOST TOWN.
BEACH COMBER
CLEARANCE SALE 10-60% OFF!
CLOSED
CLOSED

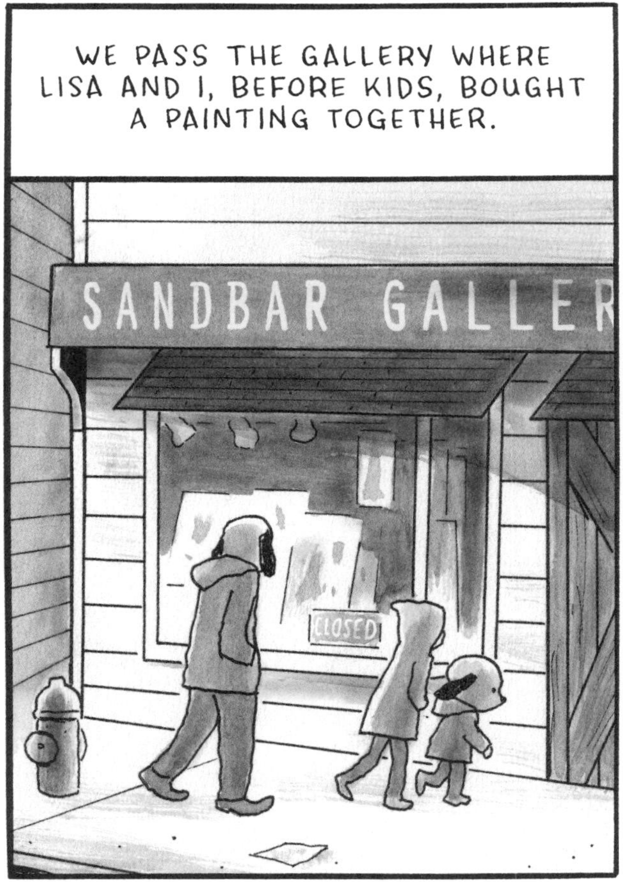
WE PASS THE GALLERY WHERE LISA AND I, BEFORE KIDS, BOUGHT A PAINTING TOGETHER.
SANDBAR GALLER
CLOSED

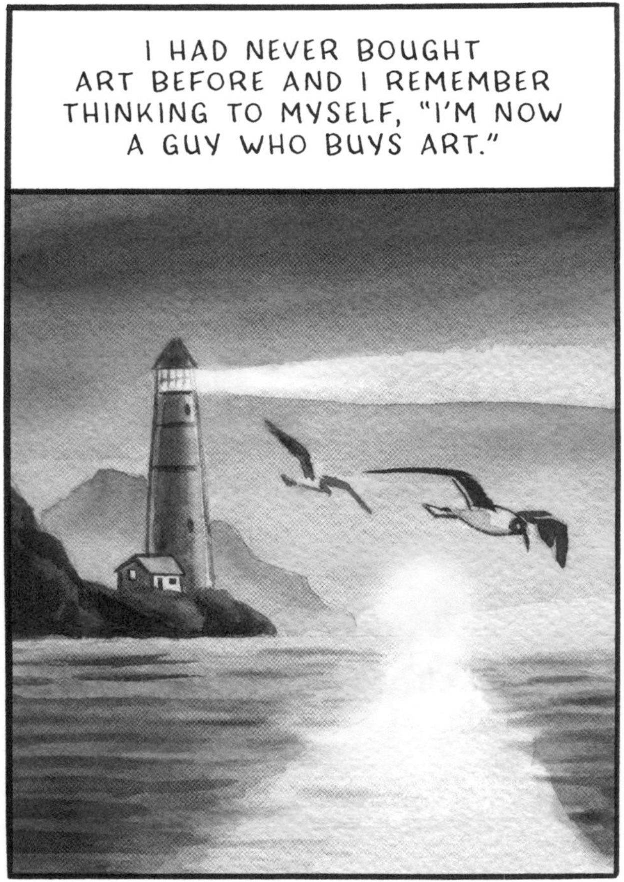
I HAD NEVER BOUGHT ART BEFORE AND I REMEMBER THINKING TO MYSELF, "I'M NOW A GUY WHO BUYS ART."

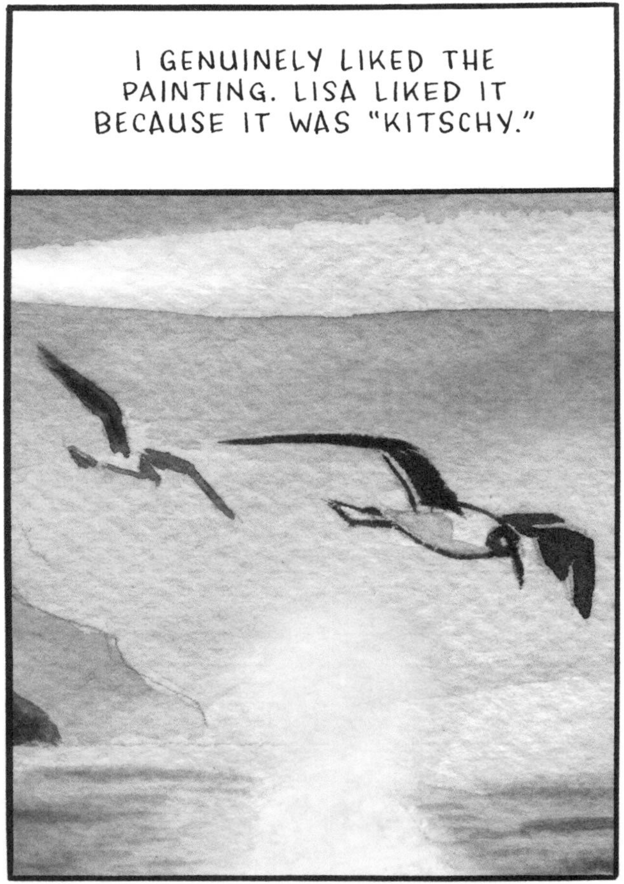
I GENUINELY LIKED THE PAINTING. LISA LIKED IT BECAUSE IT WAS "KITSCHY."

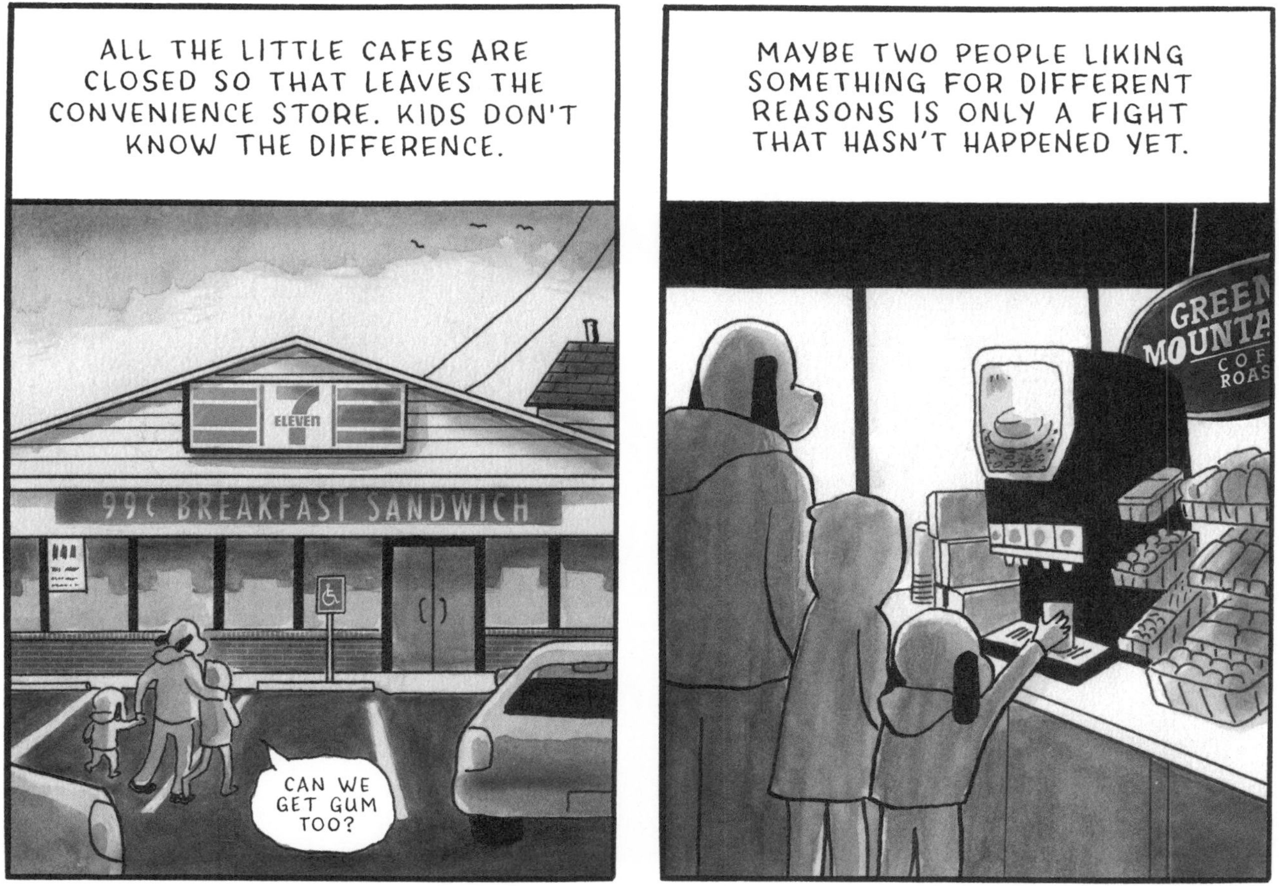
ALL THE LITTLE CAFES ARE CLOSED SO THAT LEAVES THE CONVENIENCE STORE. KIDS DON'T KNOW THE DIFFERENCE.
ELEVEN
99¢ BREAKFAST SANDWICH
CAN WE GET GUM TOO?
MAYBE TWO PEOPLE LIKING SOMETHING FOR DIFFERENT REASONS IS ONLY A FIGHT THAT HASN'T HAPPENED YET.

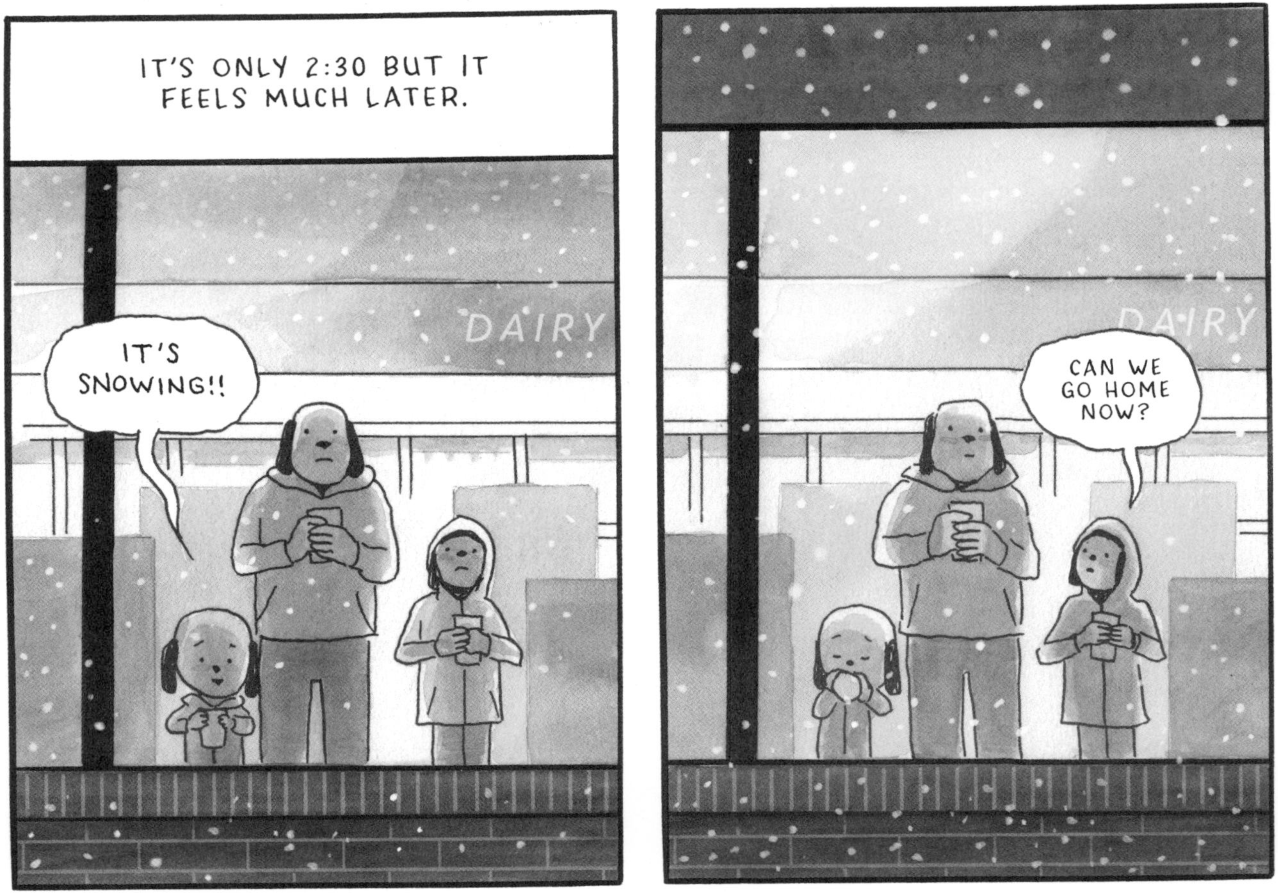
IT'S ONLY 2:30 BUT IT FEELS MUCH LATER.
DAIRY
IT'S SNOWING!!
DAIRY
CAN WE GO HOME NOW?

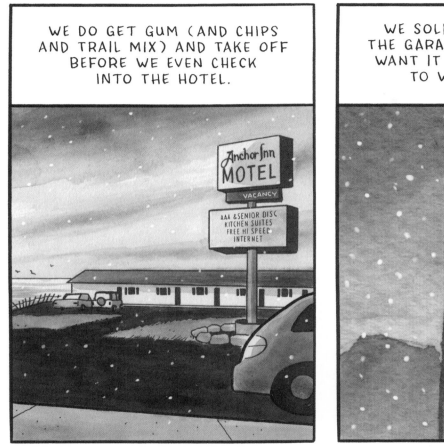

WE DO GET GUM (AND CHIPS AND TRAIL MIX) AND TAKE OFF BEFORE WE EVEN CHECK INTO THE HOTEL.

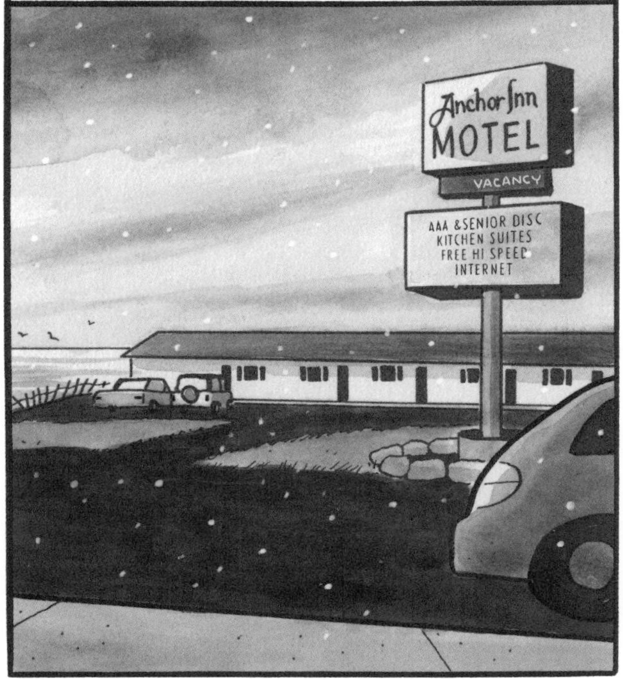
Anchor Inn
MOTEL
VACANCY
AAA &SENIOR DISC
KITCHEN SUITES
FREE HI SPEED
INTERNET

WE SOLD THE PAINTING AT THE GARAGE SALE. LISA DIDN'T WANT IT SO I WASN'T GOING TO WANT IT EITHER.

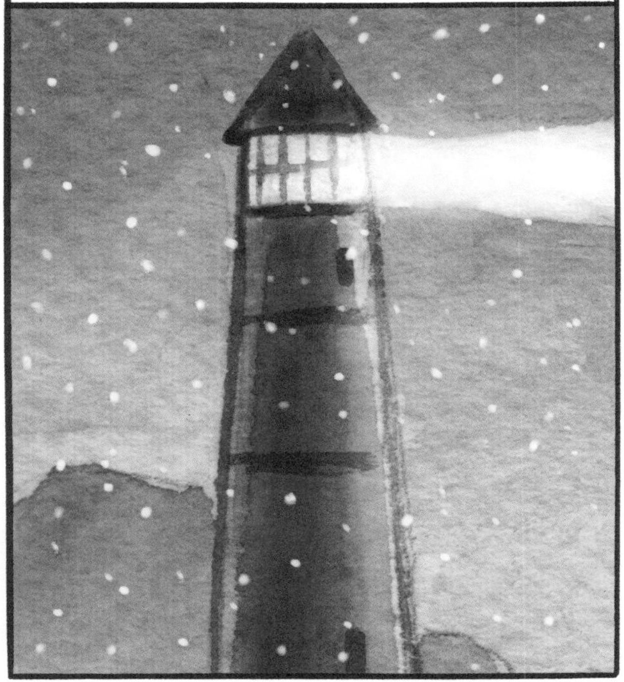

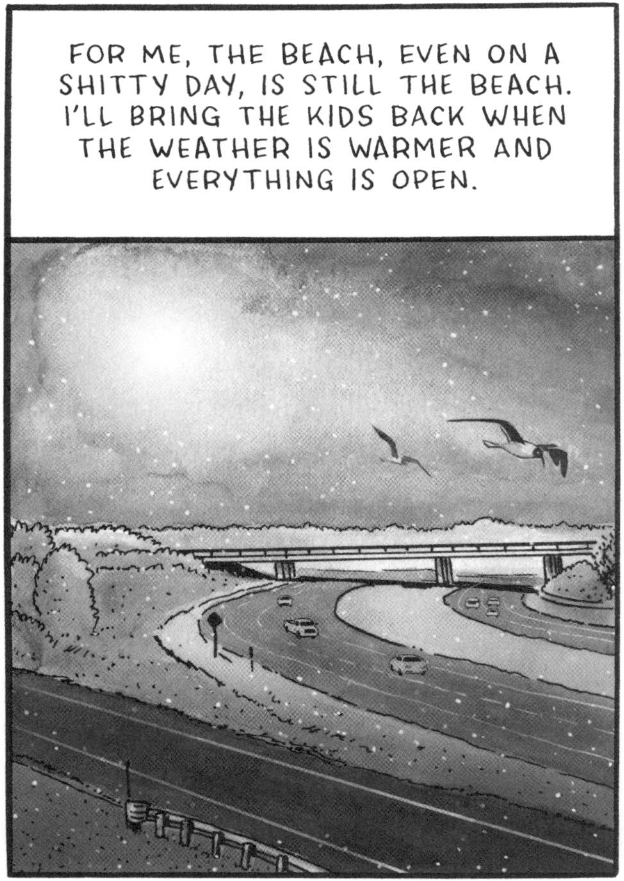
FOR ME, THE BEACH, EVEN ON A SHITTY DAY, IS STILL THE BEACH. I'LL BRING THE KIDS BACK WHEN THE WEATHER IS WARMER AND EVERYTHING IS OPEN.

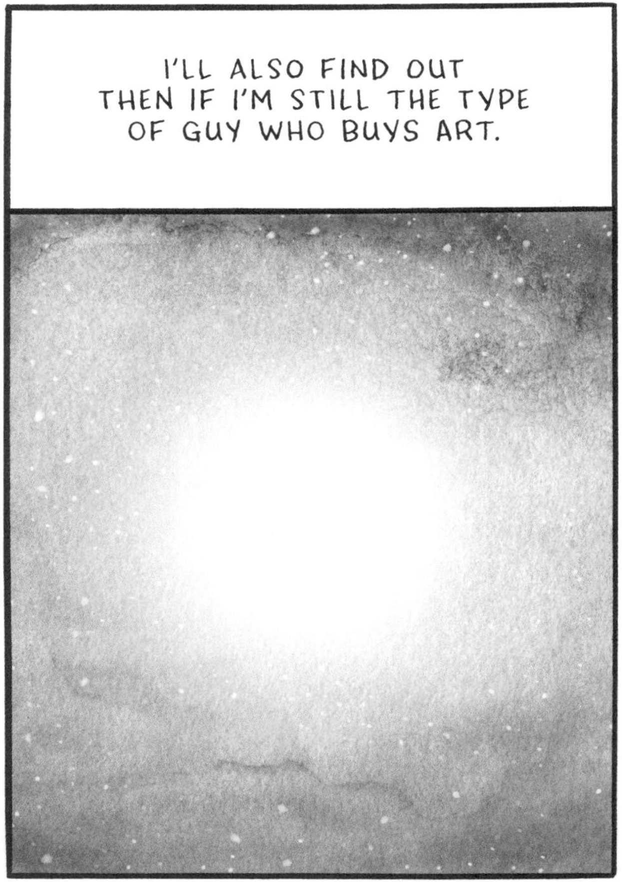
I'LL ALSO FIND OUT THEN IF I'M STILL THE TYPE OF GUY WHO BUYS ART.

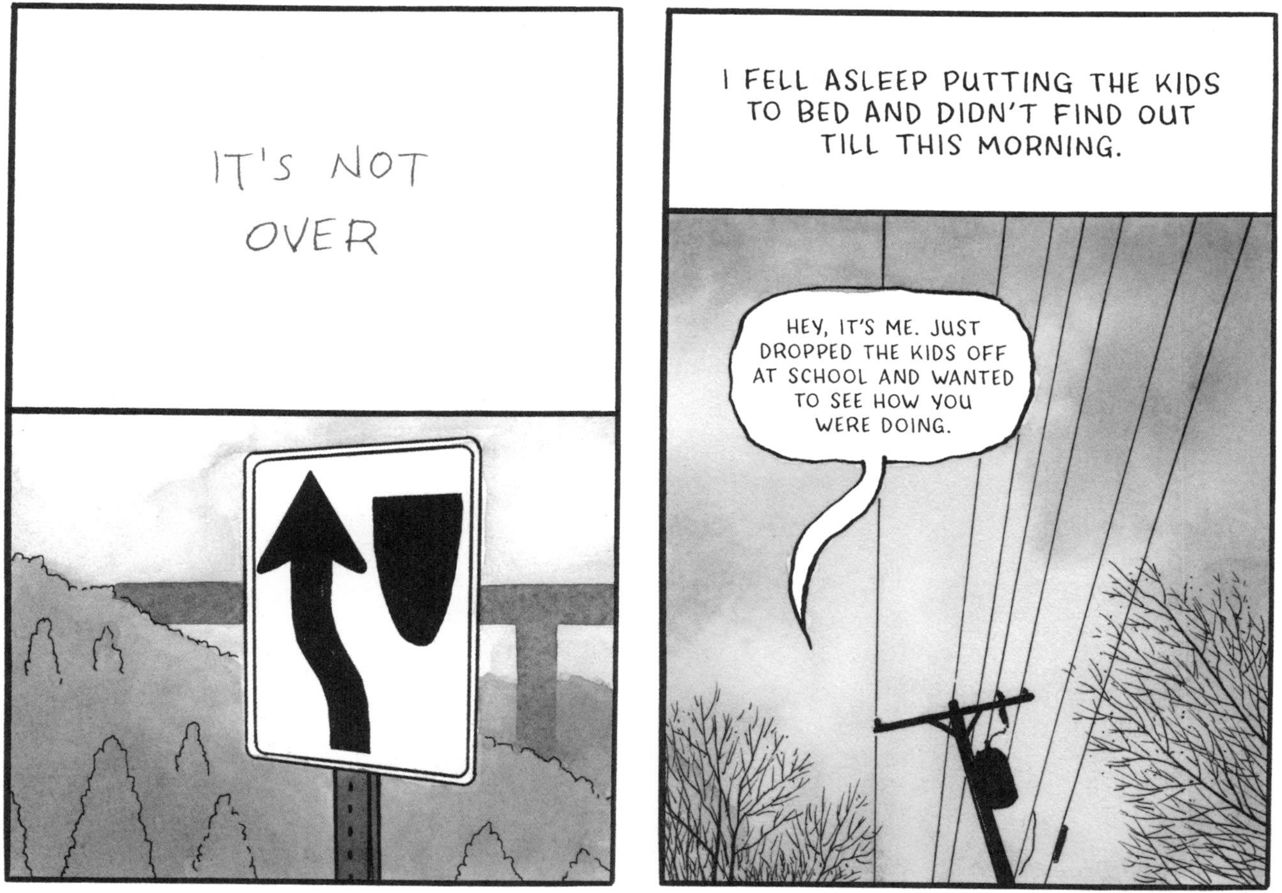
IT'S NOT OVER
I FELL ASLEEP PUTTING THE KIDS TO BED AND DIDN'T FIND OUT TILL THIS MORNING.
HEY, IT'S ME. JUST DROPPED THE KIDS OFF AT SCHOOL AND WANTED TO SEE HOW YOU WERE DOING.

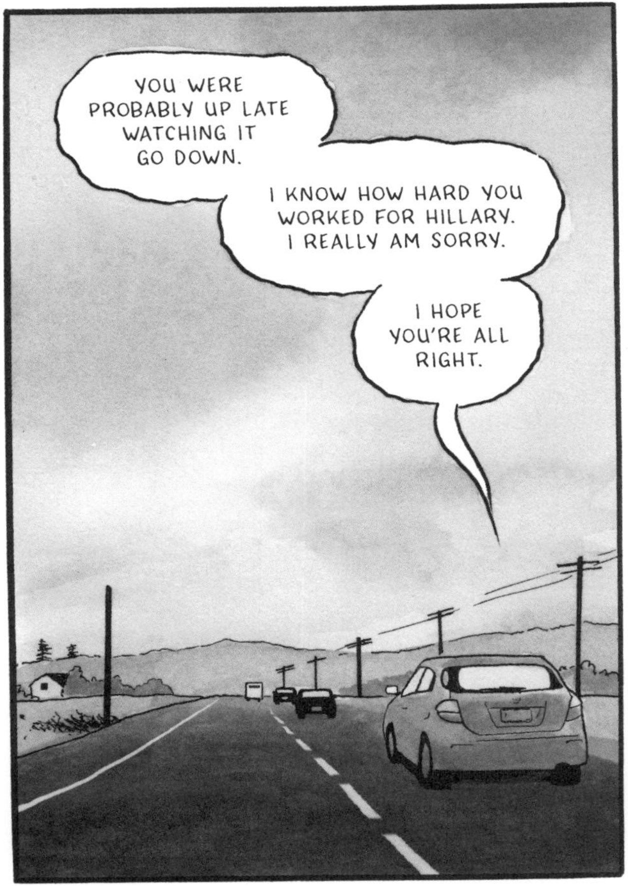
YOU WERE PROBABLY UP LATE WATCHING IT GO DOWN.
I KNOW HOW HARD YOU WORKED FOR HILLARY. I REALLY AM SORRY.
I HOPE YOU'RE ALL RIGHT.

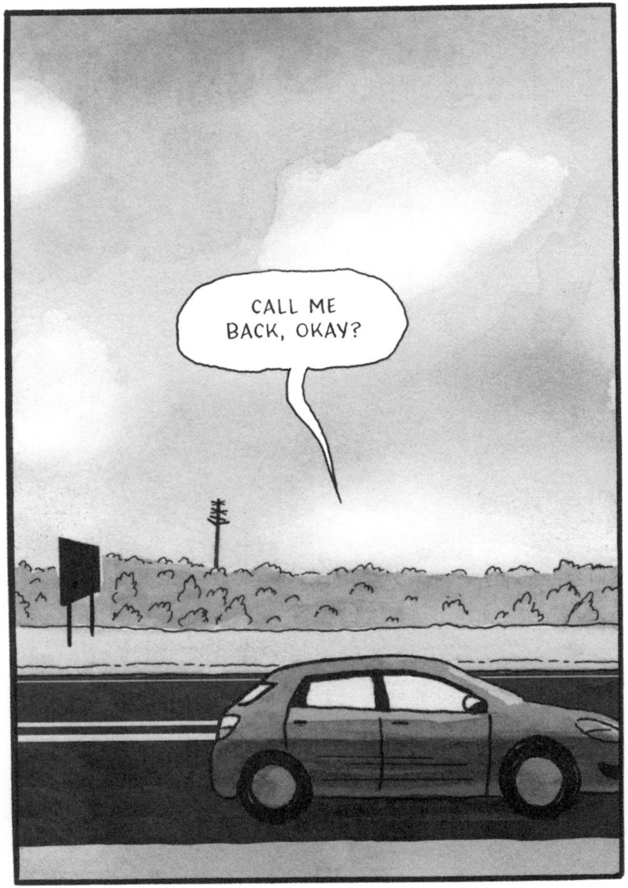
CALL ME BACK, OKAY?

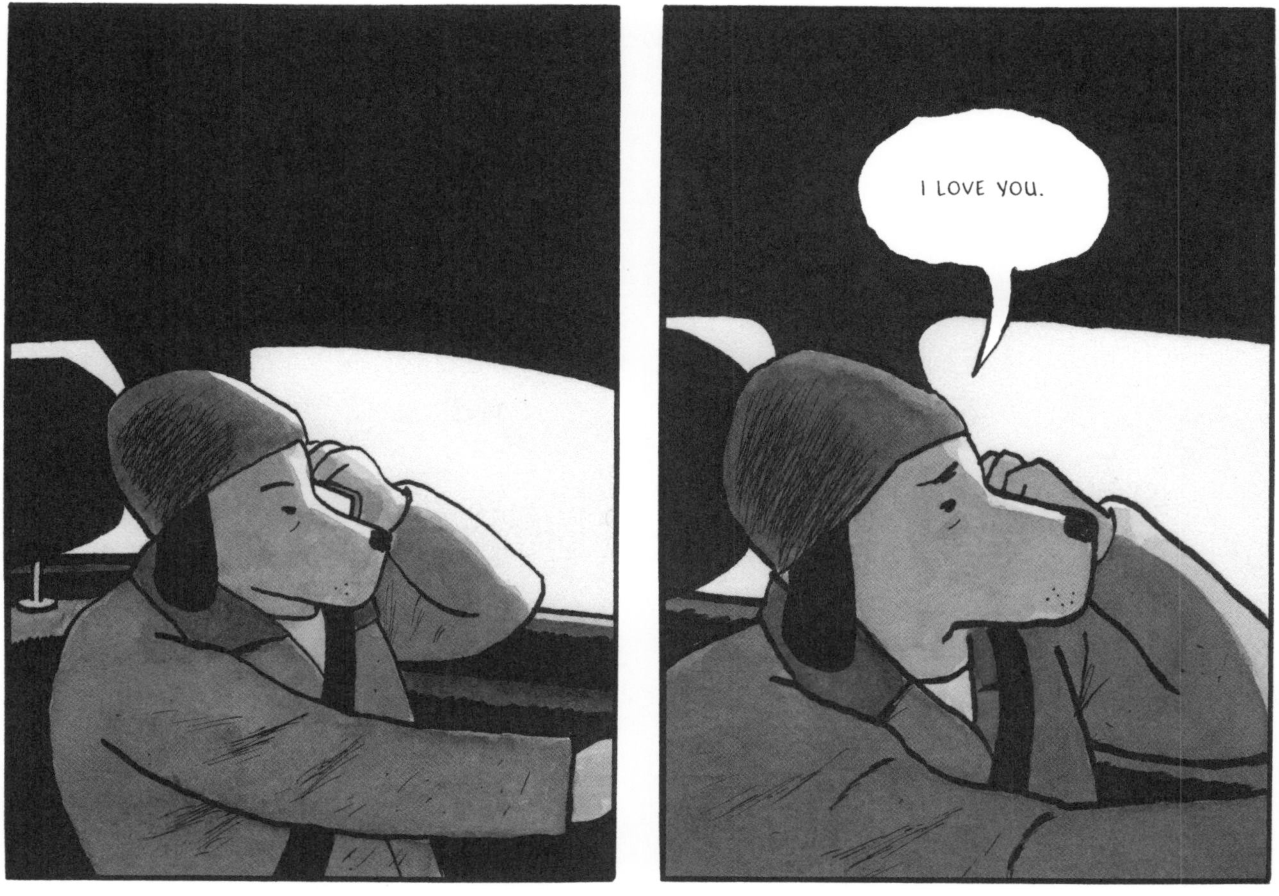
I LOVE YOU.

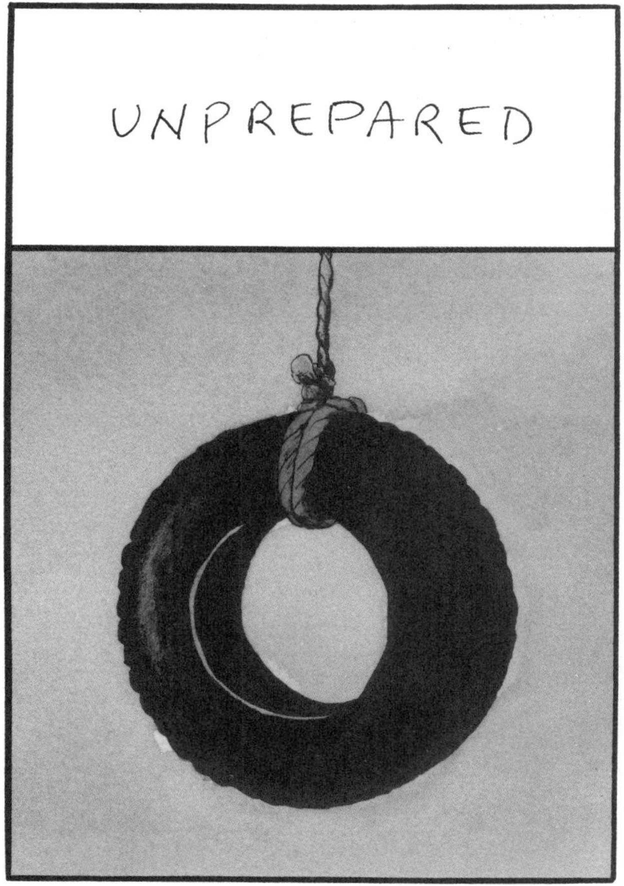
UNPREPARED

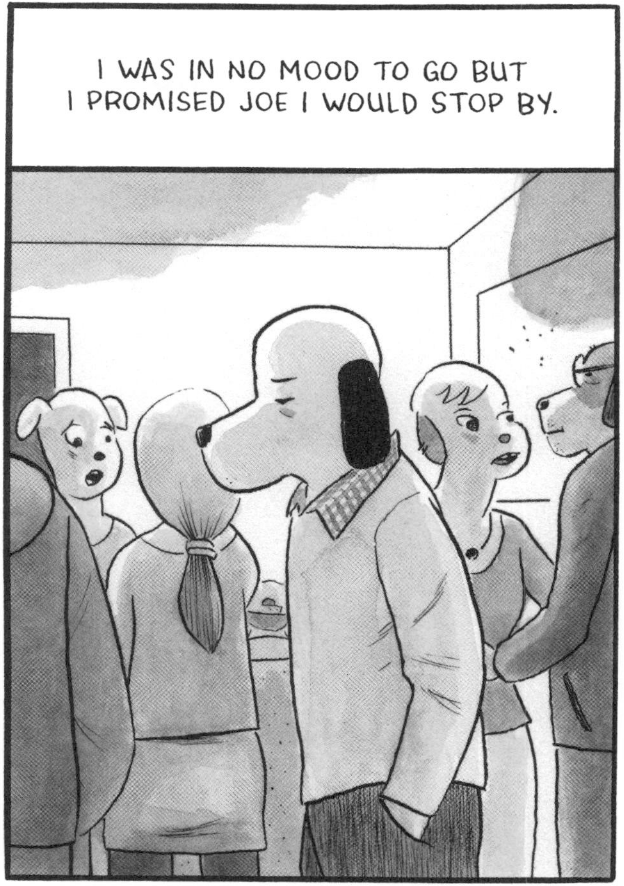
I WAS IN NO MOOD TO GO BUT
I PROMISED JOE I WOULD STOP BY.

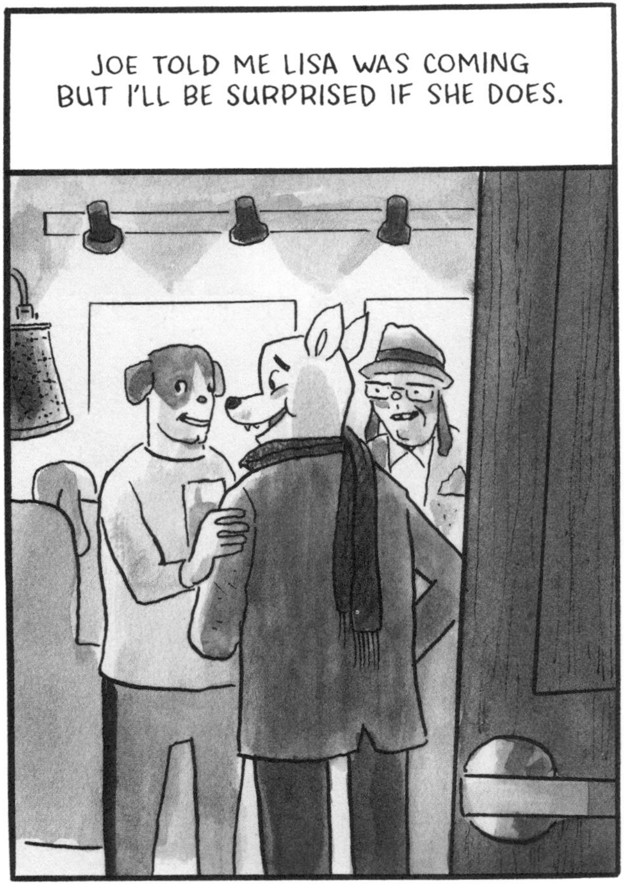
JOE TOLD ME LISA WAS COMING BUT I'LL BE SURPRISED IF SHE DOES.

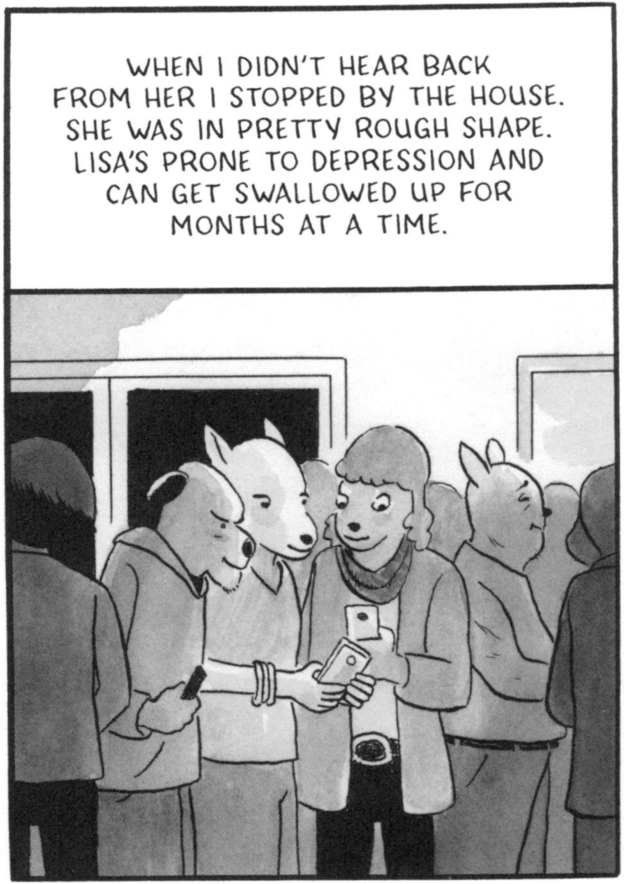
WHEN I DIDN'T HEAR BACK FROM HER I STOPPED BY THE HOUSE. SHE WAS IN PRETTY ROUGH SHAPE. LISA'S PRONE TO DEPRESSION AND CAN GET SWALLOWED UP FOR MONTHS AT A TIME.

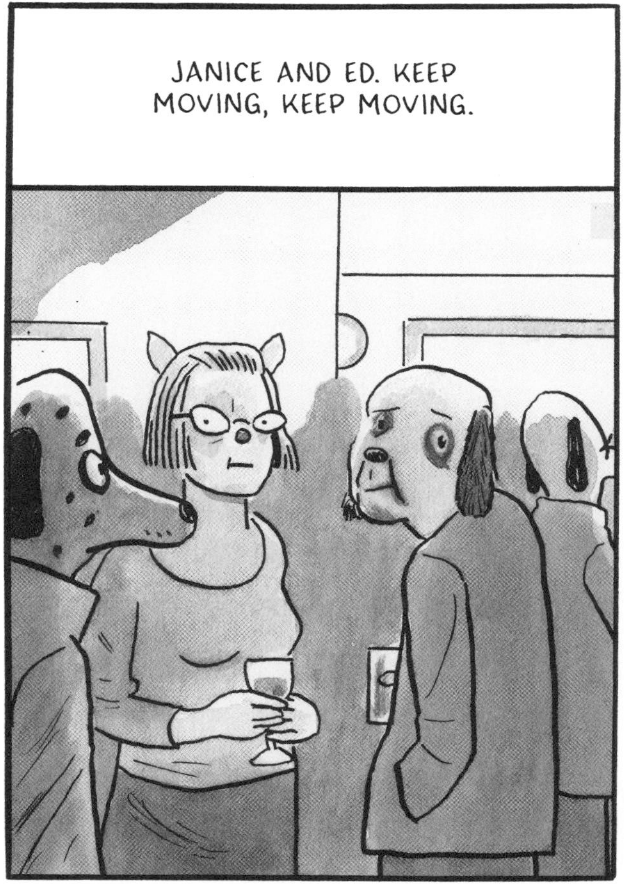
JANICE AND ED. KEEP MOVING, KEEP MOVING.

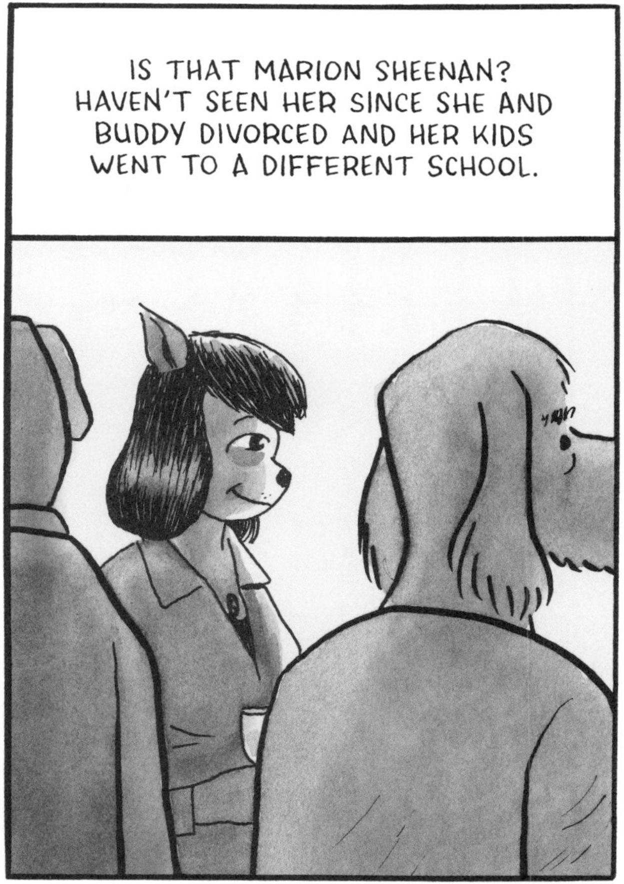
IS THAT MARION SHEENAN? HAVEN'T SEEN HER SINCE SHE AND BUDDY DIVORCED AND HER KIDS WENT TO A DIFFERENT SCHOOL.

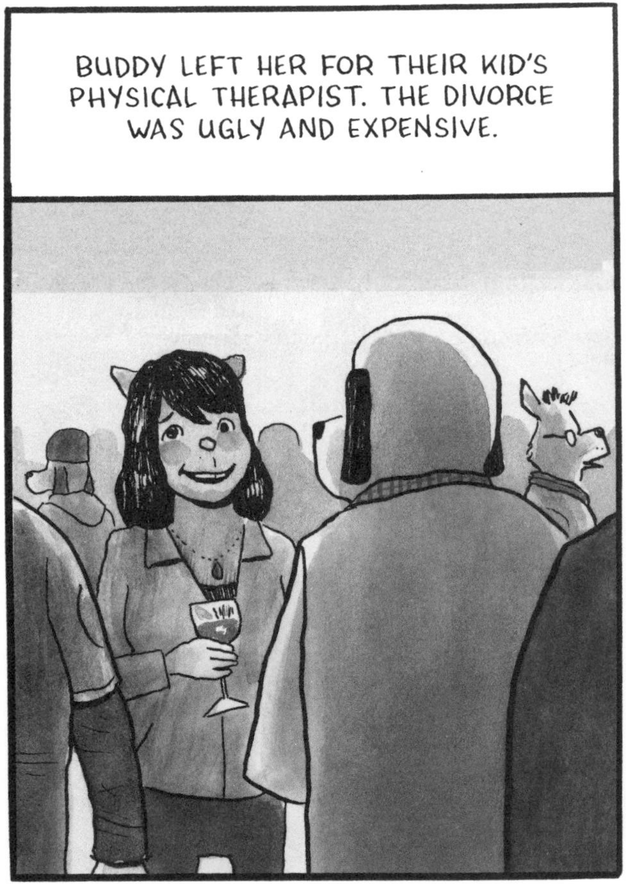
BUDDY LEFT HER FOR THEIR KID'S PHYSICAL THERAPIST. THE DIVORCE WAS UGLY AND EXPENSIVE.

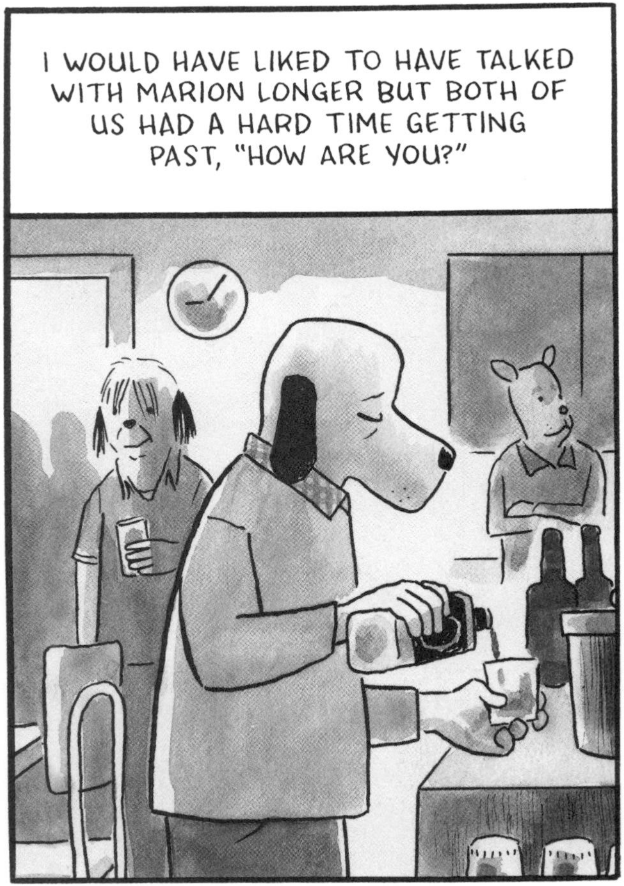
I WOULD HAVE LIKED TO HAVE TALKED WITH MARION LONGER BUT BOTH OF US HAD A HARD TIME GETTING PAST, "HOW ARE YOU?"

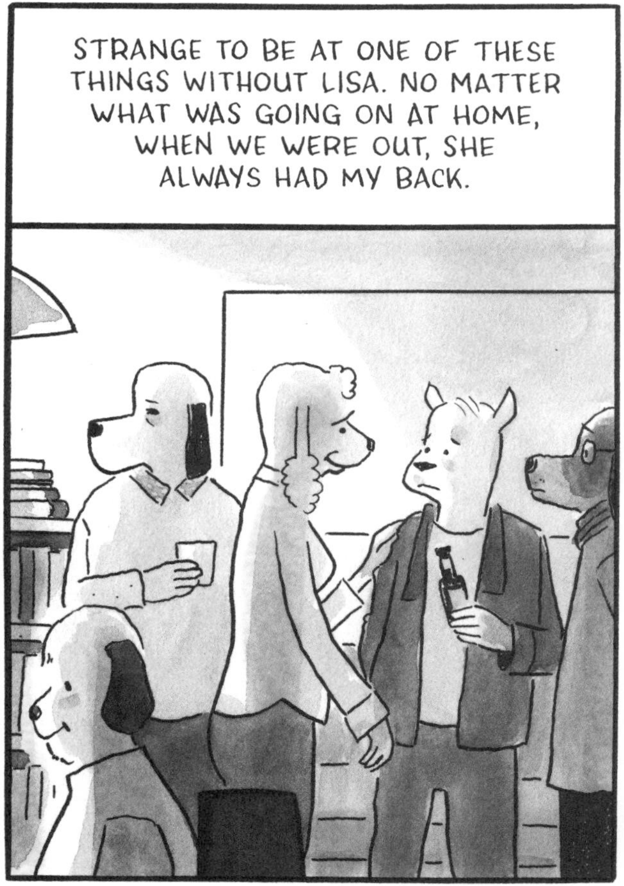
STRANGE TO BE AT ONE OF THESE THINGS WITHOUT LISA. NO MATTER WHAT WAS GOING ON AT HOME, WHEN WE WERE OUT, SHE ALWAYS HAD MY BACK.

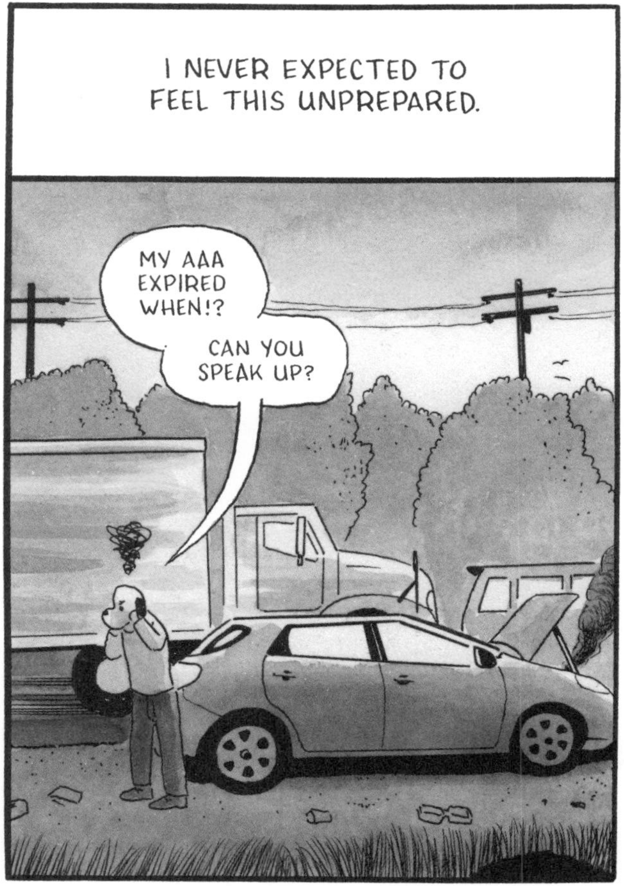
I NEVER EXPECTED TO FEEL THIS UNPREPARED.
MY AAA EXPIRED WHEN!?
CAN YOU SPEAK UP?

BIG THINGS, LITTLE THINGS—EVERY DAY IT'S SOMETHING ELSE.

MOM KNOWS JEREMY ONLY LIKES GRAPE JELLY.

I MESSED UP WHEN I FORGOT THE PERMISSION FORM FOR SUZIE'S FIELD TRIP AND SHE WAS LEFT WITH THE FIRST GRADERS ALL DAY.

I ADMITTED MY MISTAKE BUT WHY THE FUCK DIDN'T THE SCHOOL CALL ME OR LISA THAT MORNING? THAT'S TOTAL BULLSHIT. IF THE PRINCIPAL DIDN'T ALREADY KNOW WHAT I THOUGHT OF HER SHE DOES NOW.

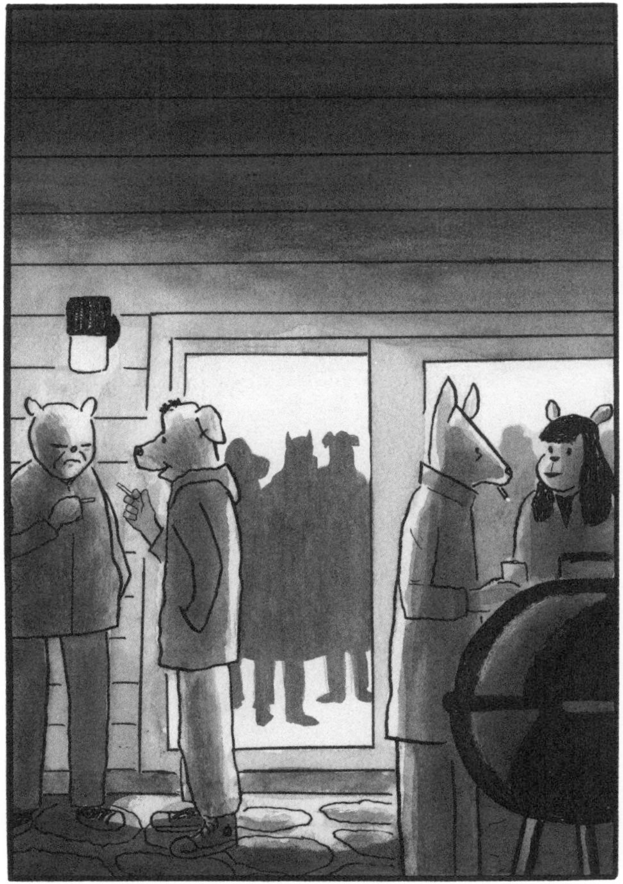

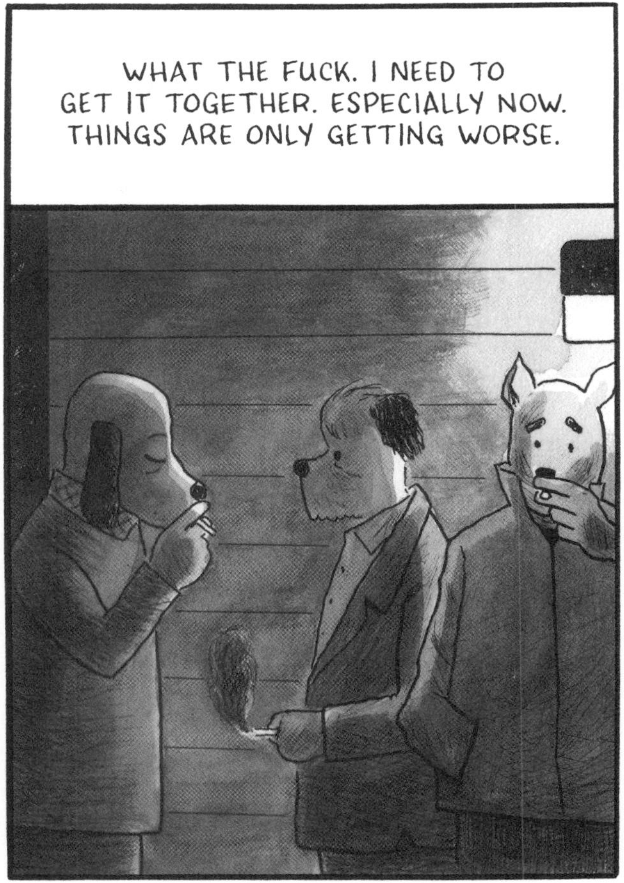
WHAT THE FUCK. I NEED TO GET IT TOGETHER. ESPECIALLY NOW. THINGS ARE ONLY GETTING WORSE.

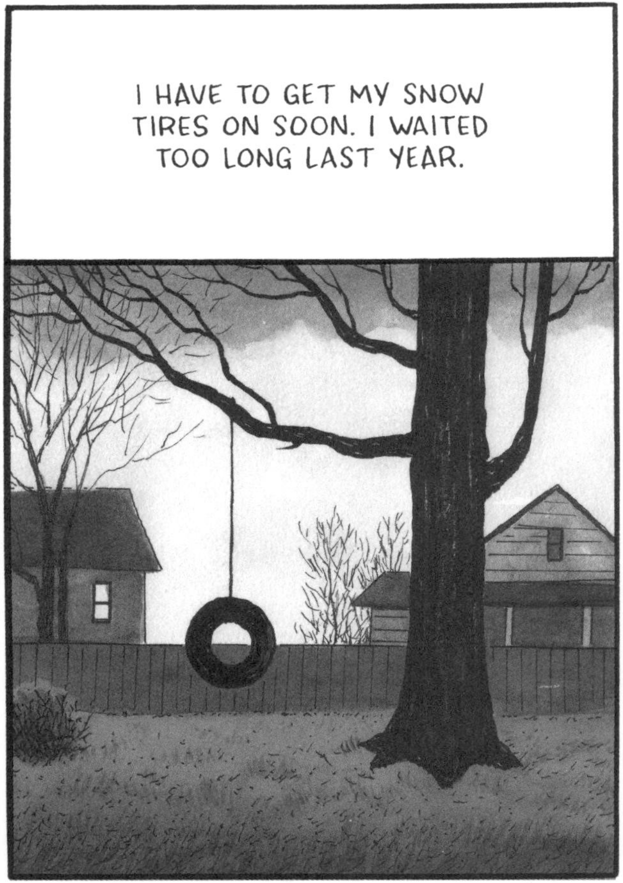
I HAVE TO GET MY SNOW TIRES ON SOON. I WAITED TOO LONG LAST YEAR.

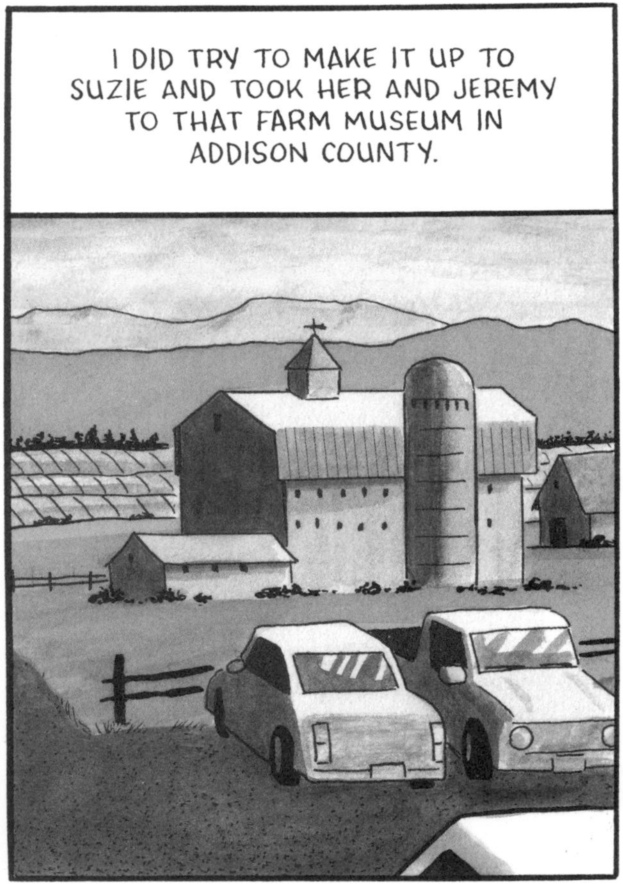
I DID TRY TO MAKE IT UP TO SUZIE AND TOOK HER AND JEREMY TO THAT FARM MUSEUM IN ADDISON COUNTY.

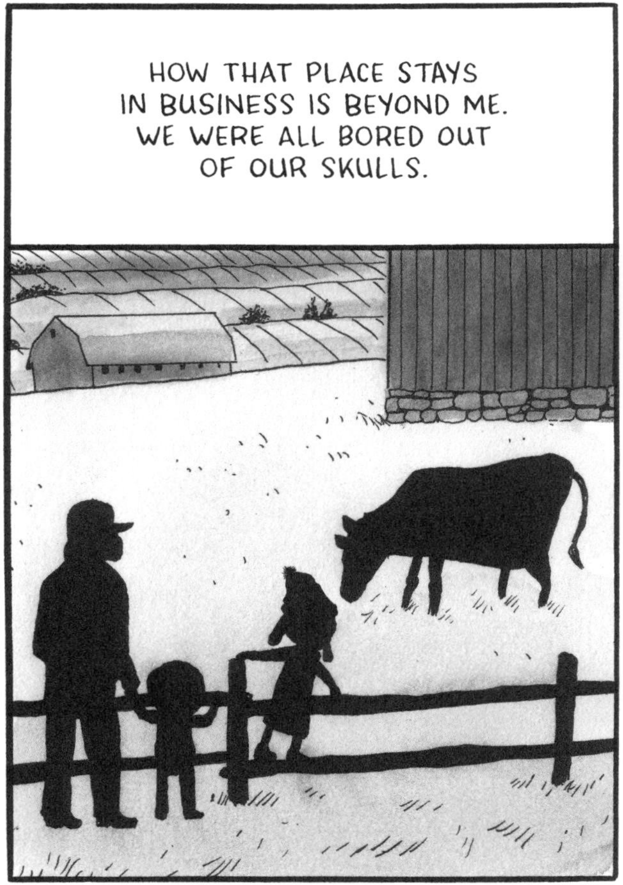
HOW THAT PLACE STAYS IN BUSINESS IS BEYOND ME. WE WERE ALL BORED OUT OF OUR SKULLS.

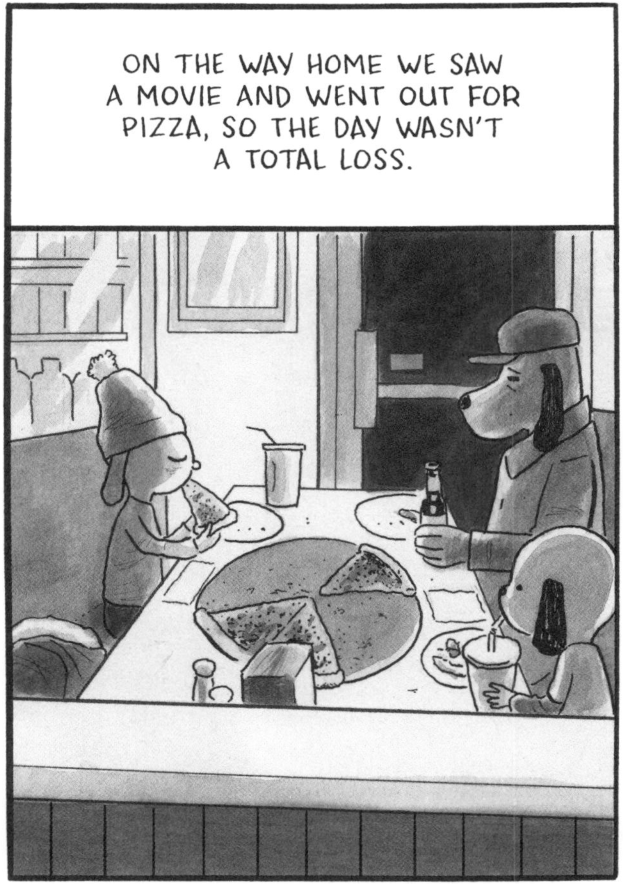
ON THE WAY HOME WE SAW A MOVIE AND WENT OUT FOR PIZZA, SO THE DAY WASN'T A TOTAL LOSS.

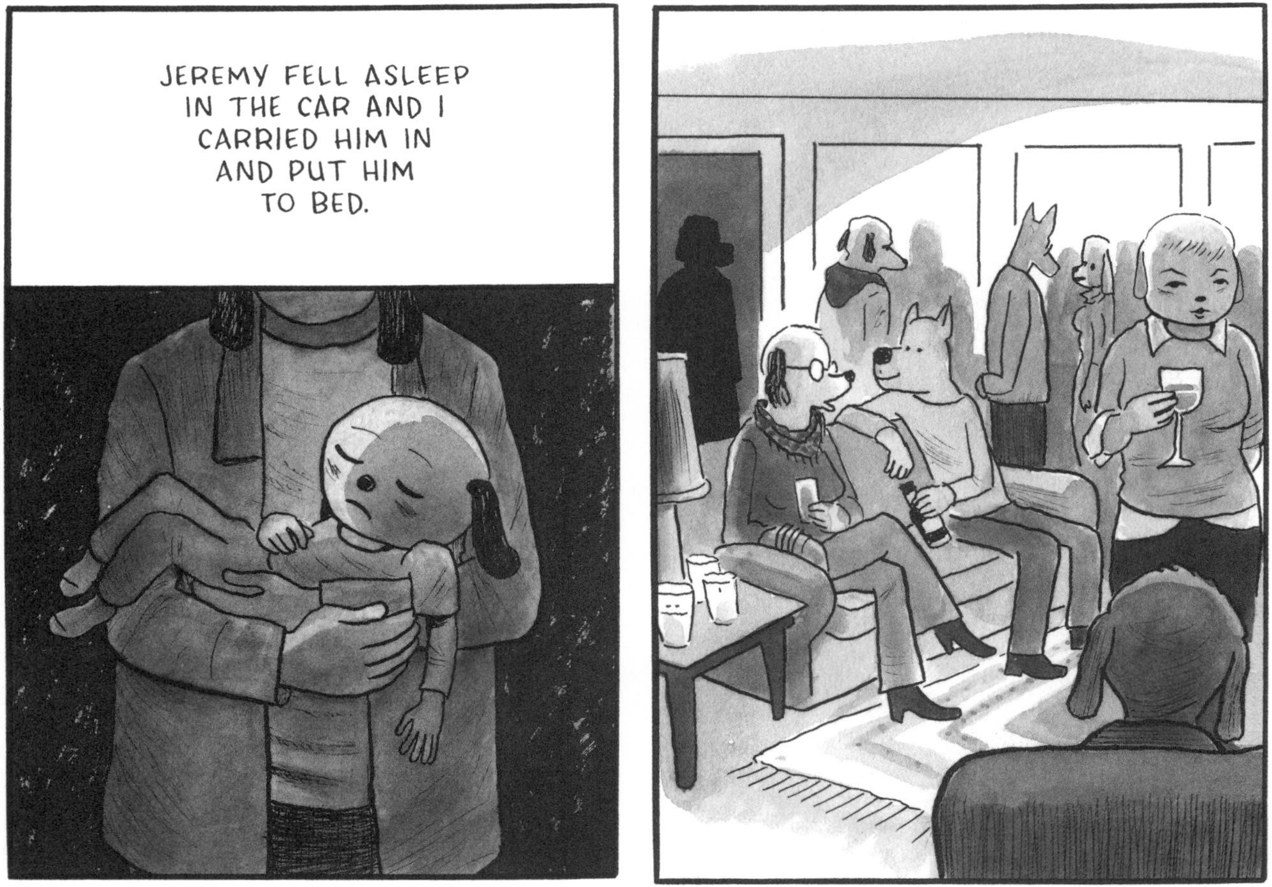
JEREMY FELL ASLEEP IN THE CAR AND I CARRIED HIM IN AND PUT HIM TO BED.

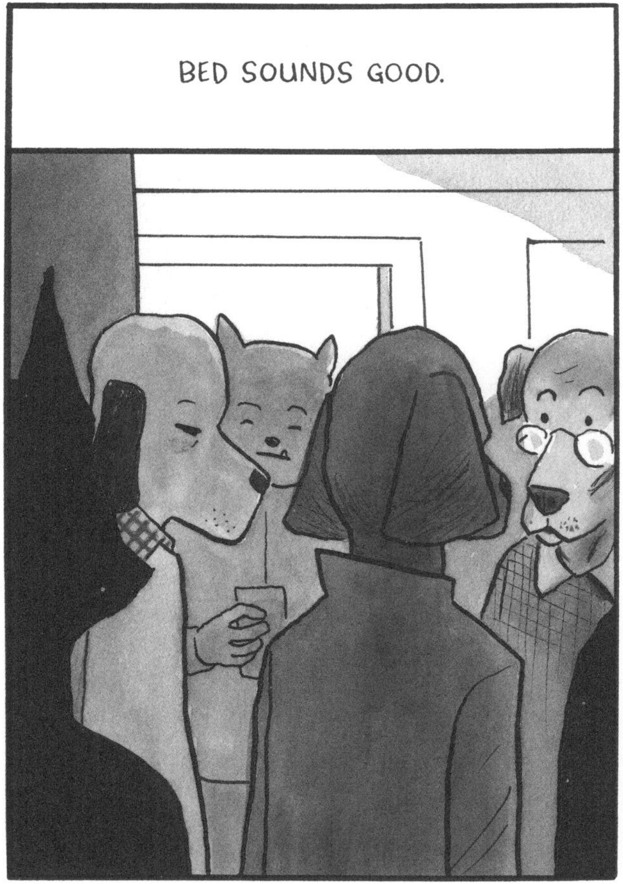
BED SOUNDS GOOD.
3

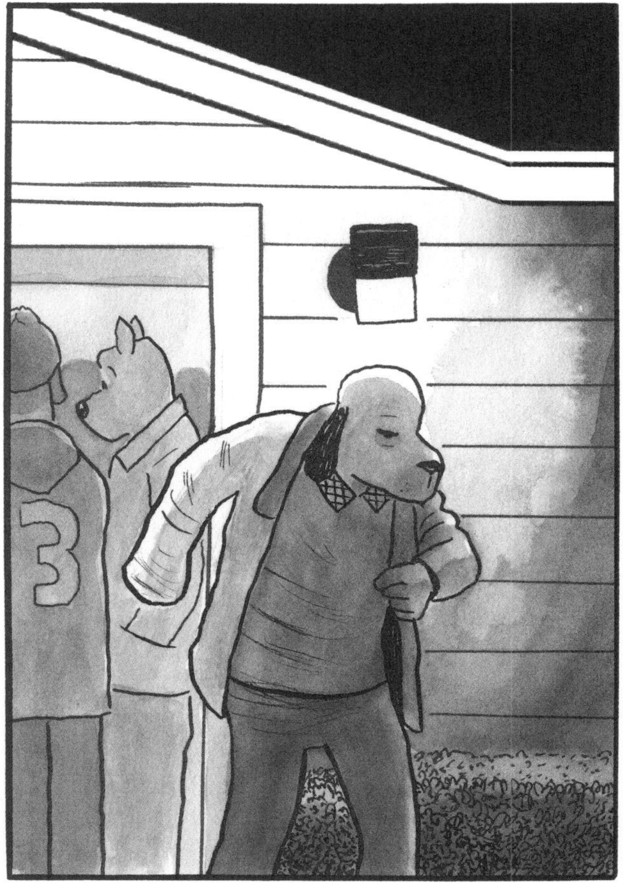
3

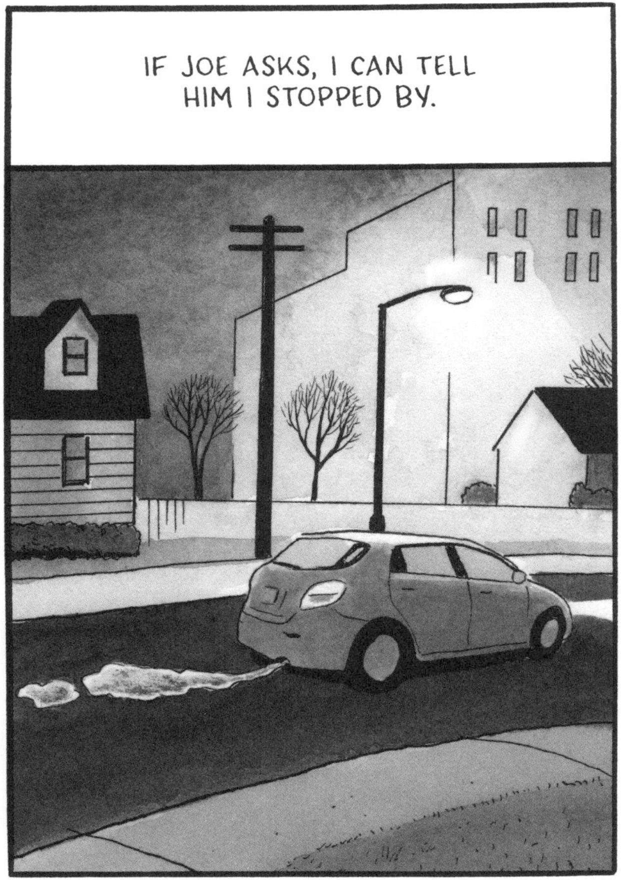
IF JOE ASKS, I CAN TELL HIM I STOPPED BY.

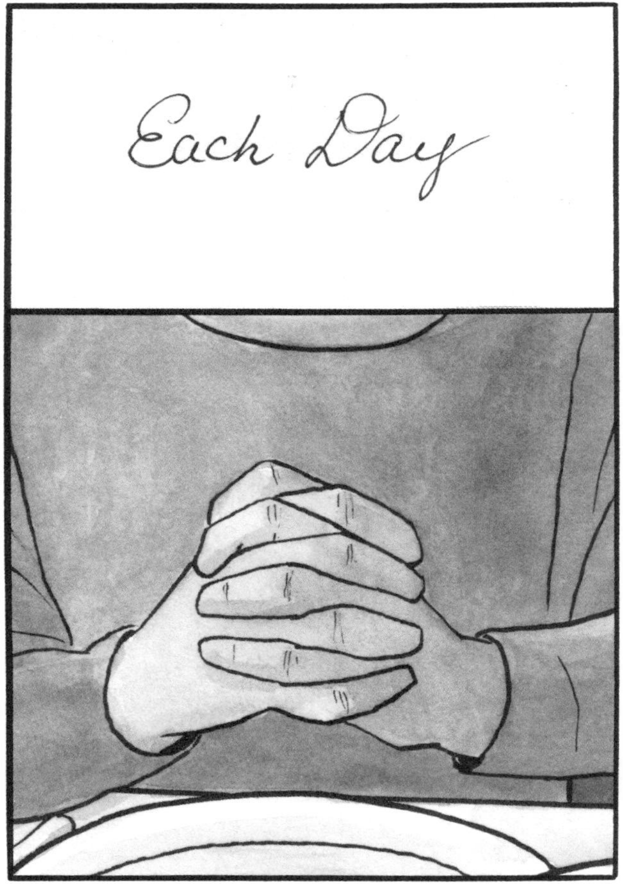
Each Day

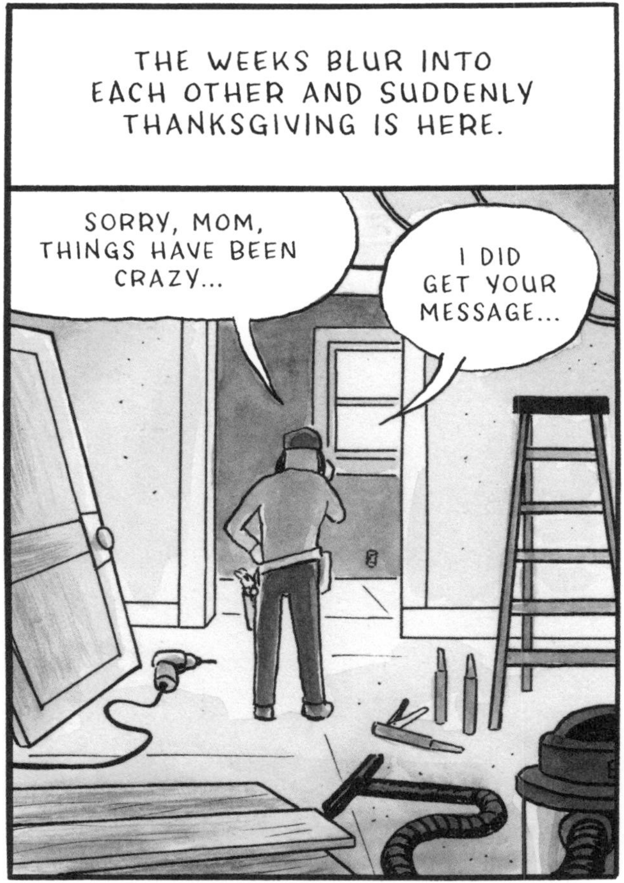
THE WEEKS BLUR INTO EACH OTHER AND SUDDENLY THANKSGIVING IS HERE.
SORRY, MOM, THINGS HAVE BEEN CRAZY...
I DID GET YOUR MESSAGE...

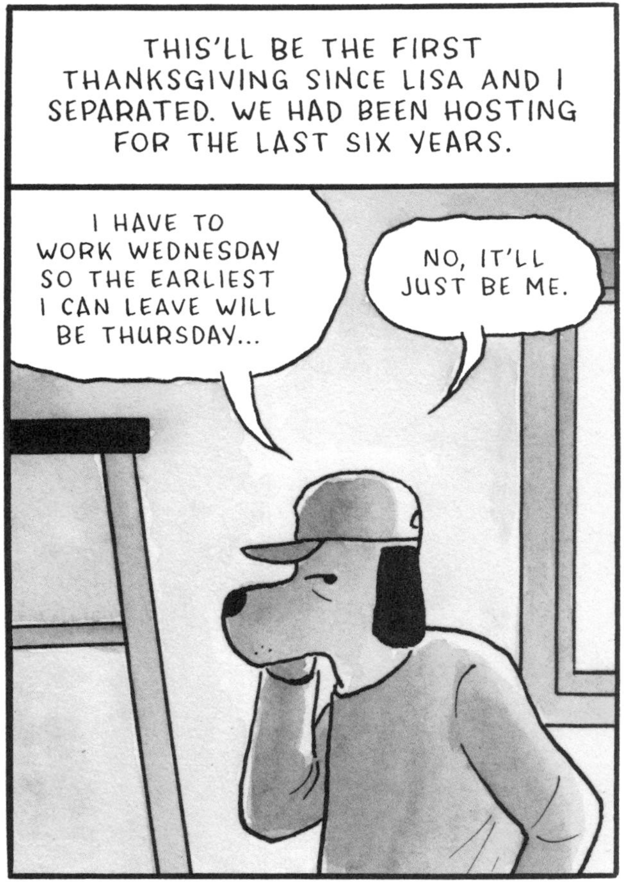
THIS'LL BE THE FIRST THANKSGIVING SINCE LISA AND I SEPARATED. WE HAD BEEN HOSTING FOR THE LAST SIX YEARS.
I HAVE TO WORK WEDNESDAY SO THE EARLIEST I CAN LEAVE WILL BE THURSDAY...
NO, IT'LL JUST BE ME.

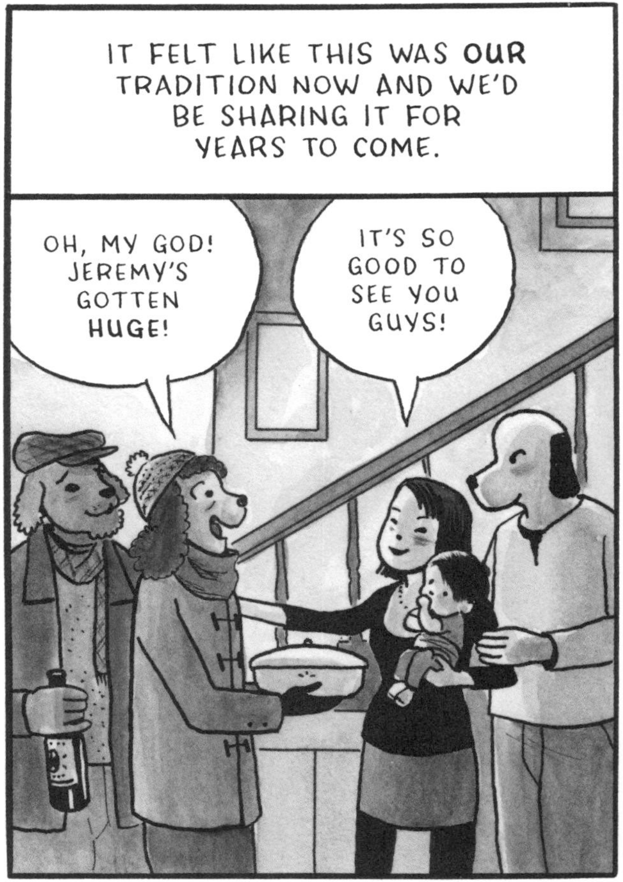
IT FELT LIKE THIS WAS **OUR** TRADITION NOW AND WE'D BE SHARING IT FOR YEARS TO COME.
OH, MY GOD! JEREMY'S GOTTEN **HUGE!**
IT'S SO GOOD TO SEE YOU GUYS!

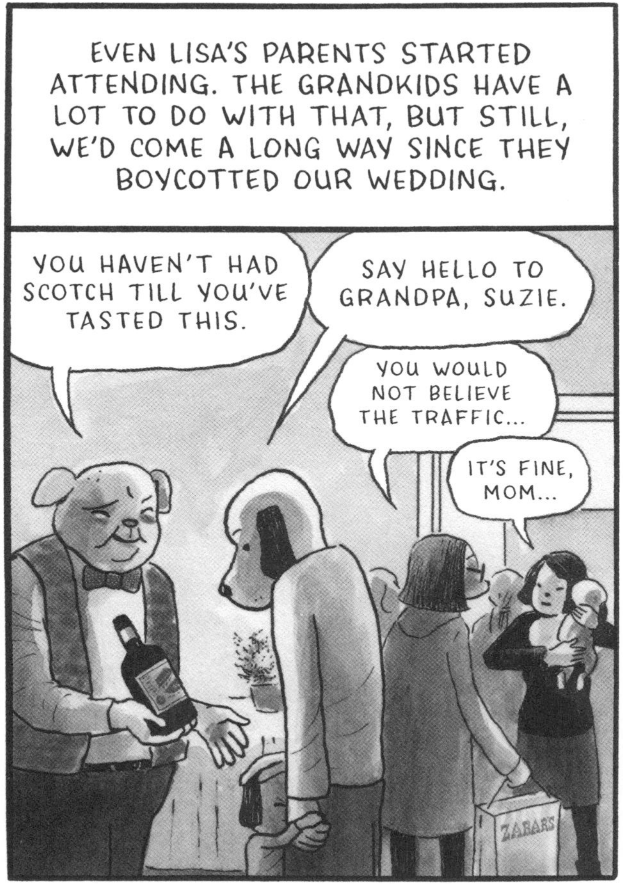
EVEN LISA'S PARENTS STARTED ATTENDING. THE GRANDKIDS HAVE A LOT TO DO WITH THAT, BUT STILL, WE'D COME A LONG WAY SINCE THEY BOYCOTTED OUR WEDDING.
YOU HAVEN'T HAD SCOTCH TILL YOU'VE TASTED THIS.
SAY HELLO TO GRANDPA, SUZIE.
YOU WOULD NOT BELIEVE THE TRAFFIC...
IT'S FINE, MOM...
ZABAR'S

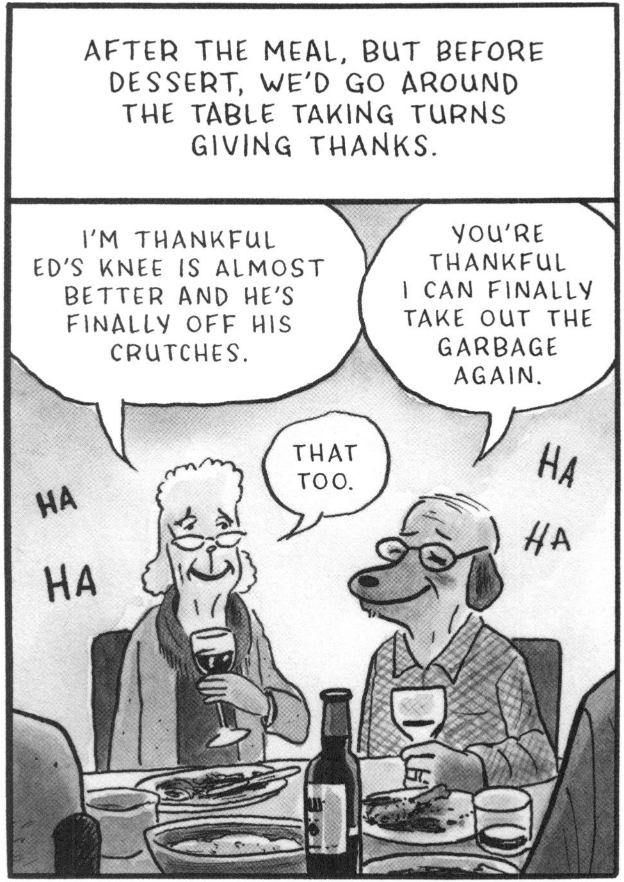
AFTER THE MEAL, BUT BEFORE DESSERT, WE'D GO AROUND THE TABLE TAKING TURNS GIVING THANKS.
I'M THANKFUL ED'S KNEE IS ALMOST BETTER AND HE'S FINALLY OFF HIS CRUTCHES.
YOU'RE THANKFUL I CAN FINALLY TAKE OUT THE GARBAGE AGAIN.
THAT TOO.
HA
HA
HA
HA

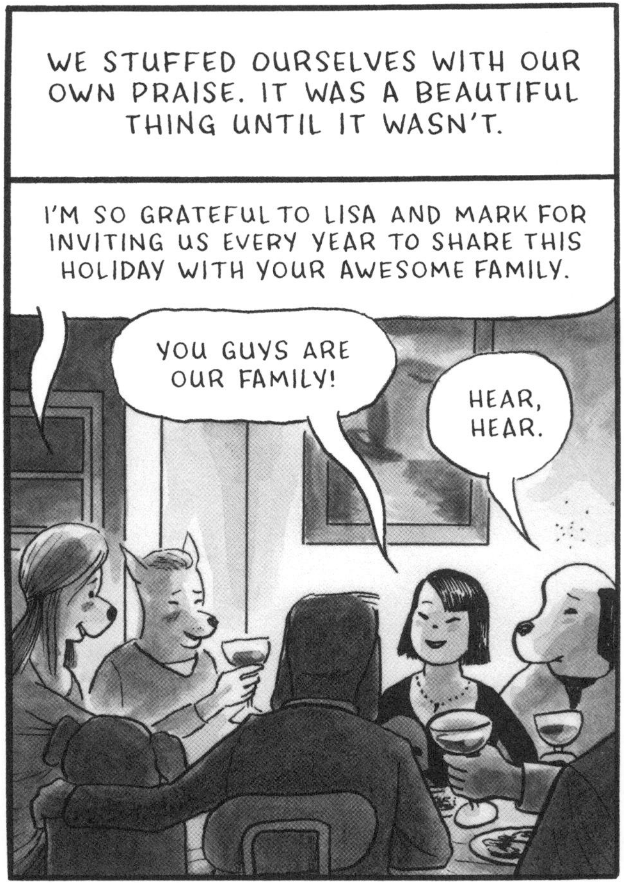
WE STUFFED OURSELVES WITH OUR OWN PRAISE. IT WAS A BEAUTIFUL THING UNTIL IT WASN'T.
I'M SO GRATEFUL TO LISA AND MARK FOR INVITING US EVERY YEAR TO SHARE THIS HOLIDAY WITH YOUR AWESOME FAMILY.
YOU GUYS ARE OUR FAMILY!
HEAR, HEAR.

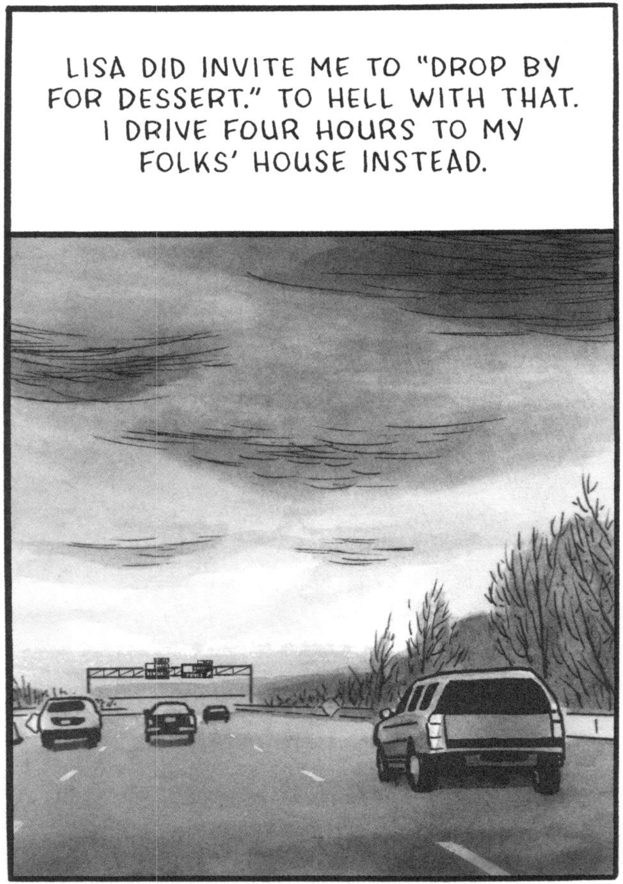
LISA DID INVITE ME TO "DROP BY FOR DESSERT." TO HELL WITH THAT. I DRIVE FOUR HOURS TO MY FOLKS' HOUSE INSTEAD.

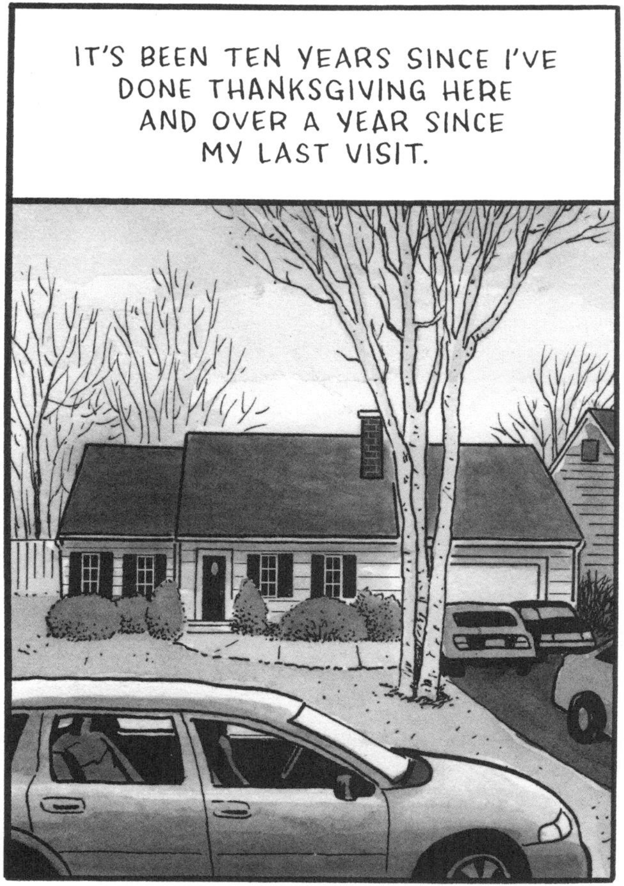
IT'S BEEN TEN YEARS SINCE I'VE DONE THANKSGIVING HERE AND OVER A YEAR SINCE MY LAST VISIT.

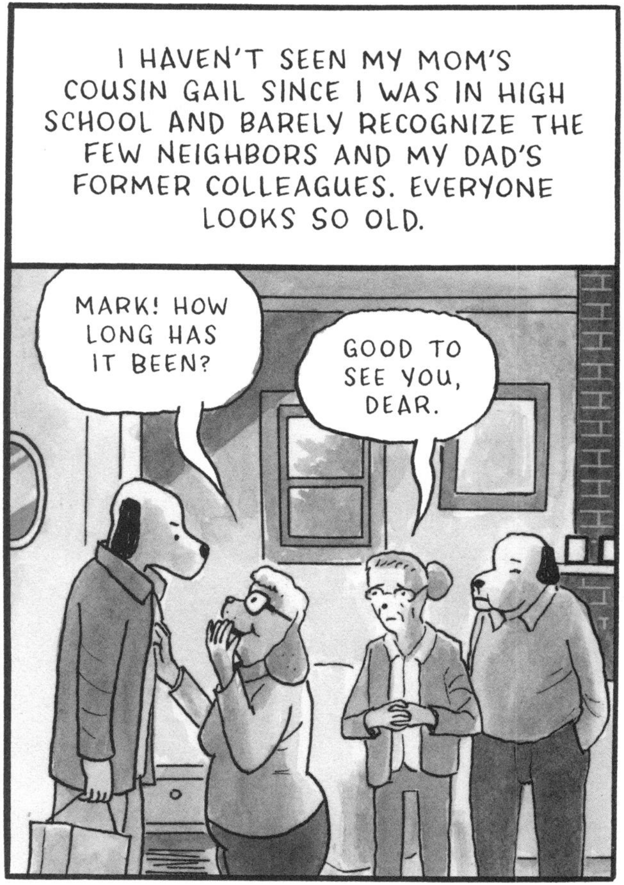
I HAVEN'T SEEN MY MOM'S COUSIN GAIL SINCE I WAS IN HIGH SCHOOL AND BARELY RECOGNIZE THE FEW NEIGHBORS AND MY DAD'S FORMER COLLEAGUES. EVERYONE LOOKS SO OLD.
MARK! HOW LONG HAS IT BEEN?
GOOD TO SEE YOU, DEAR.

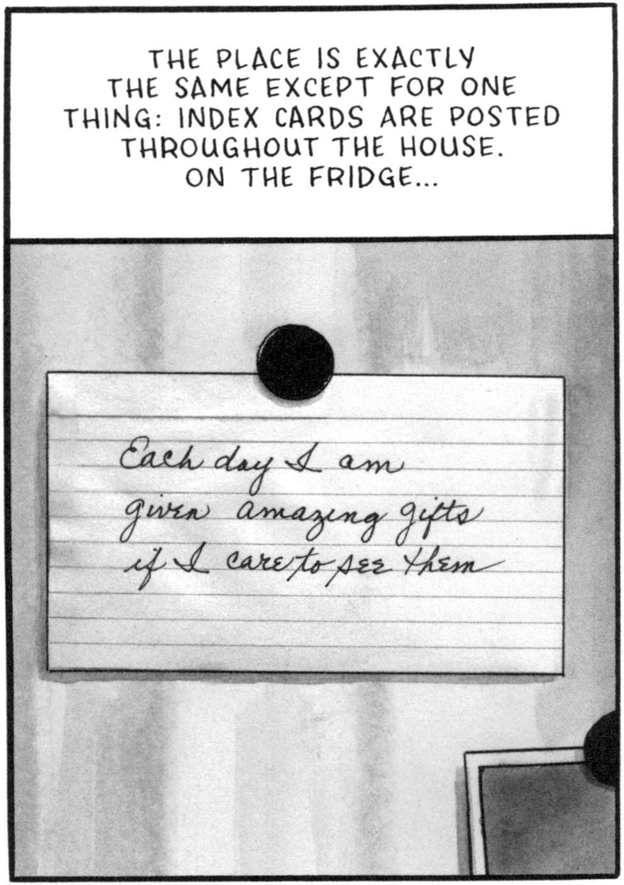
THE PLACE IS EXACTLY THE SAME EXCEPT FOR ONE THING: INDEX CARDS ARE POSTED THROUGHOUT THE HOUSE. ON THE FRIDGE...
Each day I am given amazing gifts if I care to see them

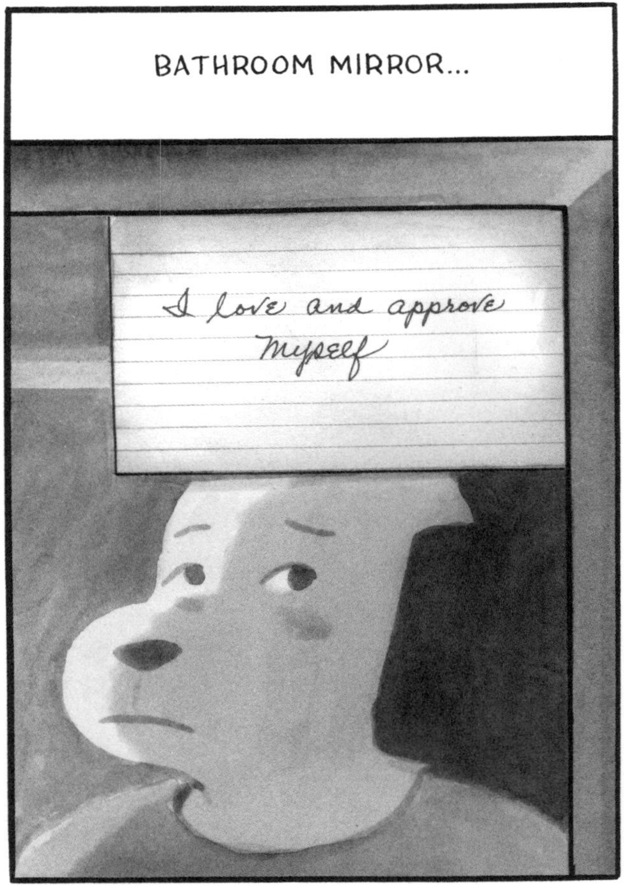
BATHROOM MIRROR...
I love and approve myself

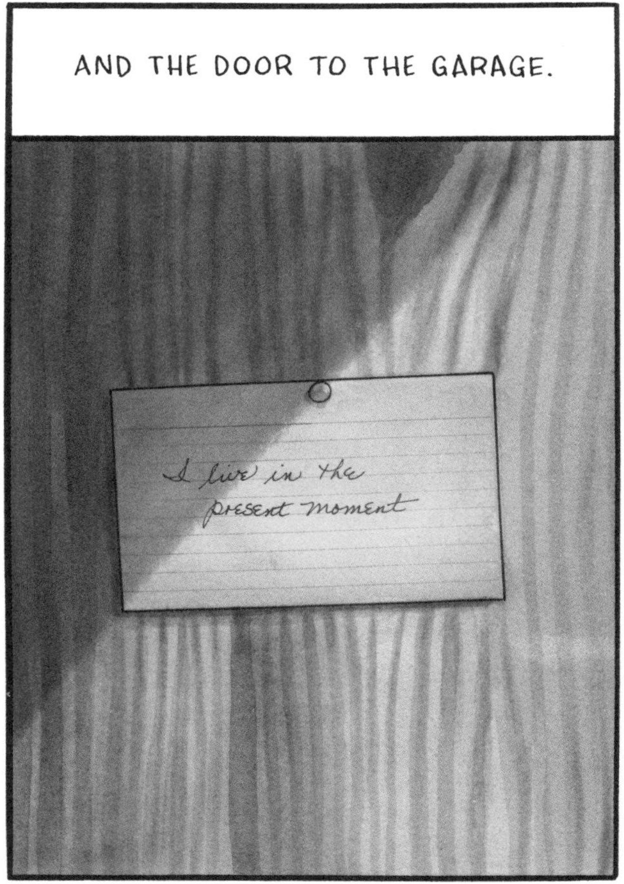
AND THE DOOR TO THE GARAGE.
I live in the present moment

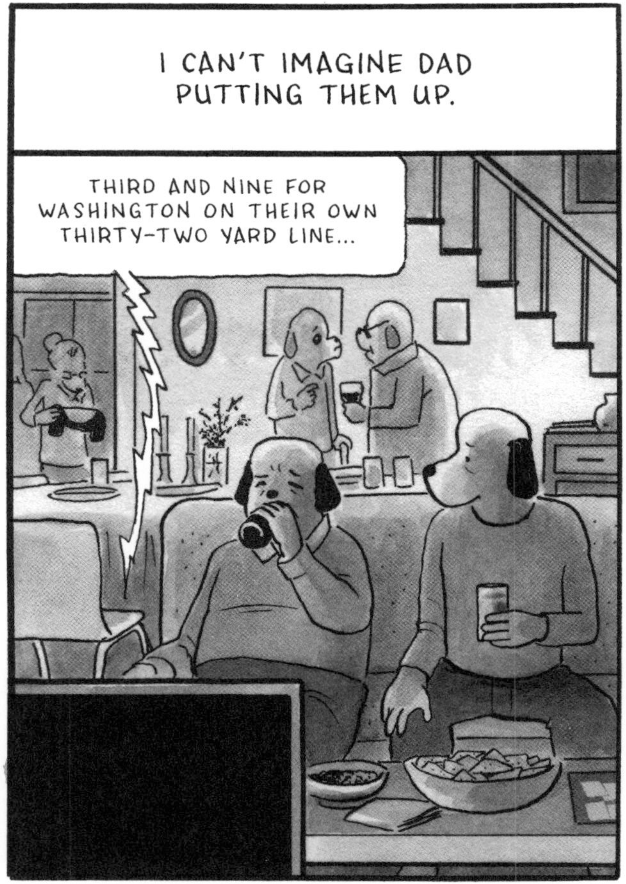
I CAN'T IMAGINE DAD PUTTING THEM UP.
THIRD AND NINE FOR WASHINGTON ON THEIR OWN THIRTY-TWO YARD LINE...

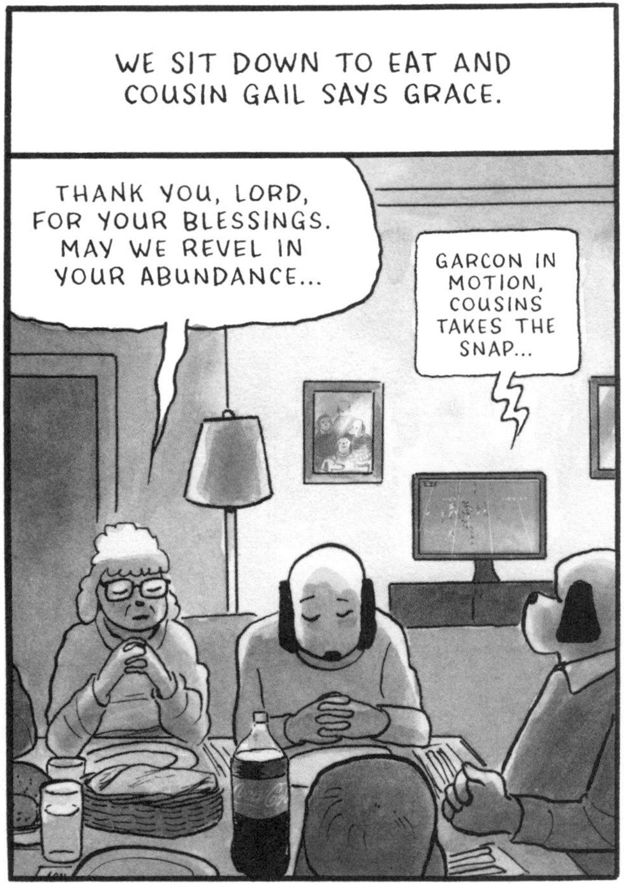
WE SIT DOWN TO EAT AND COUSIN GAIL SAYS GRACE.
THANK YOU, LORD, FOR YOUR BLESSINGS. MAY WE REVEL IN YOUR ABUNDANCE...
GARCON IN MOTION, COUSINS TAKES THE SNAP...

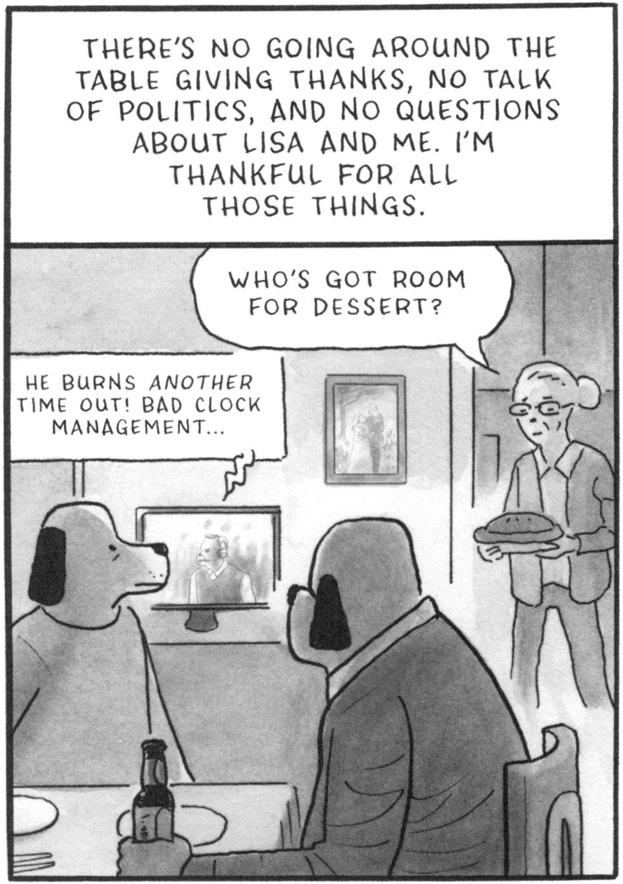
THERE'S NO GOING AROUND THE TABLE GIVING THANKS, NO TALK OF POLITICS, AND NO QUESTIONS ABOUT LISA AND ME. I'M THANKFUL FOR ALL THOSE THINGS.
WHO'S GOT ROOM FOR DESSERT?
HE BURNS *ANOTHER* TIME OUT! BAD CLOCK MANAGEMENT...

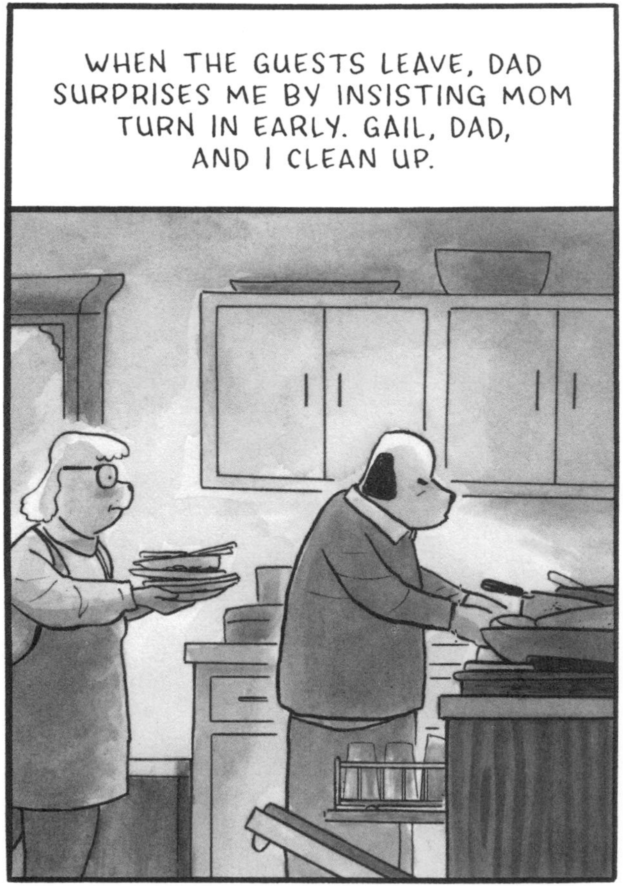
WHEN THE GUESTS LEAVE, DAD SURPRISES ME BY INSISTING MOM TURN IN EARLY. GAIL, DAD, AND I CLEAN UP.

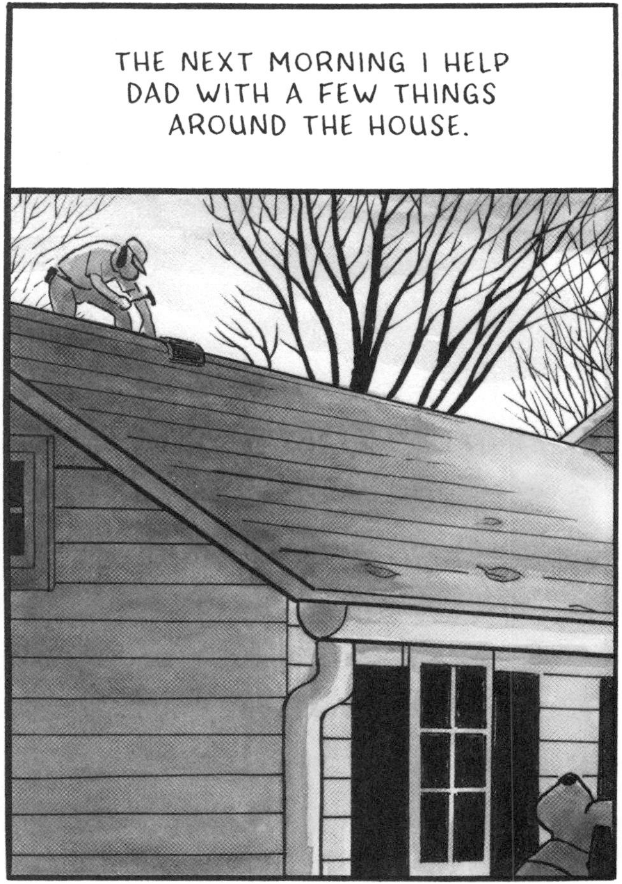
THE NEXT MORNING I HELP DAD WITH A FEW THINGS AROUND THE HOUSE.

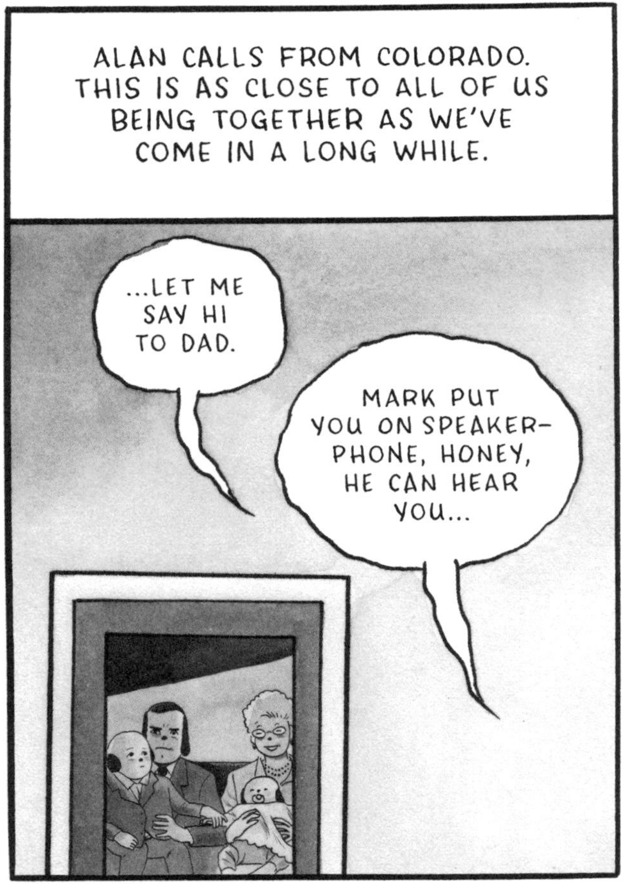
ALAN CALLS FROM COLORADO. THIS IS AS CLOSE TO ALL OF US BEING TOGETHER AS WE'VE COME IN A LONG WHILE.
...LET ME SAY HI TO DAD.
MARK PUT YOU ON SPEAKER-PHONE, HONEY, HE CAN HEAR YOU...

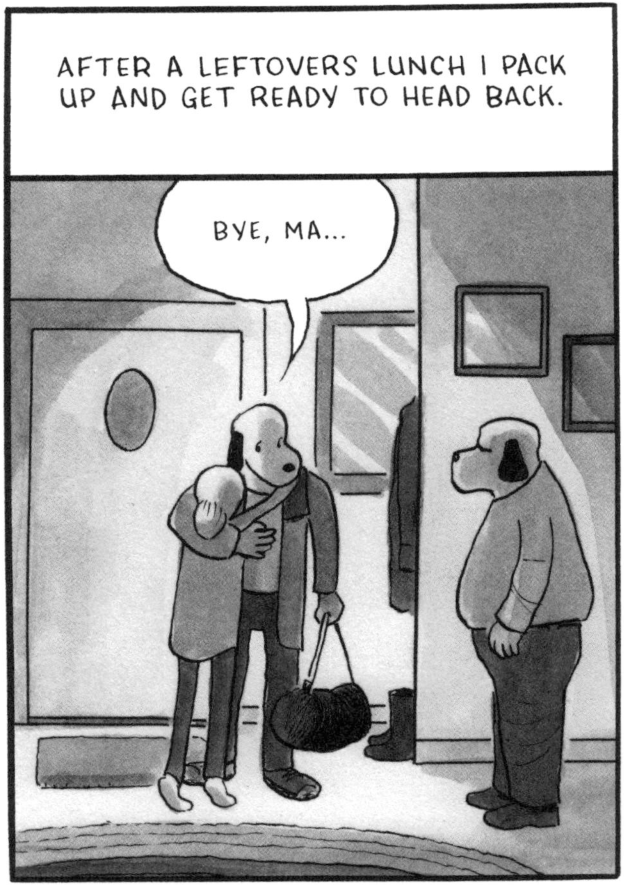
AFTER A LEFTOVERS LUNCH I PACK UP AND GET READY TO HEAD BACK.
BYE, MA...

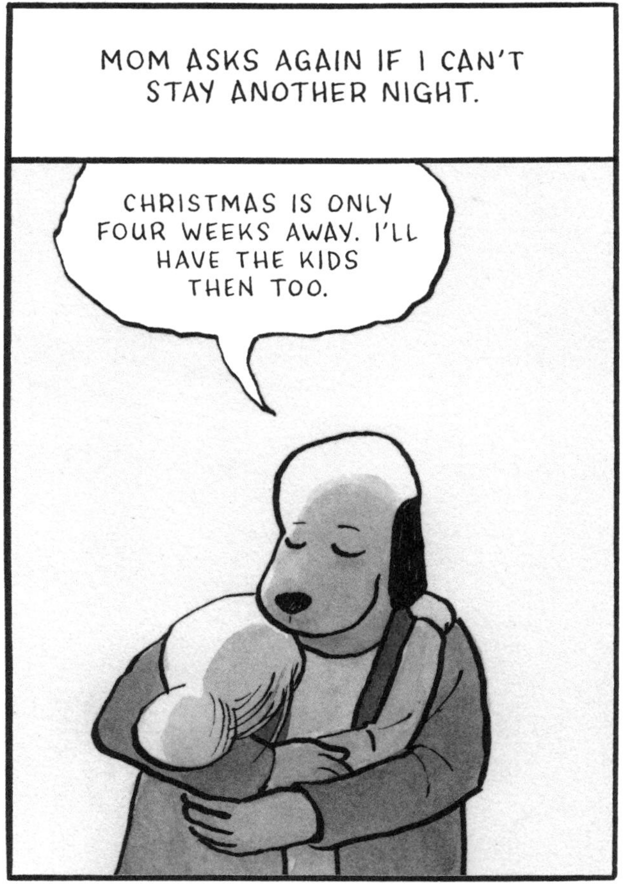
MOM ASKS AGAIN IF I CAN'T STAY ANOTHER NIGHT.
CHRISTMAS IS ONLY FOUR WEEKS AWAY. I'LL HAVE THE KIDS THEN TOO.

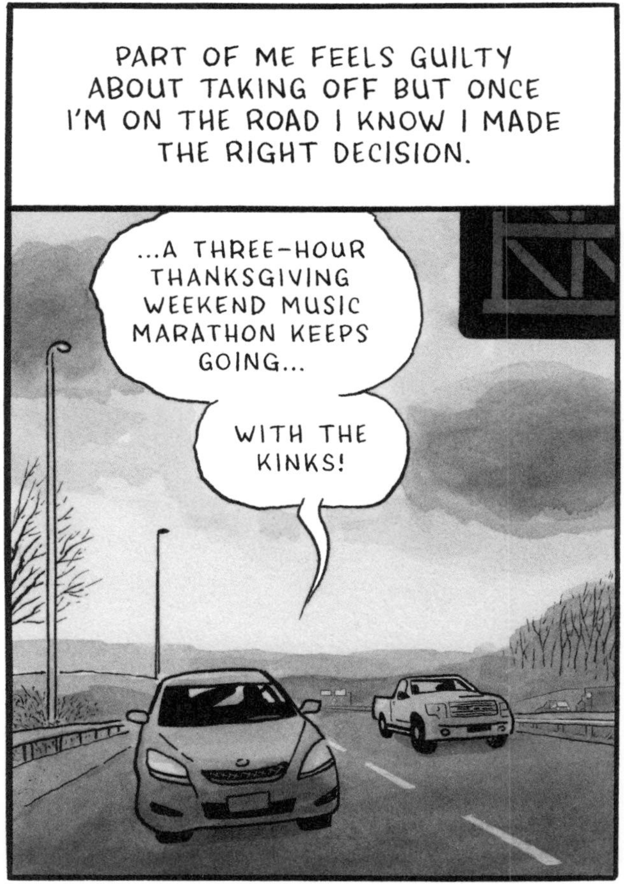
PART OF ME FEELS GUILTY ABOUT TAKING OFF BUT ONCE I'M ON THE ROAD I KNOW I MADE THE RIGHT DECISION.
...A THREE-HOUR THANKSGIVING WEEKEND MUSIC MARATHON KEEPS GOING...
WITH THE KINKS!

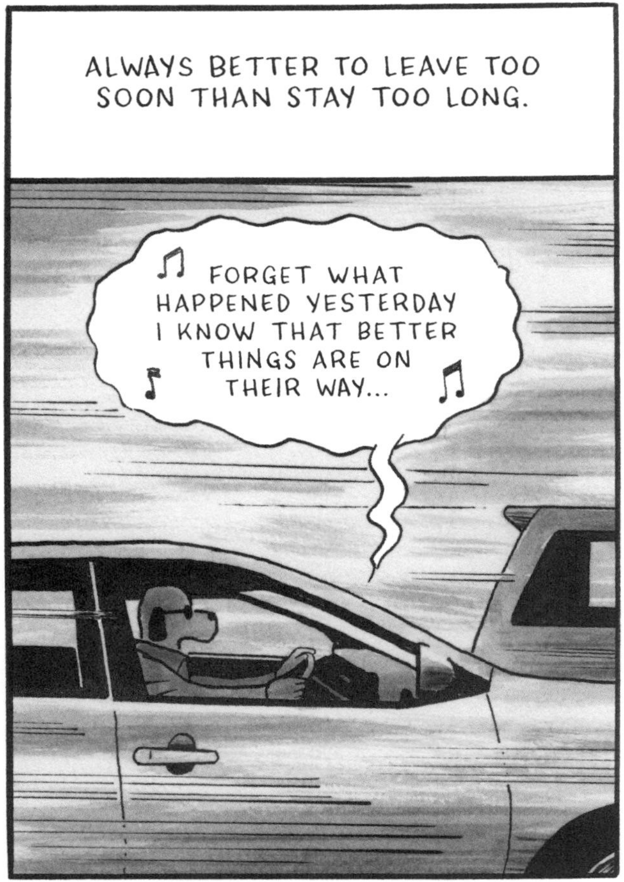
ALWAYS BETTER TO LEAVE TOO SOON THAN STAY TOO LONG.
FORGET WHAT HAPPENED YESTERDAY I KNOW THAT BETTER THINGS ARE ON THEIR WAY...

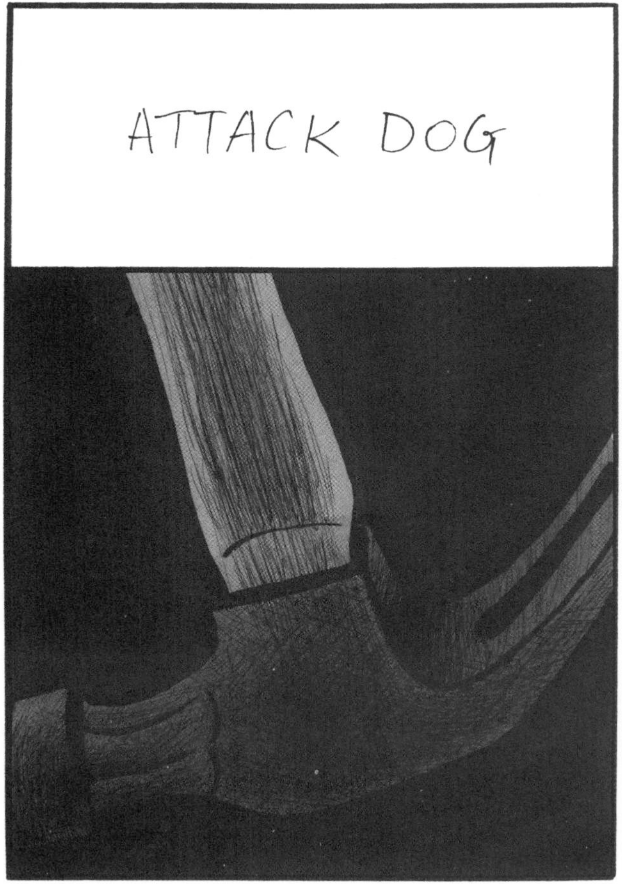
ATTACK DOG

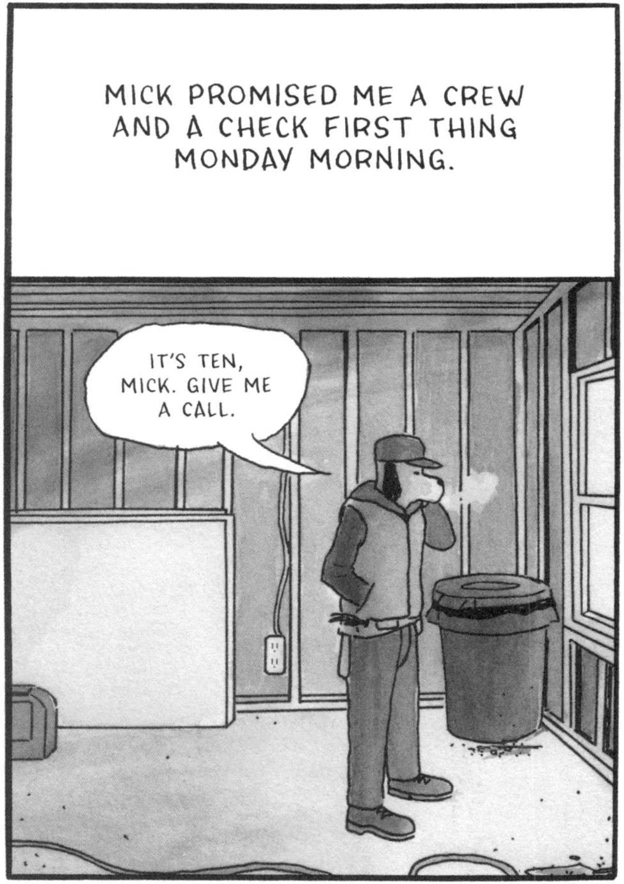
MICK PROMISED ME A CREW AND A CHECK FIRST THING MONDAY MORNING.
IT'S TEN, MICK. GIVE ME A CALL.

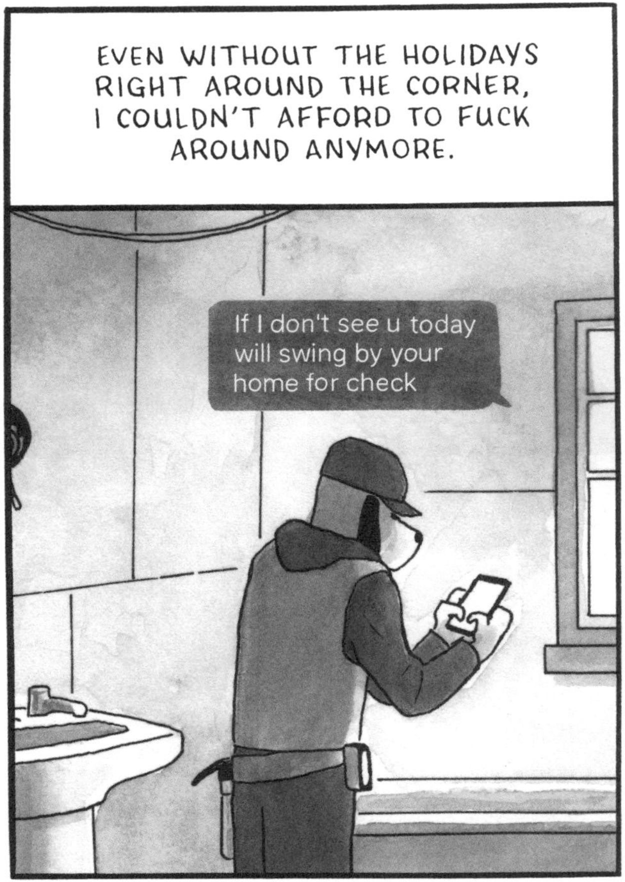
EVEN WITHOUT THE HOLIDAYS RIGHT AROUND THE CORNER, I COULDN'T AFFORD TO FUCK AROUND ANYMORE.
If I don't see u today will swing by your home for check

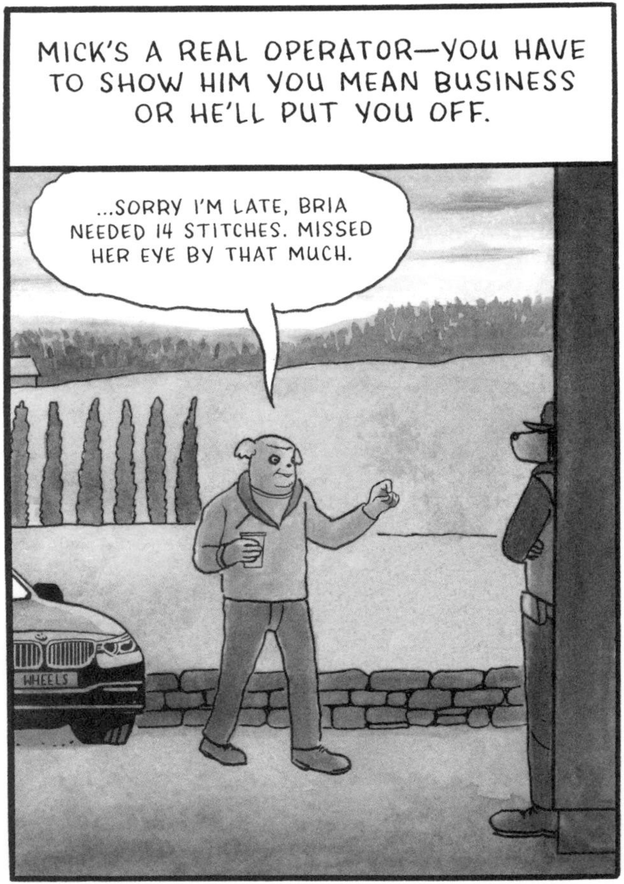
MICK'S A REAL OPERATOR—YOU HAVE TO SHOW HIM YOU MEAN BUSINESS OR HE'LL PUT YOU OFF.
...SORRY I'M LATE, BRIA NEEDED 14 STITCHES. MISSED HER EYE BY THAT MUCH.
WHEELS

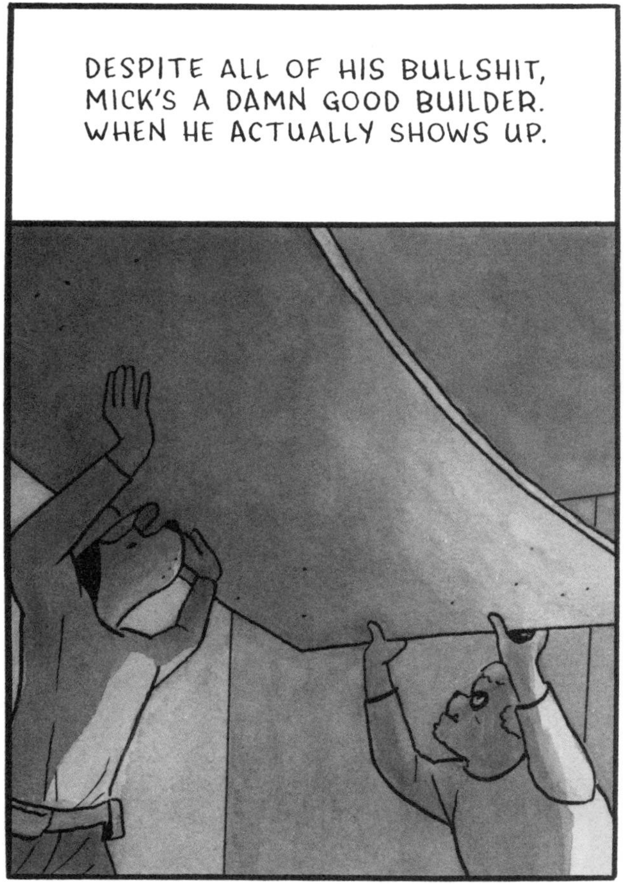
DESPITE ALL OF HIS BULLSHIT, MICK'S A DAMN GOOD BUILDER. WHEN HE ACTUALLY SHOWS UP.

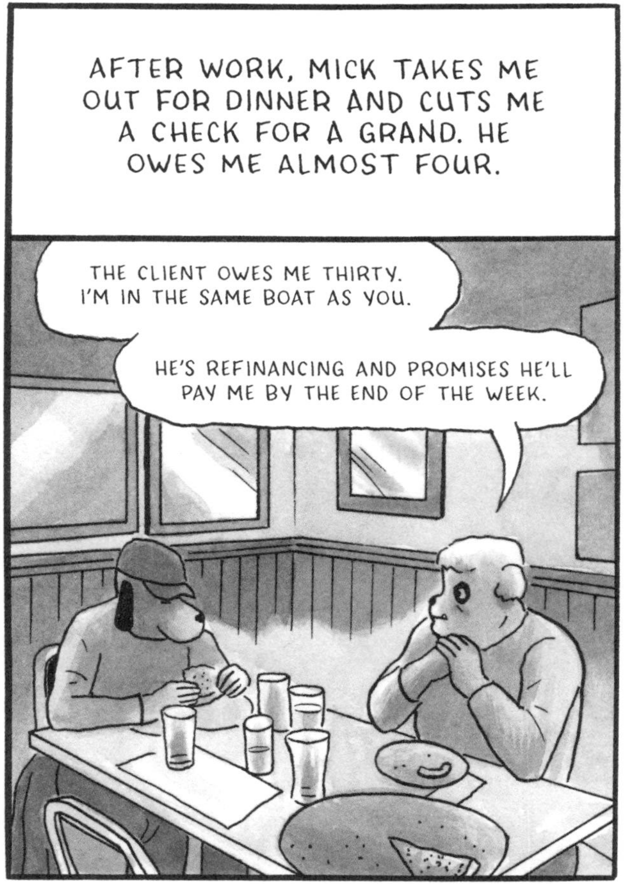
AFTER WORK, MICK TAKES ME OUT FOR DINNER AND CUTS ME A CHECK FOR A GRAND. HE OWES ME ALMOST FOUR.
THE CLIENT OWES ME THIRTY. I'M IN THE SAME BOAT AS YOU.
HE'S REFINANCING AND PROMISES HE'LL PAY ME BY THE END OF THE WEEK.

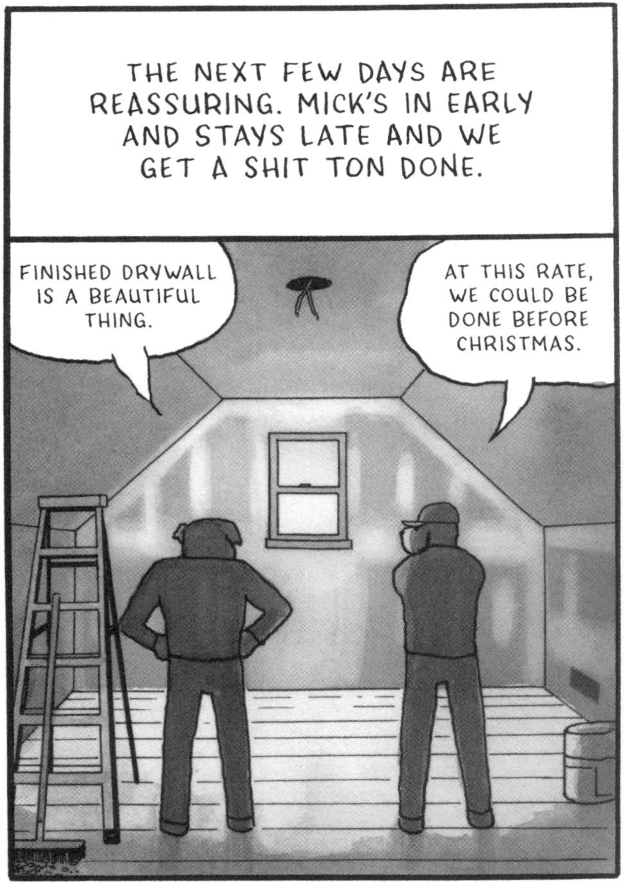
THE NEXT FEW DAYS ARE REASSURING. MICK'S IN EARLY AND STAYS LATE AND WE GET A SHIT TON DONE.
FINISHED DRYWALL IS A BEAUTIFUL THING.
AT THIS RATE, WE COULD BE DONE BEFORE CHRISTMAS.

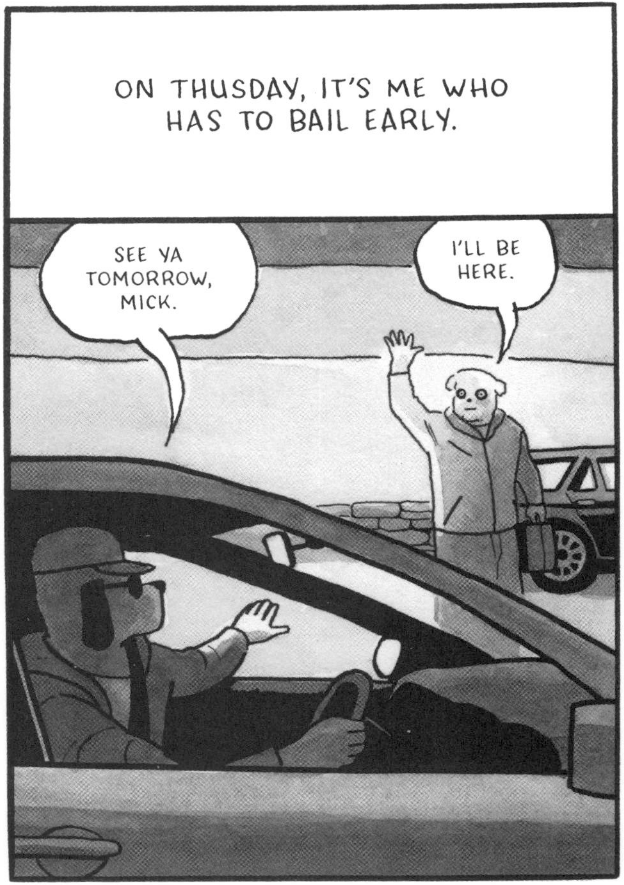
ON THUSDAY, IT'S ME WHO HAS TO BAIL EARLY.
SEE YA TOMORROW, MICK.
I'LL BE HERE.

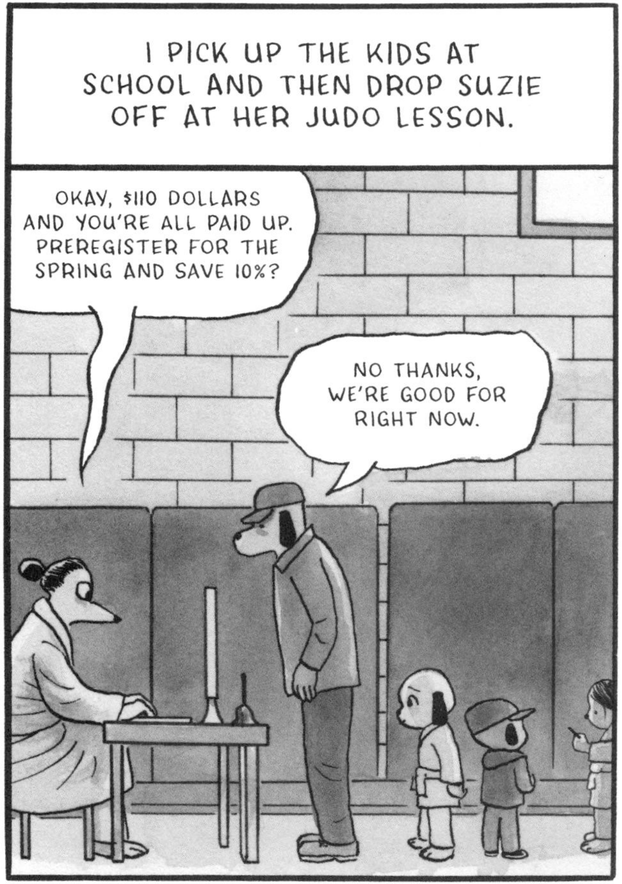
I PICK UP THE KIDS AT SCHOOL AND THEN DROP SUZIE OFF AT HER JUDO LESSON.
OKAY, $110 DOLLARS AND YOU'RE ALL PAID UP. PREREGISTER FOR THE SPRING AND SAVE 10%?
NO THANKS, WE'RE GOOD FOR RIGHT NOW.

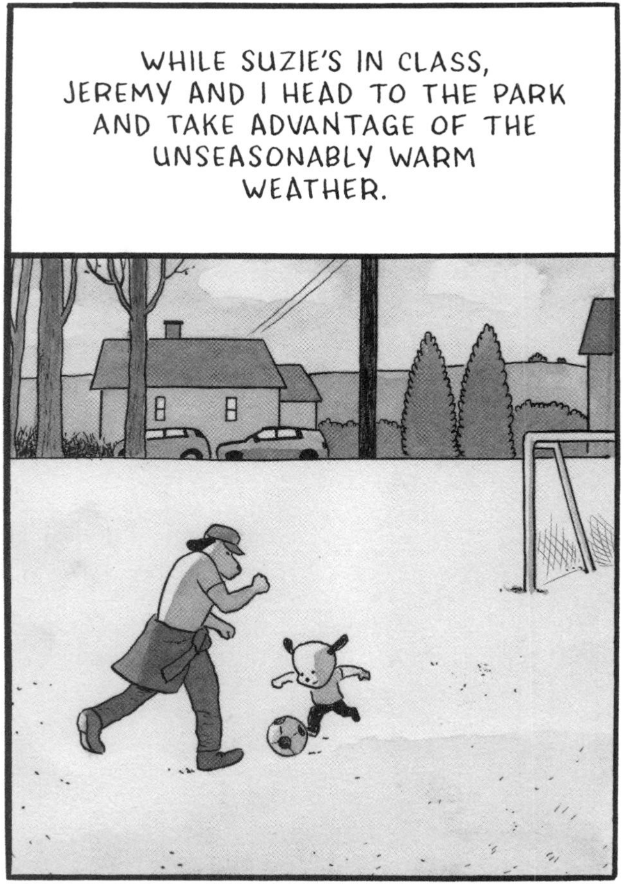
WHILE SUZIE'S IN CLASS, JEREMY AND I HEAD TO THE PARK AND TAKE ADVANTAGE OF THE UNSEASONABLY WARM WEATHER.

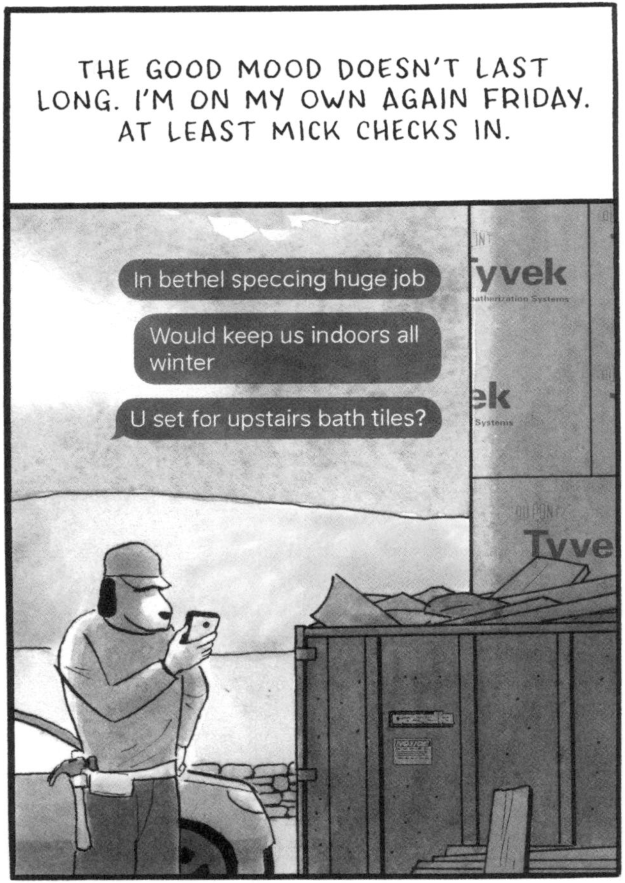
THE GOOD MOOD DOESN'T LAST LONG. I'M ON MY OWN AGAIN FRIDAY. AT LEAST MICK CHECKS IN.
In bethel speccing huge job
Would keep us indoors all winter
U set for upstairs bath tiles?

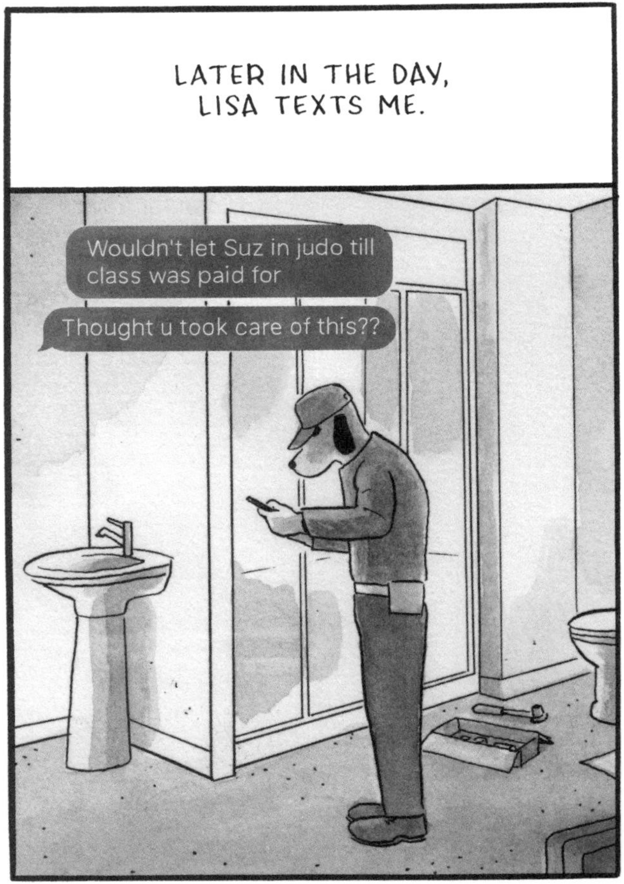
LATER IN THE DAY, LISA TEXTS ME.
Wouldn't let Suz in judo till class was paid for
Thought u took care of this??

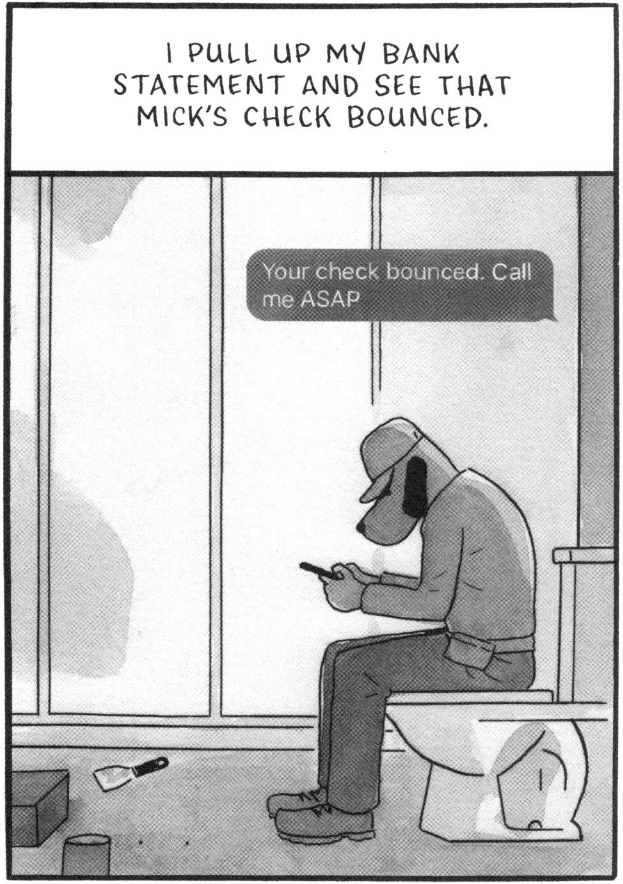
I PULL UP MY BANK STATEMENT AND SEE THAT MICK'S CHECK BOUNCED.
Your check bounced. Call me ASAP

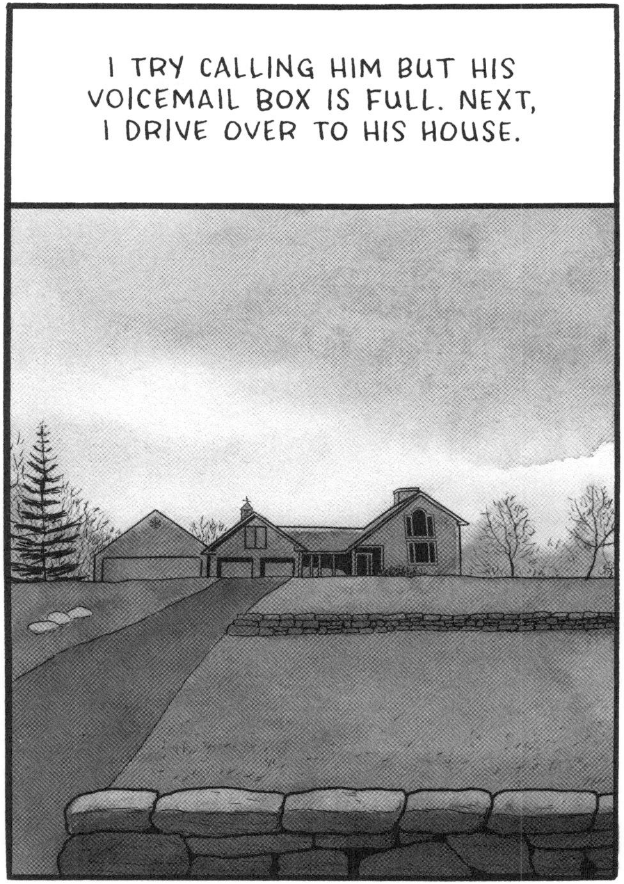
I TRY CALLING HIM BUT HIS VOICEMAIL BOX IS FULL. NEXT, I DRIVE OVER TO HIS HOUSE.

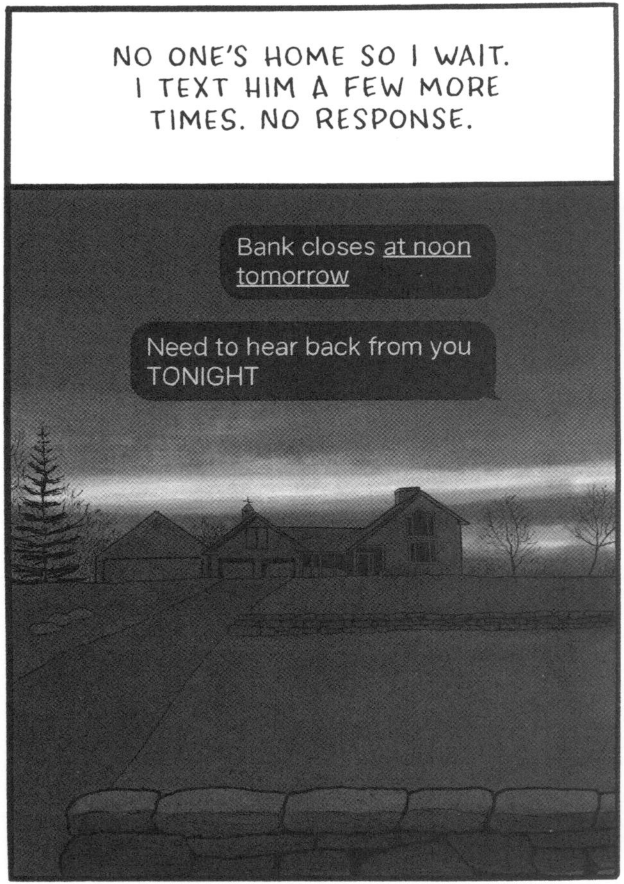
NO ONE'S HOME SO I WAIT. I TEXT HIM A FEW MORE TIMES. NO RESPONSE.
Bank closes at noon tomorrow
Need to hear back from you TONIGHT

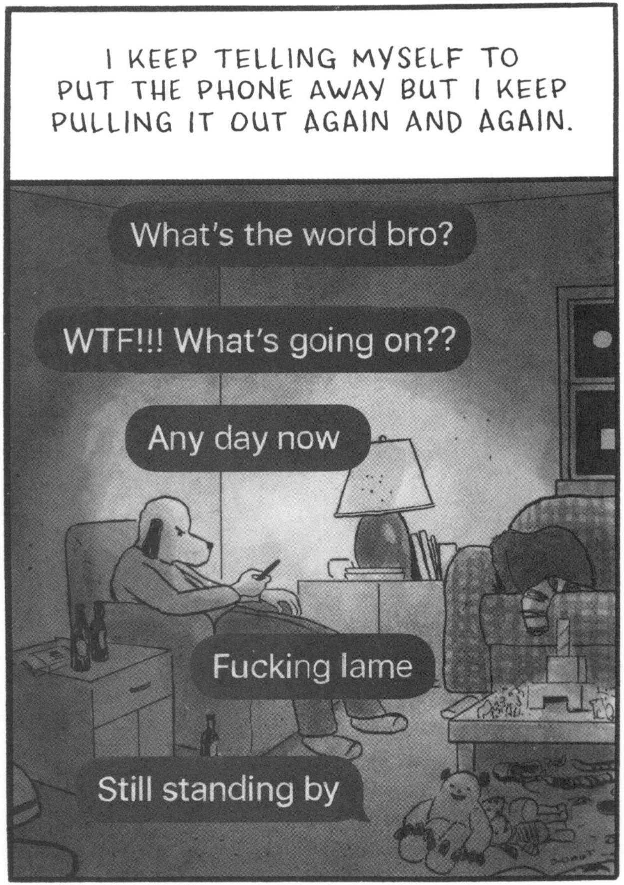
I KEEP TELLING MYSELF TO PUT THE PHONE AWAY BUT I KEEP PULLING IT OUT AGAIN AND AGAIN.
What's the word bro?
WTF!!! What's going on??
Any day now
Fucking lame
Still standing by

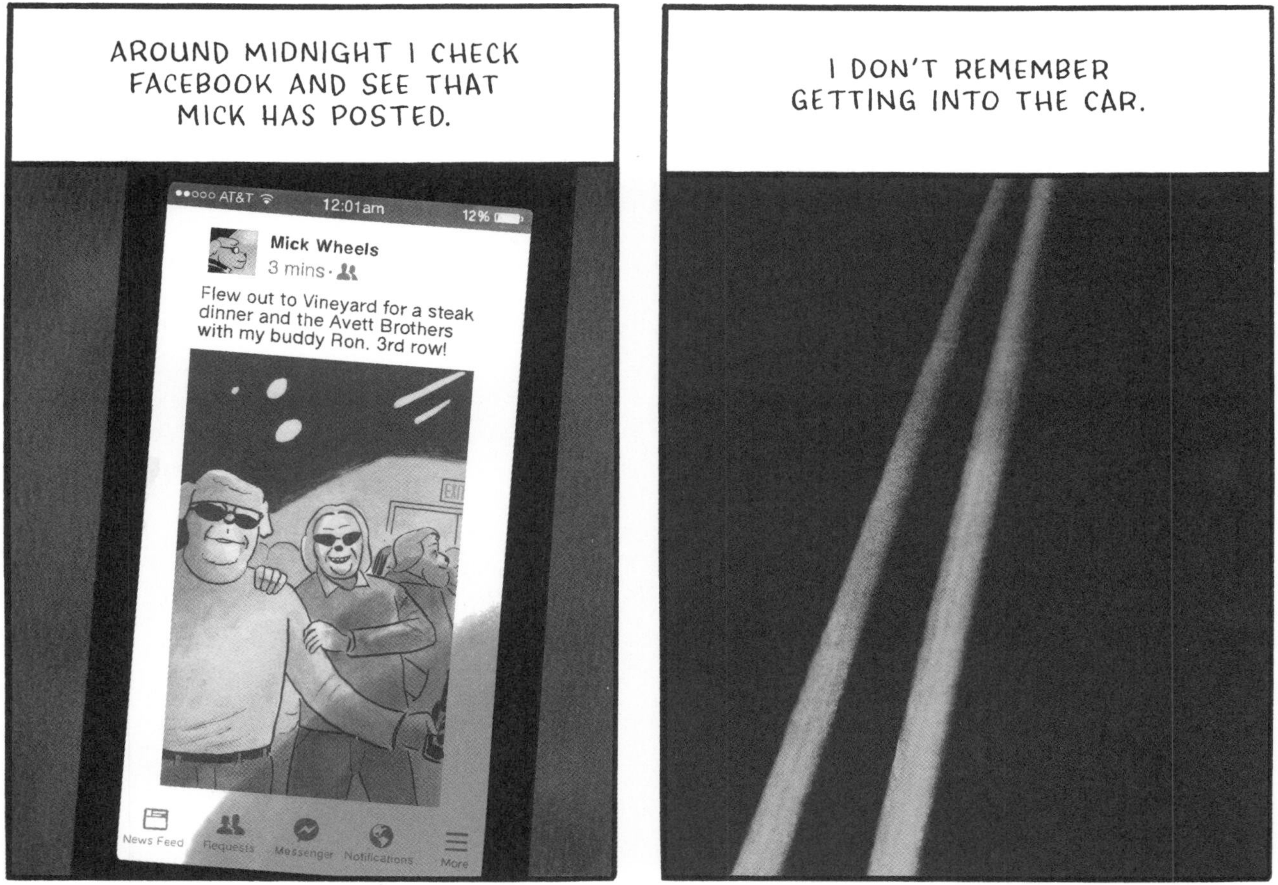
AROUND MIDNIGHT I CHECK FACEBOOK AND SEE THAT MICK HAS POSTED.
AT&T
12:01am
12%
Mick Wheels
3 mins ·
Flew out to Vineyard for a steak dinner and the Avett Brothers with my buddy Ron. 3rd row!
EXIT
News Feed
Requests
Messenger
Notifications
More
I DON'T REMEMBER GETTING INTO THE CAR.

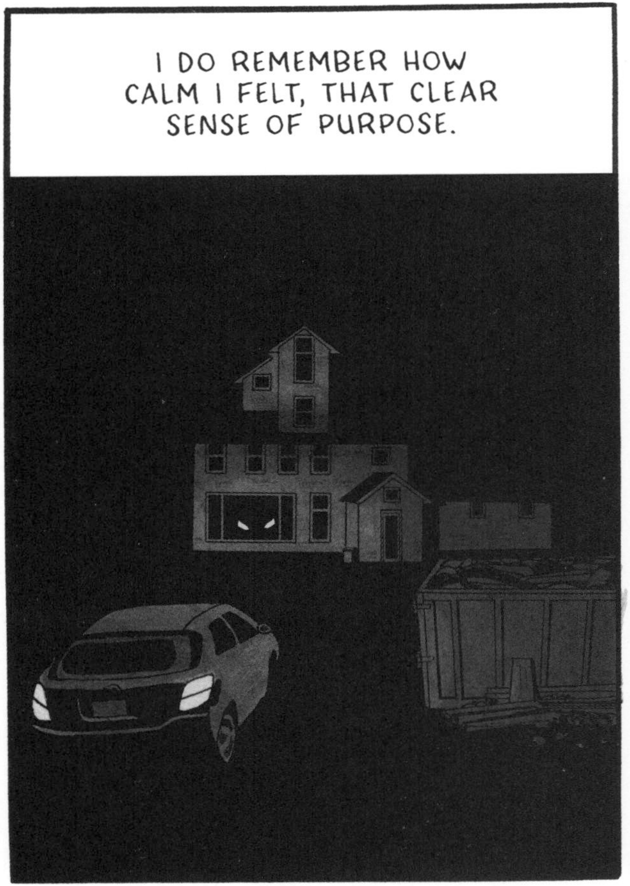
I DO REMEMBER HOW CALM I FELT, THAT CLEAR SENSE OF PURPOSE.

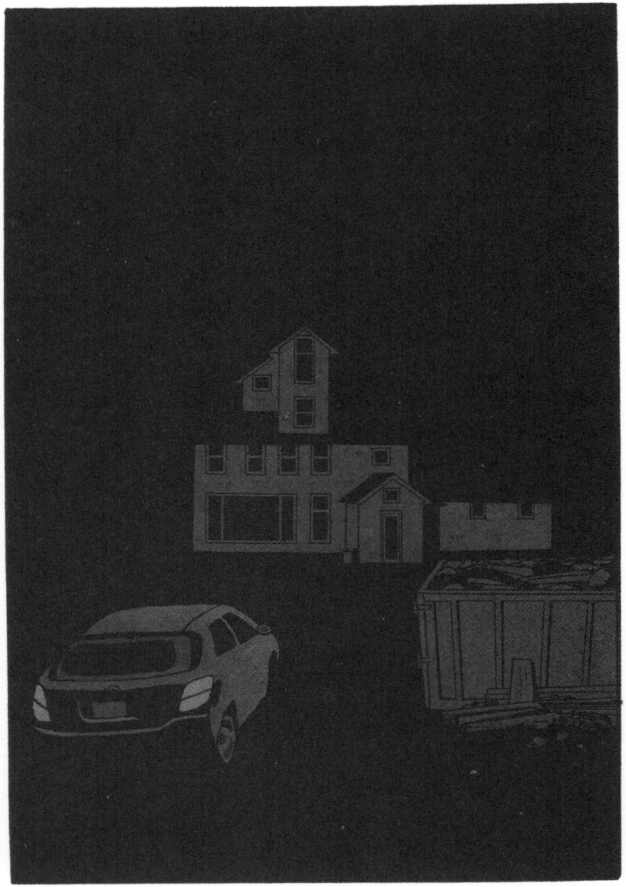

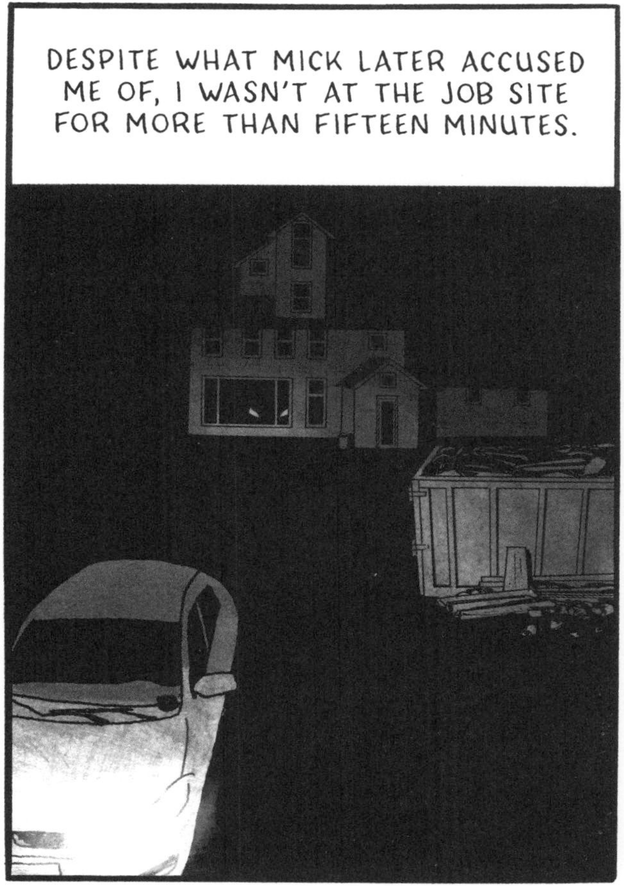
DESPITE WHAT MICK LATER ACCUSED ME OF, I WASN'T AT THE JOB SITE FOR MORE THAN FIFTEEN MINUTES.

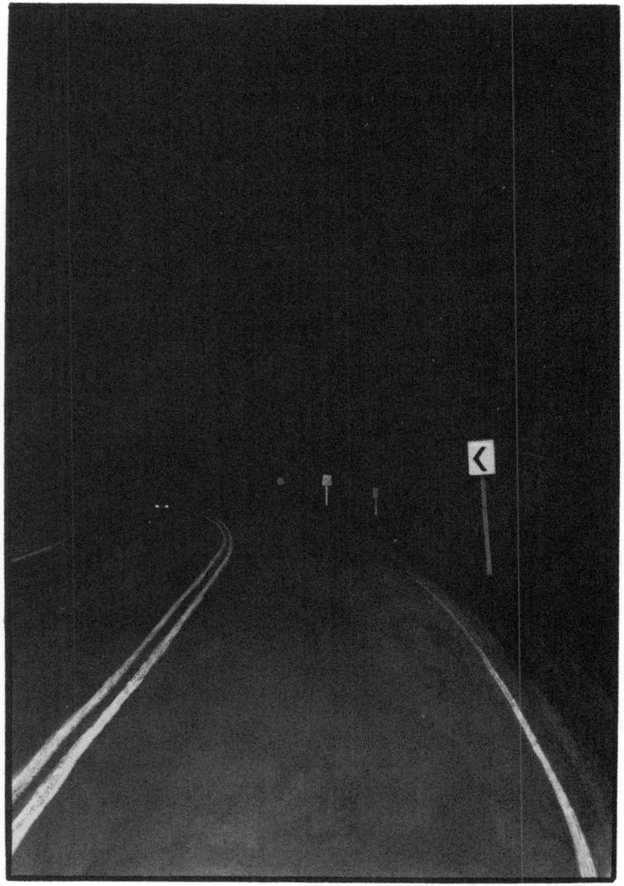

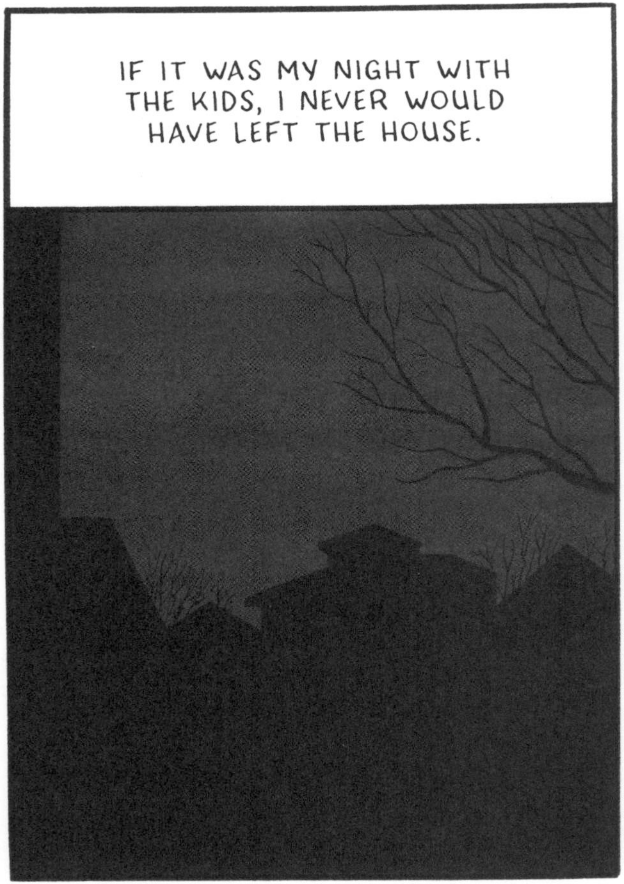
IF IT WAS MY NIGHT WITH THE KIDS, I NEVER WOULD HAVE LEFT THE HOUSE.

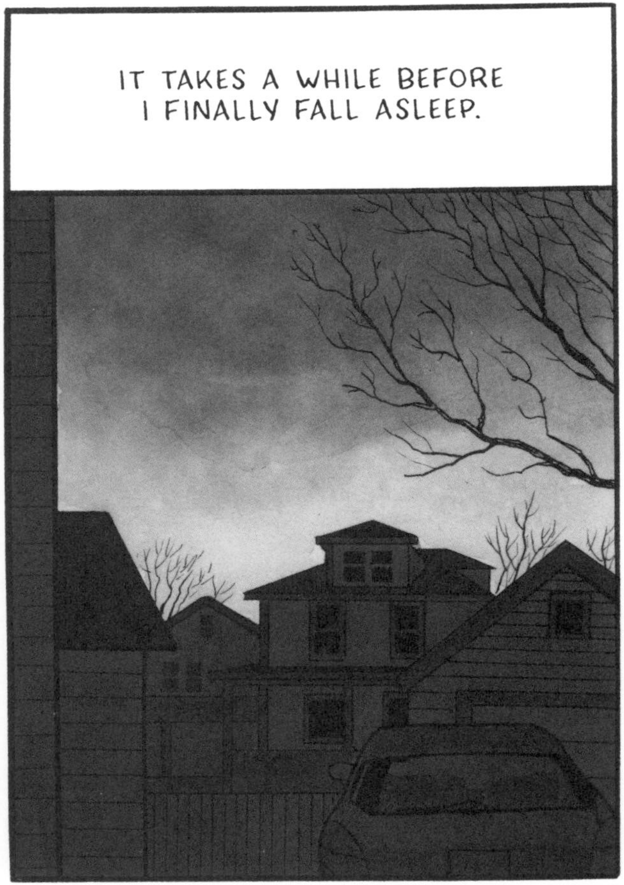
IT TAKES A WHILE BEFORE I FINALLY FALL ASLEEP.

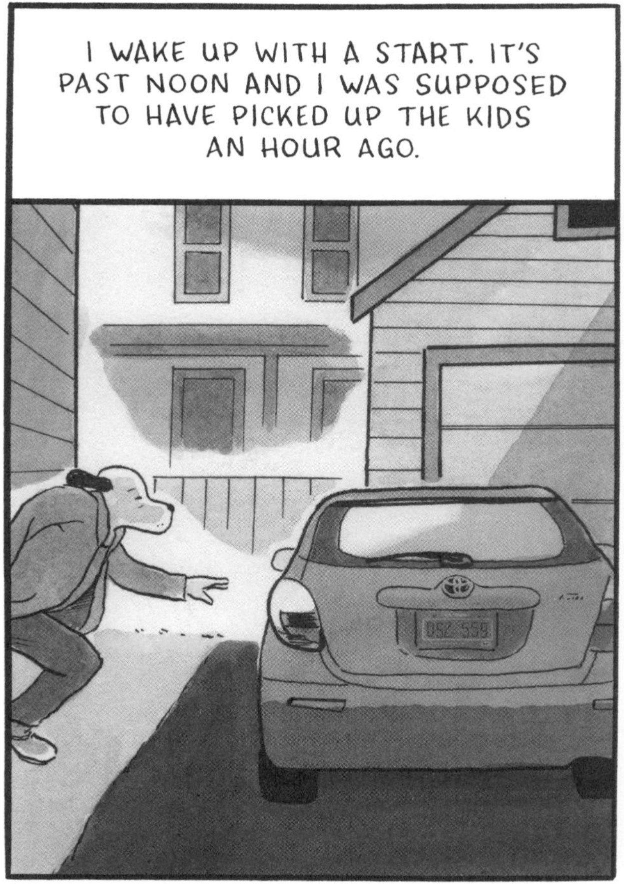
I WAKE UP WITH A START. IT'S PAST NOON AND I WAS SUPPOSED TO HAVE PICKED UP THE KIDS AN HOUR AGO.

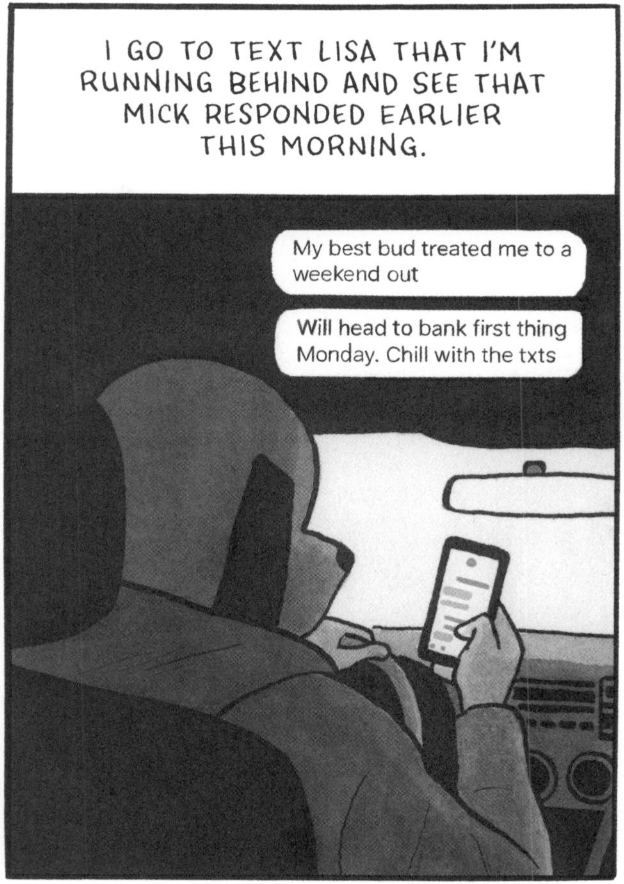
I GO TO TEXT LISA THAT I'M RUNNING BEHIND AND SEE THAT MICK RESPONDED EARLIER THIS MORNING.
My best bud treated me to a weekend out
Will head to bank first thing Monday. Chill with the txts

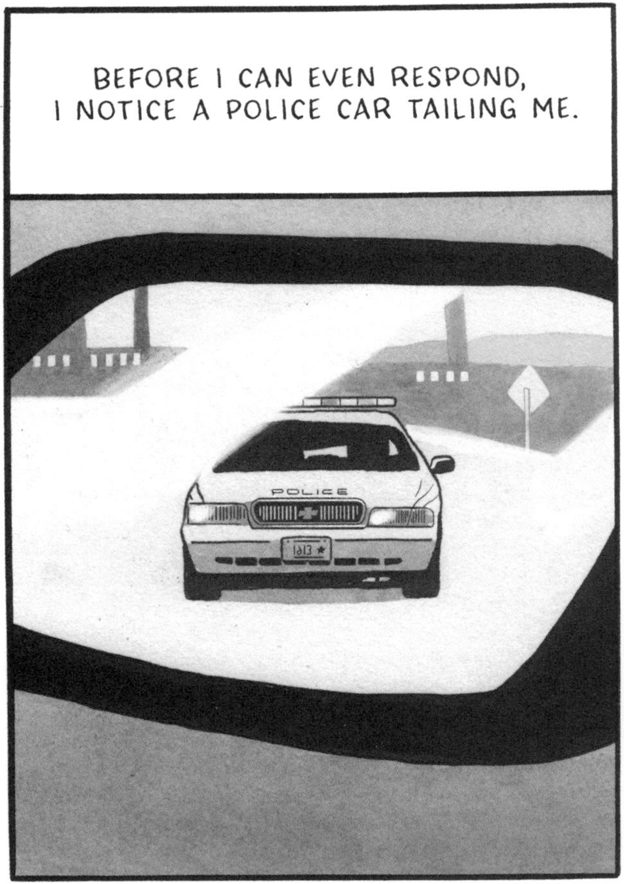
BEFORE I CAN EVEN RESPOND, I NOTICE A POLICE CAR TAILING ME.
POLICE

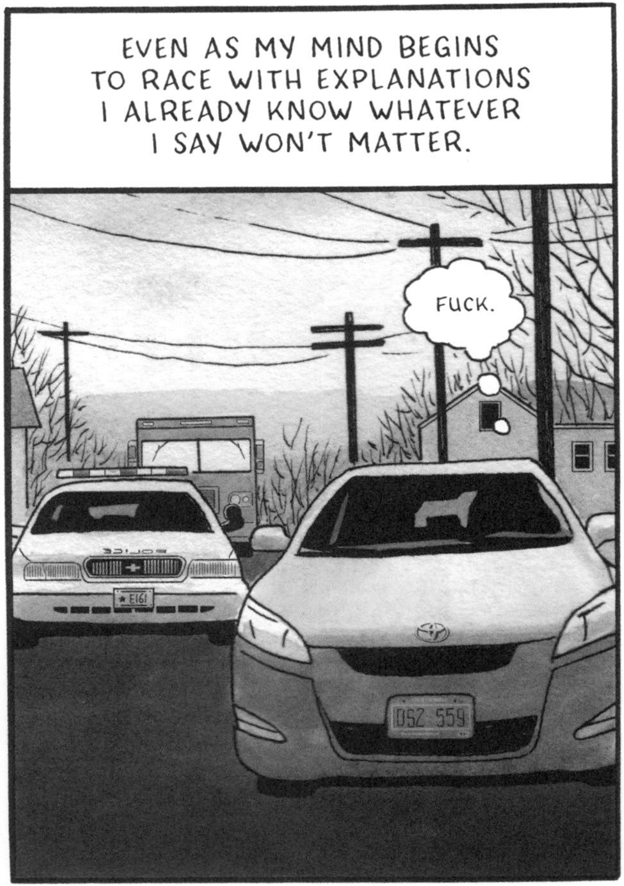
EVEN AS MY MIND BEGINS TO RACE WITH EXPLANATIONS I ALREADY KNOW WHATEVER I SAY WON'T MATTER.
FUCK.

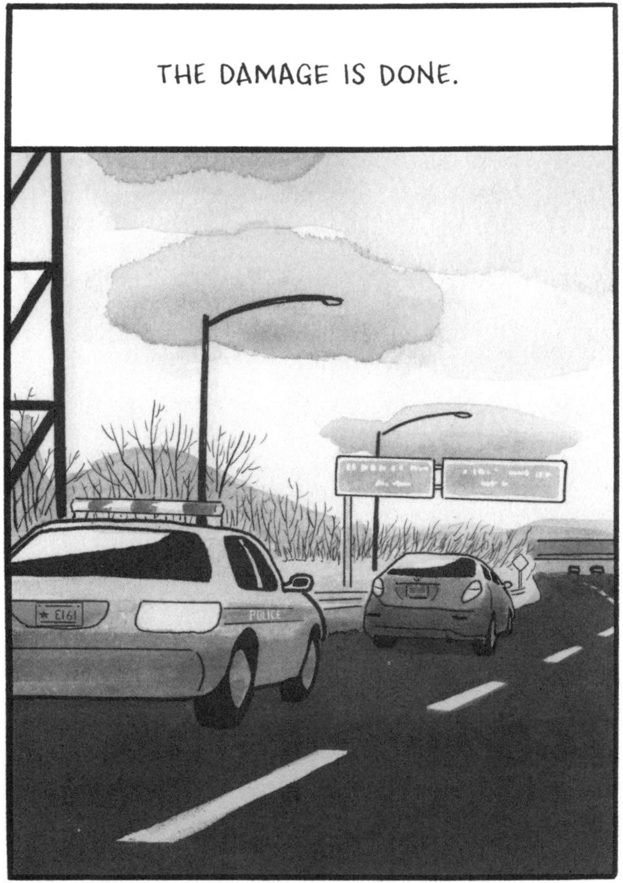
THE DAMAGE IS DONE.
POLICE

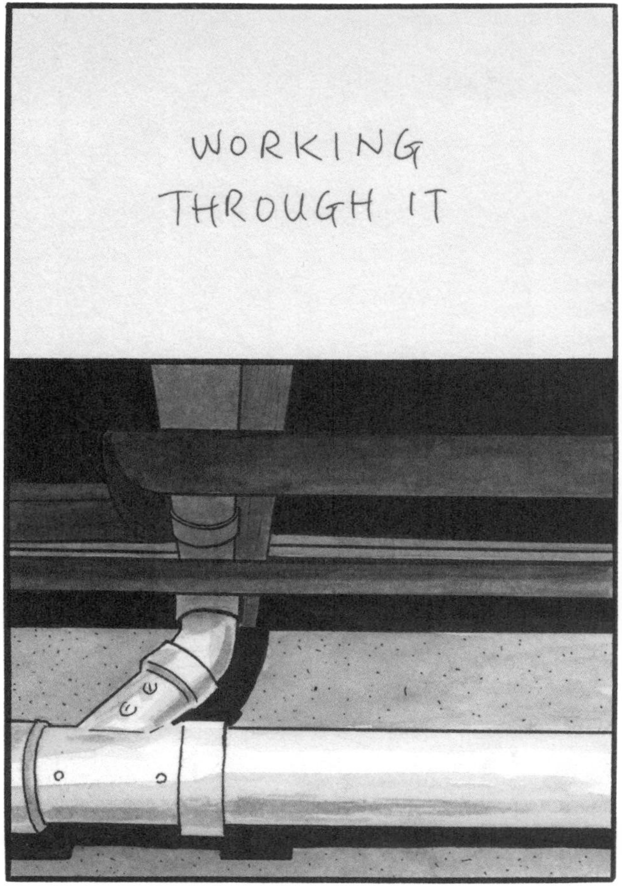
WORKING THROUGH IT

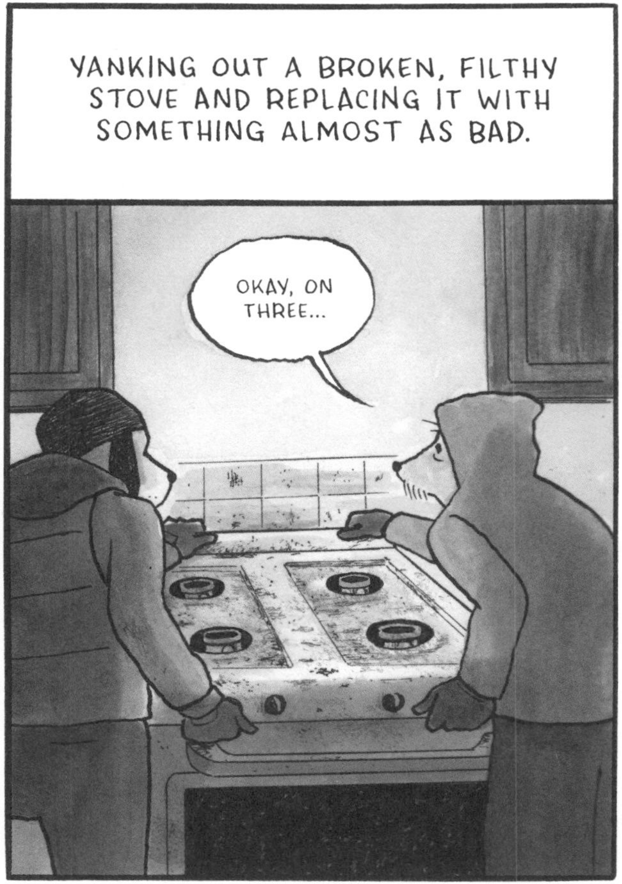
YANKING OUT A BROKEN, FILTHY STOVE AND REPLACING IT WITH SOMETHING ALMOST AS BAD.
OKAY, ON THREE...

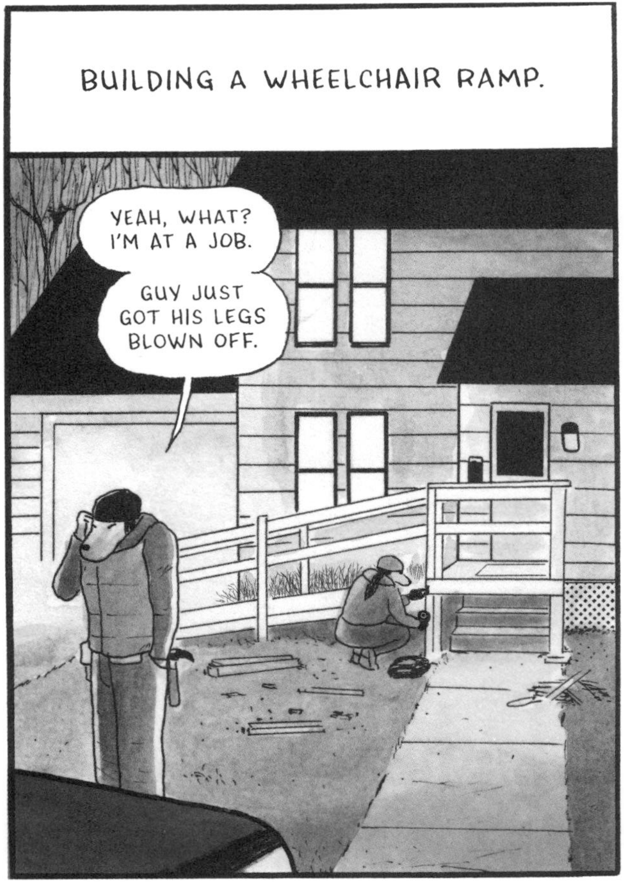
BUILDING A WHEELCHAIR RAMP.
YEAH, WHAT? I'M AT A JOB.
GUY JUST GOT HIS LEGS BLOWN OFF.

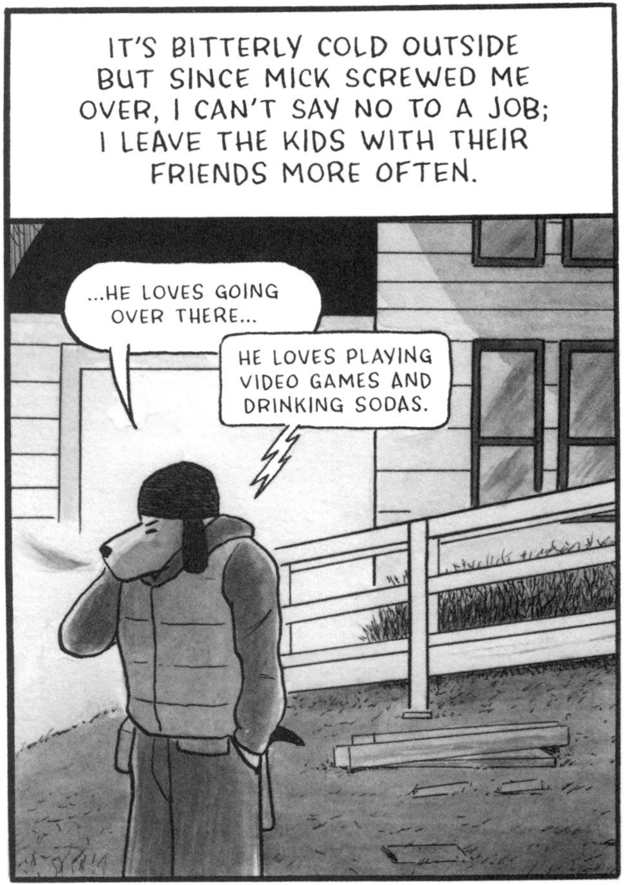
IT'S BITTERLY COLD OUTSIDE BUT SINCE MICK SCREWED ME OVER, I CAN'T SAY NO TO A JOB; I LEAVE THE KIDS WITH THEIR FRIENDS MORE OFTEN.
...HE LOVES GOING OVER THERE...
HE LOVES PLAYING VIDEO GAMES AND DRINKING SODAS.

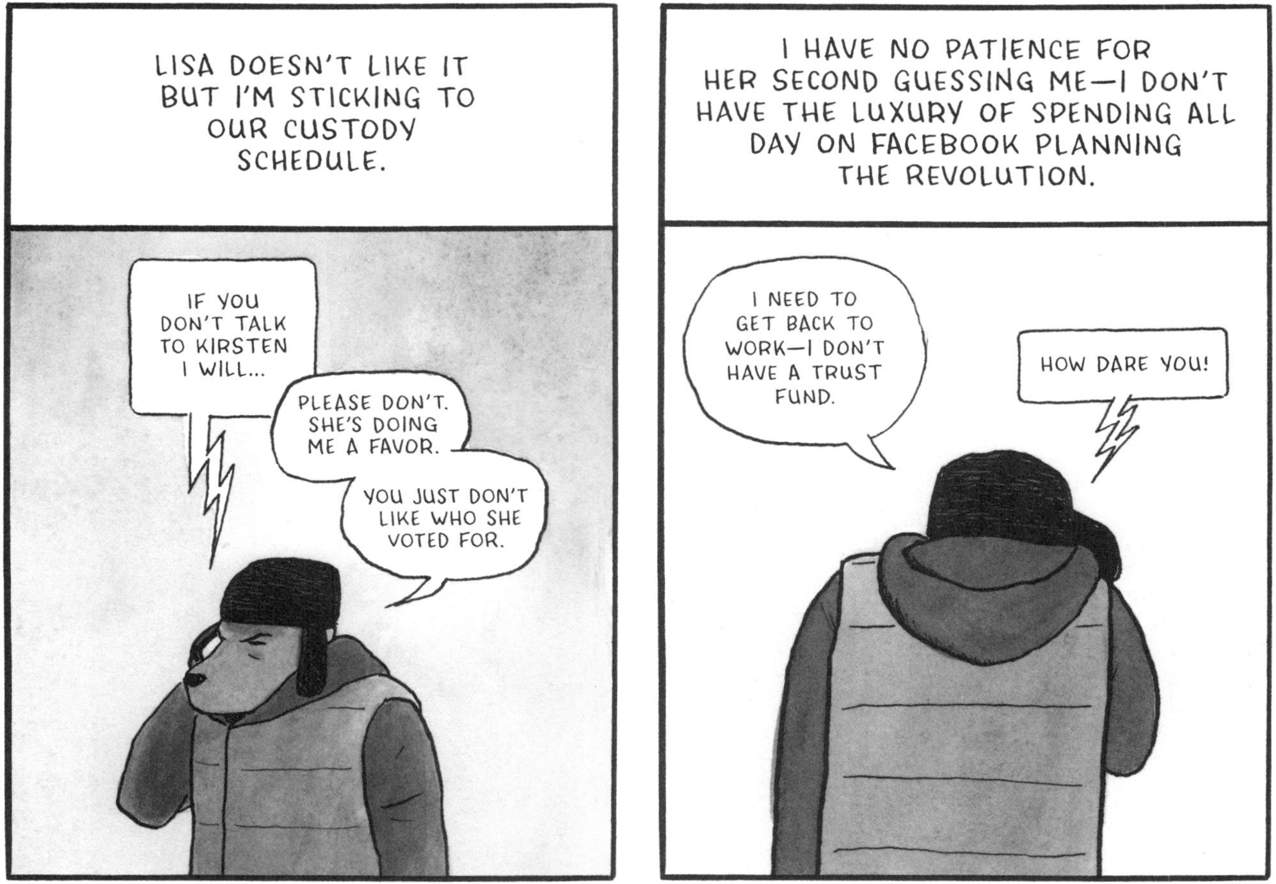
LISA DOESN'T LIKE IT BUT I'M STICKING TO OUR CUSTODY SCHEDULE.
IF YOU DON'T TALK TO KIRSTEN I WILL...
PLEASE DON'T. SHE'S DOING ME A FAVOR.
YOU JUST DON'T LIKE WHO SHE VOTED FOR.
I HAVE NO PATIENCE FOR HER SECOND GUESSING ME—I DON'T HAVE THE LUXURY OF SPENDING ALL DAY ON FACEBOOK PLANNING THE REVOLUTION.
I NEED TO GET BACK TO WORK—I DON'T HAVE A TRUST FUND.
HOW DARE YOU!

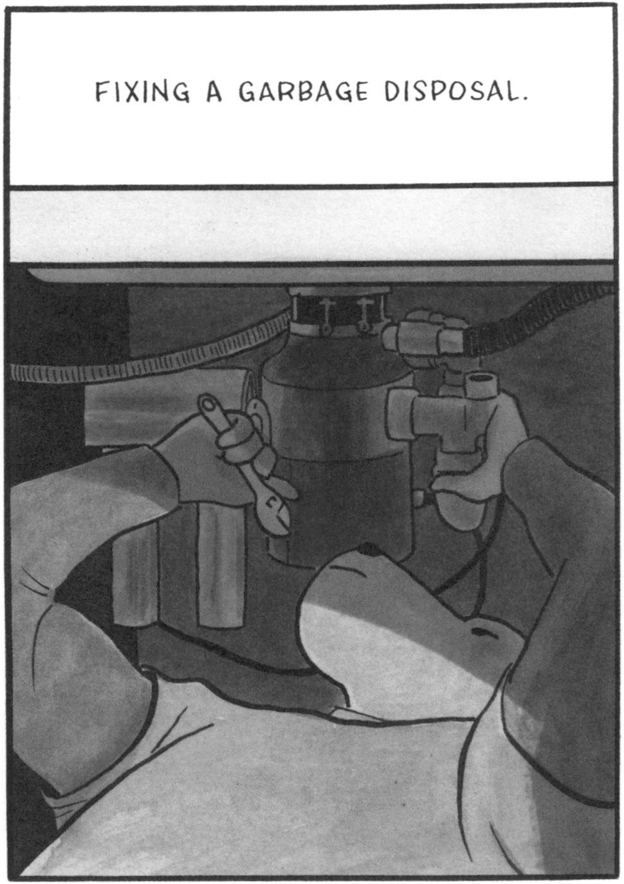
FIXING A GARBAGE DISPOSAL.

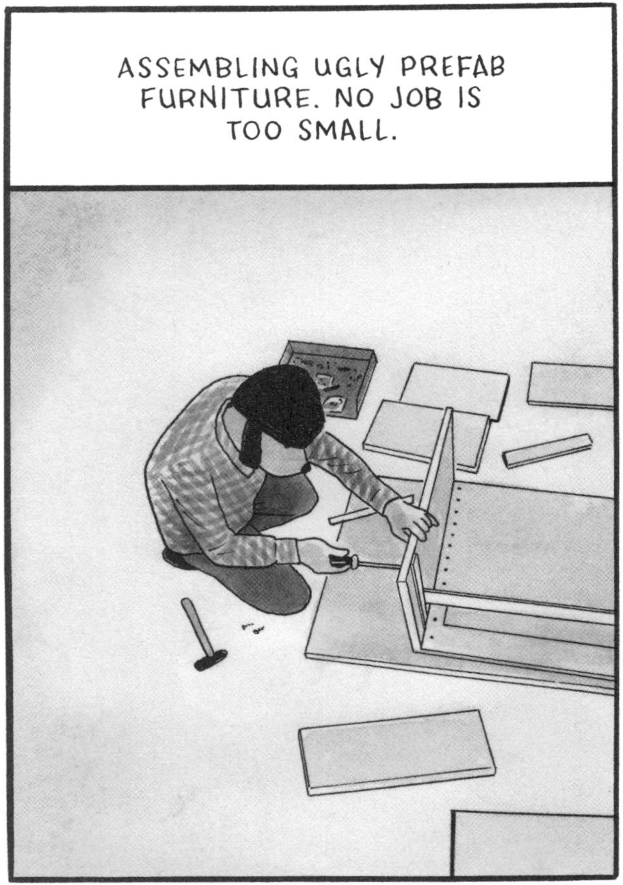
ASSEMBLING UGLY PREFAB FURNITURE. NO JOB IS TOO SMALL.

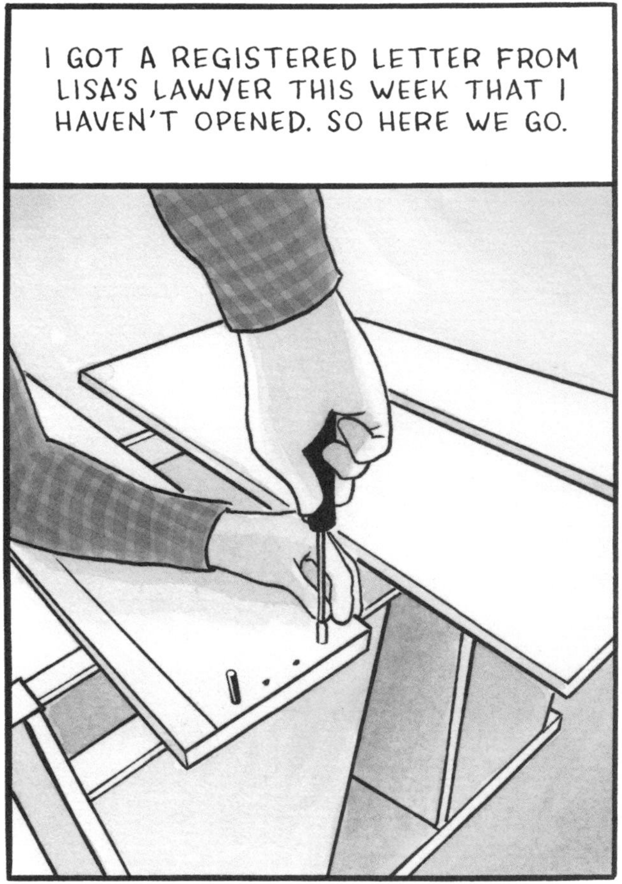
I GOT A REGISTERED LETTER FROM LISA'S LAWYER THIS WEEK THAT I HAVEN'T OPENED. SO HERE WE GO.

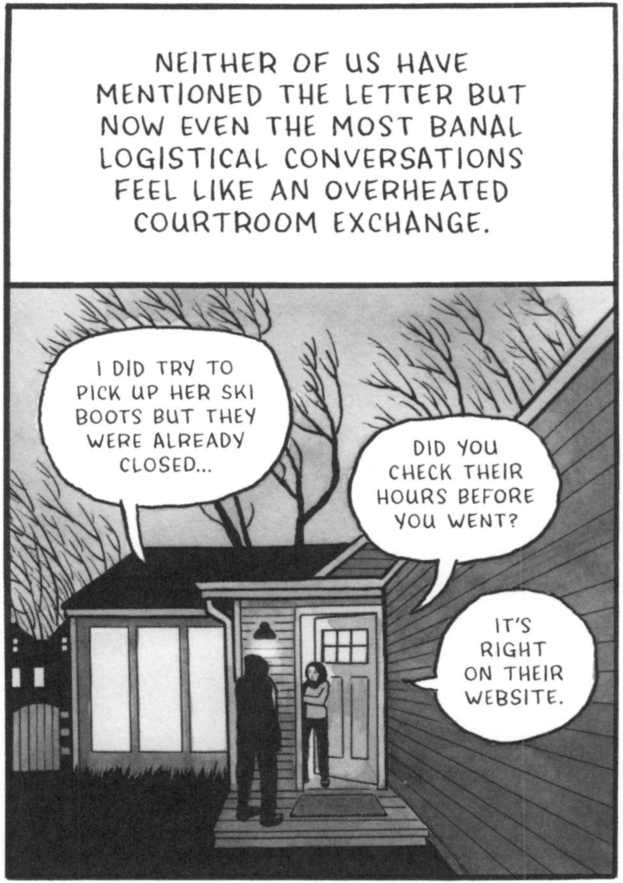
NEITHER OF US HAVE MENTIONED THE LETTER BUT NOW EVEN THE MOST BANAL LOGISTICAL CONVERSATIONS FEEL LIKE AN OVERHEATED COURTROOM EXCHANGE.
I DID TRY TO PICK UP HER SKI BOOTS BUT THEY WERE ALREADY CLOSED...
DID YOU CHECK THEIR HOURS BEFORE YOU WENT?
IT'S RIGHT ON THEIR WEBSITE.

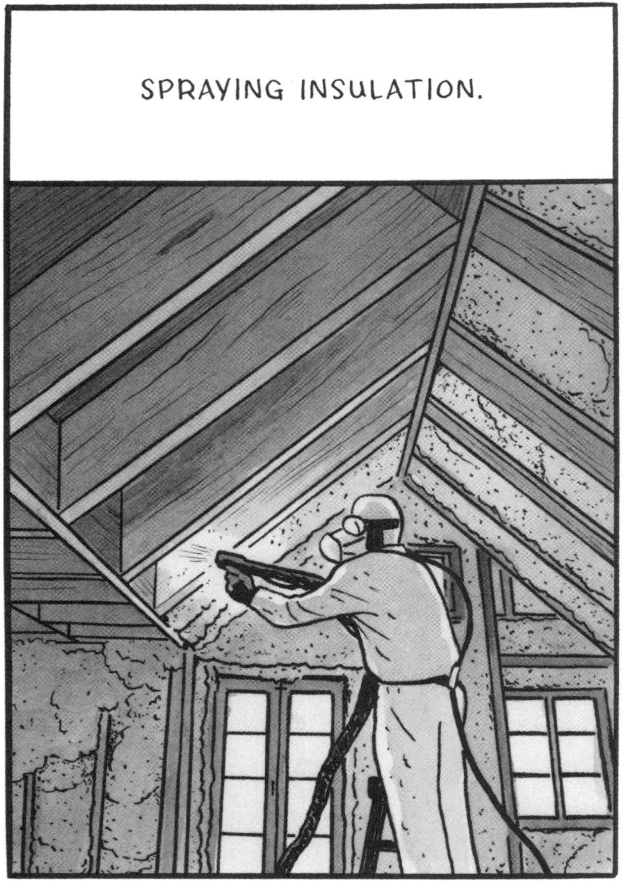
SPRAYING INSULATION.

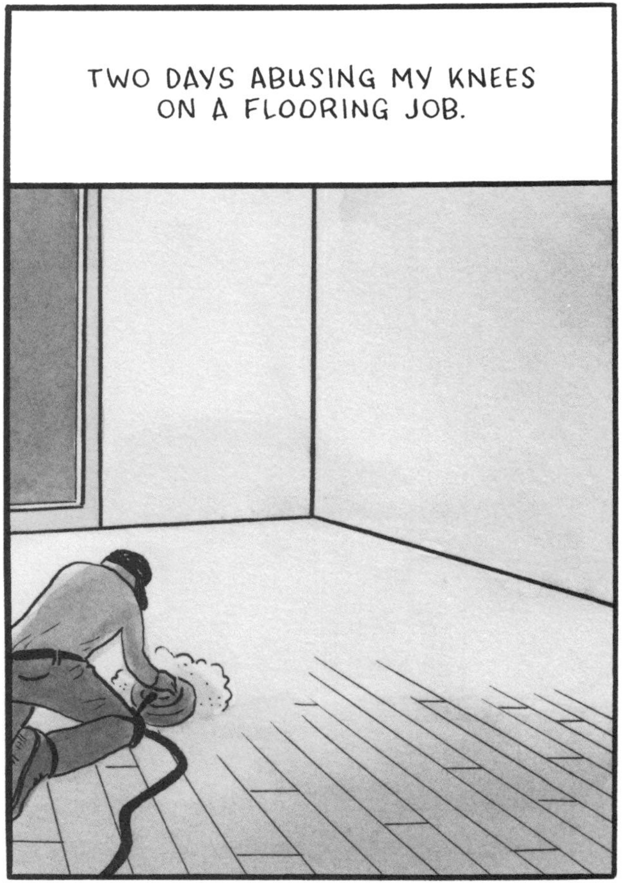
TWO DAYS ABUSING MY KNEES ON A FLOORING JOB.

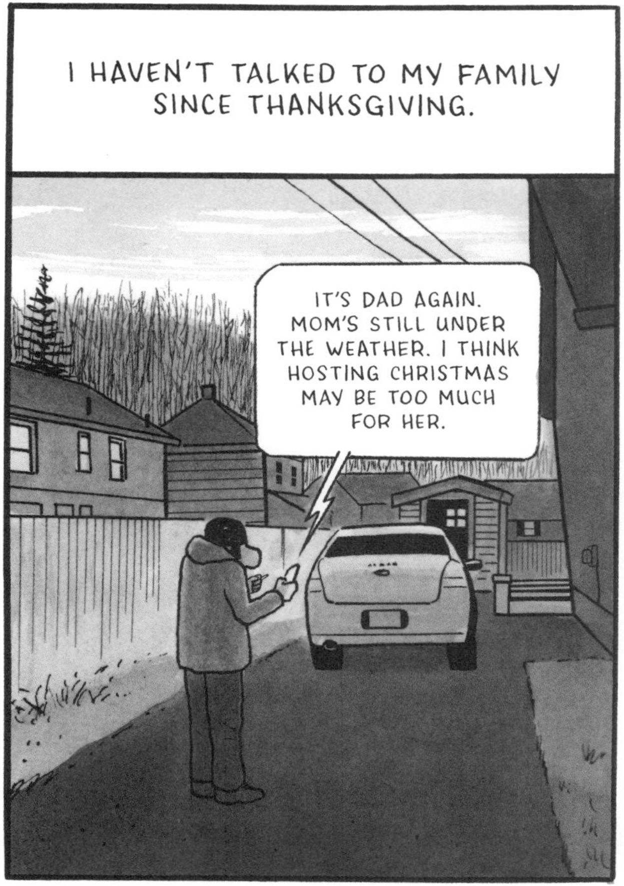
I HAVEN'T TALKED TO MY FAMILY SINCE THANKSGIVING.
IT'S DAD AGAIN. MOM'S STILL UNDER THE WEATHER. I THINK HOSTING CHRISTMAS MAY BE TOO MUCH FOR HER.

I'M IN NO HURRY TO CALL ANYONE BACK. I DON'T NEED TO ENDURE ONE OF DAD'S LONG JUDGEMENTAL SILENCES OR LISTEN TO ALAN TELL ME "I TOLD YOU SO."

WOULD HAVING A LAWYER EARLIER HAVE CHANGED ANYTHING? WOULD ANYTHING HAVE CHANGED ANYTHING?

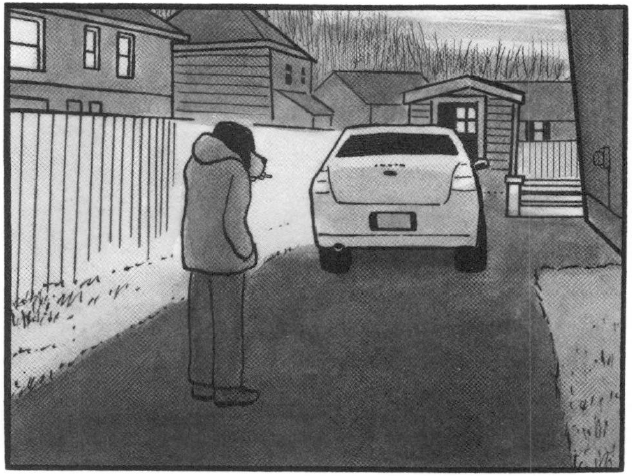

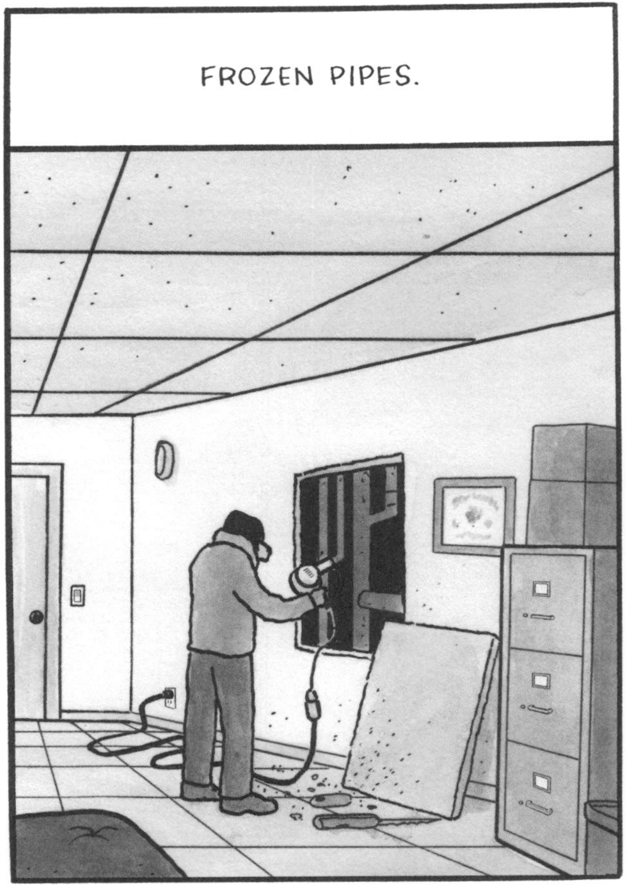
FROZEN PIPES.

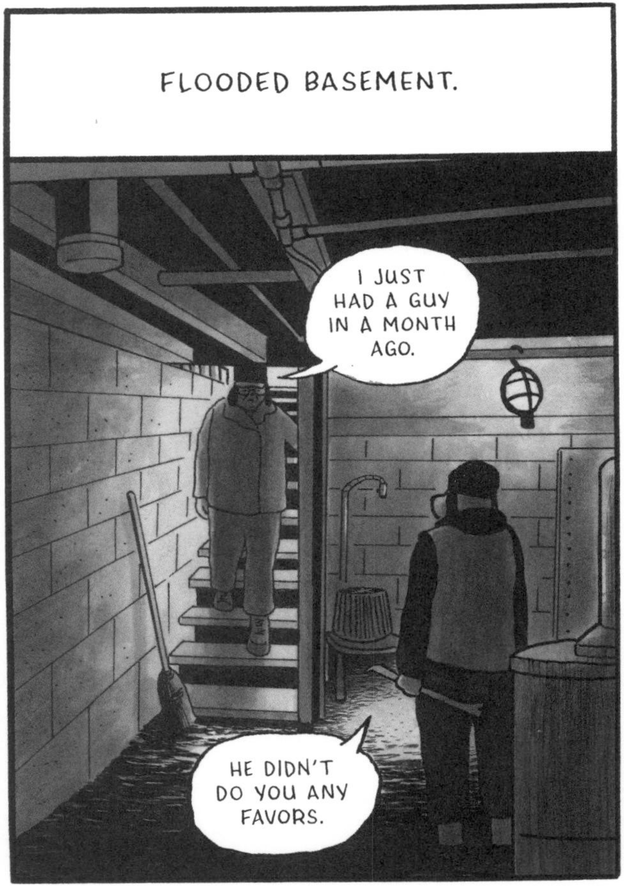
FLOODED BASEMENT.
I JUST HAD A GUY IN A MONTH AGO.
HE DIDN'T DO YOU ANY FAVORS.

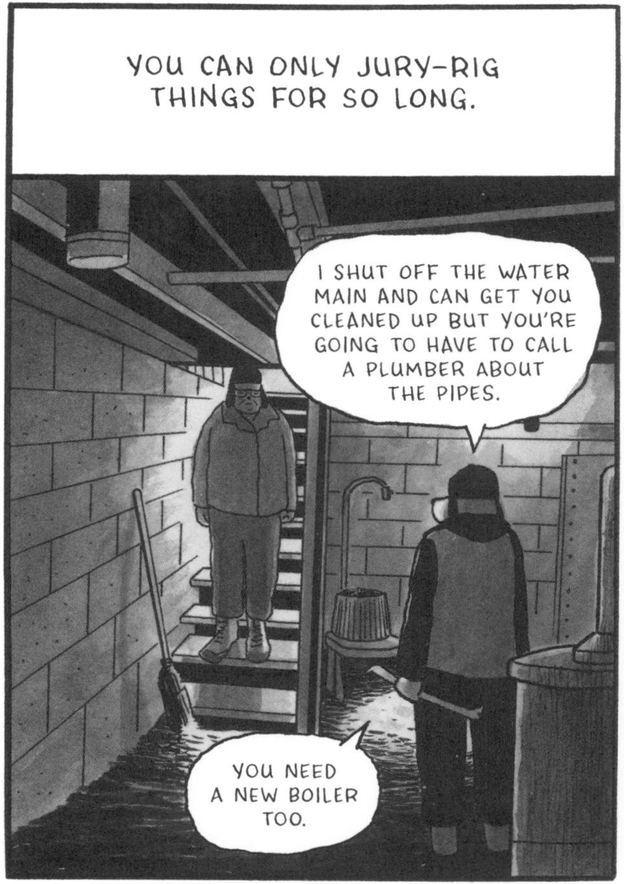
YOU CAN ONLY JURY-RIG THINGS FOR SO LONG.
I SHUT OFF THE WATER MAIN AND CAN GET YOU CLEANED UP BUT YOU'RE GOING TO HAVE TO CALL A PLUMBER ABOUT THE PIPES.
YOU NEED A NEW BOILER TOO.

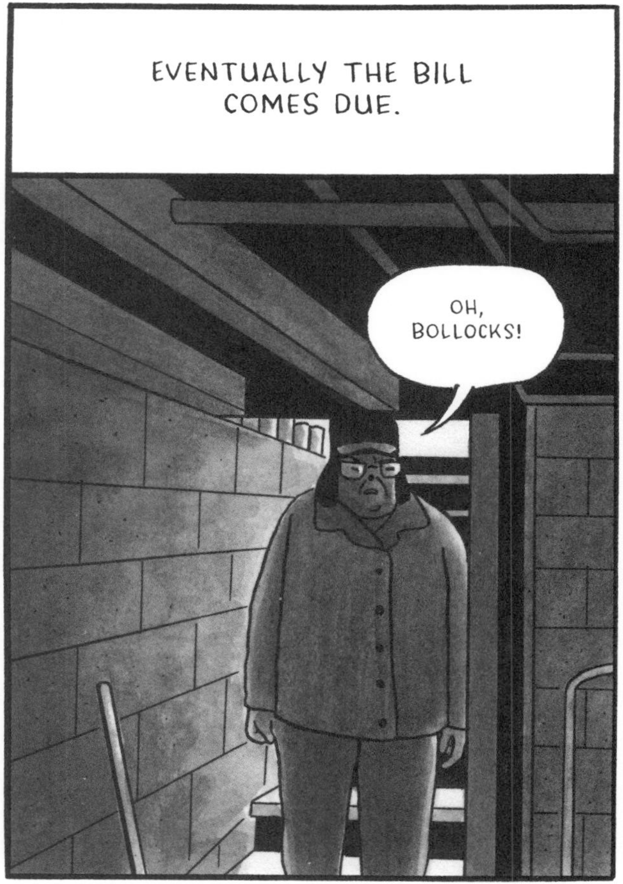
EVENTUALLY THE BILL COMES DUE.
OH, BOLLOCKS!

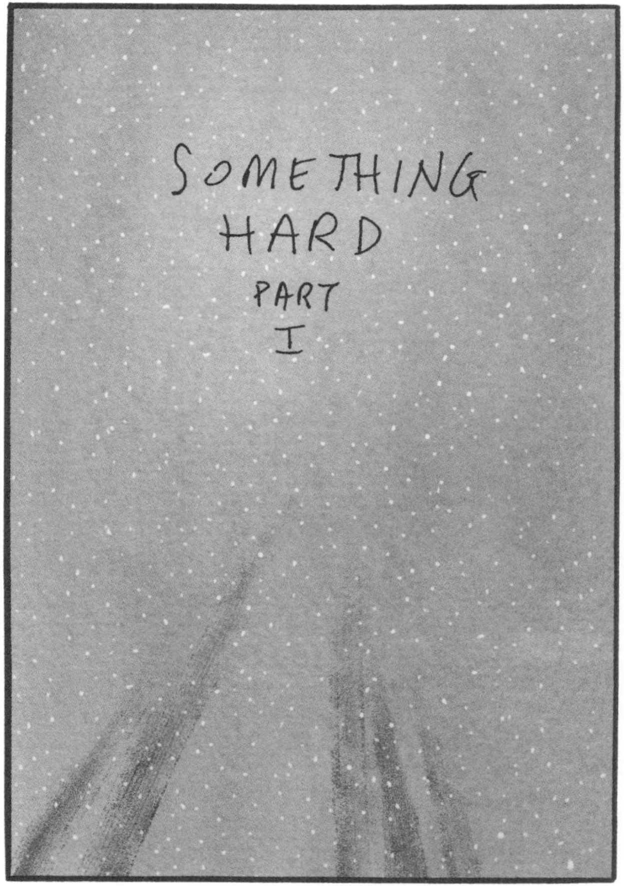
SOMETHING
HARD
PART
I

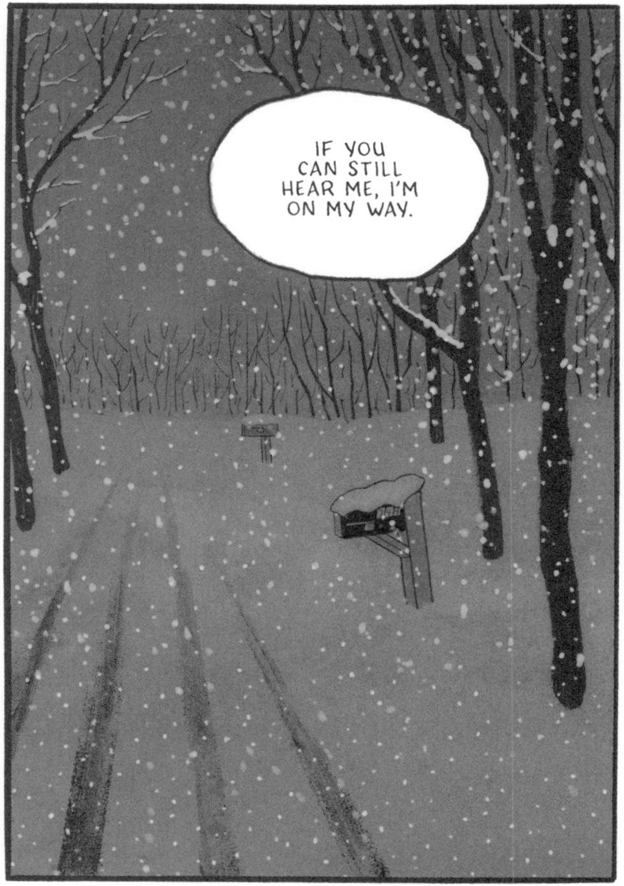
IF YOU CAN STILL HEAR ME, I'M ON MY WAY.

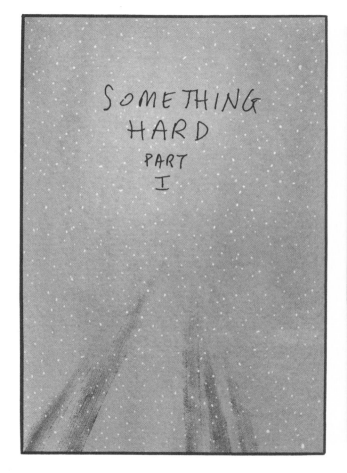

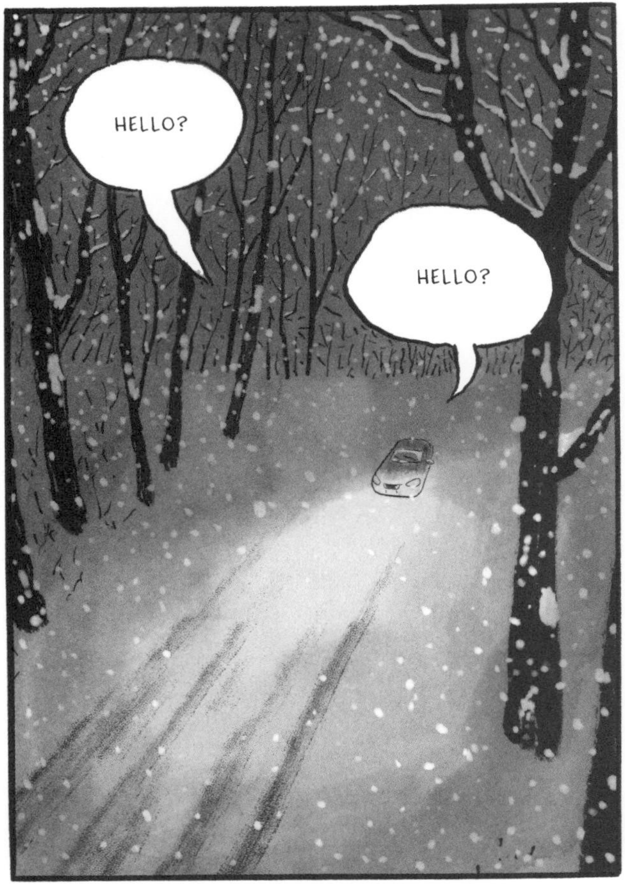
HELLO?
HELLO?

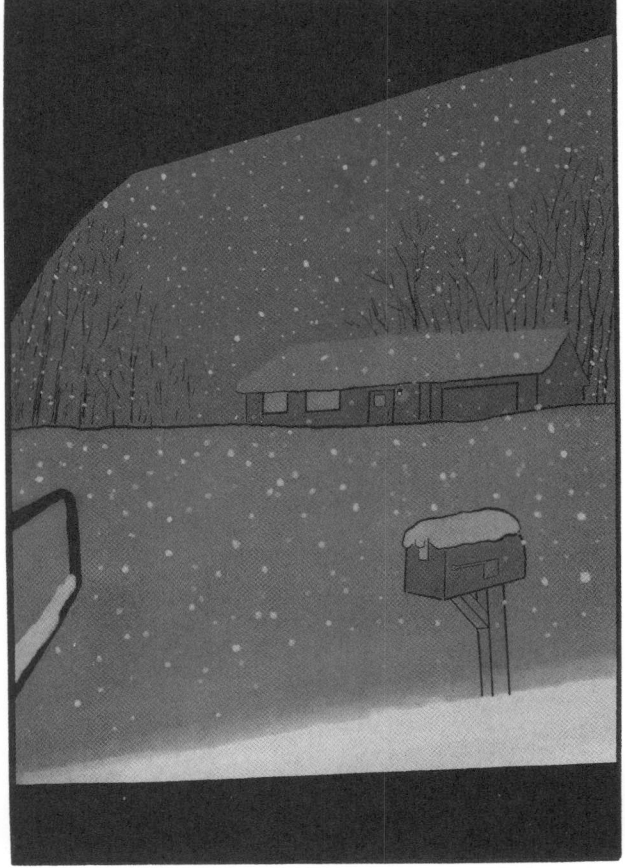

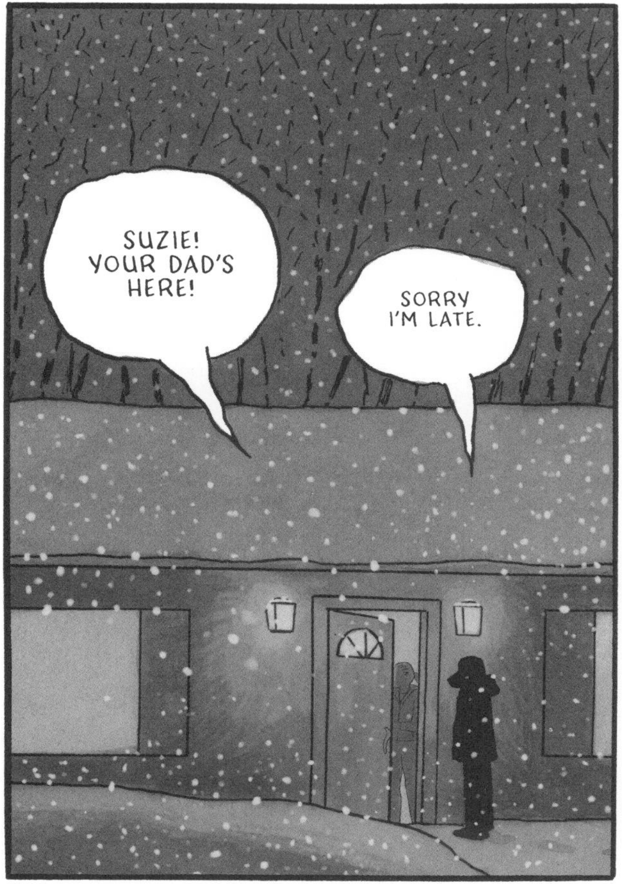
SUZIE! YOUR DAD'S HERE!
SORRY I'M LATE.

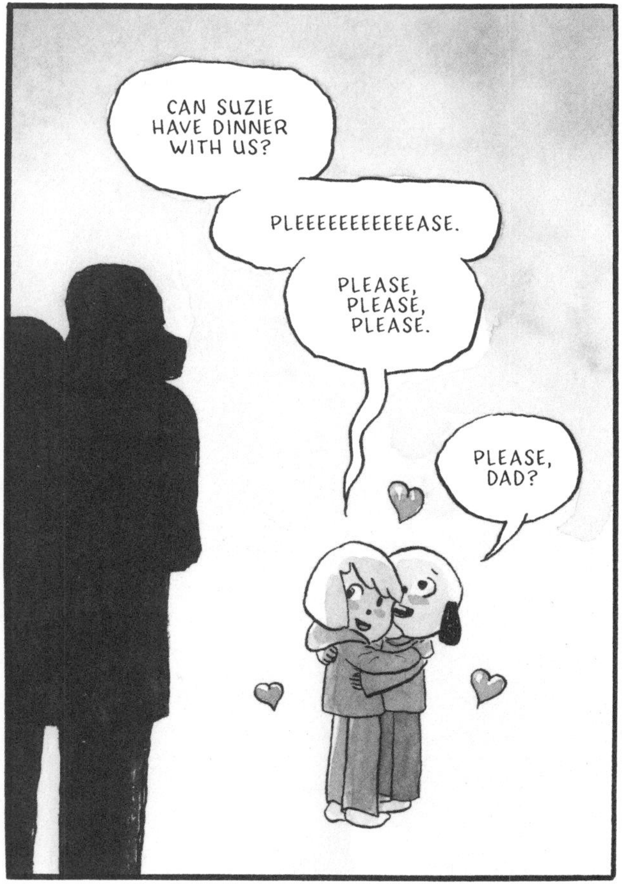
CAN SUZIE HAVE DINNER WITH US?
PLEEEEEEEEEEEEASE.
PLEASE, PLEASE, PLEASE.
PLEASE, DAD?

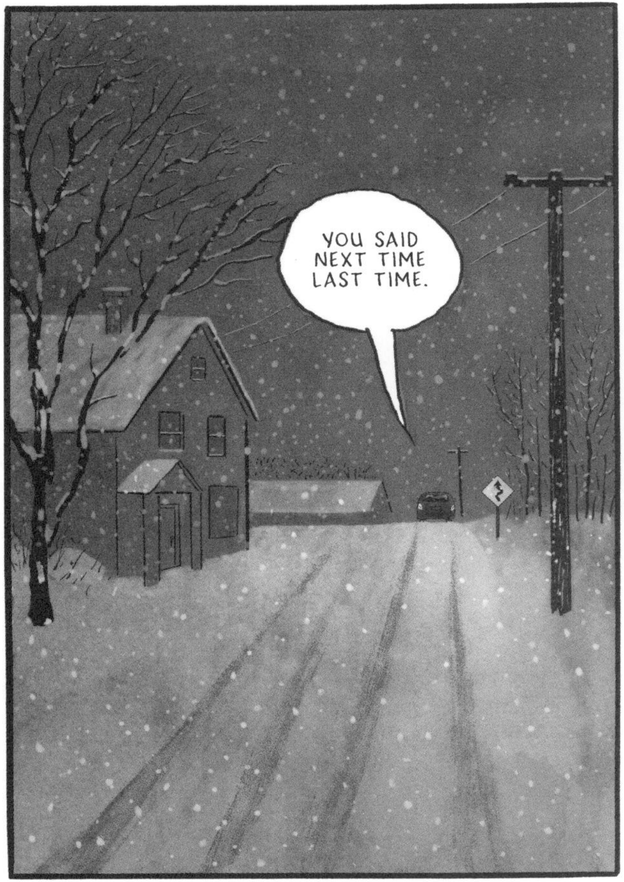
YOU SAID NEXT TIME LAST TIME.

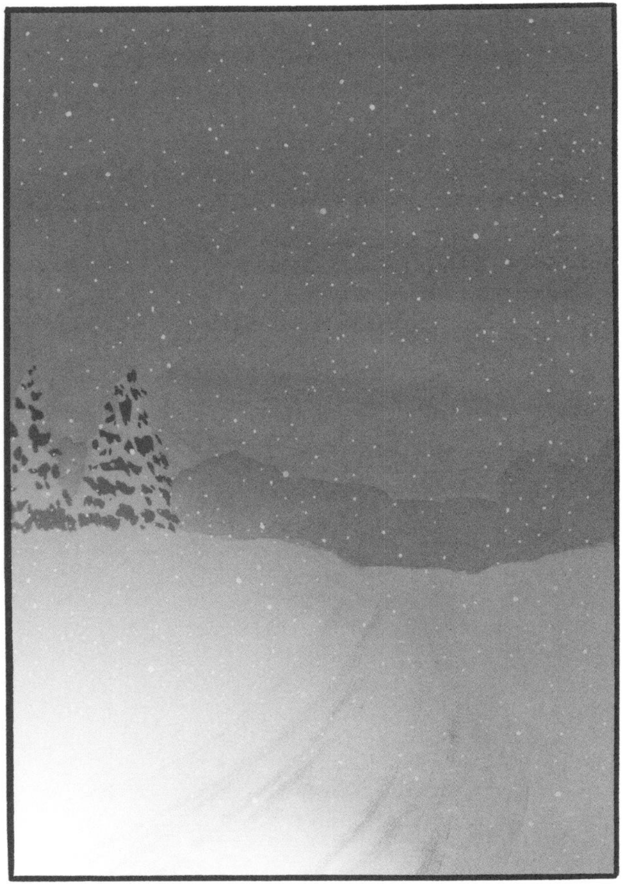

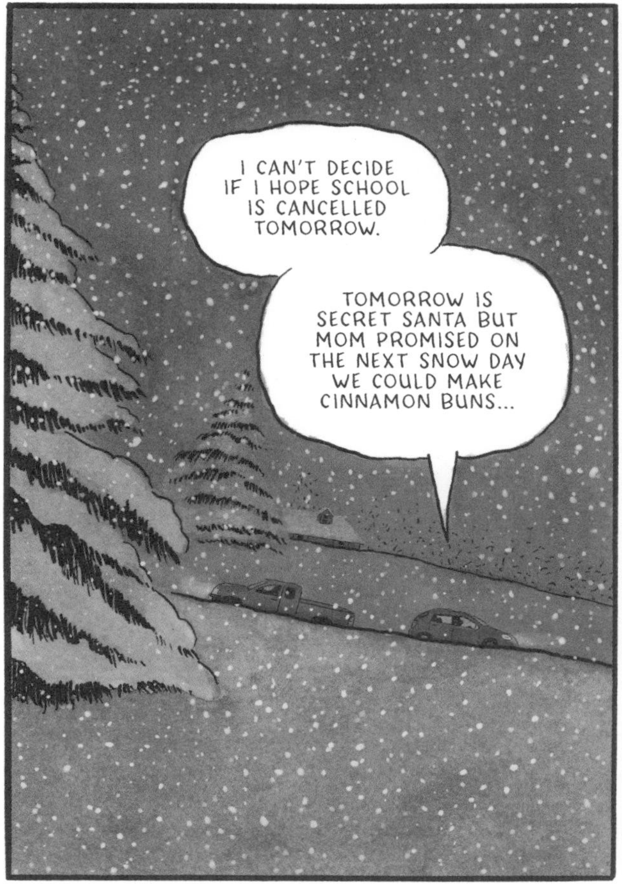
I CAN'T DECIDE IF I HOPE SCHOOL IS CANCELLED TOMORROW.
TOMORROW IS SECRET SANTA BUT MOM PROMISED ON THE NEXT SNOW DAY WE COULD MAKE CINNAMON BUNS...

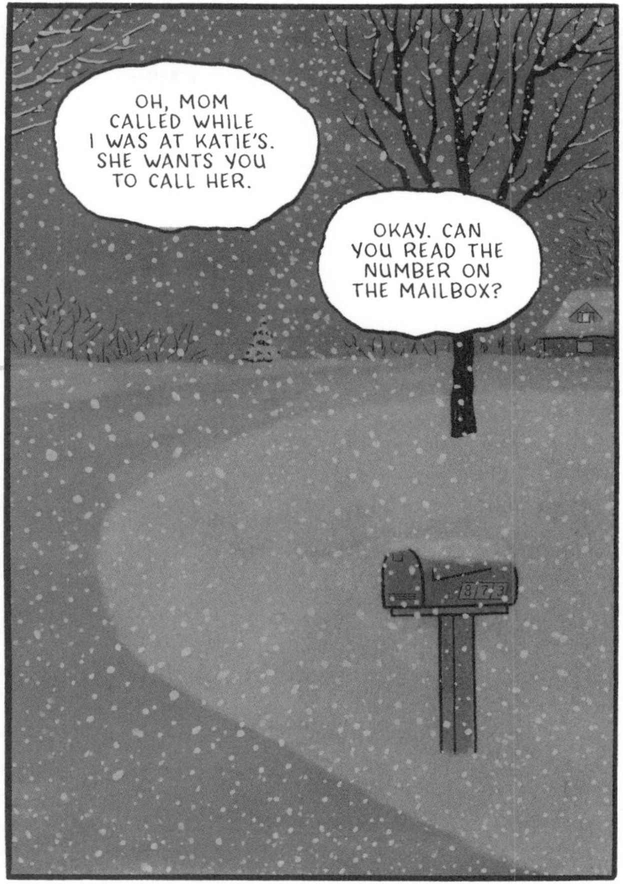
OH, MOM CALLED WHILE I WAS AT KATIE'S. SHE WANTS YOU TO CALL HER.
OKAY. CAN YOU READ THE NUMBER ON THE MAILBOX?

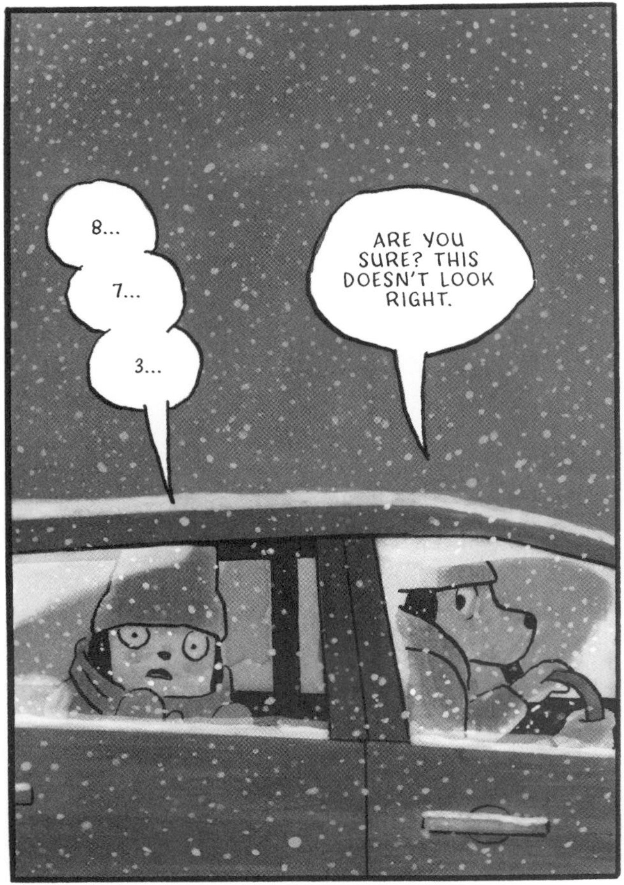
8...
7...
3...
ARE YOU SURE? THIS DOESN'T LOOK RIGHT.

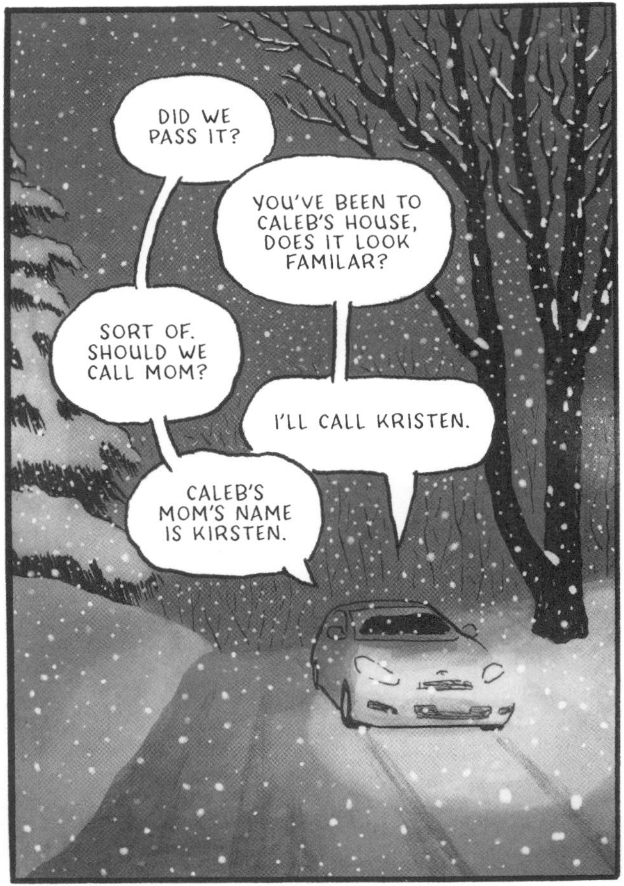
DID WE PASS IT?
YOU'VE BEEN TO CALEB'S HOUSE, DOES IT LOOK FAMILAR?
SORT OF. SHOULD WE CALL MOM?
I'LL CALL KRISTEN.
CALEB'S MOM'S NAME IS KIRSTEN.

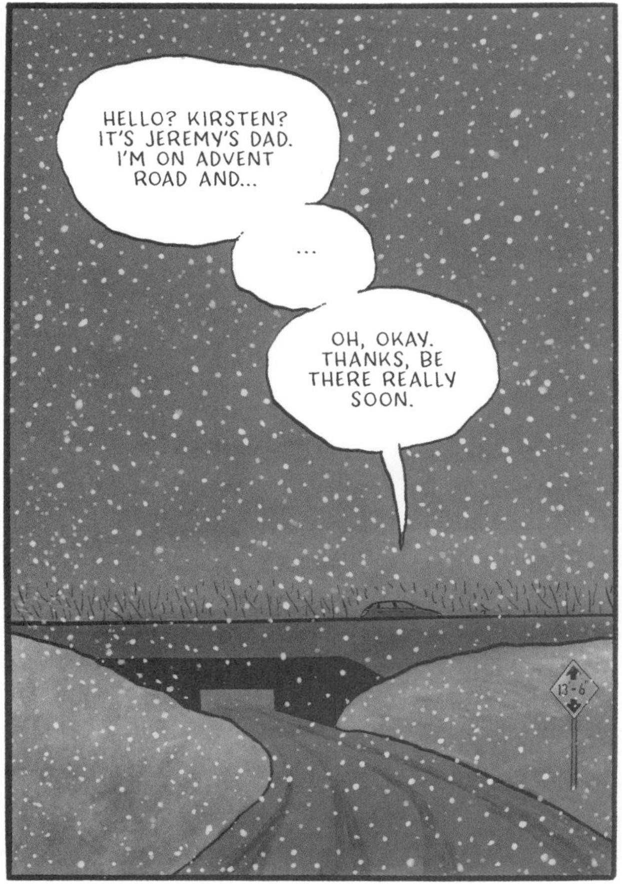
HELLO? KIRSTEN? IT'S JEREMY'S DAD. I'M ON ADVENT ROAD AND...
...
OH, OKAY. THANKS, BE THERE REALLY SOON.
13'-6"

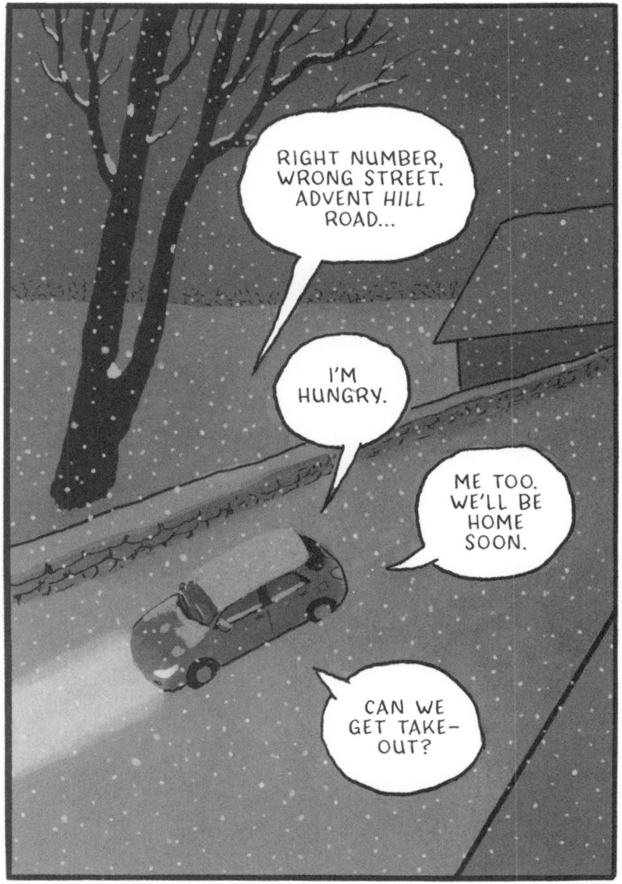
RIGHT NUMBER, WRONG STREET. ADVENT *HILL* ROAD...
I'M HUNGRY.
ME TOO. WE'LL BE HOME SOON.
CAN WE GET TAKE-OUT?

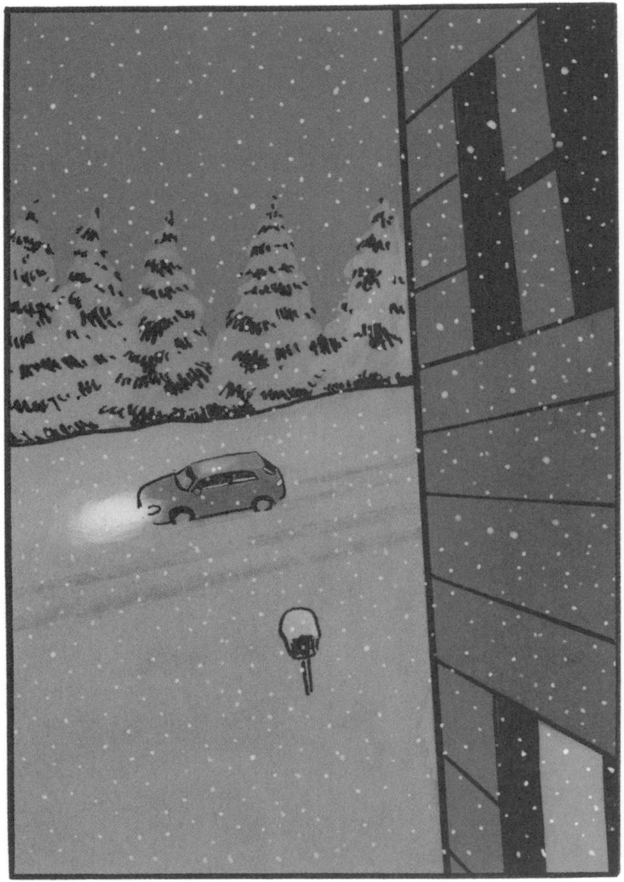

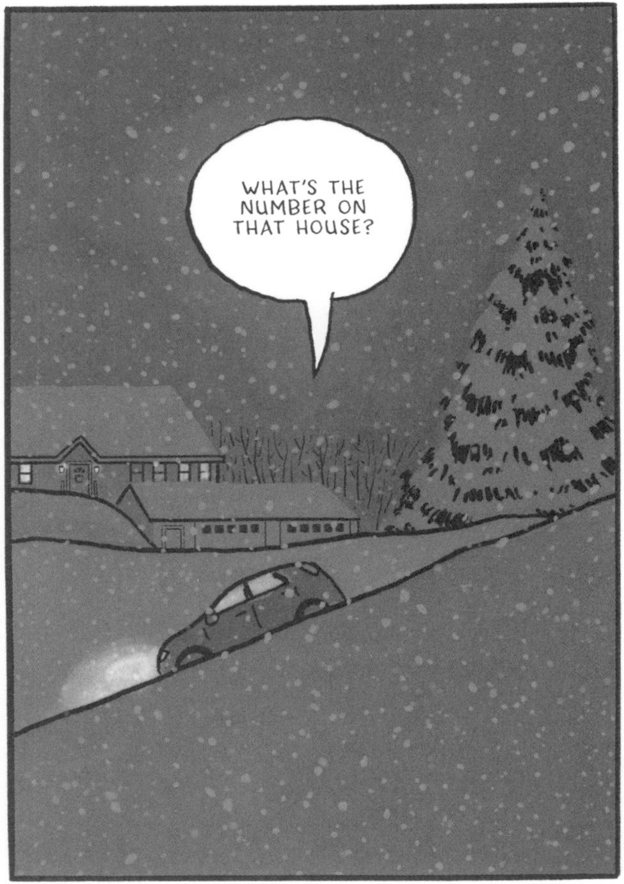
WHAT'S THE NUMBER ON THAT HOUSE?

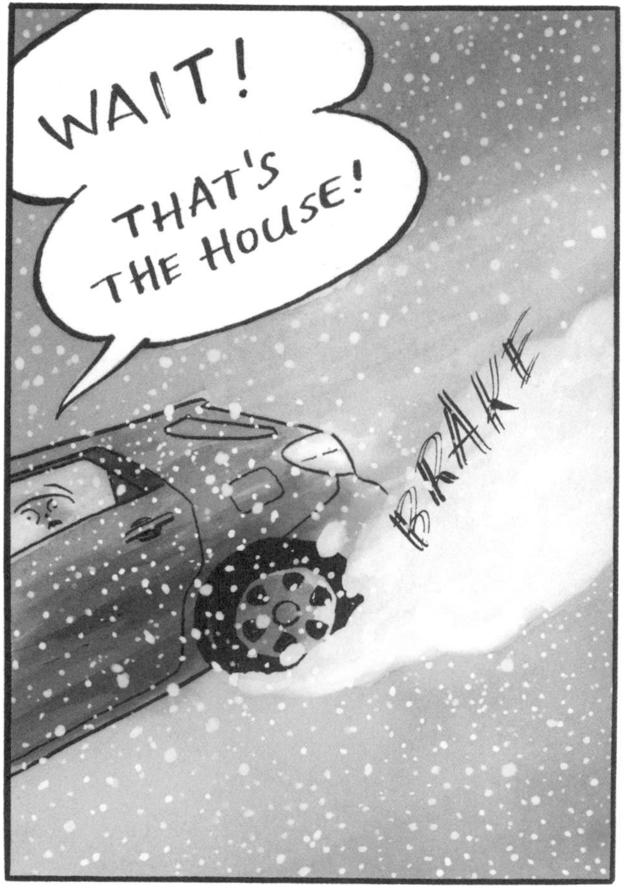
WAIT!
THAT'S THE HOUSE!
BRAKE

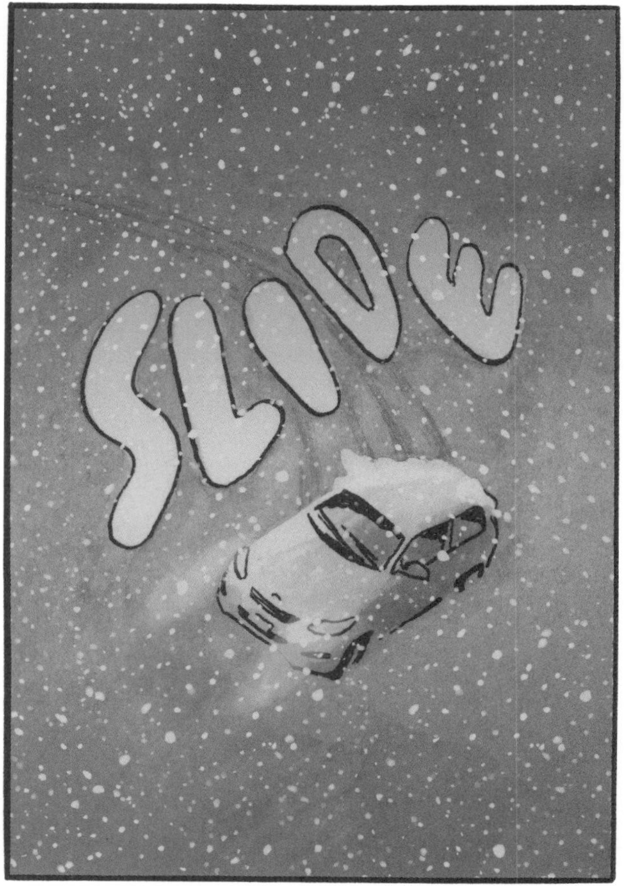
SLIDE

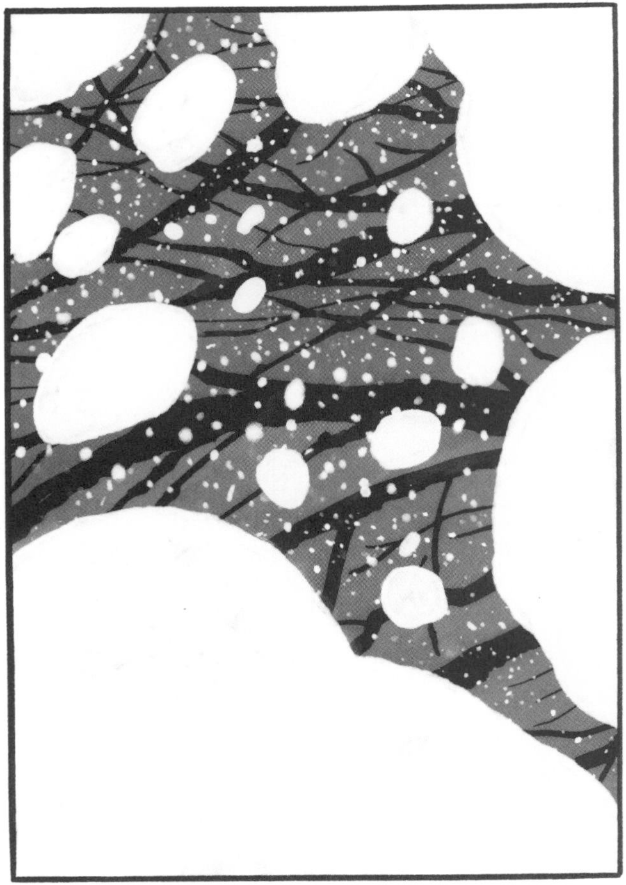

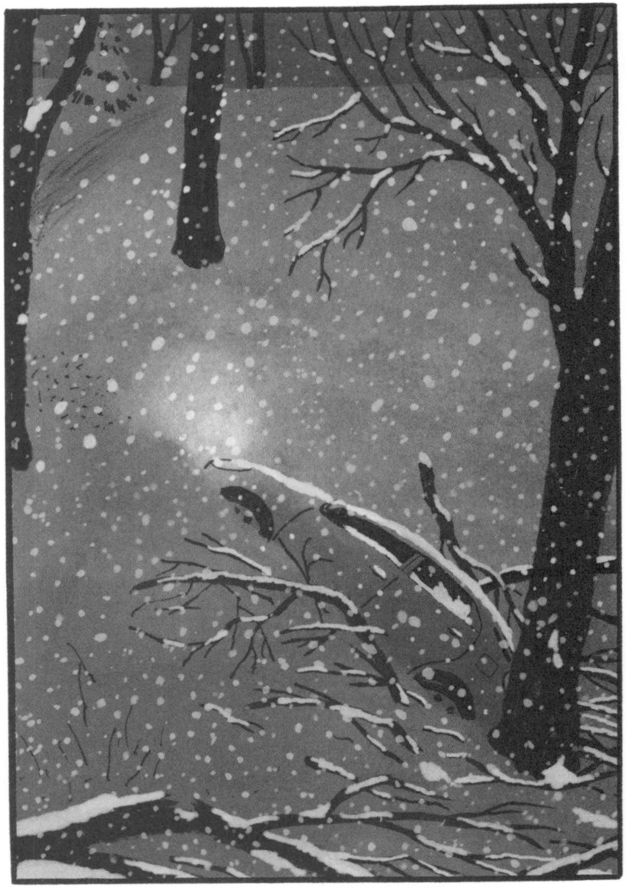

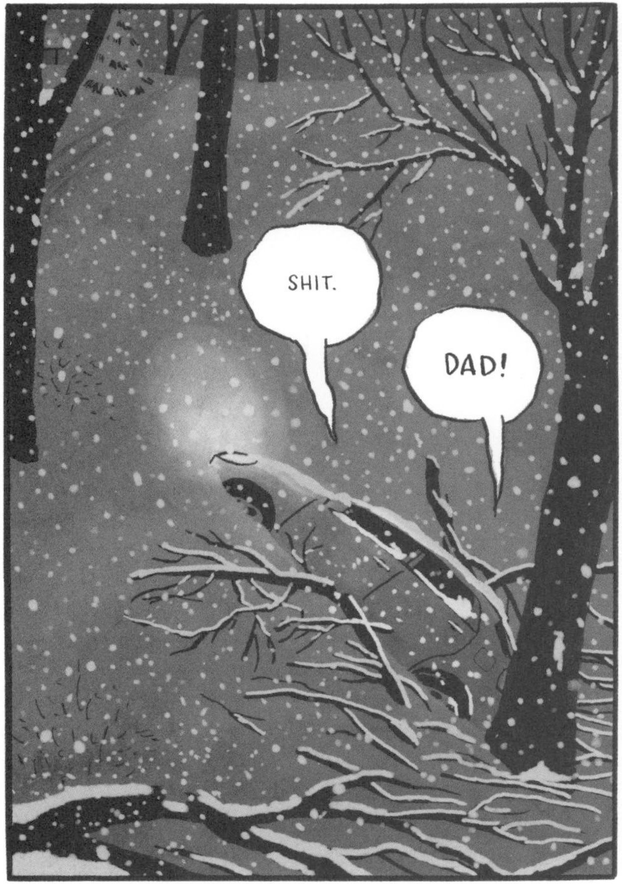
SHIT.
DAD!

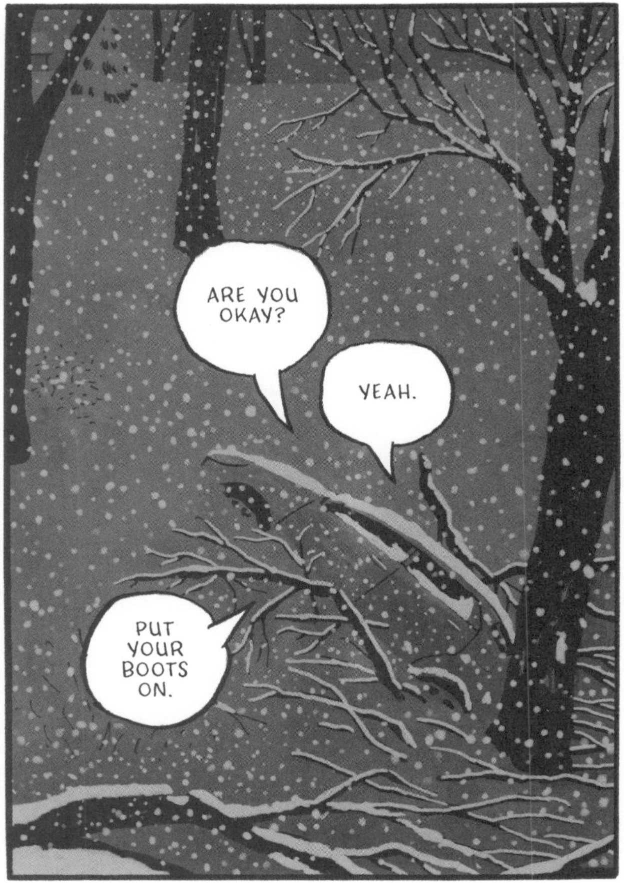
ARE YOU OKAY?
YEAH.
PUT YOUR BOOTS ON.

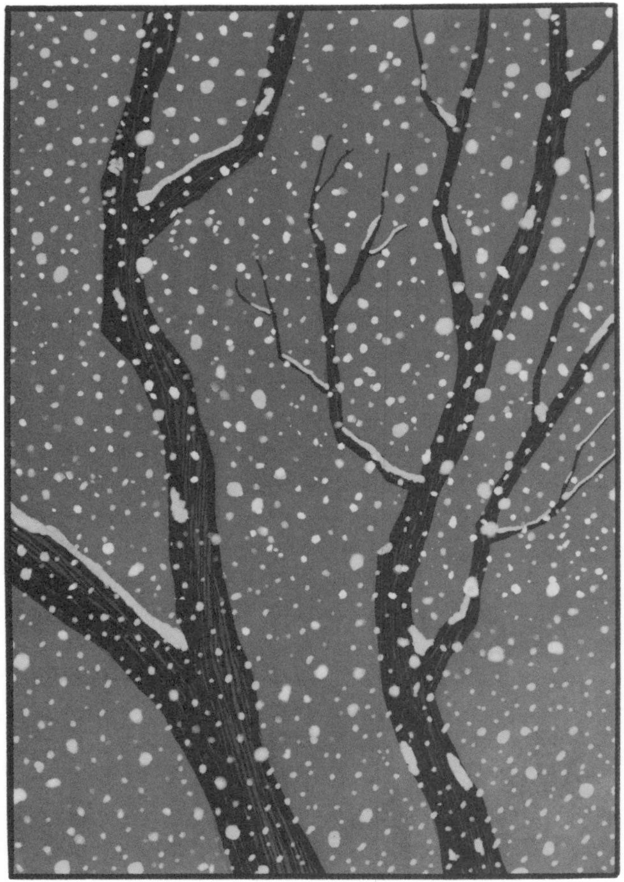

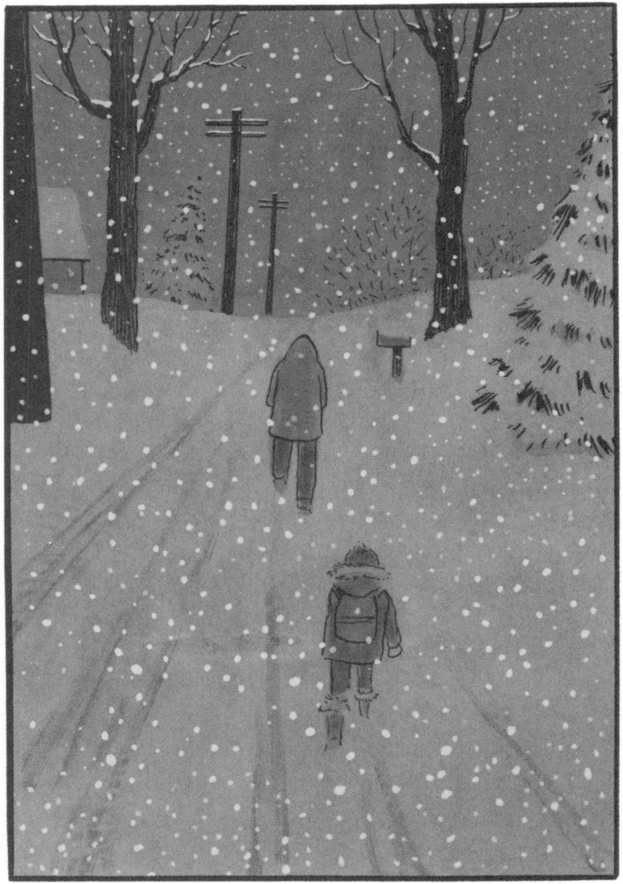

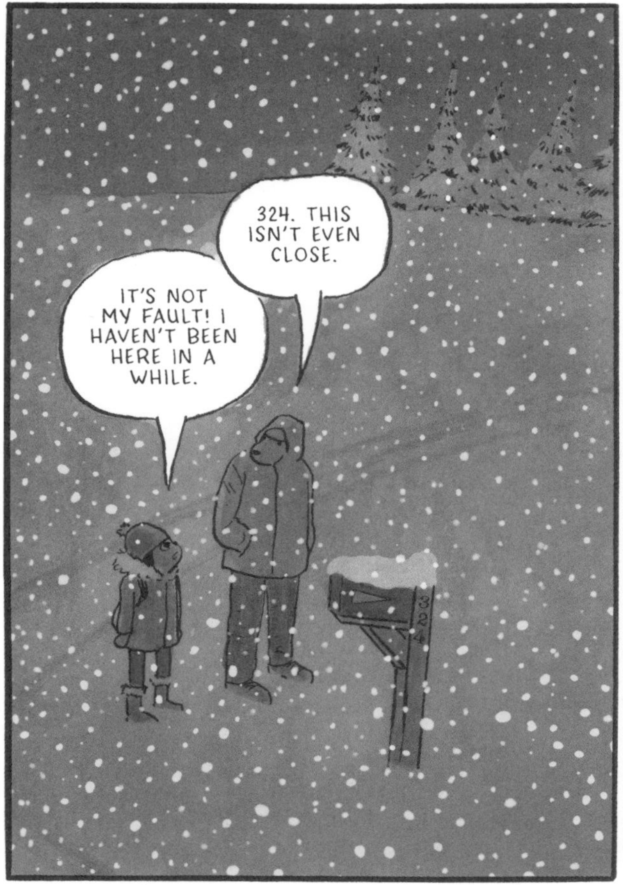
324. THIS ISN'T EVEN CLOSE.
IT'S NOT MY FAULT! I HAVEN'T BEEN HERE IN A WHILE.

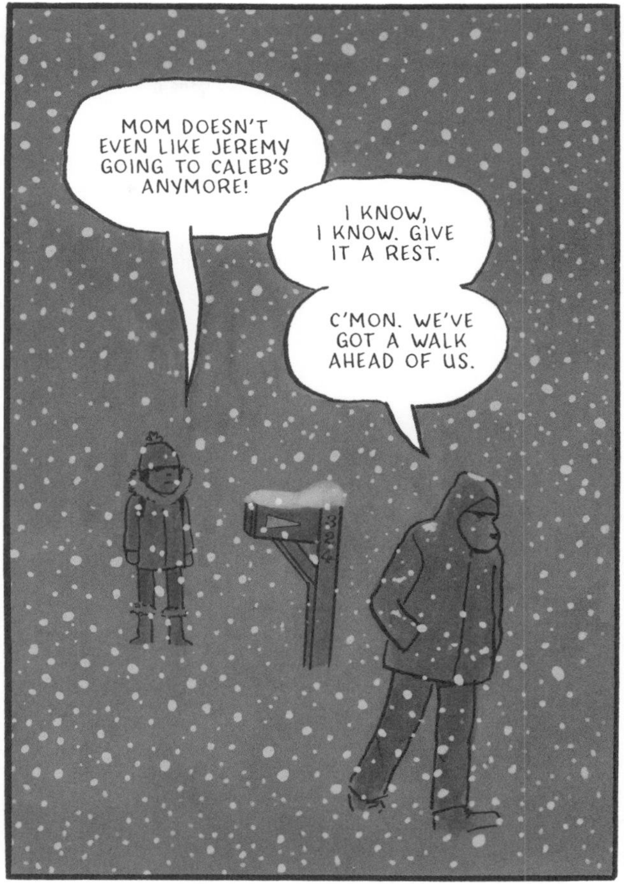
MOM DOESN'T EVEN LIKE JEREMY GOING TO CALEB'S ANYMORE!
I KNOW, I KNOW. GIVE IT A REST.
C'MON. WE'VE GOT A WALK AHEAD OF US.

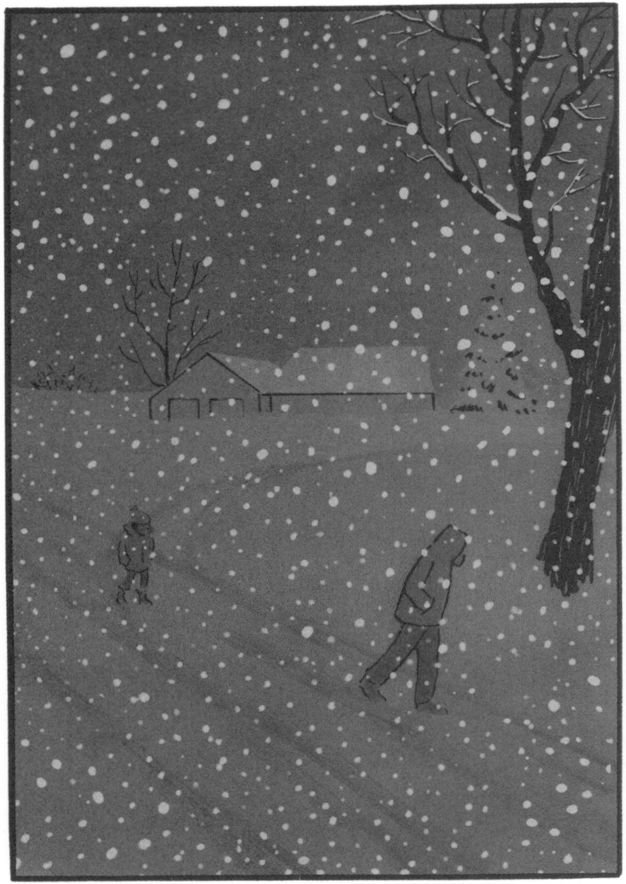

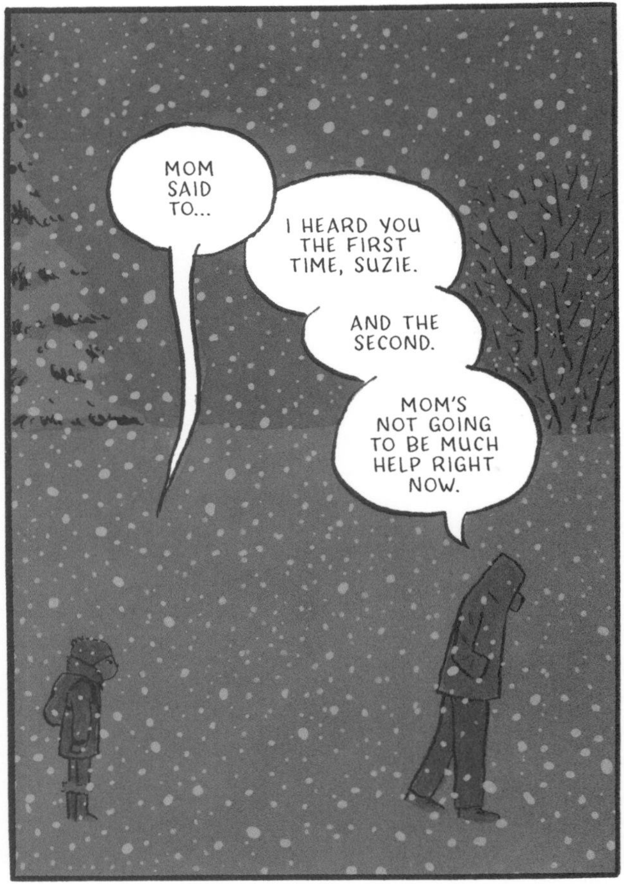
MOM SAID TO...
I HEARD YOU THE FIRST TIME, SUZIE.
AND THE SECOND.
MOM'S NOT GOING TO BE MUCH HELP RIGHT NOW.

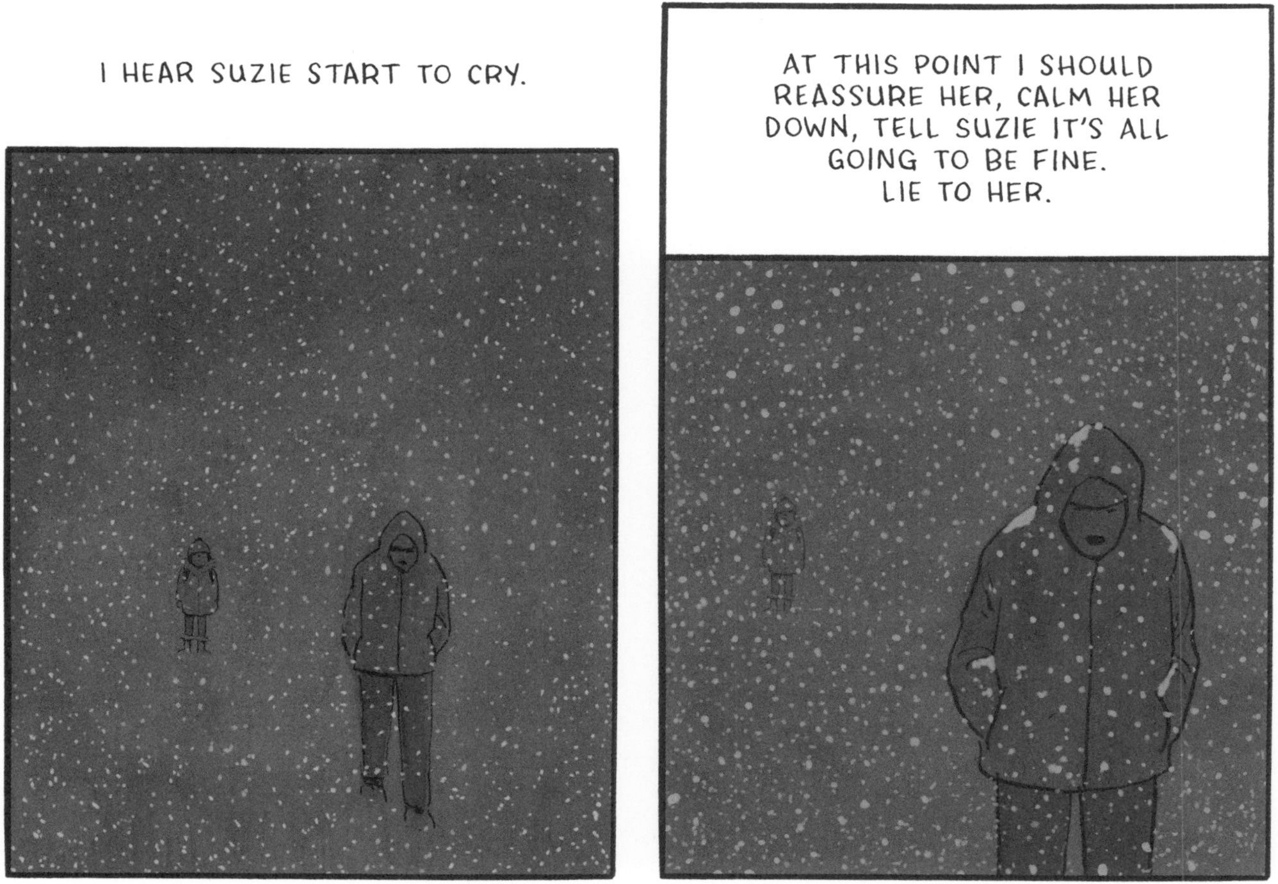
I HEAR SUZIE START TO CRY.
AT THIS POINT I SHOULD REASSURE HER, CALM HER DOWN, TELL SUZIE IT'S ALL GOING TO BE FINE. LIE TO HER.

BUT SOMETHING HARD INSIDE ME
PREVENTS ME FROM DOING SO.

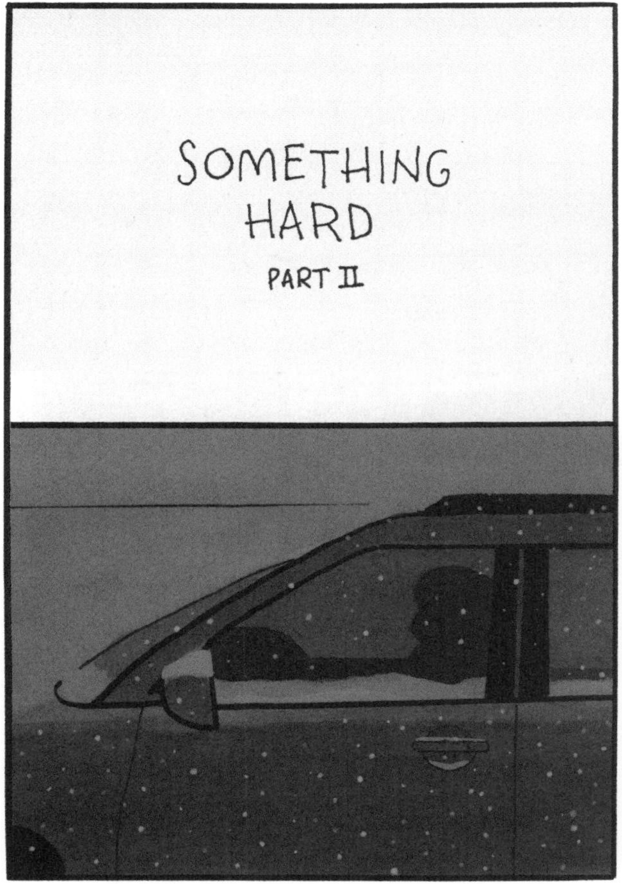
SOMETHING
HARD
PART II

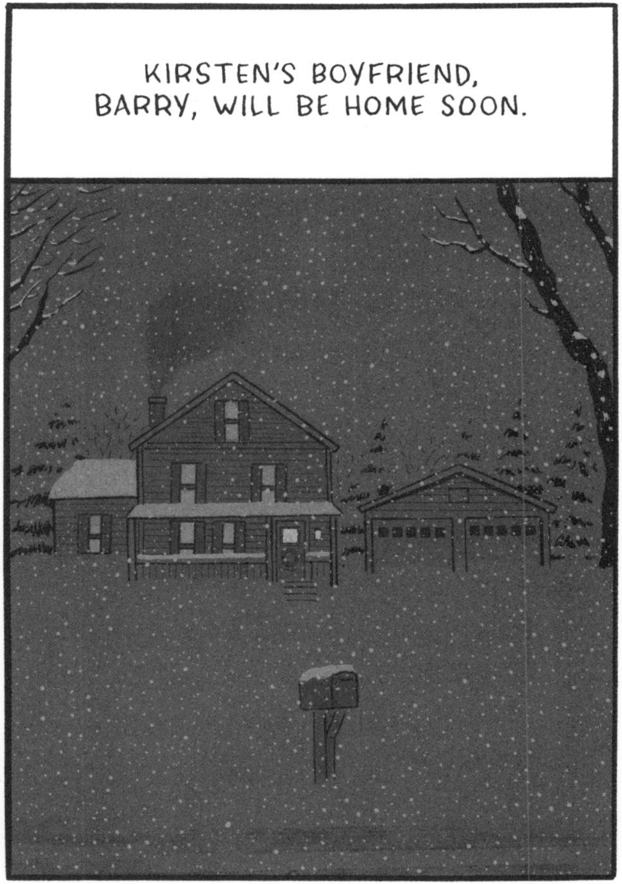
KIRSTEN'S BOYFRIEND,
BARRY, WILL BE HOME SOON.

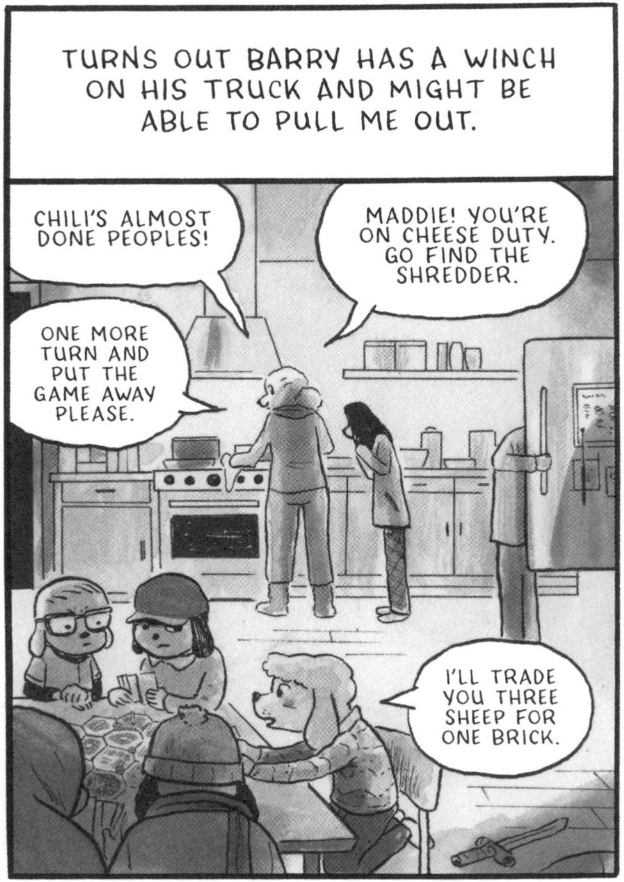
TURNS OUT BARRY HAS A WINCH ON HIS TRUCK AND MIGHT BE ABLE TO PULL ME OUT.
CHILI'S ALMOST DONE PEOPLES!
MADDIE! YOU'RE ON CHEESE DUTY. GO FIND THE SHREDDER.
ONE MORE TURN AND PUT THE GAME AWAY PLEASE.
I'LL TRADE YOU THREE SHEEP FOR ONE BRICK.

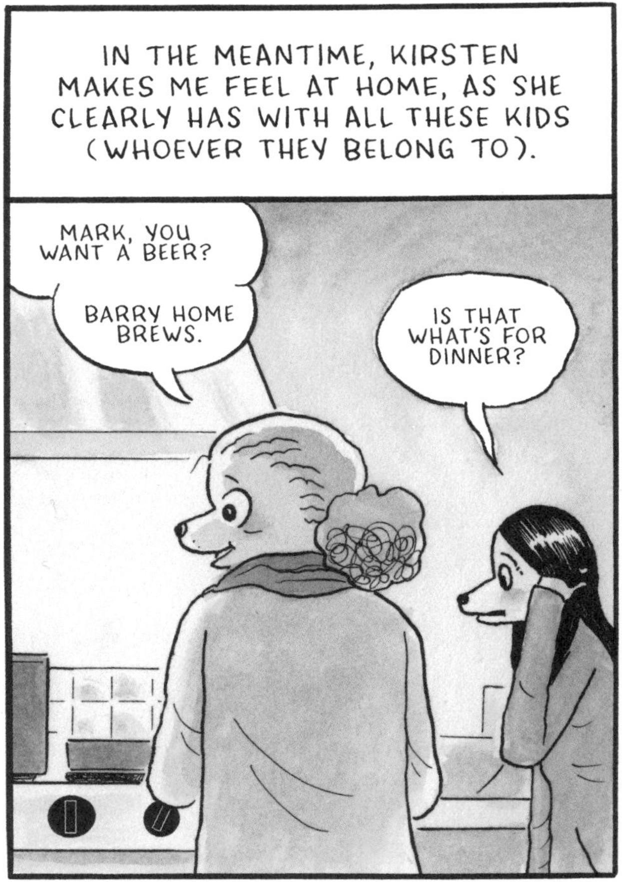
IN THE MEANTIME, KIRSTEN MAKES ME FEEL AT HOME, AS SHE CLEARLY HAS WITH ALL THESE KIDS (WHOEVER THEY BELONG TO).
MARK, YOU WANT A BEER?
BARRY HOME BREWS.
IS THAT WHAT'S FOR DINNER?

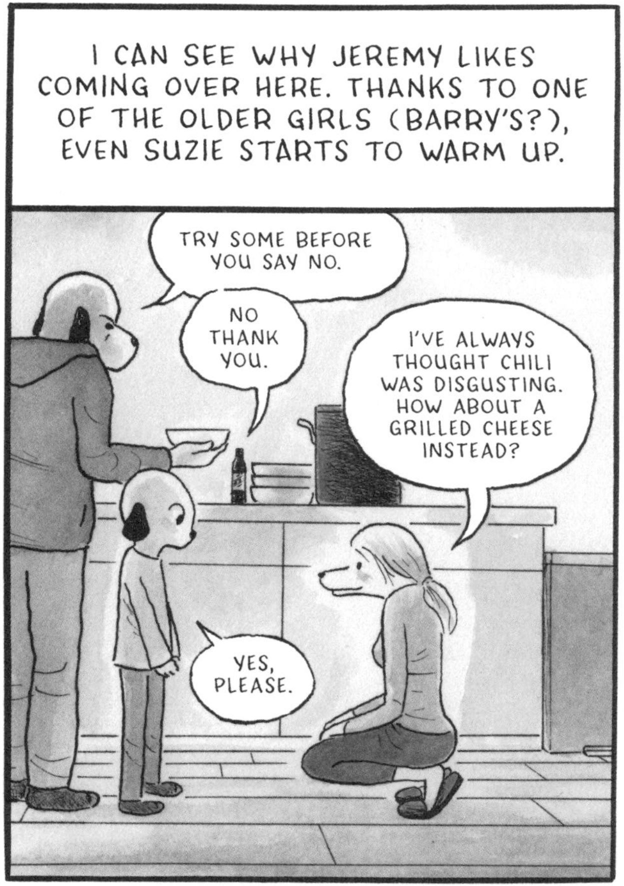
I CAN SEE WHY JEREMY LIKES COMING OVER HERE. THANKS TO ONE OF THE OLDER GIRLS (BARRY'S?), EVEN SUZIE STARTS TO WARM UP.
TRY SOME BEFORE YOU SAY NO.
NO THANK YOU.
I'VE ALWAYS THOUGHT CHILI WAS DISGUSTING. HOW ABOUT A GRILLED CHEESE INSTEAD?
YES, PLEASE.

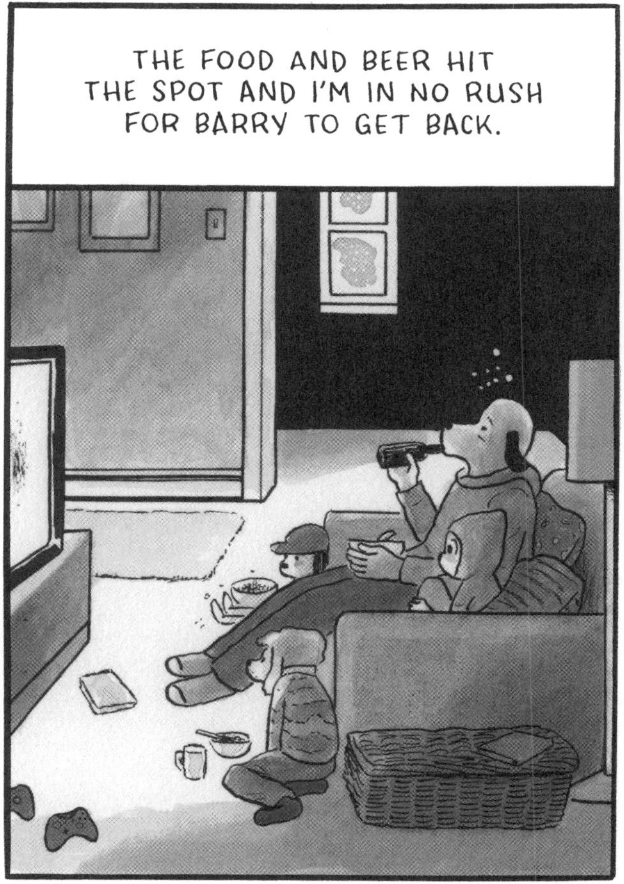
THE FOOD AND BEER HIT THE SPOT AND I'M IN NO RUSH FOR BARRY TO GET BACK.

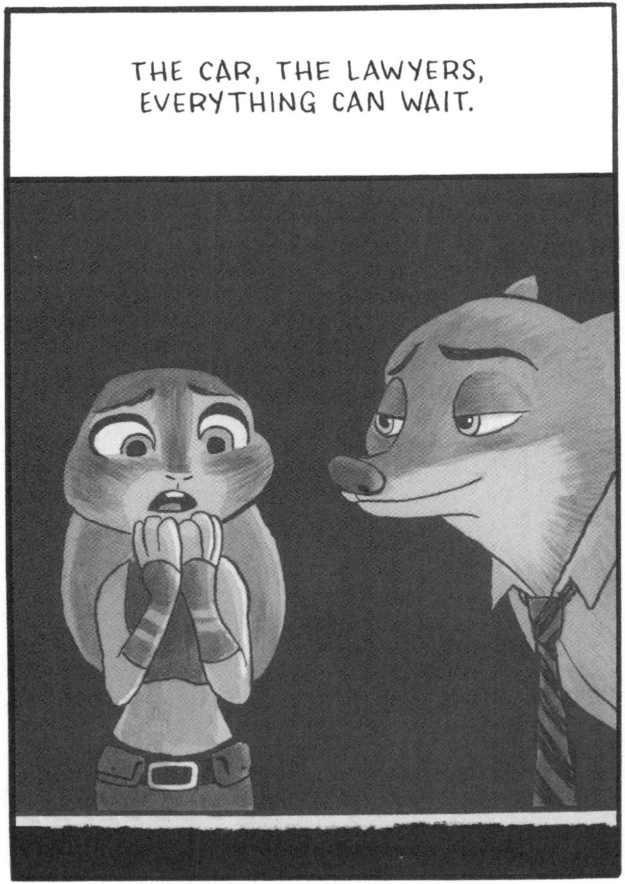
THE CAR, THE LAWYERS, EVERYTHING CAN WAIT.

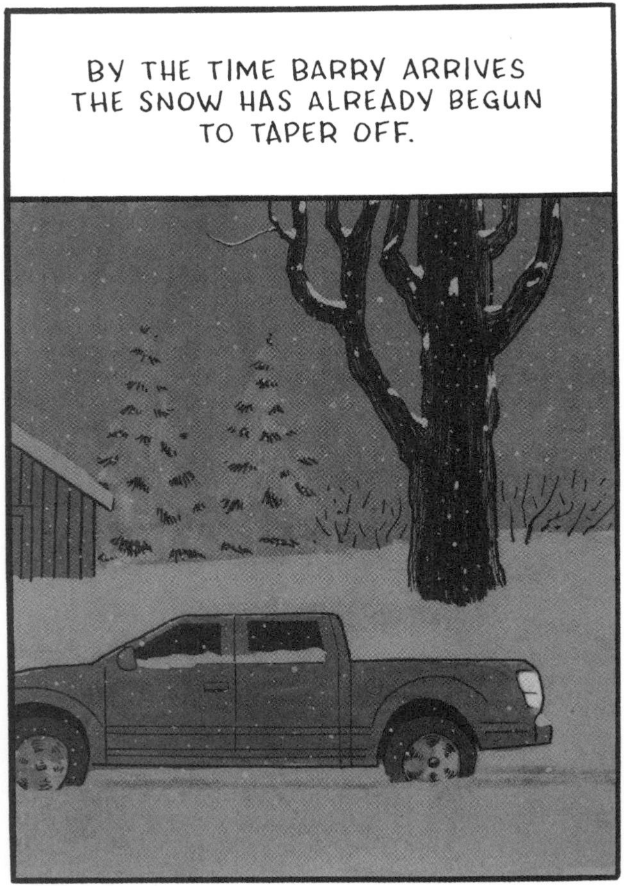
BY THE TIME BARRY ARRIVES THE SNOW HAS ALREADY BEGUN TO TAPER OFF.

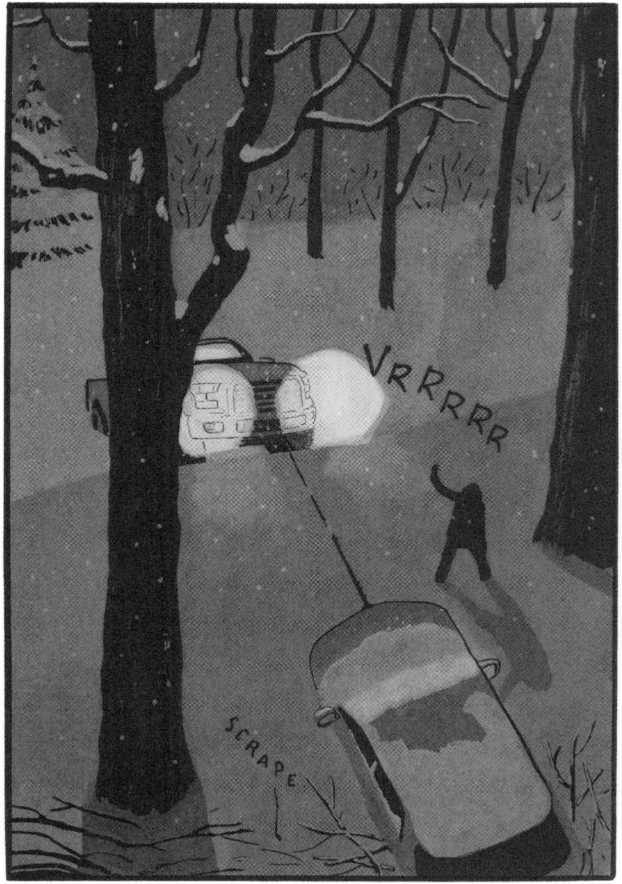
VRRRRRR
SCRAPE

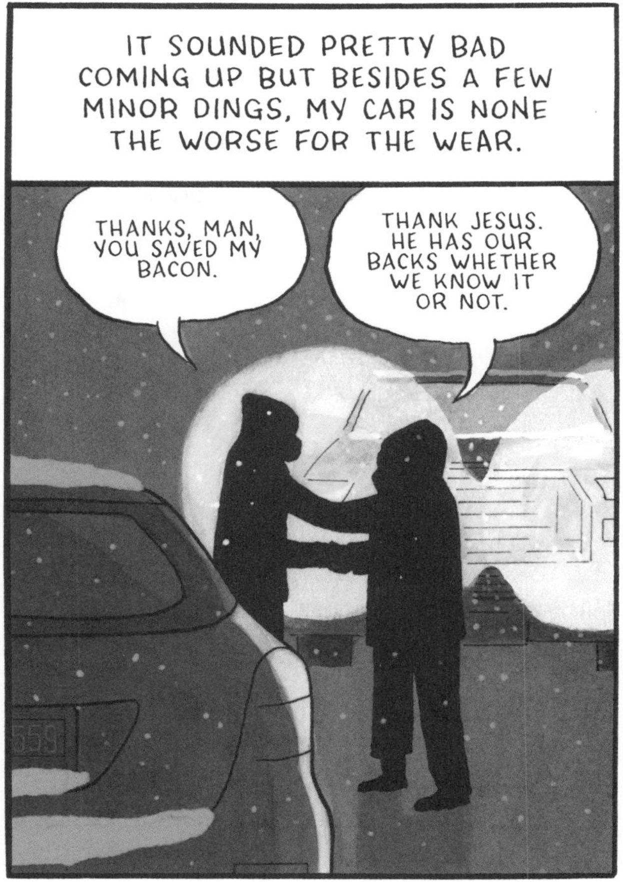
IT SOUNDED PRETTY BAD COMING UP BUT BESIDES A FEW MINOR DINGS, MY CAR IS NONE THE WORSE FOR THE WEAR.
THANKS, MAN, YOU SAVED MY BACON.
THANK JESUS. HE HAS OUR BACKS WHETHER WE KNOW IT OR NOT.

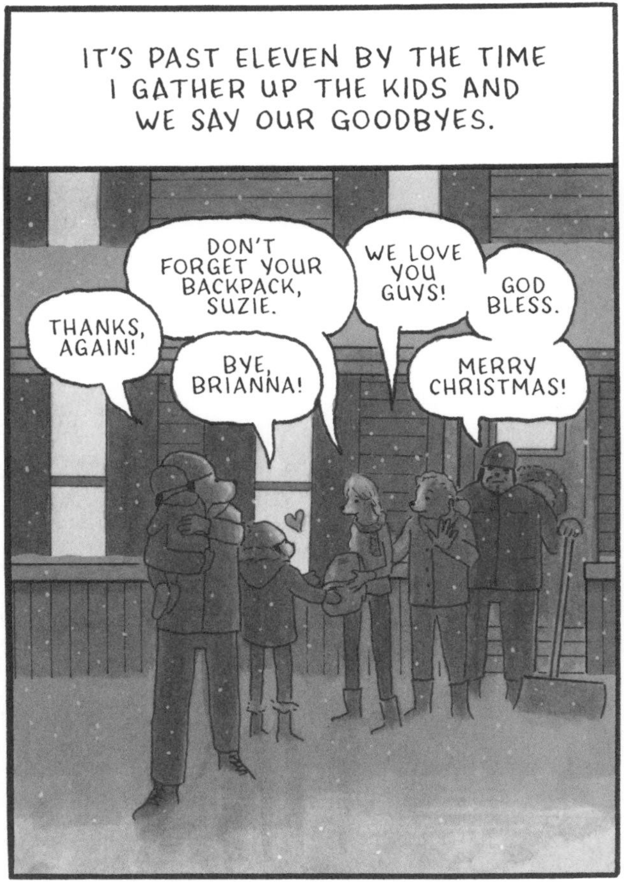
IT'S PAST ELEVEN BY THE TIME I GATHER UP THE KIDS AND WE SAY OUR GOODBYES.
THANKS, AGAIN!
DON'T FORGET YOUR BACKPACK, SUZIE.
BYE, BRIANNA!
WE LOVE YOU GUYS!
GOD BLESS.
MERRY CHRISTMAS!

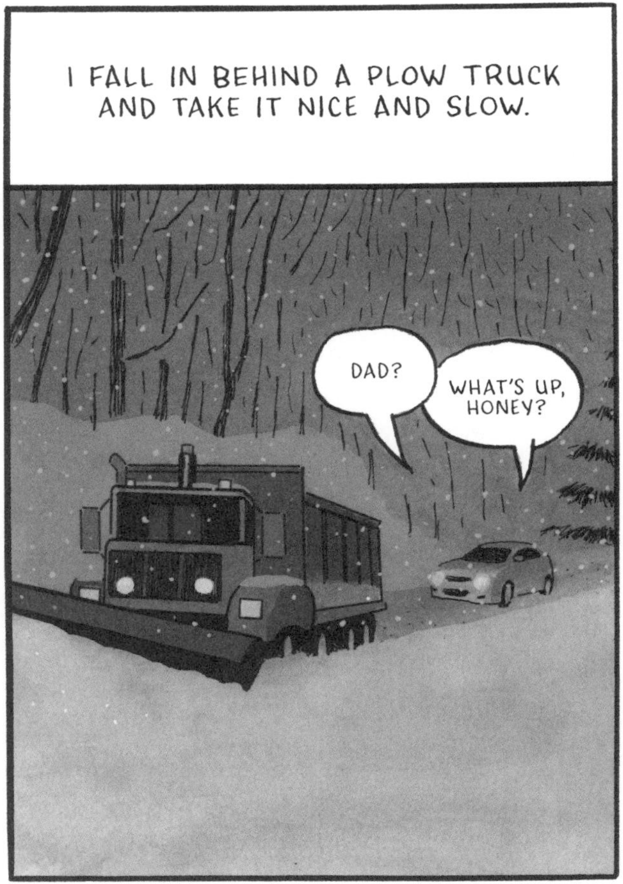
I FALL IN BEHIND A PLOW TRUCK AND TAKE IT NICE AND SLOW.
DAD?
WHAT'S UP, HONEY?

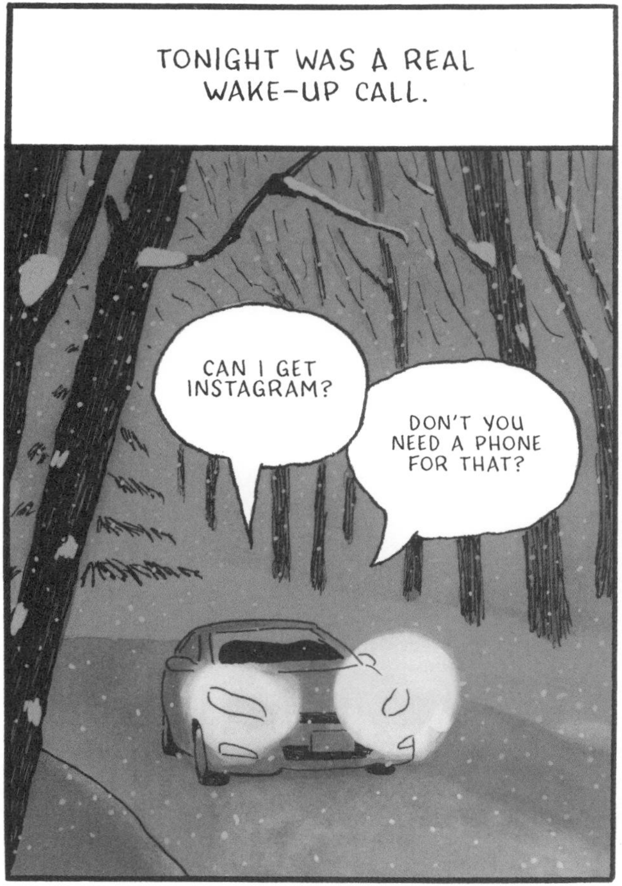
TONIGHT WAS A REAL WAKE-UP CALL.
CAN I GET INSTAGRAM?
DON'T YOU NEED A PHONE FOR THAT?

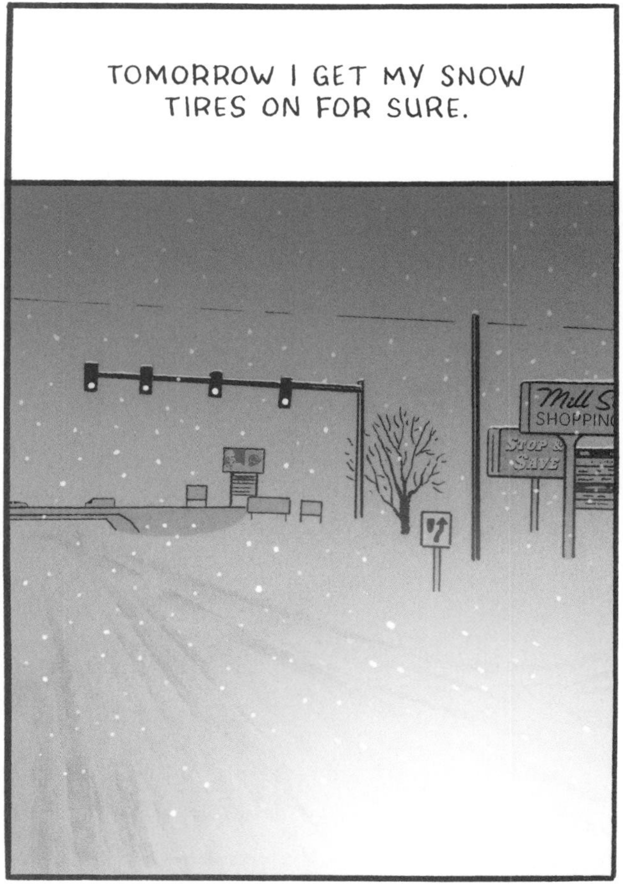
TOMORROW I GET MY SNOW TIRES ON FOR SURE.

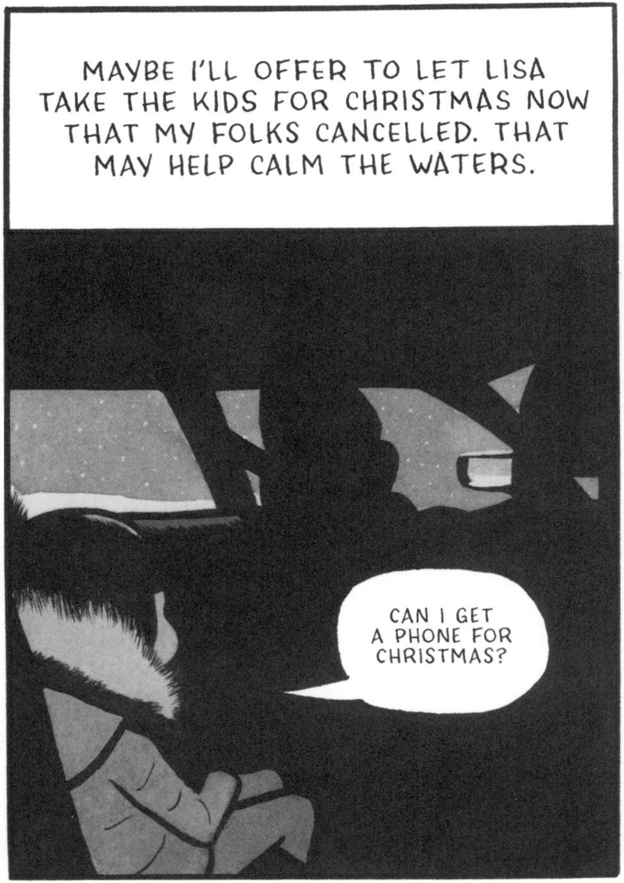
MAYBE I'LL OFFER TO LET LISA TAKE THE KIDS FOR CHRISTMAS NOW THAT MY FOLKS CANCELLED. THAT MAY HELP CALM THE WATERS.
CAN I GET A PHONE FOR CHRISTMAS?

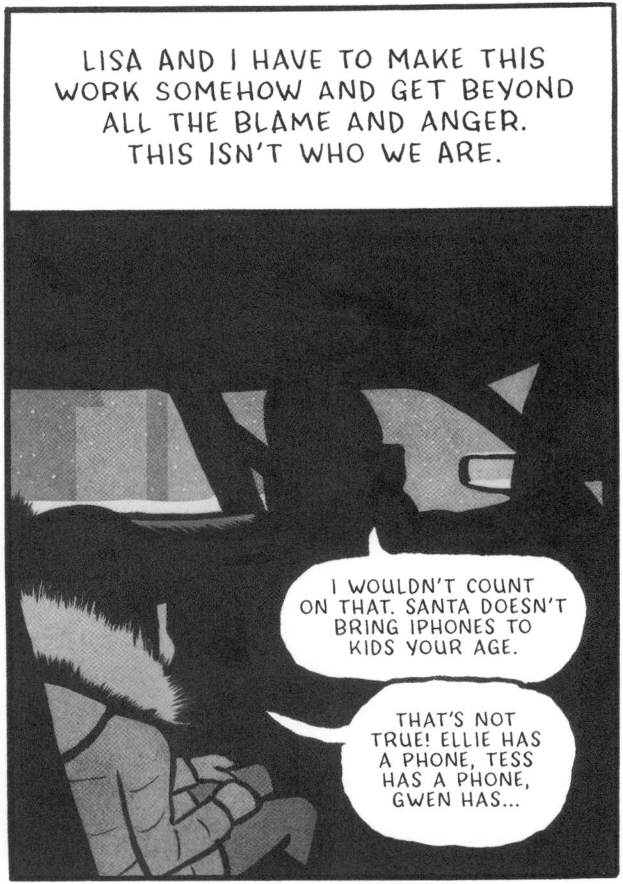
LISA AND I HAVE TO MAKE THIS WORK SOMEHOW AND GET BEYOND ALL THE BLAME AND ANGER. THIS ISN'T WHO WE ARE.
I WOULDN'T COUNT ON THAT. SANTA DOESN'T BRING IPHONES TO KIDS YOUR AGE.
THAT'S NOT TRUE! ELLIE HAS A PHONE, TESS HAS A PHONE, GWEN HAS...

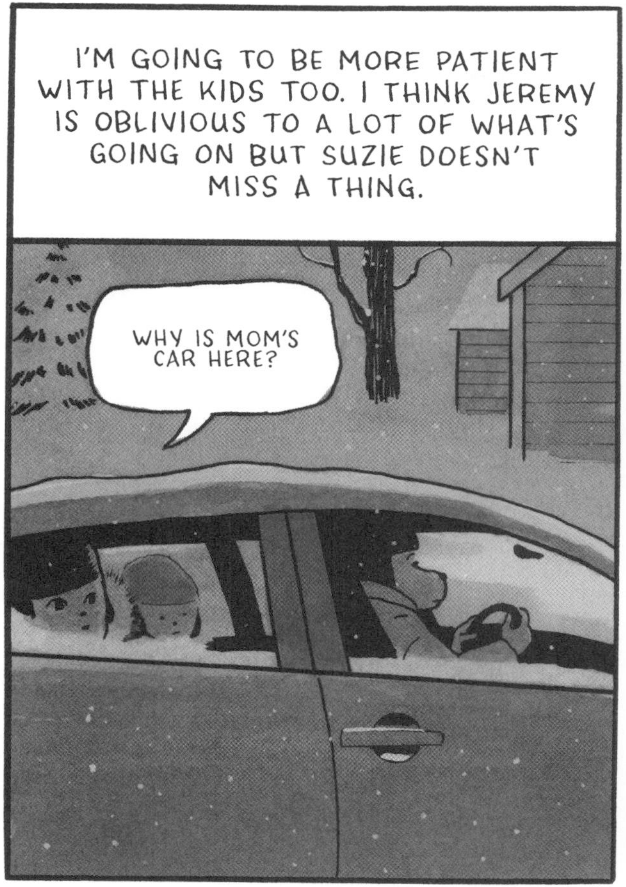
I'M GOING TO BE MORE PATIENT WITH THE KIDS TOO. I THINK JEREMY IS OBLIVIOUS TO A LOT OF WHAT'S GOING ON BUT SUZIE DOESN'T MISS A THING.
WHY IS MOM'S CAR HERE?
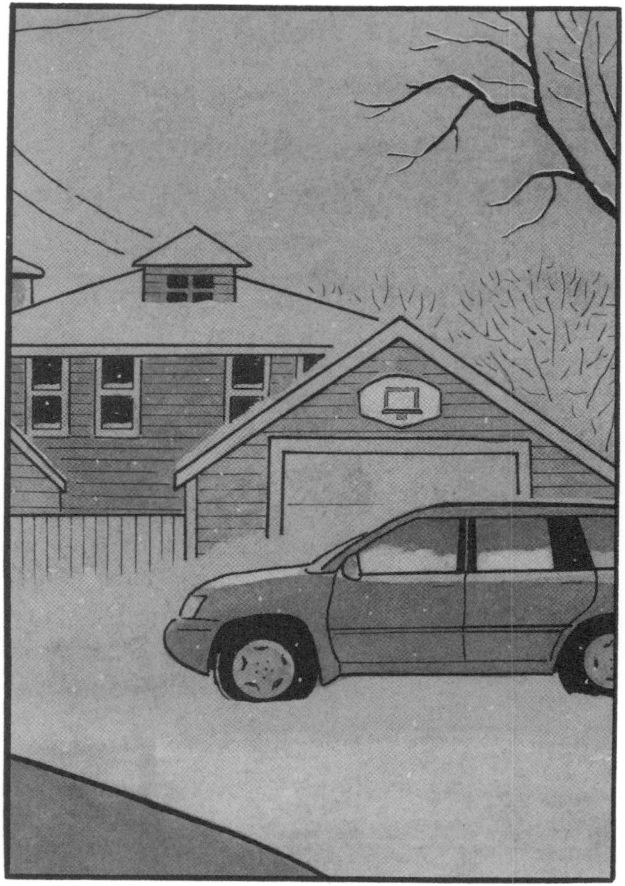

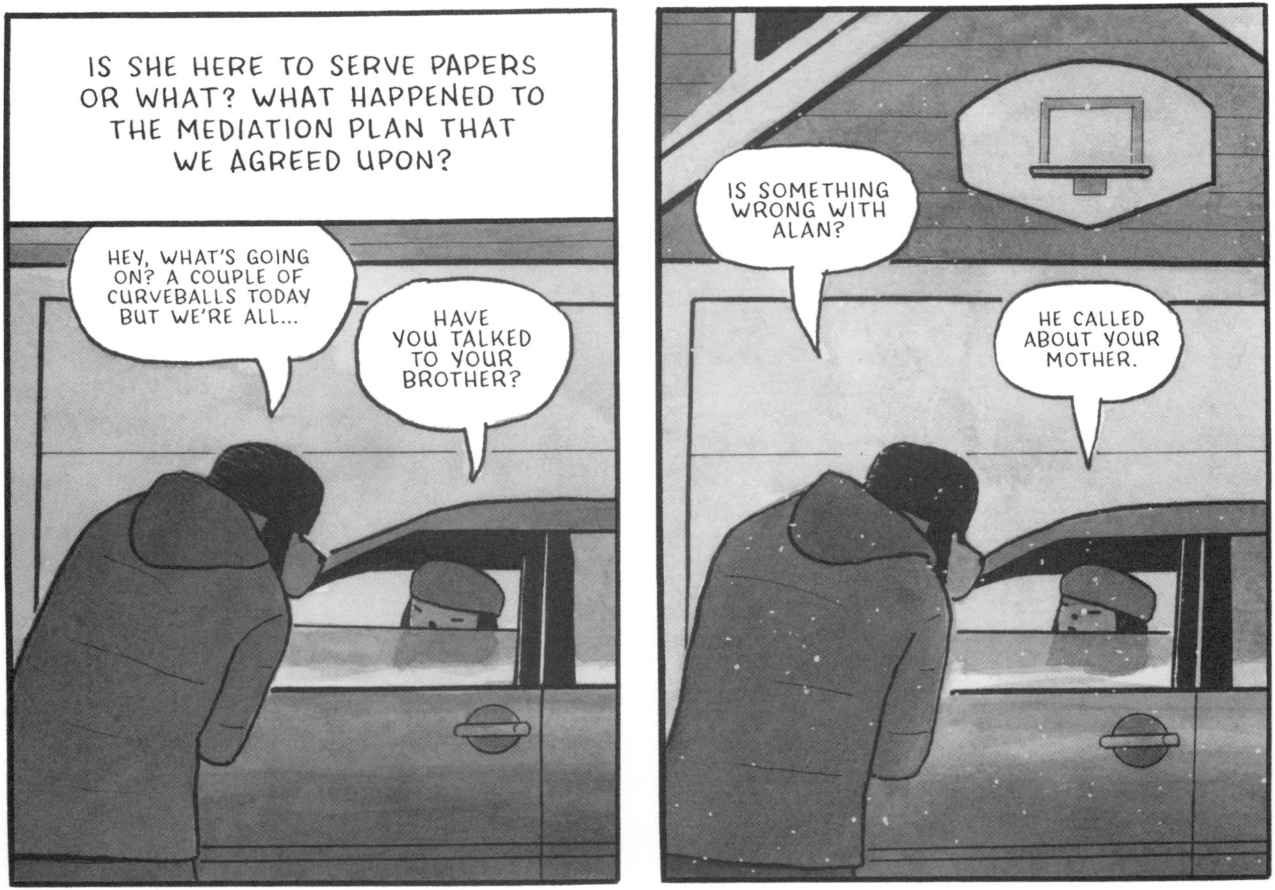
IS SHE HERE TO SERVE PAPERS OR WHAT? WHAT HAPPENED TO THE MEDIATION PLAN THAT WE AGREED UPON?
HEY, WHAT'S GOING ON? A COUPLE OF CURVEBALLS TODAY BUT WE'RE ALL...
HAVE YOU TALKED TO YOUR BROTHER?
IS SOMETHING WRONG WITH ALAN?
HE CALLED ABOUT YOUR MOTHER.

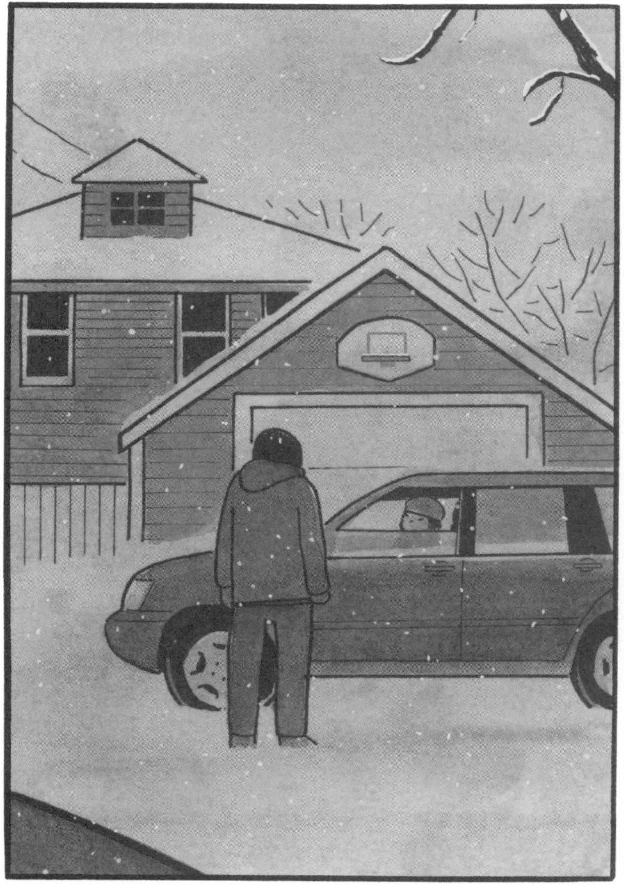

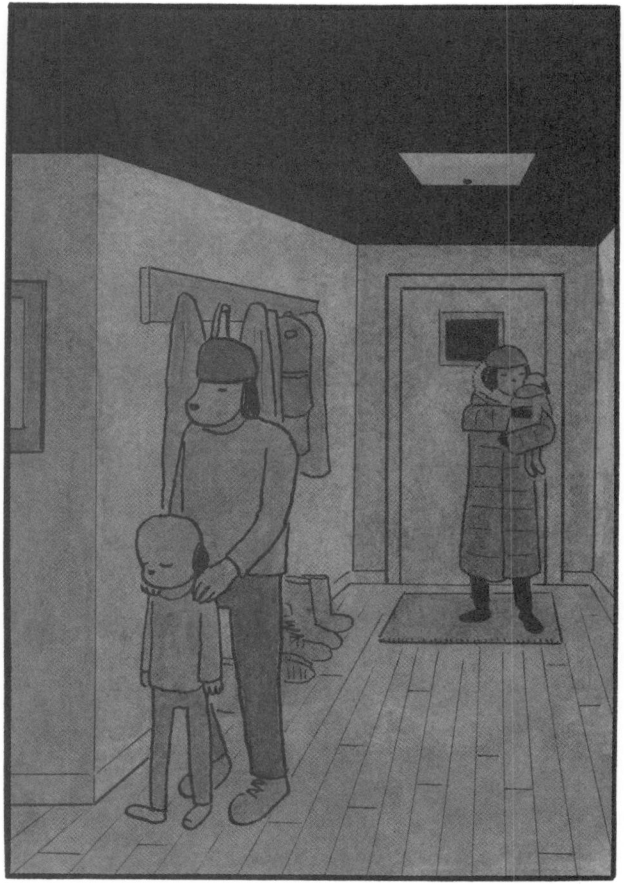

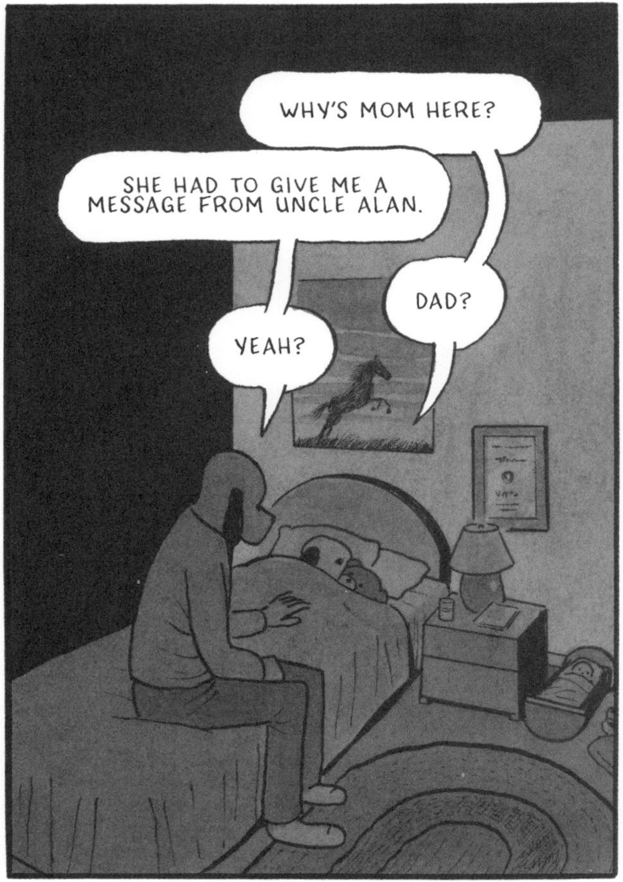
WHY'S MOM HERE?
SHE HAD TO GIVE ME A MESSAGE FROM UNCLE ALAN.
DAD?
YEAH?

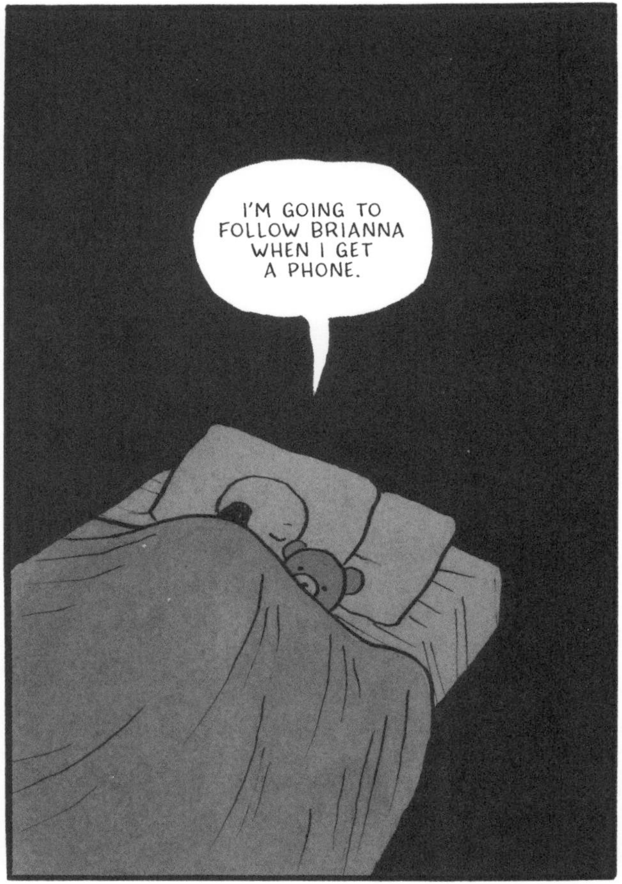
I'M GOING TO FOLLOW BRIANNA WHEN I GET A PHONE.

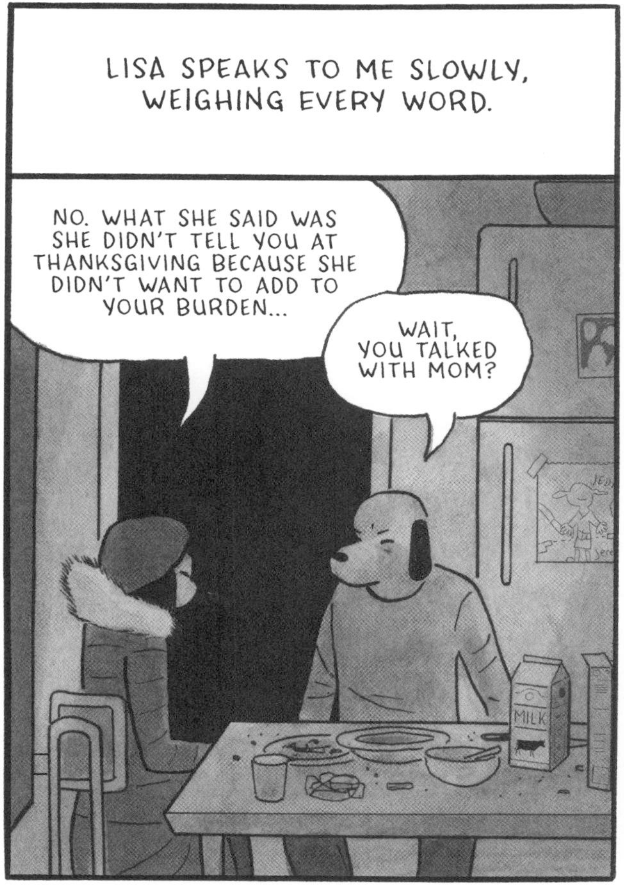
LISA SPEAKS TO ME SLOWLY, WEIGHING EVERY WORD.
NO. WHAT SHE SAID WAS SHE DIDN'T TELL YOU AT THANKSGIVING BECAUSE SHE DIDN'T WANT TO ADD TO YOUR BURDEN...
WAIT, YOU TALKED WITH MOM?
MILK

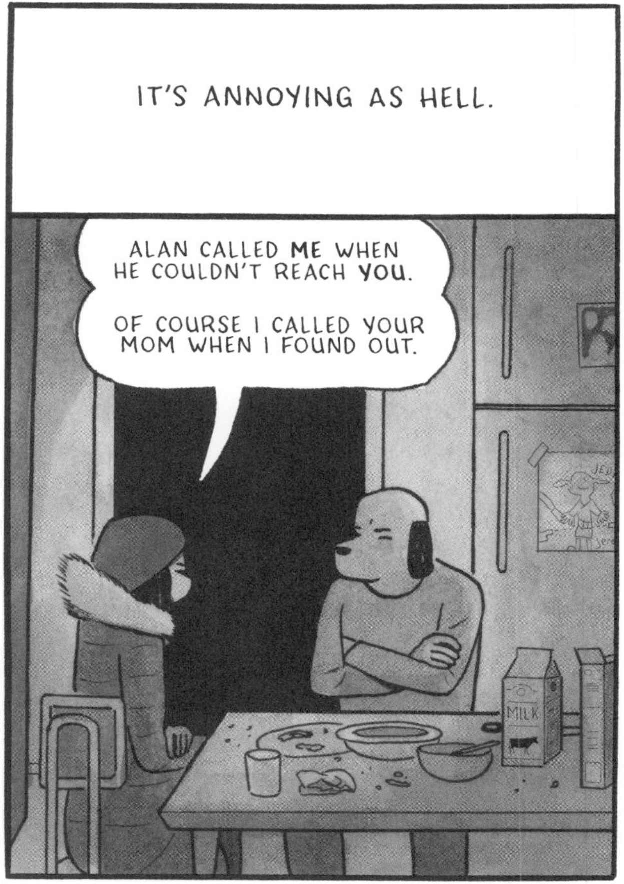
IT'S ANNOYING AS HELL.
ALAN CALLED **ME** WHEN HE COULDN'T REACH **YOU**.
OF COURSE I CALLED YOUR MOM WHEN I FOUND OUT.
MILK

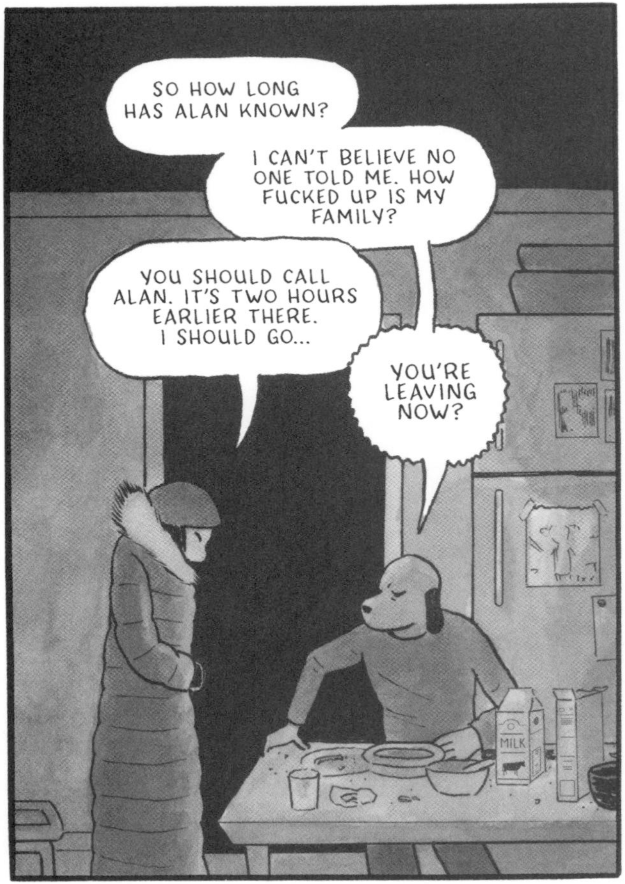
SO HOW LONG HAS ALAN KNOWN?
I CAN'T BELIEVE NO ONE TOLD ME. HOW FUCKED UP IS MY FAMILY?
YOU SHOULD CALL ALAN. IT'S TWO HOURS EARLIER THERE. I SHOULD GO...
YOU'RE LEAVING NOW?
MILK

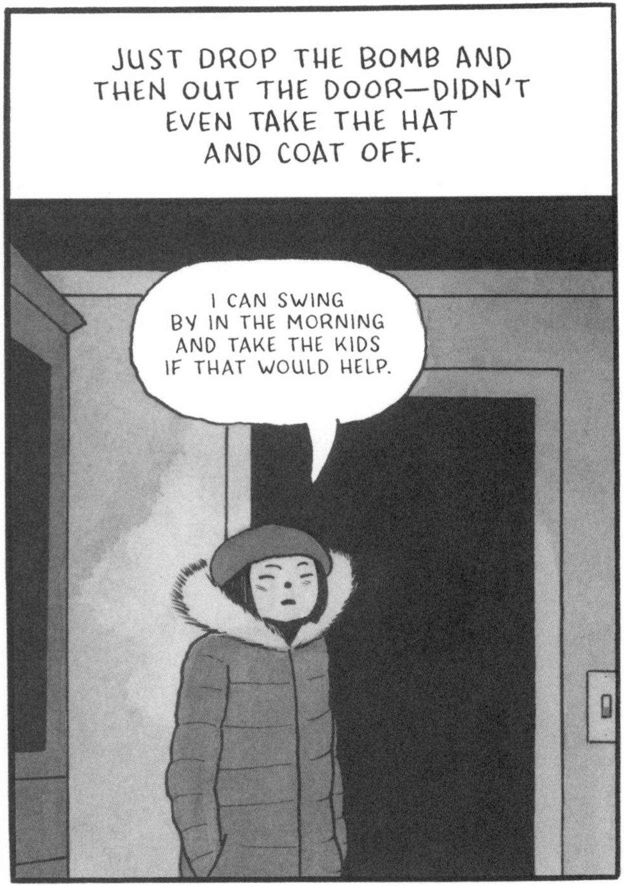
JUST DROP THE BOMB AND THEN OUT THE DOOR—DIDN'T EVEN TAKE THE HAT AND COAT OFF.
I CAN SWING BY IN THE MORNING AND TAKE THE KIDS IF THAT WOULD HELP.

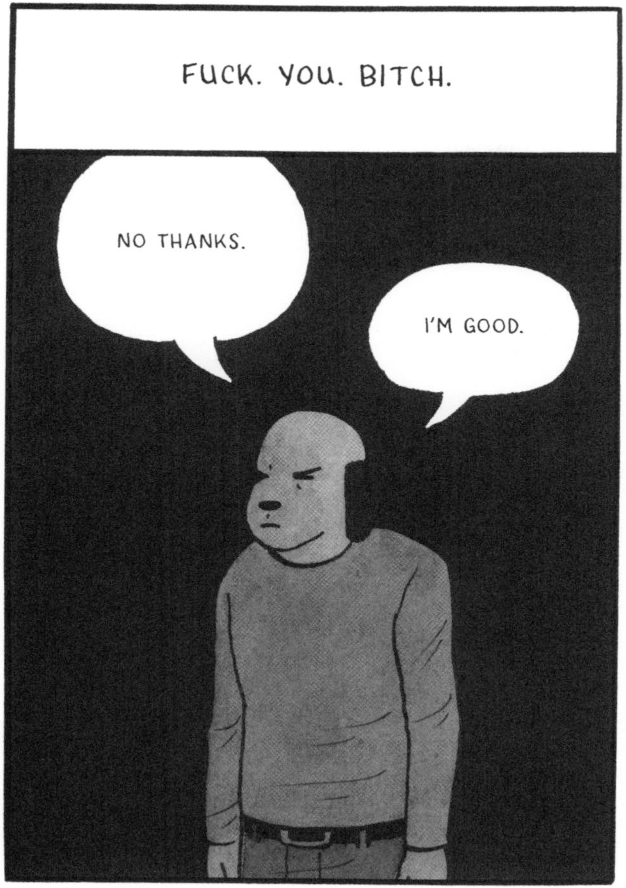
FUCK. YOU. BITCH.
NO THANKS.
I'M GOOD.

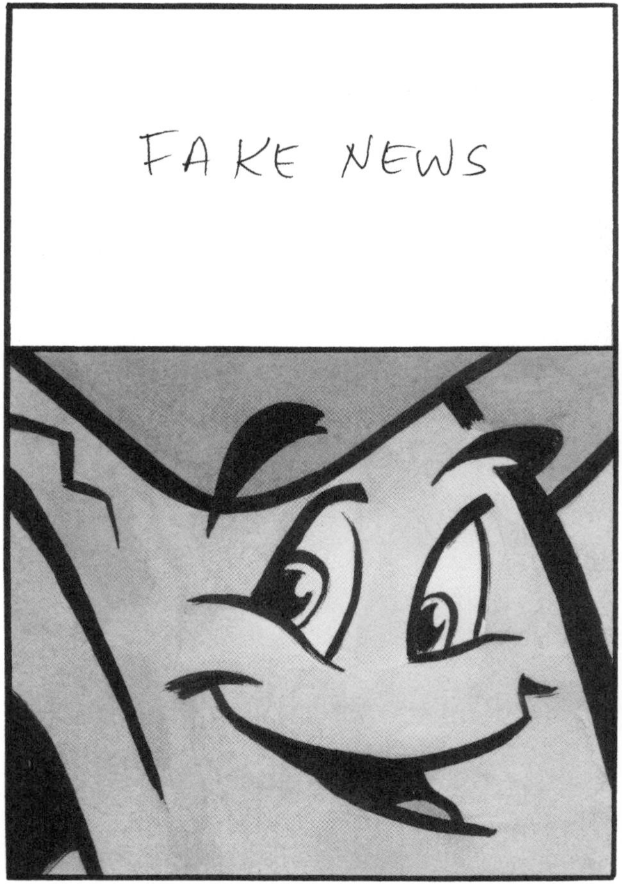
FAKE NEWS

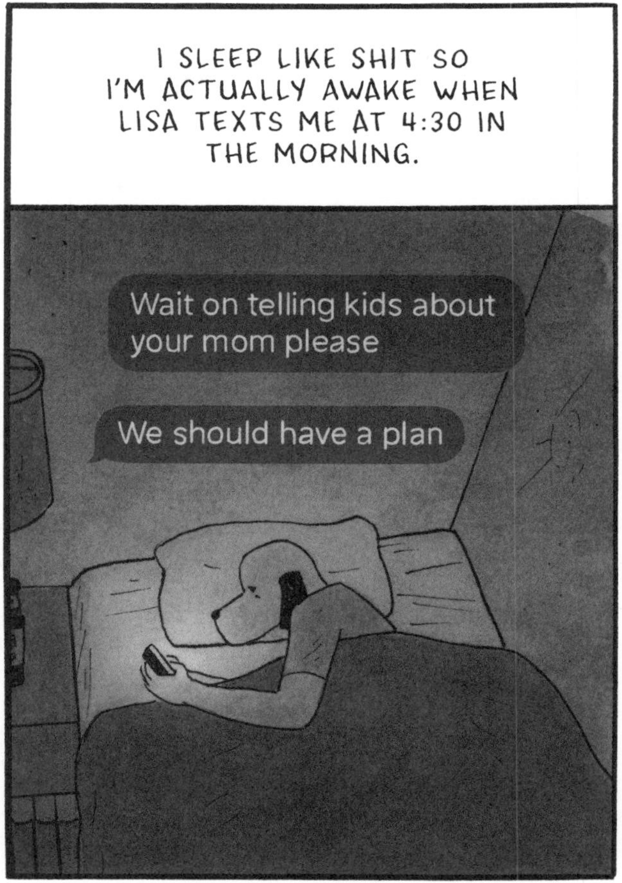
I SLEEP LIKE SHIT SO I'M ACTUALLY AWAKE WHEN LISA TEXTS ME AT 4:30 IN THE MORNING.
Wait on telling kids about your mom please
We should have a plan

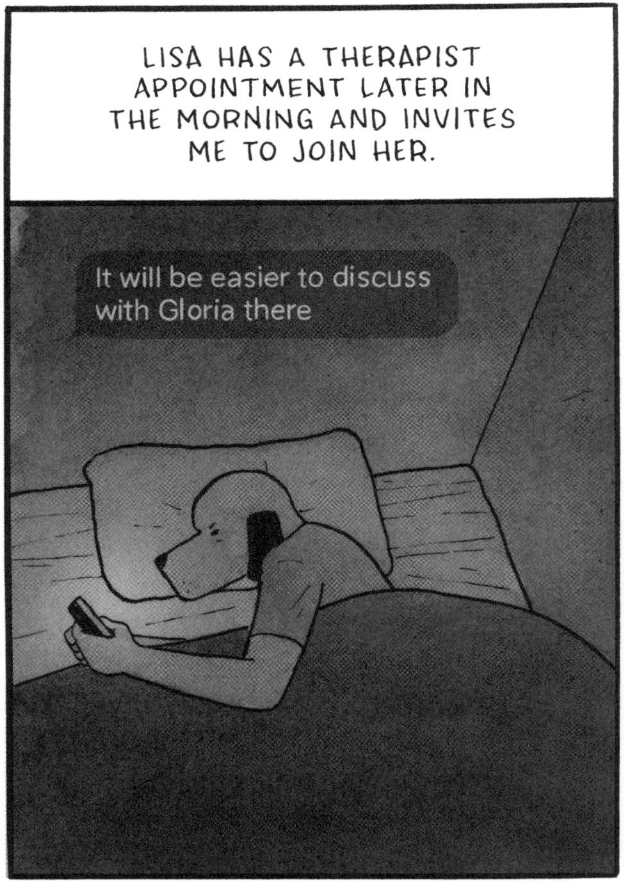
LISA HAS A THERAPIST APPOINTMENT LATER IN THE MORNING AND INVITES ME TO JOIN HER.
It will be easier to discuss with Gloria there

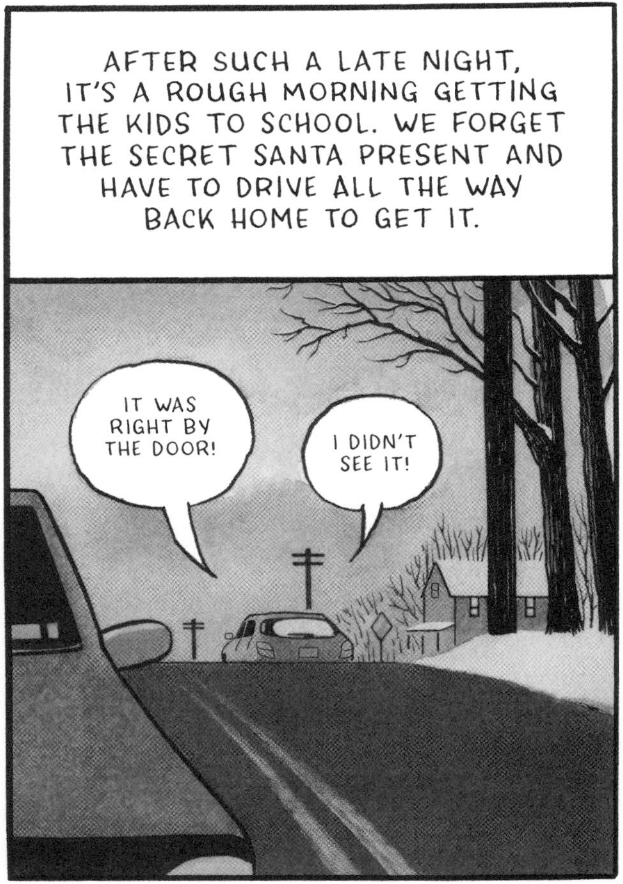
AFTER SUCH A LATE NIGHT, IT'S A ROUGH MORNING GETTING THE KIDS TO SCHOOL. WE FORGET THE SECRET SANTA PRESENT AND HAVE TO DRIVE ALL THE WAY BACK HOME TO GET IT.
IT WAS RIGHT BY THE DOOR!
I DIDN'T SEE IT!

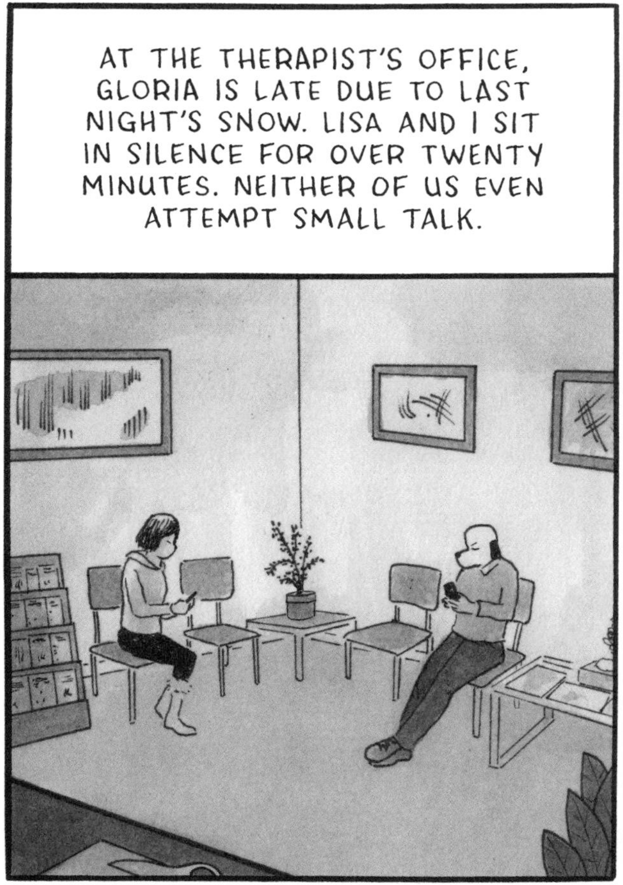
AT THE THERAPIST'S OFFICE, GLORIA IS LATE DUE TO LAST NIGHT'S SNOW. LISA AND I SIT IN SILENCE FOR OVER TWENTY MINUTES. NEITHER OF US EVEN ATTEMPT SMALL TALK.

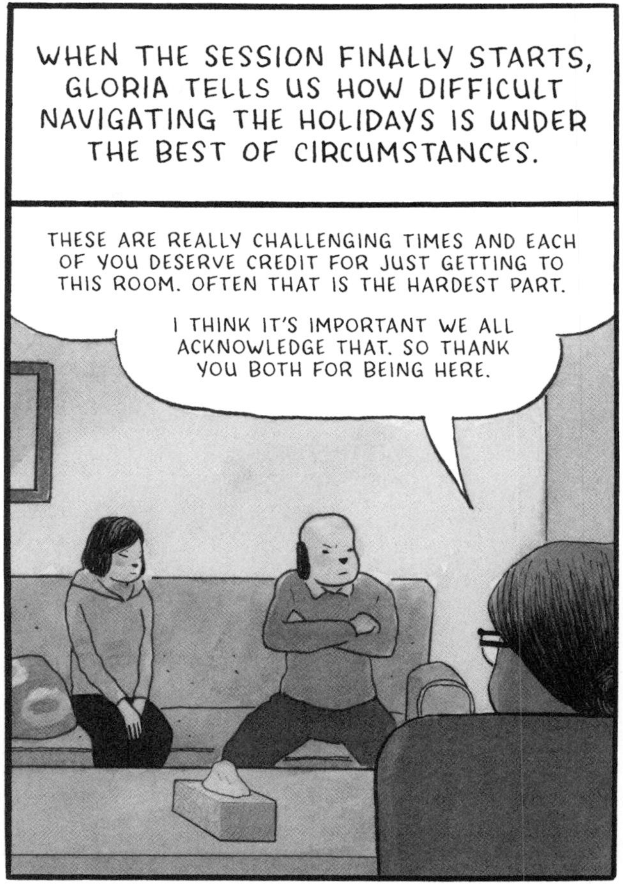
WHEN THE SESSION FINALLY STARTS, GLORIA TELLS US HOW DIFFICULT NAVIGATING THE HOLIDAYS IS UNDER THE BEST OF CIRCUMSTANCES.
THESE ARE REALLY CHALLENGING TIMES AND EACH OF YOU DESERVE CREDIT FOR JUST GETTING TO THIS ROOM. OFTEN THAT IS THE HARDEST PART.
I THINK IT'S IMPORTANT WE ALL ACKNOWLEDGE THAT. SO THANK YOU BOTH FOR BEING HERE.

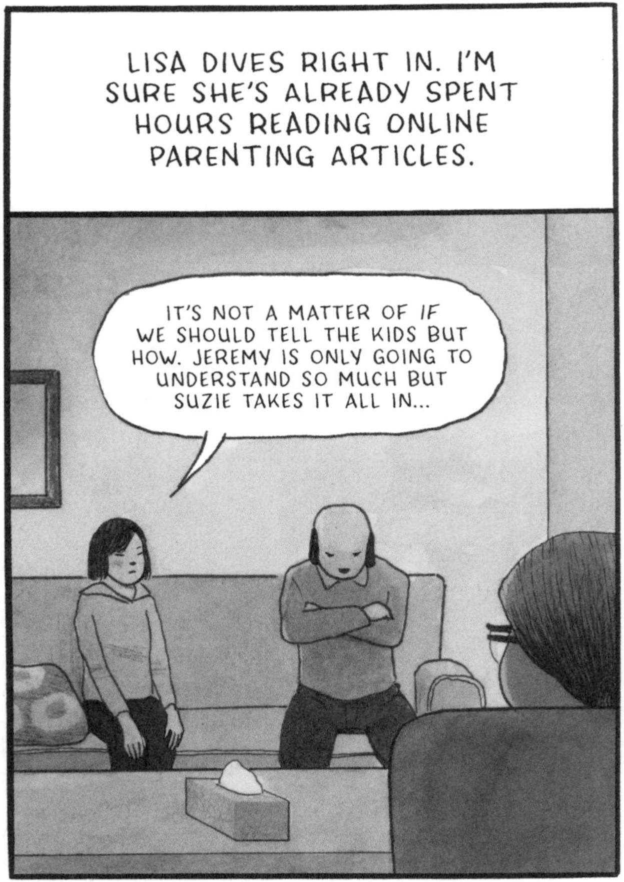
LISA DIVES RIGHT IN. I'M SURE SHE'S ALREADY SPENT HOURS READING ONLINE PARENTING ARTICLES.
IT'S NOT A MATTER OF *IF* WE SHOULD TELL THE KIDS BUT HOW. JEREMY IS ONLY GOING TO UNDERSTAND SO MUCH BUT SUZIE TAKES IT ALL IN...
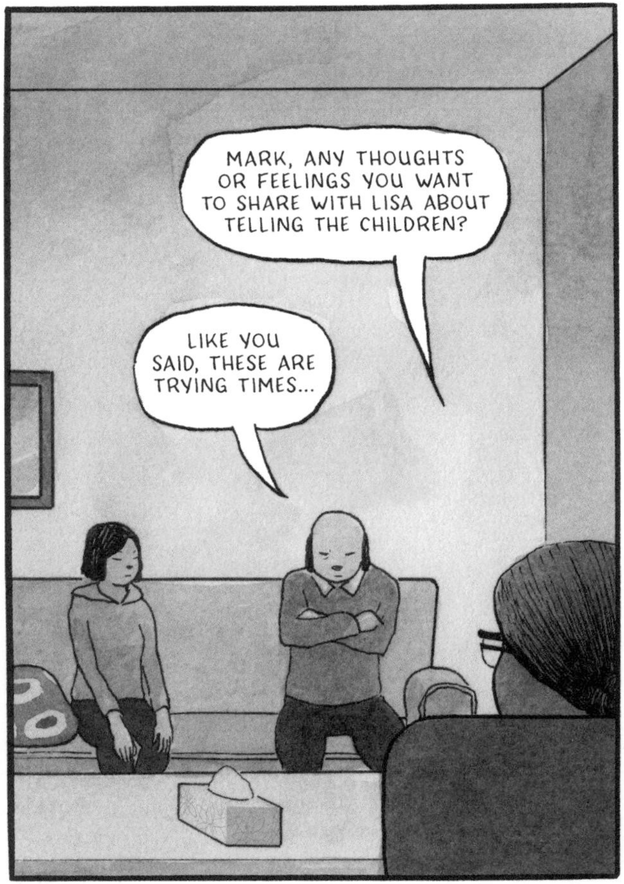
MARK, ANY THOUGHTS OR FEELINGS YOU WANT TO SHARE WITH LISA ABOUT TELLING THE CHILDREN?
LIKE YOU SAID, THESE ARE TRYING TIMES...

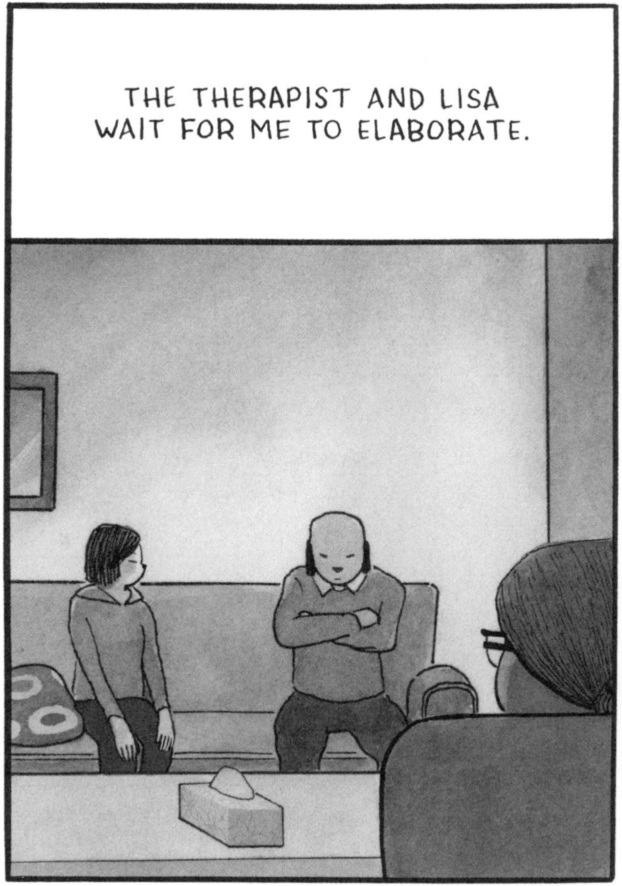
THE THERAPIST AND LISA WAIT FOR ME TO ELABORATE.

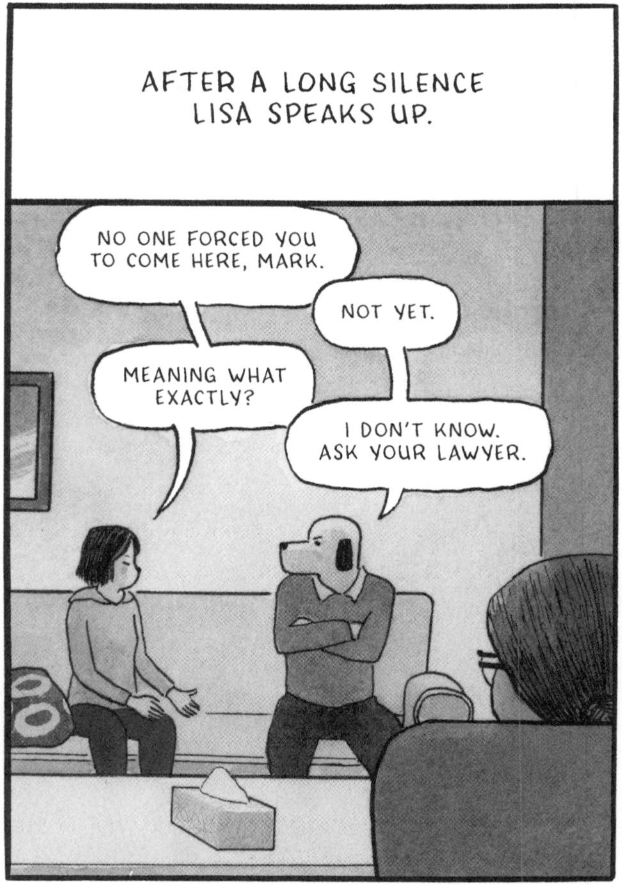
AFTER A LONG SILENCE LISA SPEAKS UP.
NO ONE FORCED YOU TO COME HERE, MARK.
NOT YET.
MEANING WHAT EXACTLY?
I DON'T KNOW. ASK YOUR LAWYER.

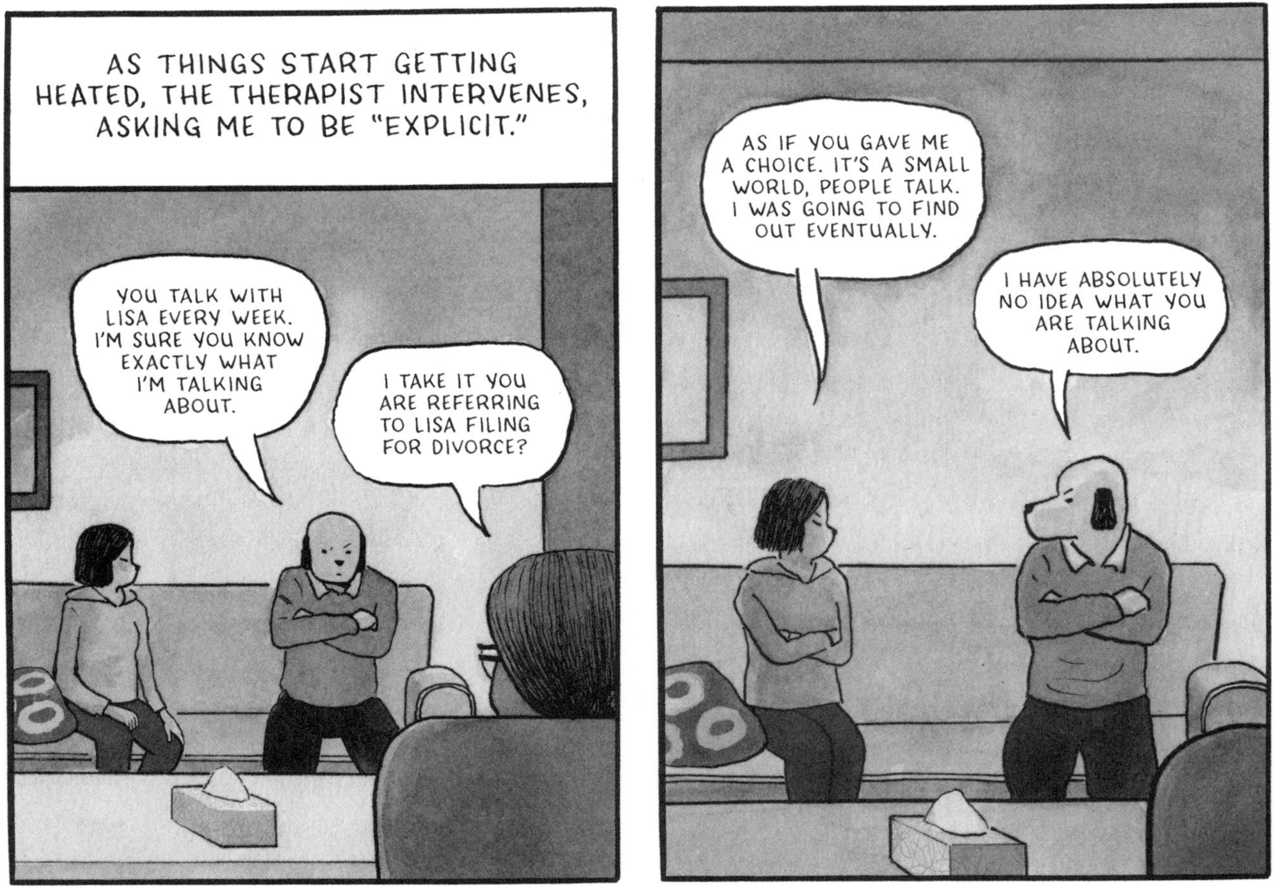
AS THINGS START GETTING HEATED, THE THERAPIST INTERVENES, ASKING ME TO BE "EXPLICIT."
YOU TALK WITH LISA EVERY WEEK. I'M SURE YOU KNOW EXACTLY WHAT I'M TALKING ABOUT.
I TAKE IT YOU ARE REFERRING TO LISA FILING FOR DIVORCE?
AS IF YOU GAVE ME A CHOICE. IT'S A SMALL WORLD, PEOPLE TALK. I WAS GOING TO FIND OUT EVENTUALLY.
I HAVE ABSOLUTELY NO IDEA WHAT YOU ARE TALKING ABOUT.

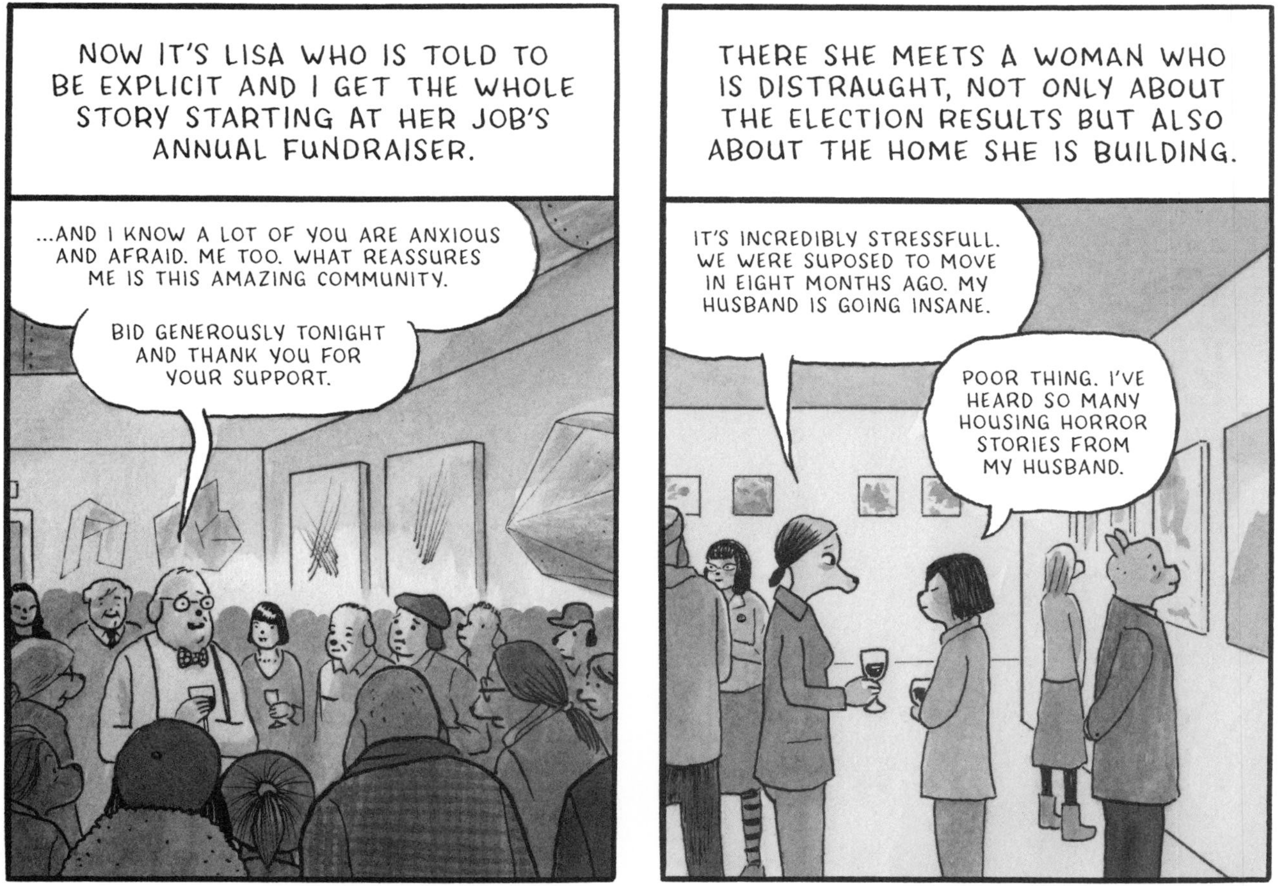
NOW IT'S LISA WHO IS TOLD TO BE EXPLICIT AND I GET THE WHOLE STORY STARTING AT HER JOB'S ANNUAL FUNDRAISER.
...AND I KNOW A LOT OF YOU ARE ANXIOUS AND AFRAID. ME TOO. WHAT REASSURES ME IS THIS AMAZING COMMUNITY.
BID GENEROUSLY TONIGHT AND THANK YOU FOR YOUR SUPPORT.
THERE SHE MEETS A WOMAN WHO IS DISTRAUGHT, NOT ONLY ABOUT THE ELECTION RESULTS BUT ALSO ABOUT THE HOME SHE IS BUILDING.
IT'S INCREDIBLY STRESSFULL. WE WERE SUPOSED TO MOVE IN EIGHT MONTHS AGO. MY HUSBAND IS GOING INSANE.
POOR THING. I'VE HEARD SO MANY HOUSING HORROR STORIES FROM MY HUSBAND.

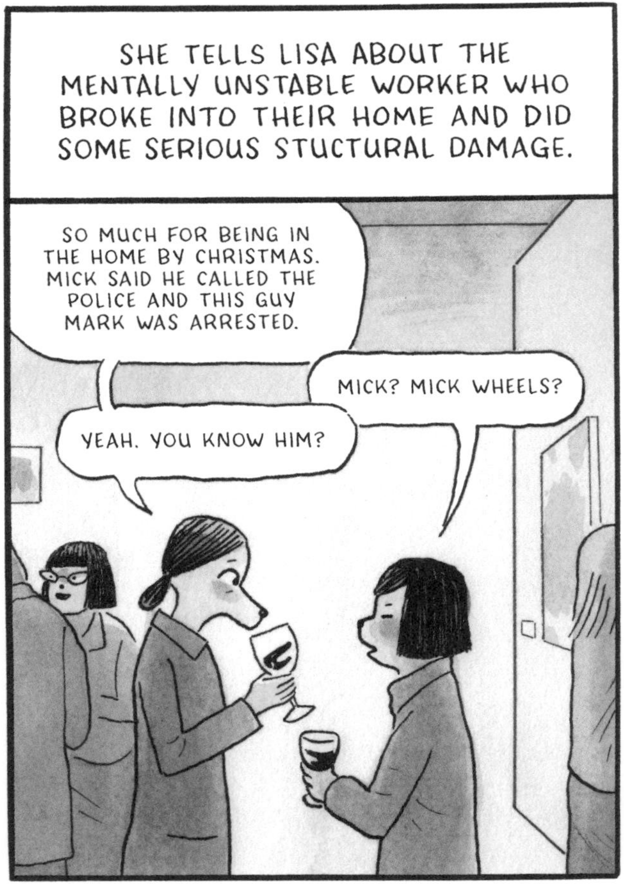
SHE TELLS LISA ABOUT THE MENTALLY UNSTABLE WORKER WHO BROKE INTO THEIR HOME AND DID SOME SERIOUS STUCTURAL DAMAGE.
SO MUCH FOR BEING IN THE HOME BY CHRISTMAS. MICK SAID HE CALLED THE POLICE AND THIS GUY MARK WAS ARRESTED.
MICK? MICK WHEELS?
YEAH. YOU KNOW HIM?

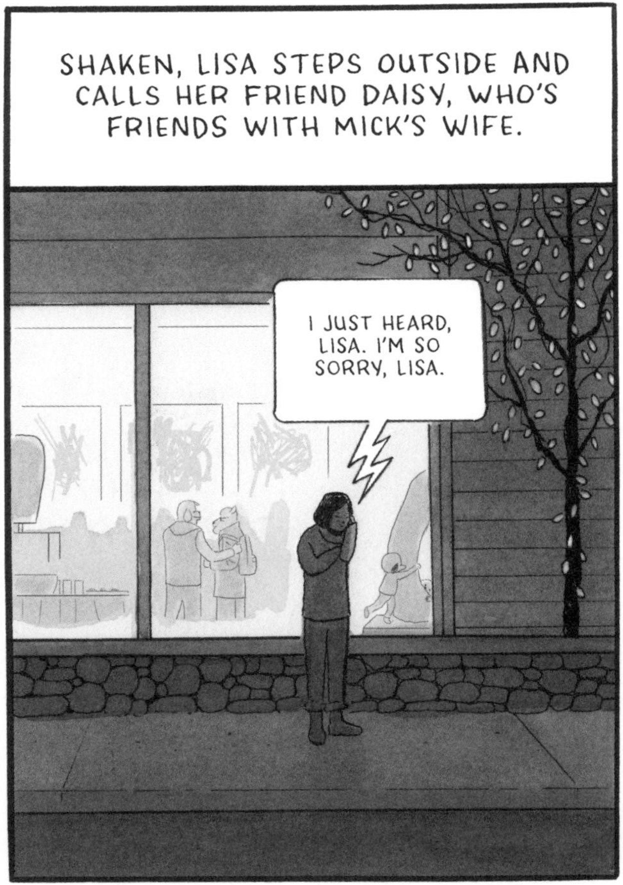
SHAKEN, LISA STEPS OUTSIDE AND CALLS HER FRIEND DAISY, WHO'S FRIENDS WITH MICK'S WIFE.
I JUST HEARD, LISA. I'M SO SORRY, LISA.

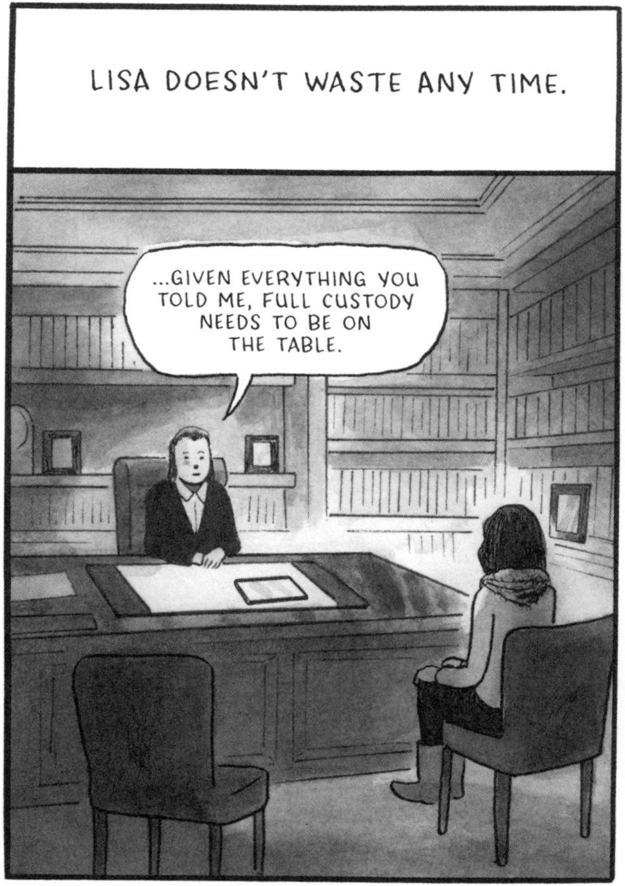
LISA DOESN'T WASTE ANY TIME.
...GIVEN EVERYTHING YOU TOLD ME, FULL CUSTODY NEEDS TO BE ON THE TABLE.

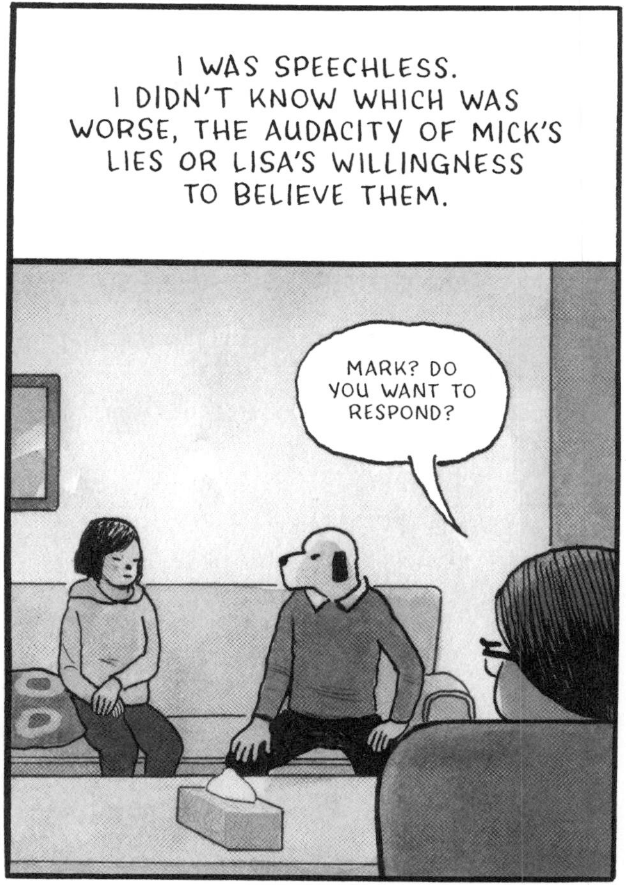
I WAS SPEECHLESS. I DIDN'T KNOW WHICH WAS WORSE, THE AUDACITY OF MICK'S LIES OR LISA'S WILLINGNESS TO BELIEVE THEM.
MARK? DO YOU WANT TO RESPOND?

I TELL LISA ABOUT THE BOUNCED CHECK, THE MONEY MICK OWES ME, AND HIS ENDLESS EXCUSES. I'M NOT PROUD OF TAKING A HAMMER TO THE DRYWALL BUT THERE WERE REASONS.

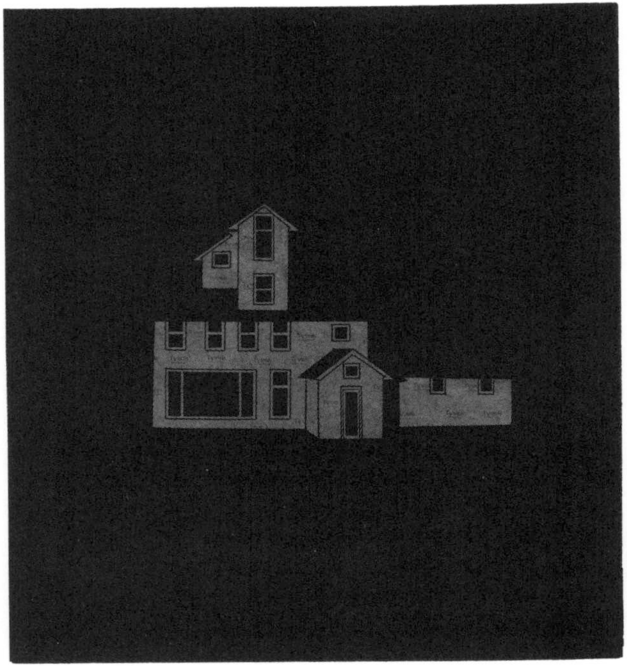

I TELL HER THAT THE CLOSEST I WAS TO BEING ARRESTED WAS BEING PULLED OVER FOR TEXTING WHILE DRIVING.

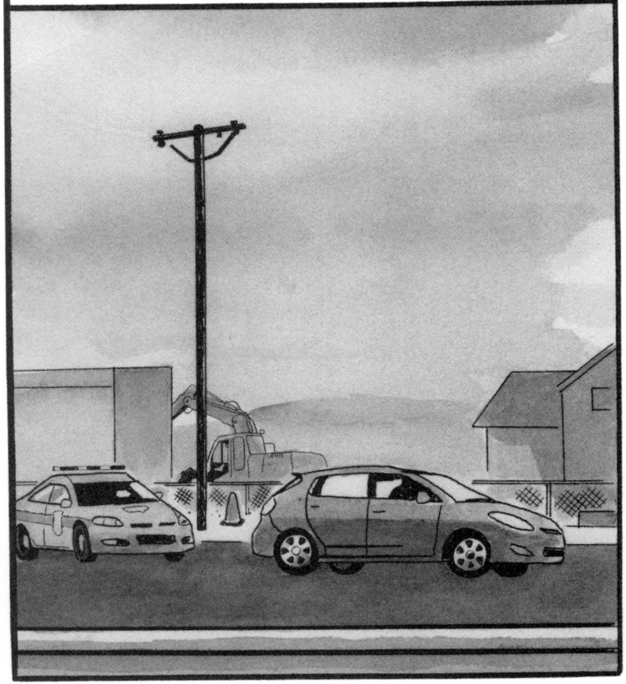

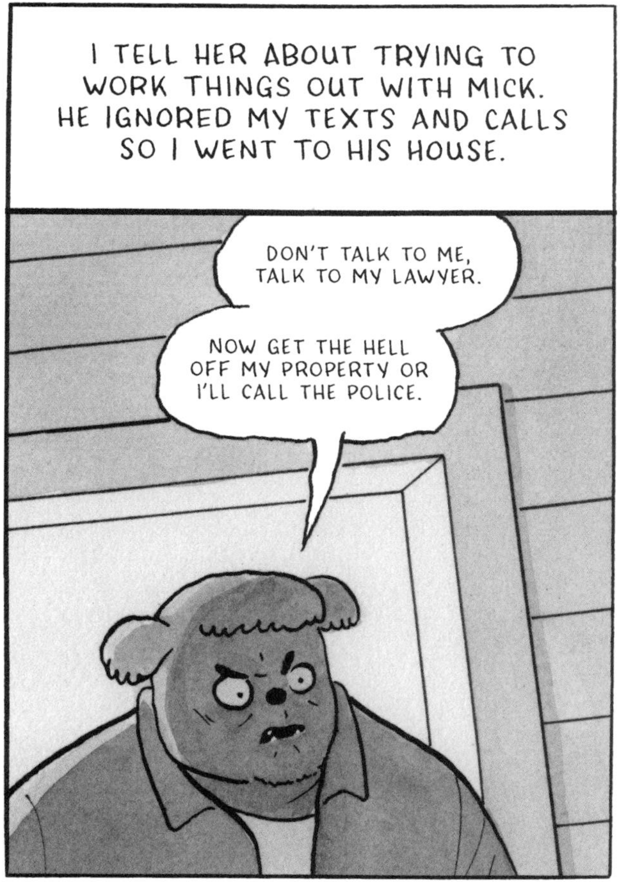
I TELL HER ABOUT TRYING TO WORK THINGS OUT WITH MICK. HE IGNORED MY TEXTS AND CALLS SO I WENT TO HIS HOUSE.
DON'T TALK TO ME, TALK TO MY LAWYER.
NOW GET THE HELL OFF MY PROPERTY OR I'LL CALL THE POLICE.

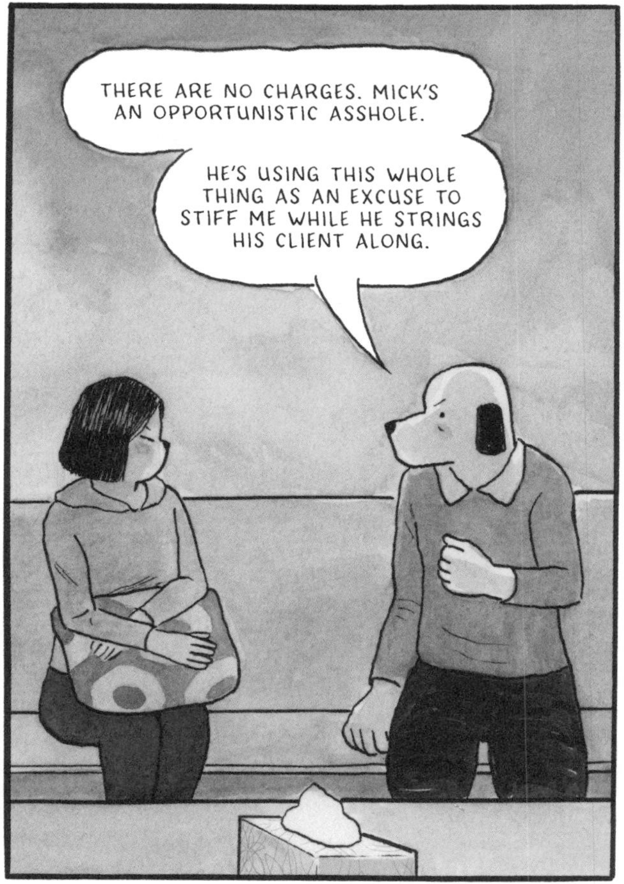
THERE ARE NO CHARGES. MICK'S AN OPPORTUNISTIC ASSHOLE.
HE'S USING THIS WHOLE THING AS AN EXCUSE TO STIFF ME WHILE HE STRINGS HIS CLIENT ALONG.

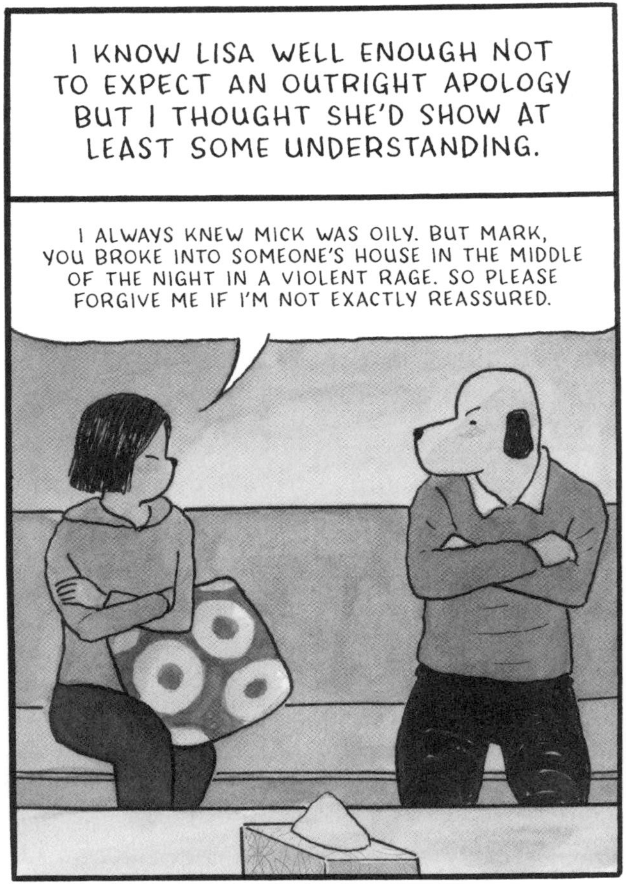
I KNOW LISA WELL ENOUGH NOT TO EXPECT AN OUTRIGHT APOLOGY BUT I THOUGHT SHE'D SHOW AT LEAST SOME UNDERSTANDING.
I ALWAYS KNEW MICK WAS OILY. BUT MARK, YOU BROKE INTO SOMEONE'S HOUSE IN THE MIDDLE OF THE NIGHT IN A VIOLENT RAGE. SO PLEASE FORGIVE ME IF I'M NOT EXACTLY REASSURED.

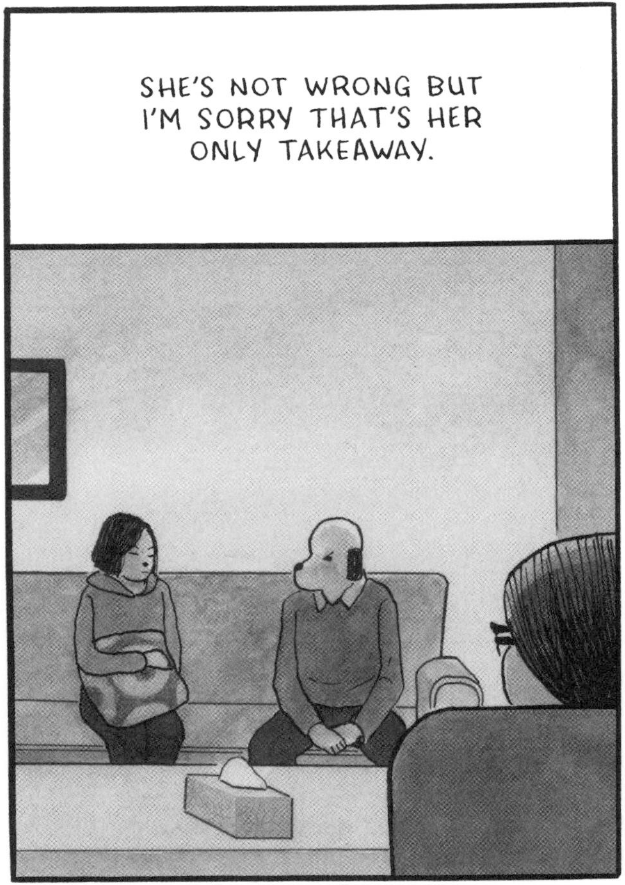
SHE'S NOT WRONG BUT I'M SORRY THAT'S HER ONLY TAKEAWAY.

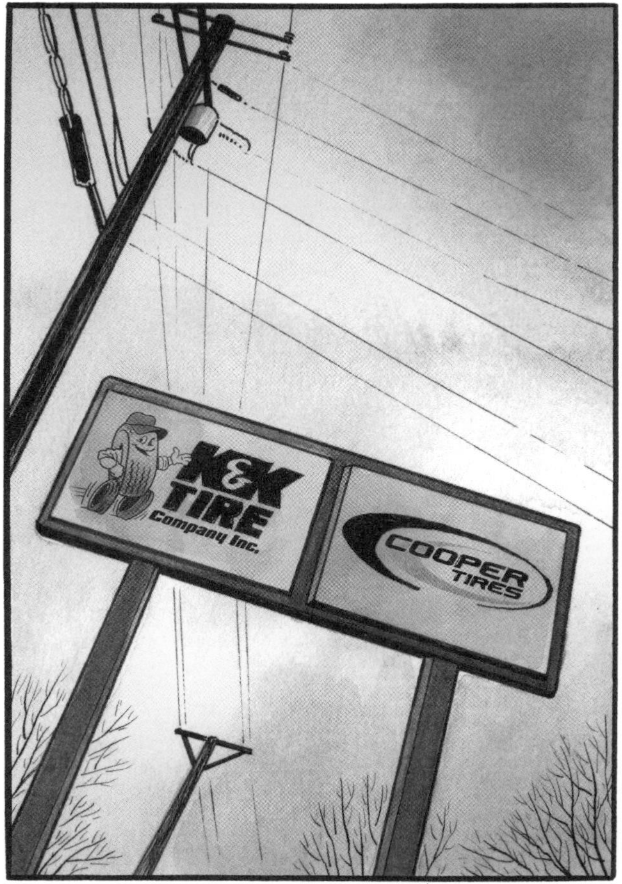
K&K TIRE Company Inc.
COOPER TIRES

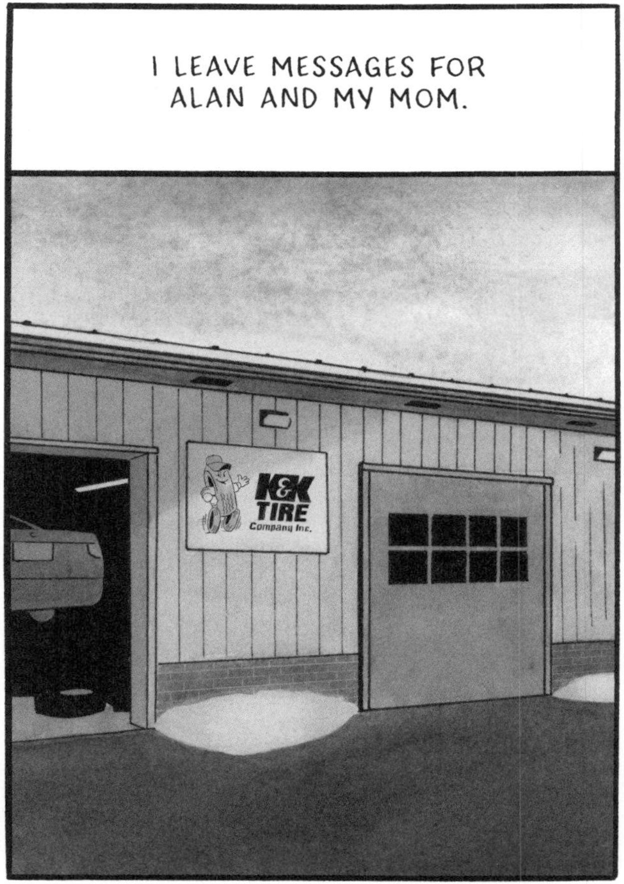
I LEAVE MESSAGES FOR ALAN AND MY MOM.
K&K TIRE Company Inc.

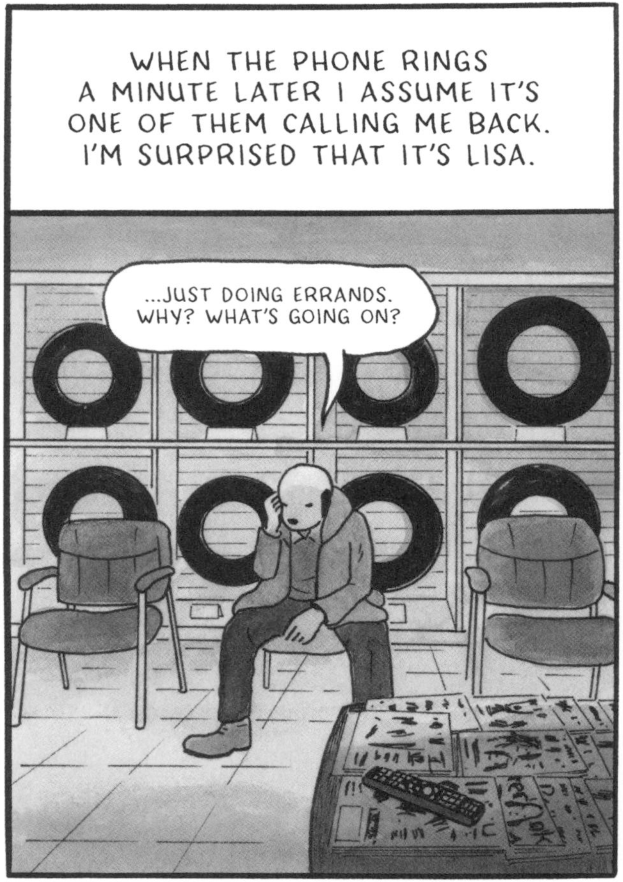
WHEN THE PHONE RINGS A MINUTE LATER I ASSUME IT'S ONE OF THEM CALLING ME BACK. I'M SURPRISED THAT IT'S LISA.
...JUST DOING ERRANDS. WHY? WHAT'S GOING ON?

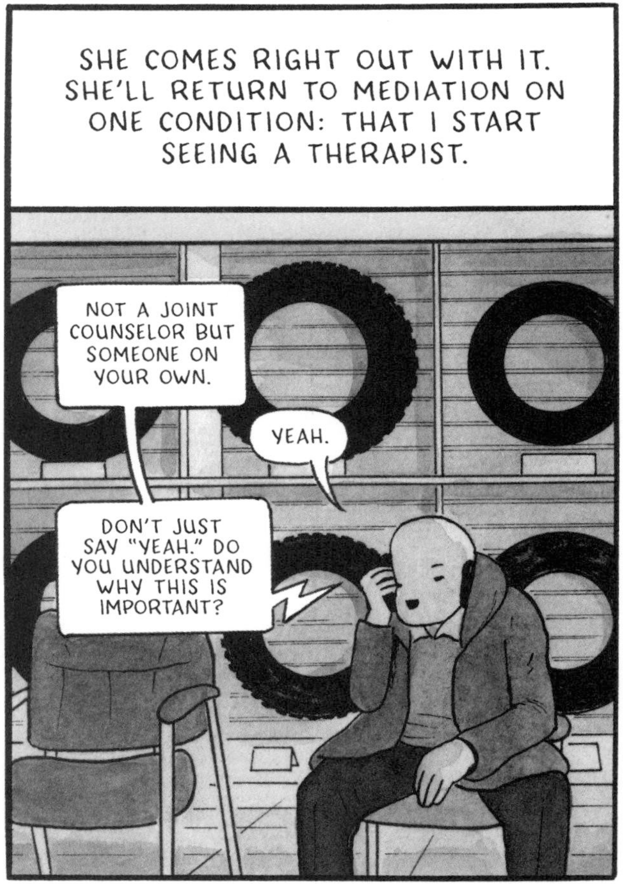
SHE COMES RIGHT OUT WITH IT. SHE'LL RETURN TO MEDIATION ON ONE CONDITION: THAT I START SEEING A THERAPIST.
NOT A JOINT COUNSELOR BUT SOMEONE ON YOUR OWN.
YEAH.
DON'T JUST SAY "YEAH." DO YOU UNDERSTAND WHY THIS IS IMPORTANT?

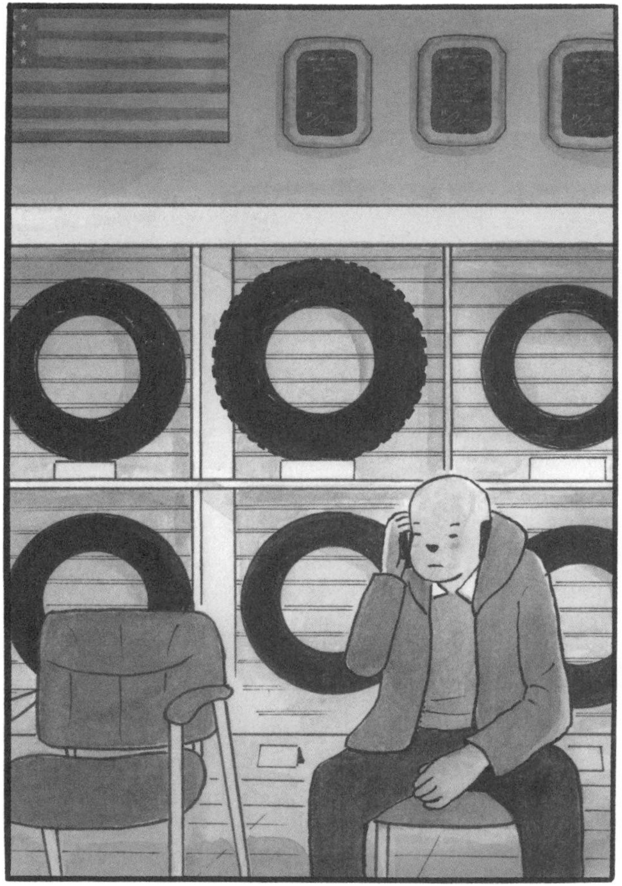

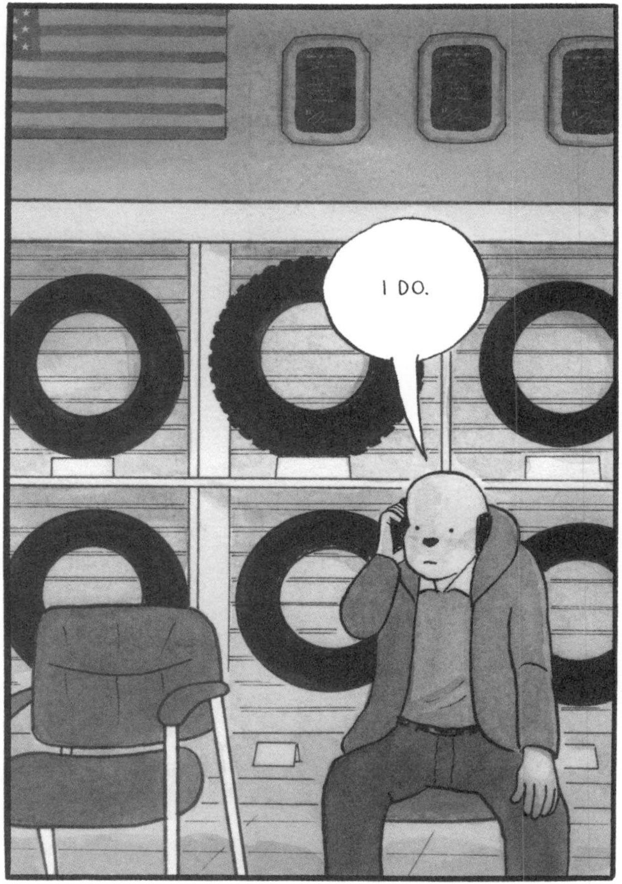
I DO.

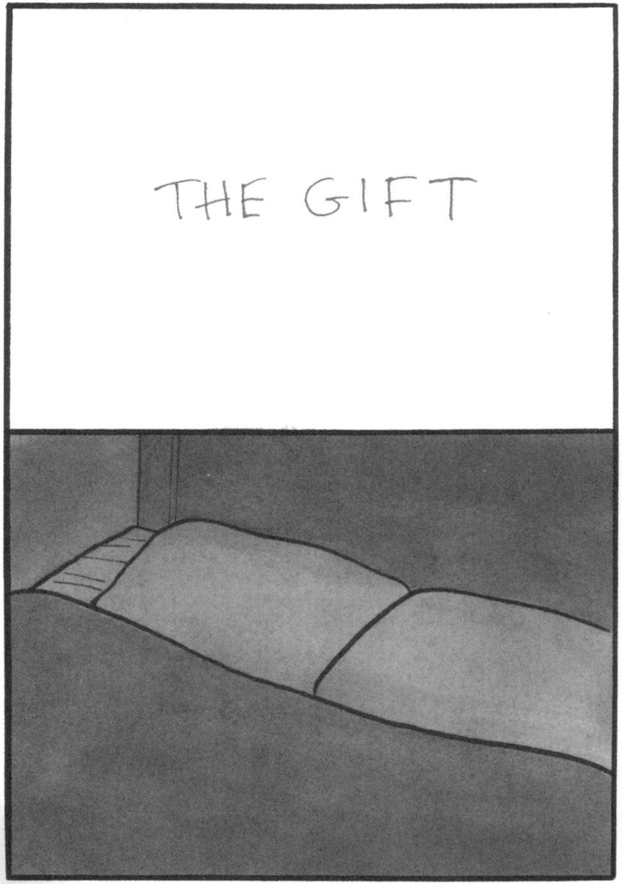
THE GIFT

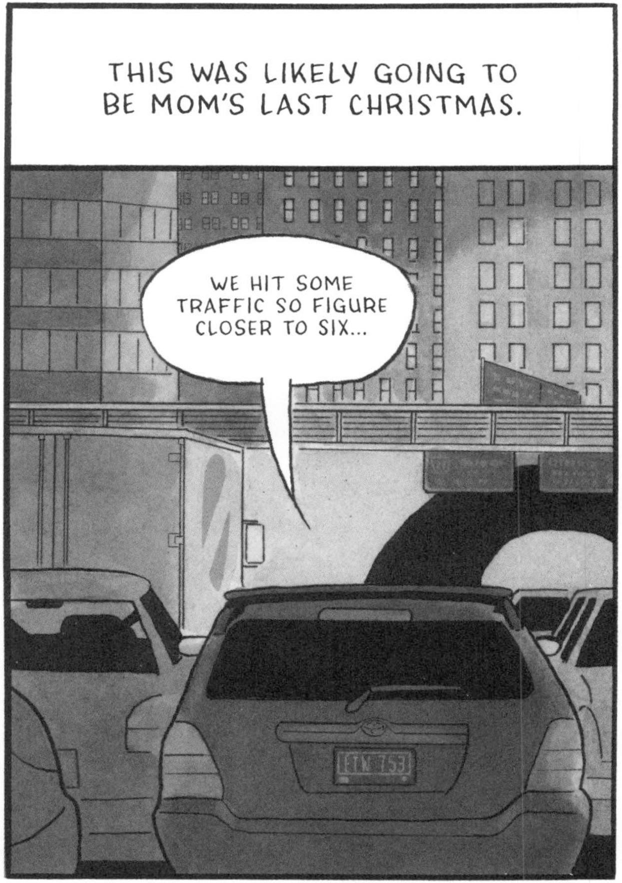
THIS WAS LIKELY GOING TO BE MOM'S LAST CHRISTMAS.
WE HIT SOME TRAFFIC SO FIGURE CLOSER TO SIX...

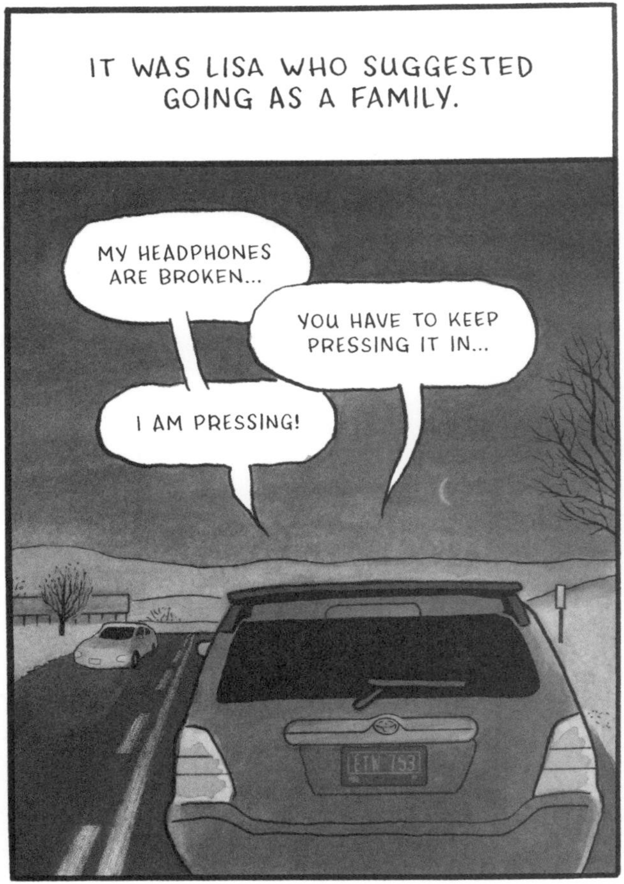
IT WAS LISA WHO SUGGESTED GOING AS A FAMILY.
MY HEADPHONES ARE BROKEN...
YOU HAVE TO KEEP PRESSING IT IN...
I AM PRESSING!
ETW 753

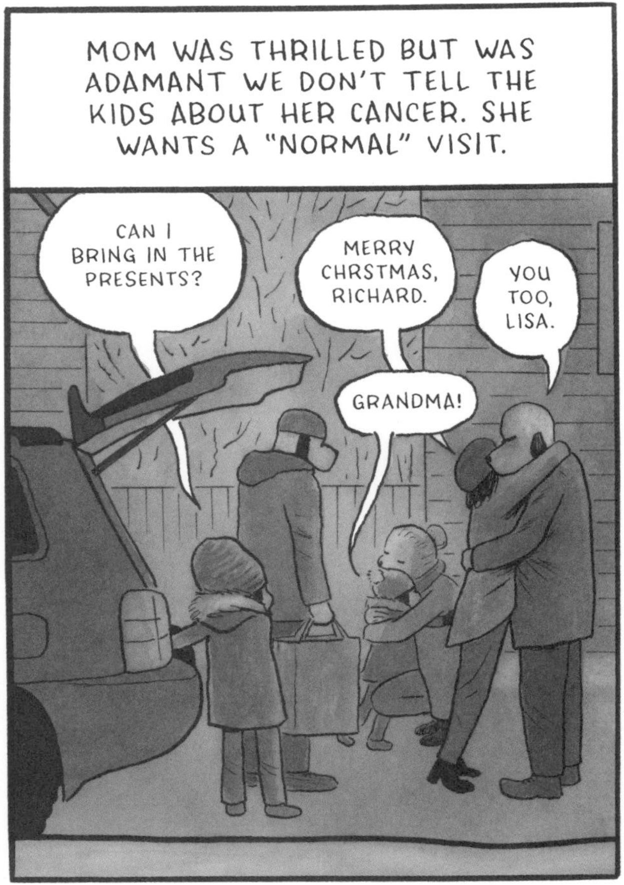
MOM WAS THRILLED BUT WAS ADAMANT WE DON'T TELL THE KIDS ABOUT HER CANCER. SHE WANTS A "NORMAL" VISIT.
CAN I BRING IN THE PRESENTS?
MERRY CHRSTMAS, RICHARD.
YOU TOO, LISA.
GRANDMA!

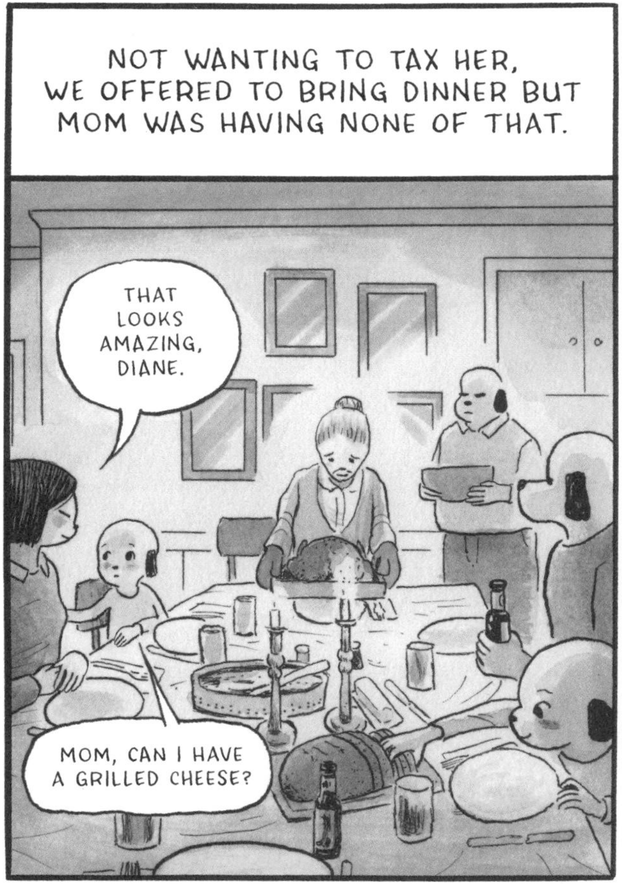
NOT WANTING TO TAX HER, WE OFFERED TO BRING DINNER BUT MOM WAS HAVING NONE OF THAT.
THAT LOOKS AMAZING, DIANE.
MOM, CAN I HAVE A GRILLED CHEESE?

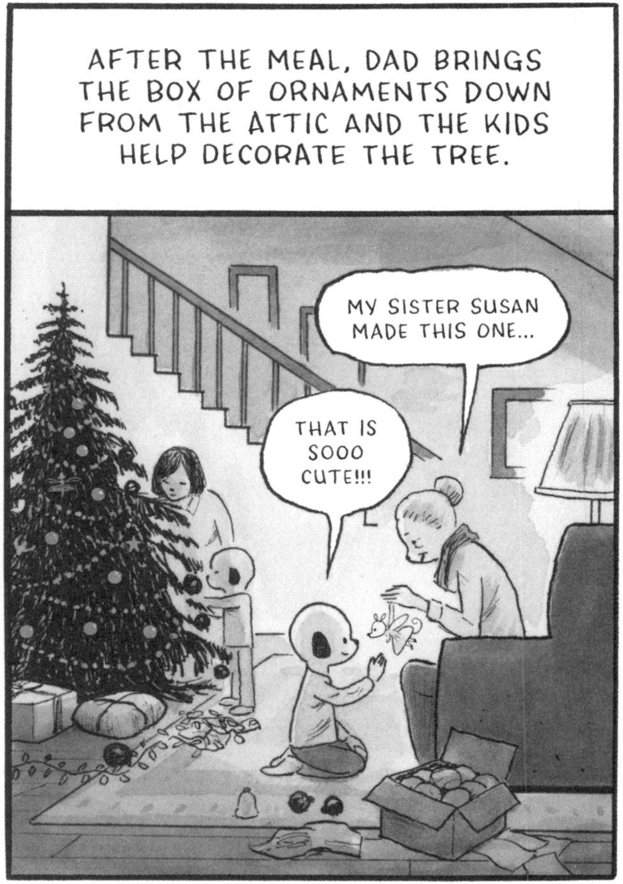
AFTER THE MEAL, DAD BRINGS THE BOX OF ORNAMENTS DOWN FROM THE ATTIC AND THE KIDS HELP DECORATE THE TREE.
MY SISTER SUSAN MADE THIS ONE...
THAT IS SOOO CUTE!!!

MOM PLIES THE KIDS WITH HOLIDAY COOKIES AND GLASS AFTER GLASS OF EGGNOG. IT DRIVES LISA CRAZY, BUT GIVEN THE CIRCUMSTANCES, SHE'S NOT GOING TO BEGRUDGE MY MOM FOR INDULGING HER ONLY GRANDKIDS.

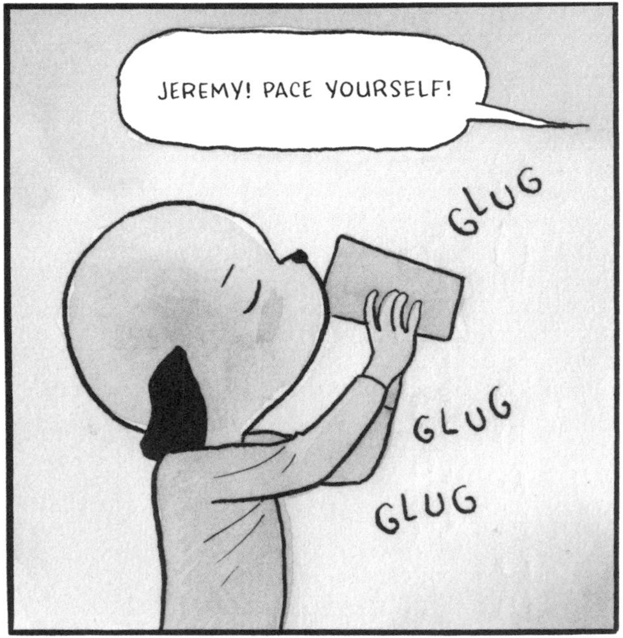
JEREMY! PACE YOURSELF!
GLUG
GLUG
GLUG

WHILE MOM AND LISA PUT THE KIDS TO BED, DAD AND I CLEAN UP.

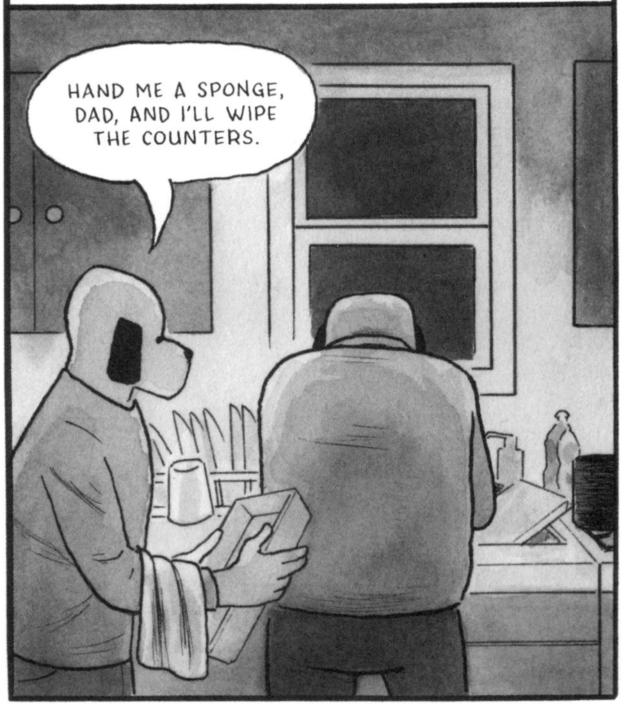
HAND ME A SPONGE, DAD, AND I'LL WIPE THE COUNTERS.

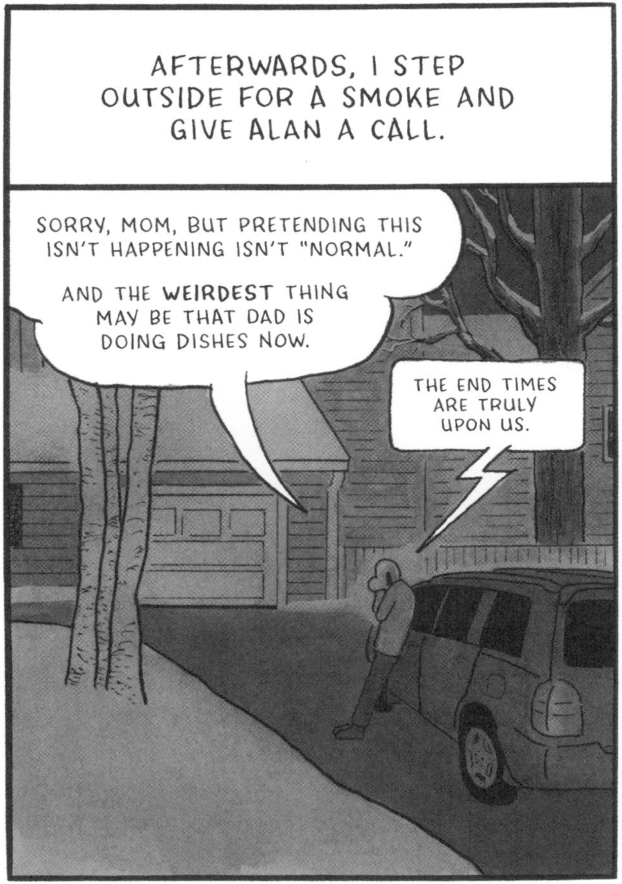
AFTERWARDS, I STEP OUTSIDE FOR A SMOKE AND GIVE ALAN A CALL.
SORRY, MOM, BUT PRETENDING THIS ISN'T HAPPENING ISN'T "NORMAL."
AND THE **WEIRDEST** THING MAY BE THAT DAD IS DOING DISHES NOW.
THE END TIMES ARE TRULY UPON US.

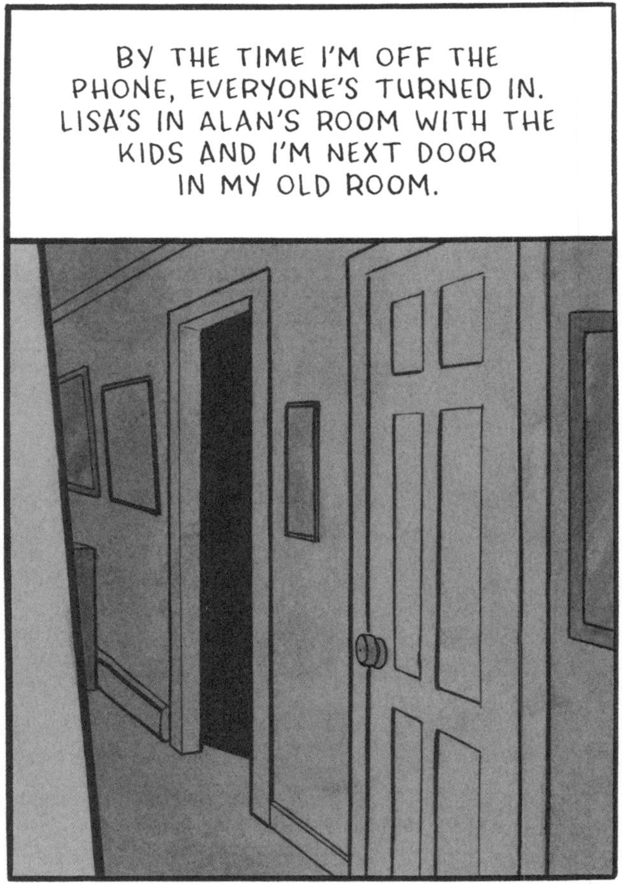
BY THE TIME I'M OFF THE PHONE, EVERYONE'S TURNED IN. LISA'S IN ALAN'S ROOM WITH THE KIDS AND I'M NEXT DOOR IN MY OLD ROOM.

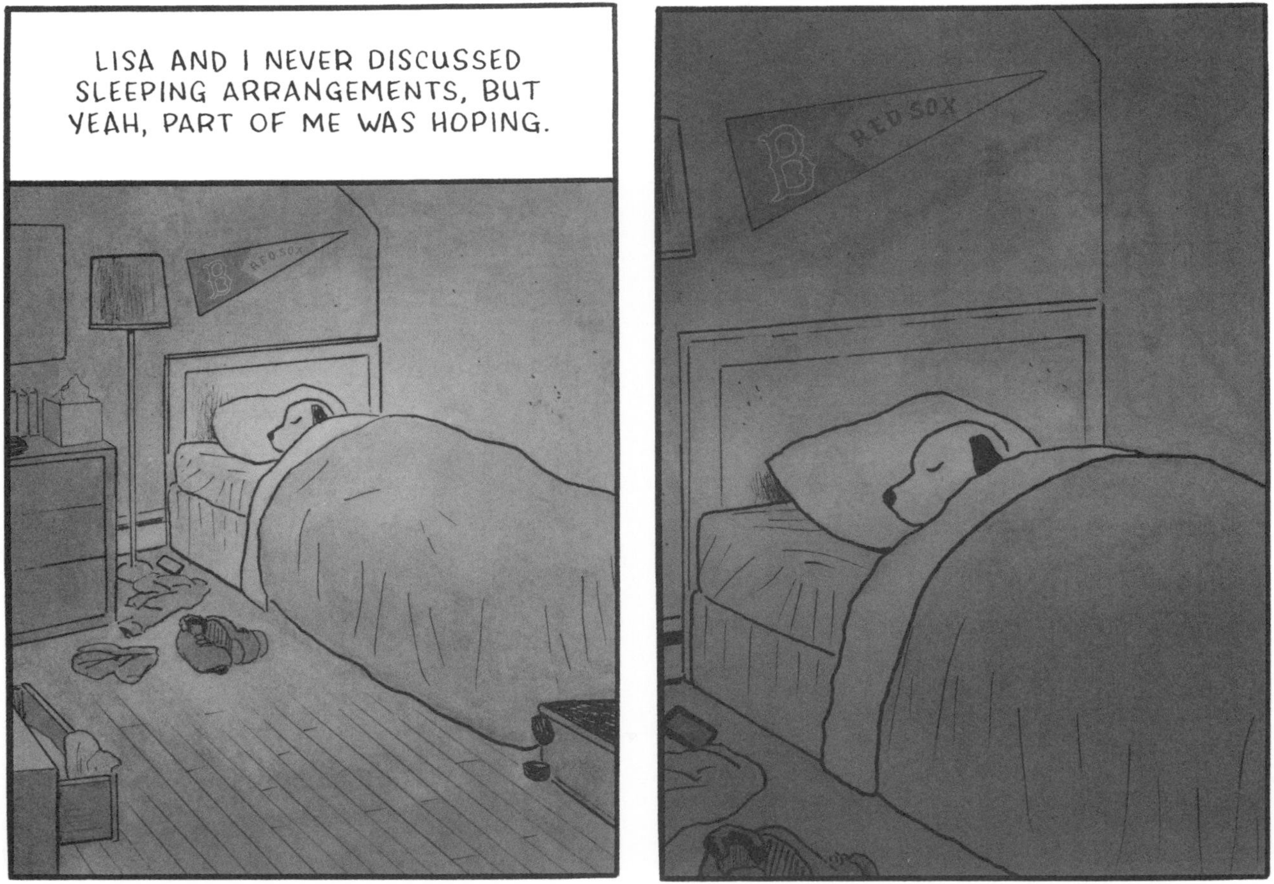
LISA AND I NEVER DISCUSSED SLEEPING ARRANGEMENTS, BUT YEAH, PART OF ME WAS HOPING.
RED SOX

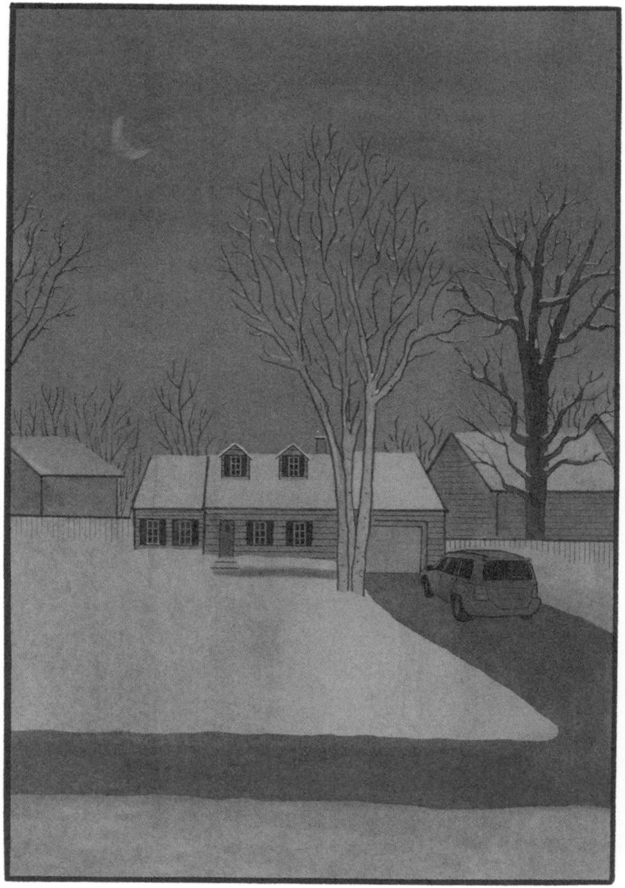

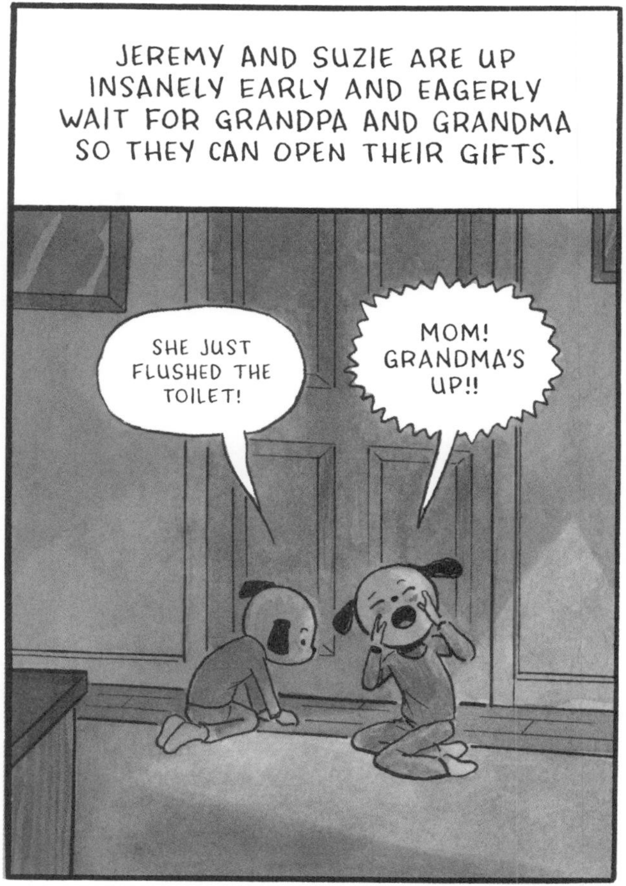
JEREMY AND SUZIE ARE UP INSANELY EARLY AND EAGERLY WAIT FOR GRANDPA AND GRANDMA SO THEY CAN OPEN THEIR GIFTS.
MOM! GRANDMA'S UP!!
SHE JUST FLUSHED THE TOILET!

DISAPPOINTMENT MINGLES WITH EXCITEMENT AS THE MOST ANTICIPATED MORNING OF THE KIDS' YEAR SPEEDS BY.

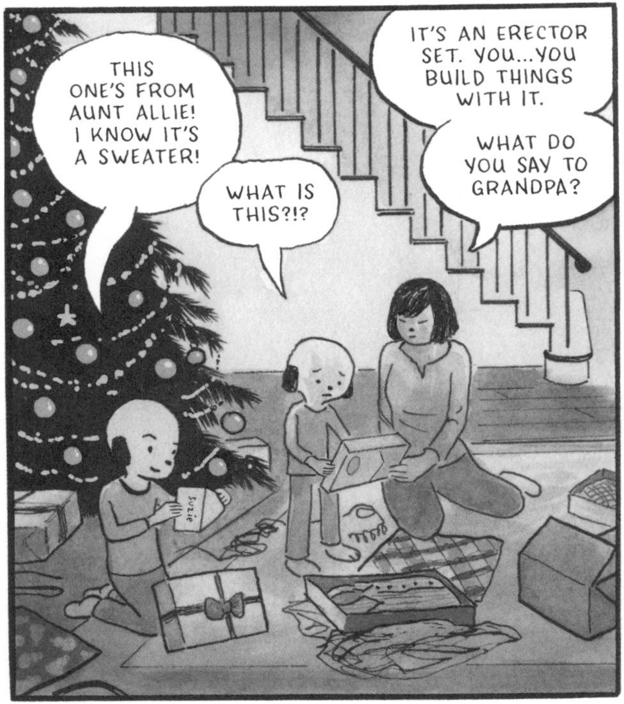

THIS ONE'S FROM AUNT ALLIE! I KNOW IT'S A SWEATER!
WHAT IS THIS?!?
IT'S AN ERECTOR SET. YOU...YOU BUILD THINGS WITH IT.
WHAT DO YOU SAY TO GRANDPA?

NEXT, THE ADULTS EXCHANGE GIFTS. WHEN WE WERE A COUPLE, LISA WAS ALWAYS THE GIFT BUYER AND FOR THIS TRIP SHE RESUMED THAT ROLE.

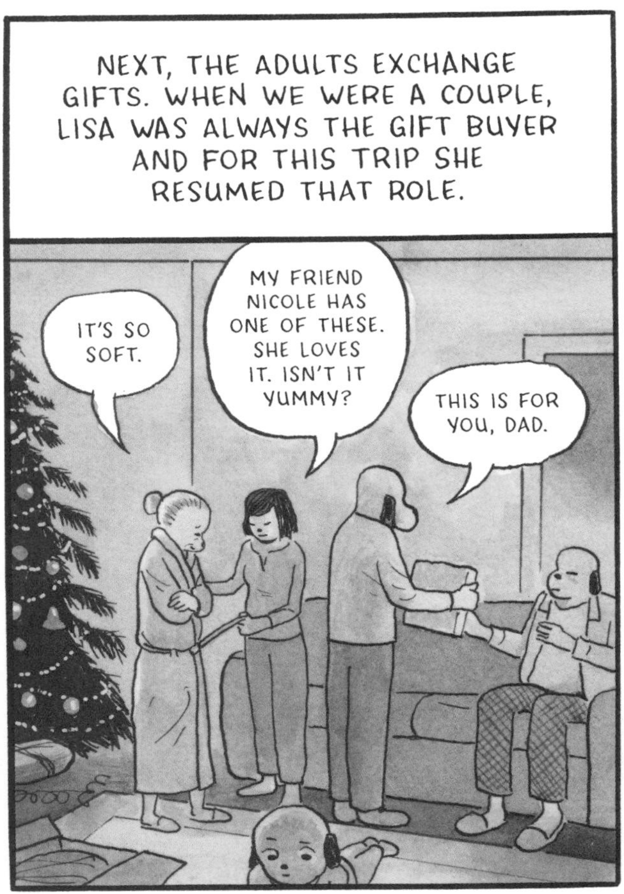

IT'S SO SOFT.
MY FRIEND NICOLE HAS ONE OF THESE. SHE LOVES IT. ISN'T IT YUMMY?
THIS IS FOR YOU, DAD.

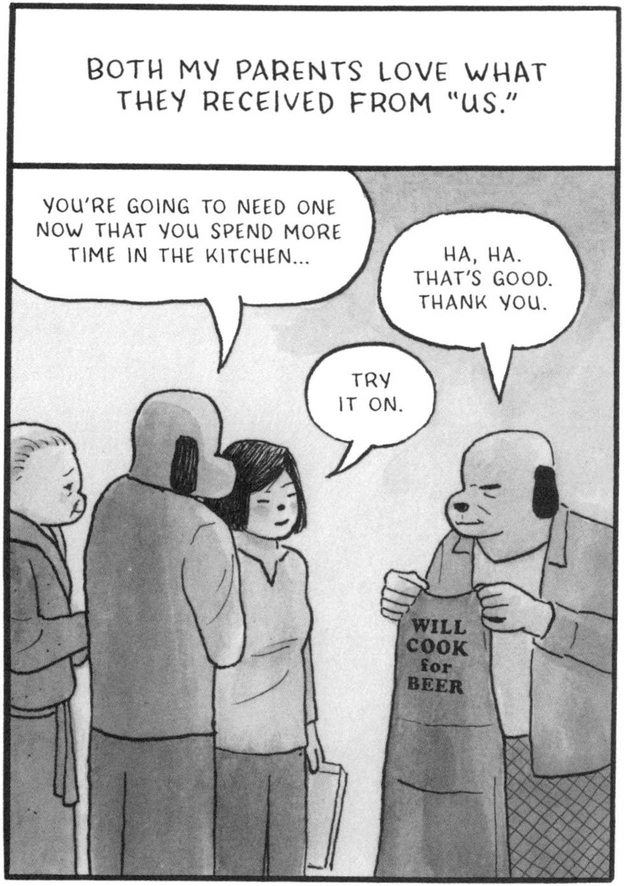
BOTH MY PARENTS LOVE WHAT THEY RECEIVED FROM "US."
YOU'RE GOING TO NEED ONE NOW THAT YOU SPEND MORE TIME IN THE KITCHEN...
TRY IT ON.
HA, HA. THAT'S GOOD. THANK YOU.
WILL COOK for BEER

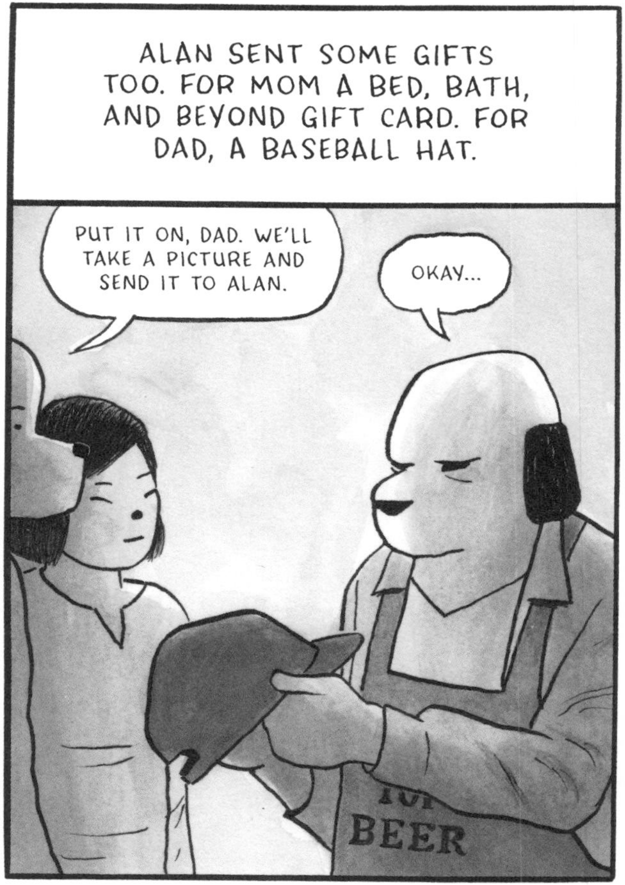
ALAN SENT SOME GIFTS TOO. FOR MOM A BED, BATH, AND BEYOND GIFT CARD. FOR DAD, A BASEBALL HAT.
PUT IT ON, DAD. WE'LL TAKE A PICTURE AND SEND IT TO ALAN.
OKAY...
BEER

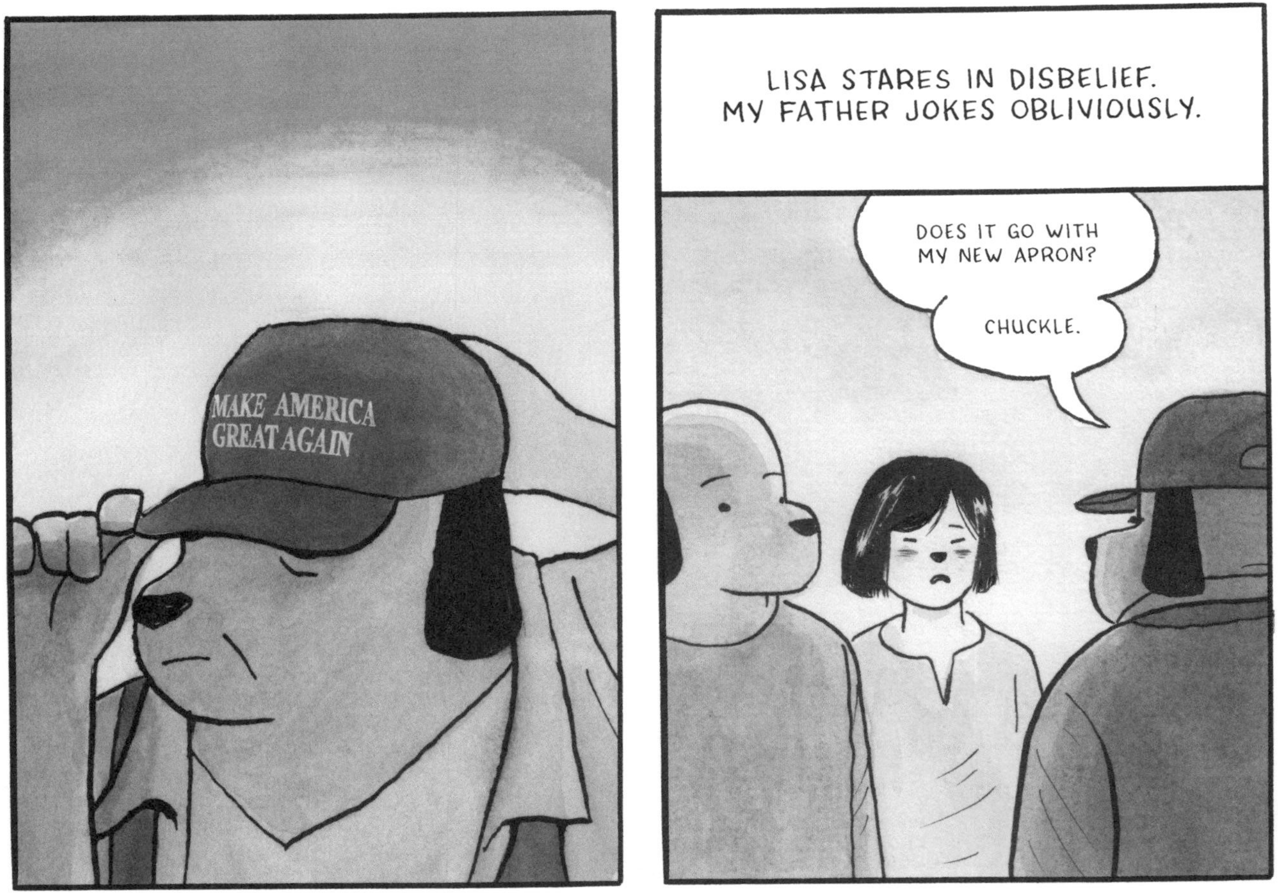
MAKE AMERICA GREAT AGAIN
LISA STARES IN DISBELIEF. MY FATHER JOKES OBLIVIOUSLY.
DOES IT GO WITH MY NEW APRON?
CHUCKLE.

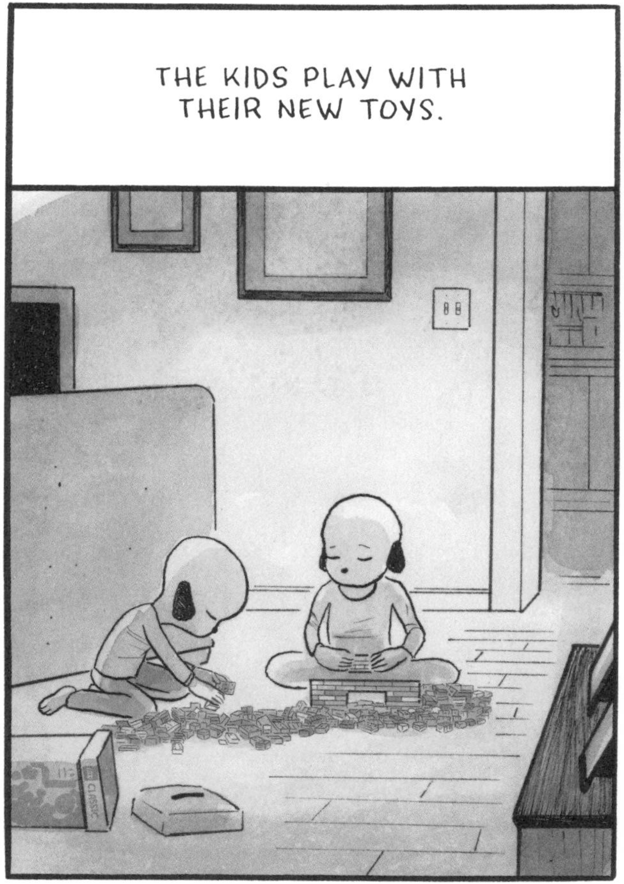
THE KIDS PLAY WITH THEIR NEW TOYS.

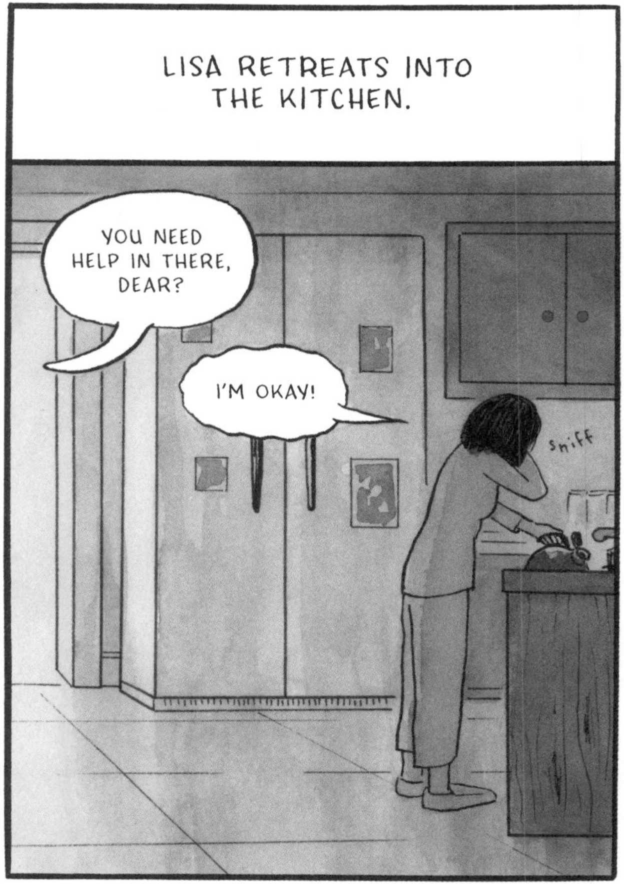
LISA RETREATS INTO THE KITCHEN.
YOU NEED HELP IN THERE, DEAR?
I'M OKAY!
sniff

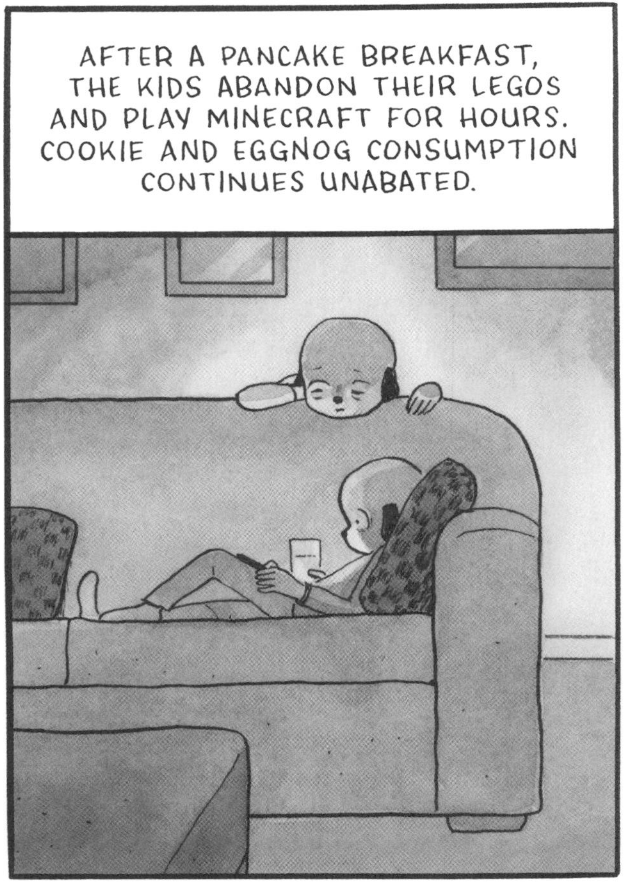
AFTER A PANCAKE BREAKFAST, THE KIDS ABANDON THEIR LEGOS AND PLAY MINECRAFT FOR HOURS. COOKIE AND EGGNOG CONSUMPTION CONTINUES UNABATED.

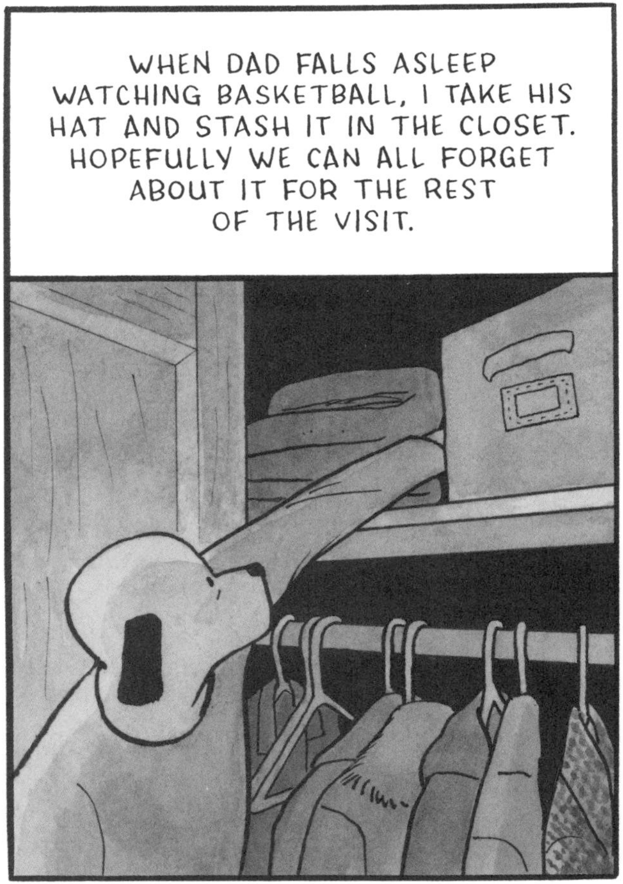
WHEN DAD FALLS ASLEEP WATCHING BASKETBALL, I TAKE HIS HAT AND STASH IT IN THE CLOSET. HOPEFULLY WE CAN ALL FORGET ABOUT IT FOR THE REST OF THE VISIT.

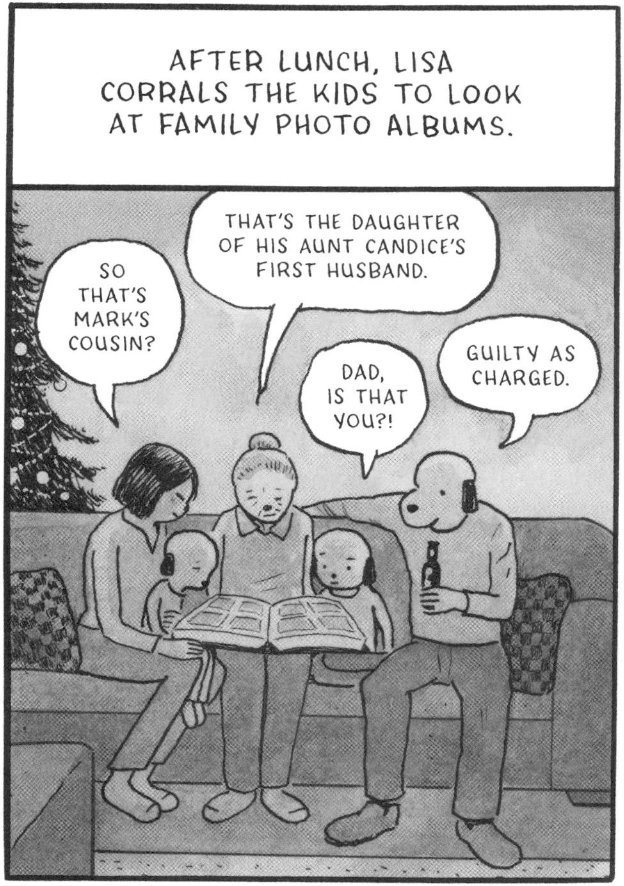
AFTER LUNCH, LISA CORRALS THE KIDS TO LOOK AT FAMILY PHOTO ALBUMS.
SO THAT'S MARK'S COUSIN?
THAT'S THE DAUGHTER OF HIS AUNT CANDICE'S FIRST HUSBAND.
DAD, IS THAT YOU?!
GUILTY AS CHARGED.

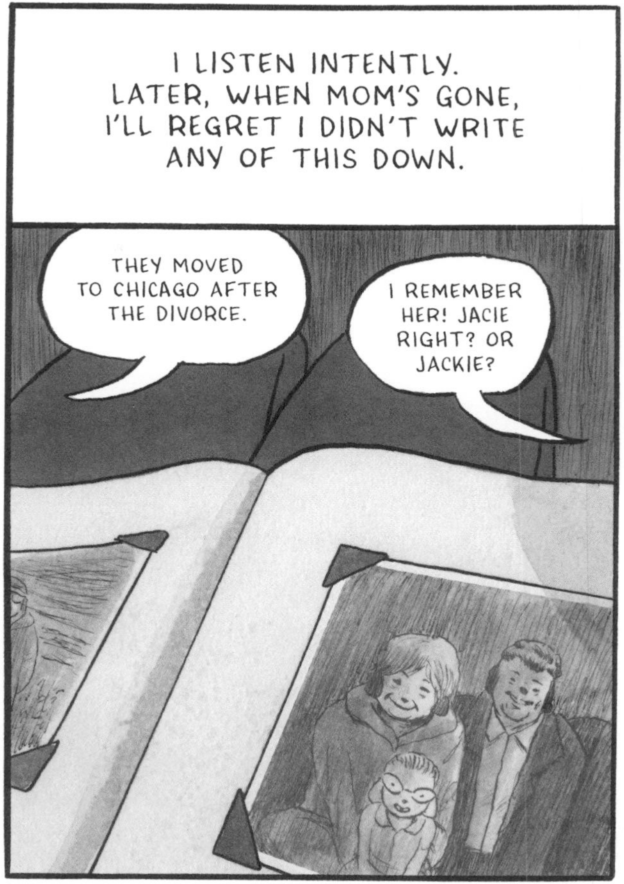
I LISTEN INTENTLY. LATER, WHEN MOM'S GONE, I'LL REGRET I DIDN'T WRITE ANY OF THIS DOWN.
THEY MOVED TO CHICAGO AFTER THE DIVORCE.
I REMEMBER HER! JACIE RIGHT? OR JACKIE?

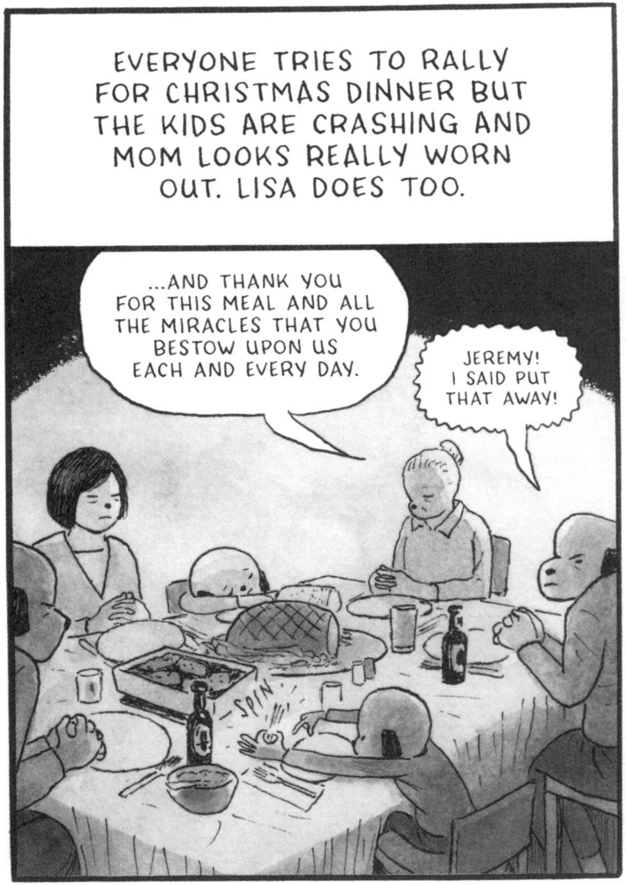
EVERYONE TRIES TO RALLY FOR CHRISTMAS DINNER BUT THE KIDS ARE CRASHING AND MOM LOOKS REALLY WORN OUT. LISA DOES TOO.
...AND THANK YOU FOR THIS MEAL AND ALL THE MIRACLES THAT YOU BESTOW UPON US EACH AND EVERY DAY.
JEREMY! I SAID PUT THAT AWAY!
SPIN

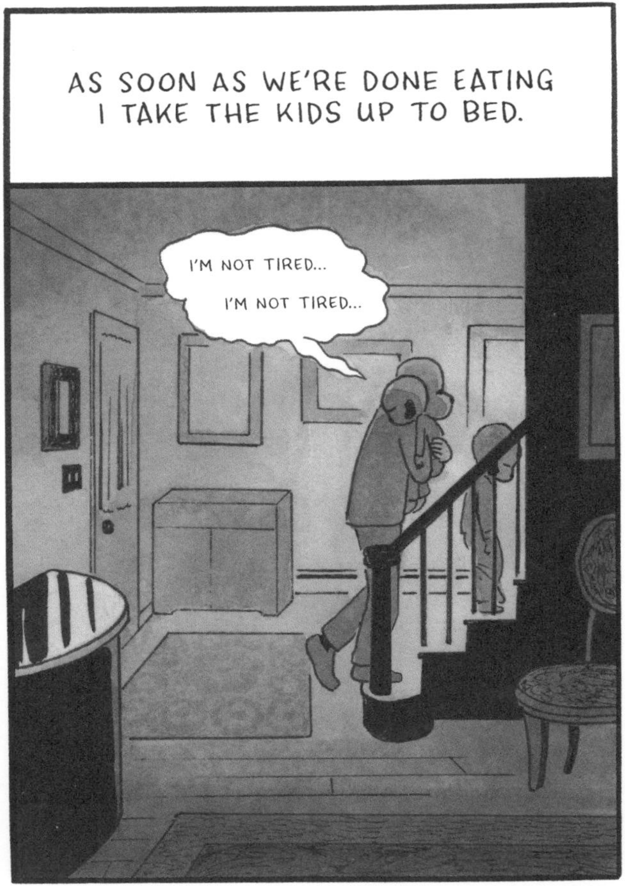
AS SOON AS WE'RE DONE EATING I TAKE THE KIDS UP TO BED.
I'M NOT TIRED...
I'M NOT TIRED...

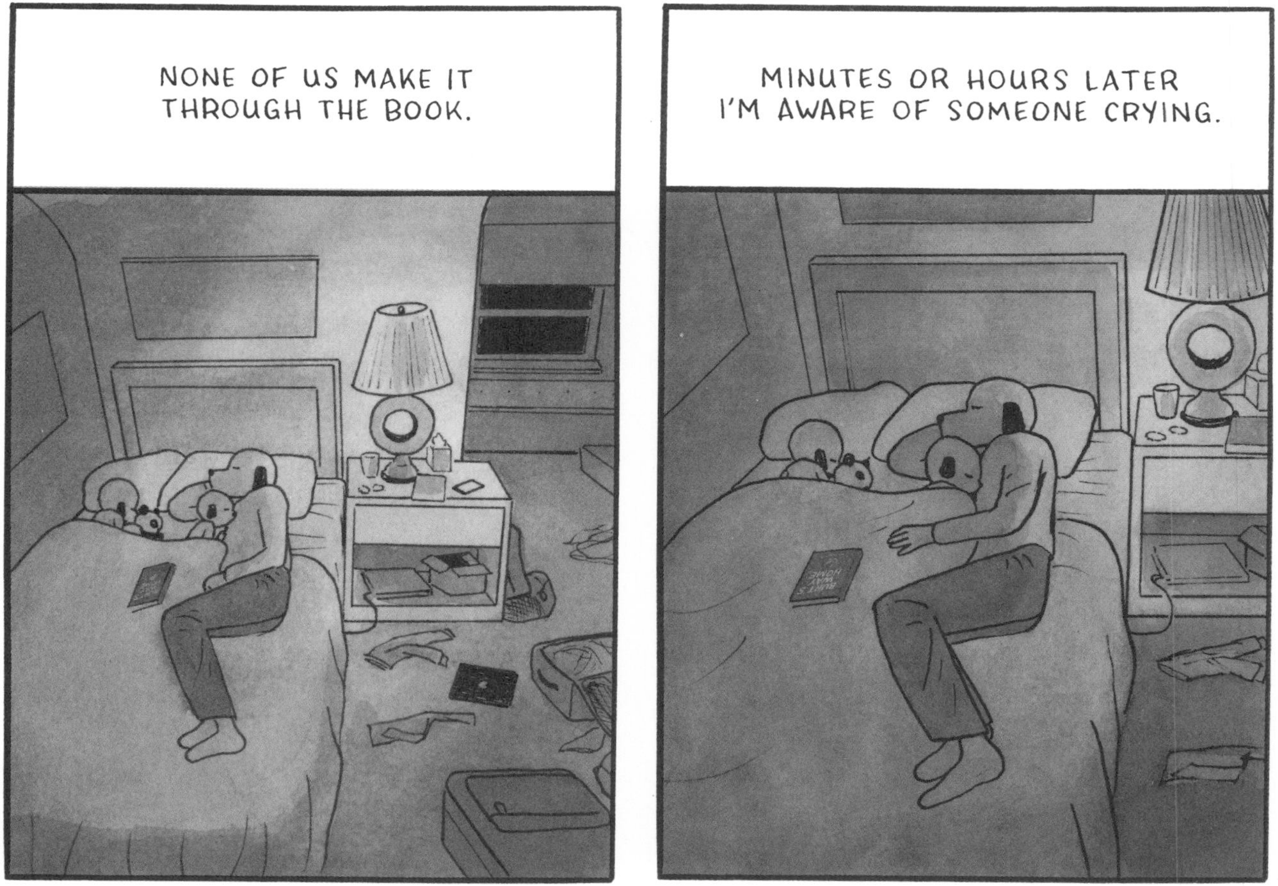
NONE OF US MAKE IT THROUGH THE BOOK.
MINUTES OR HOURS LATER I'M AWARE OF SOMEONE CRYING.

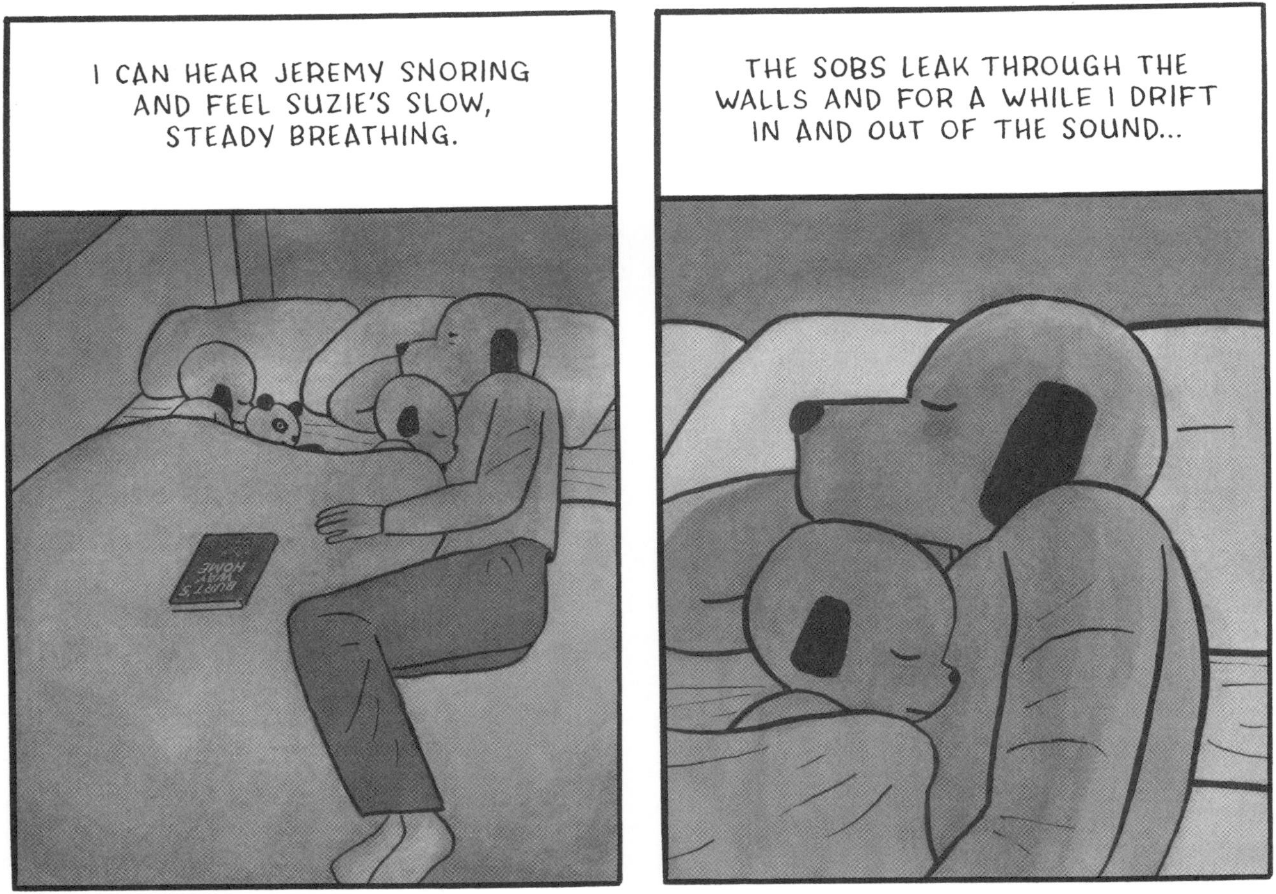
I CAN HEAR JEREMY SNORING AND FEEL SUZIE'S SLOW, STEADY BREATHING.
BURT'S WAY HOME
THE SOBS LEAK THROUGH THE WALLS AND FOR A WHILE I DRIFT IN AND OUT OF THE SOUND...

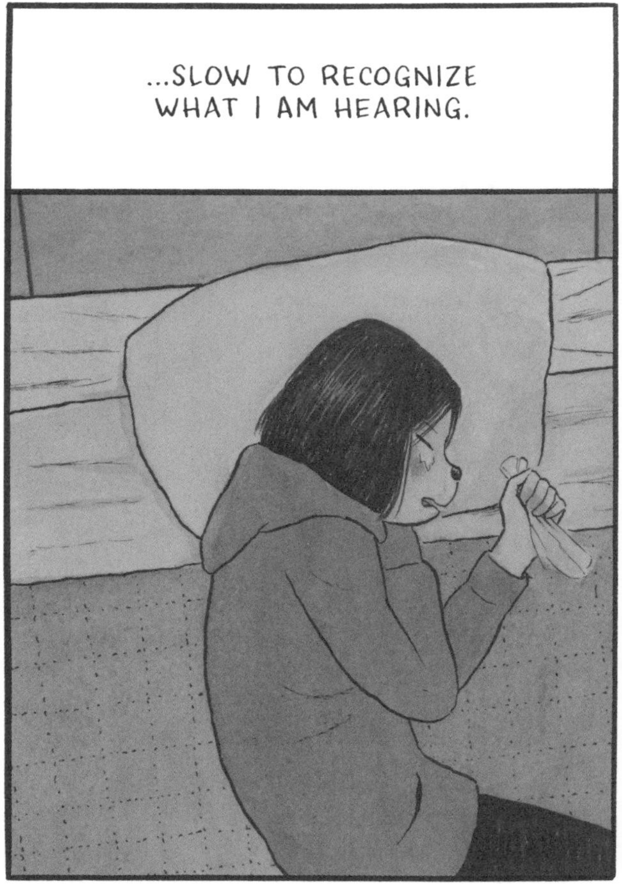
...SLOW TO RECOGNIZE WHAT I AM HEARING.

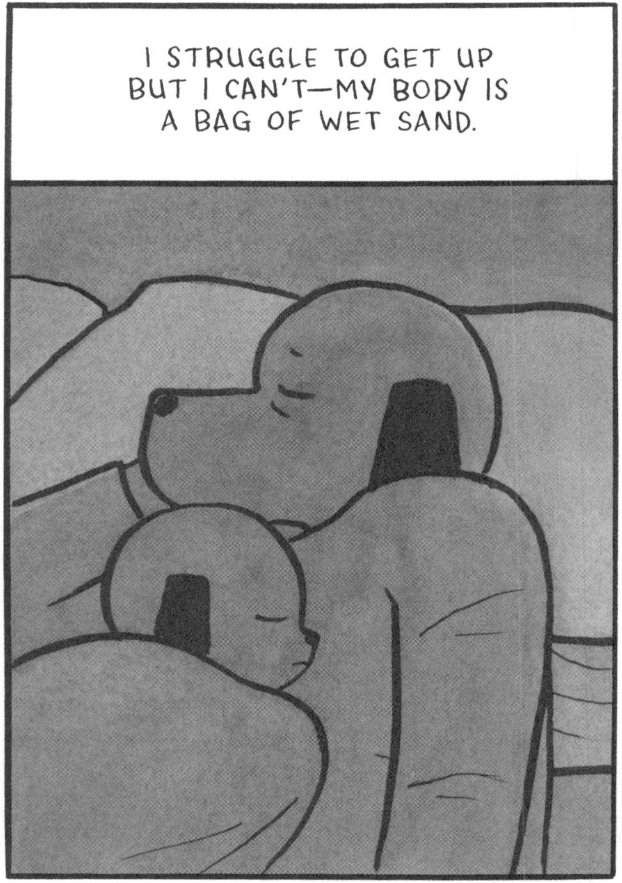
I STRUGGLE TO GET UP BUT I CAN'T—MY BODY IS A BAG OF WET SAND.

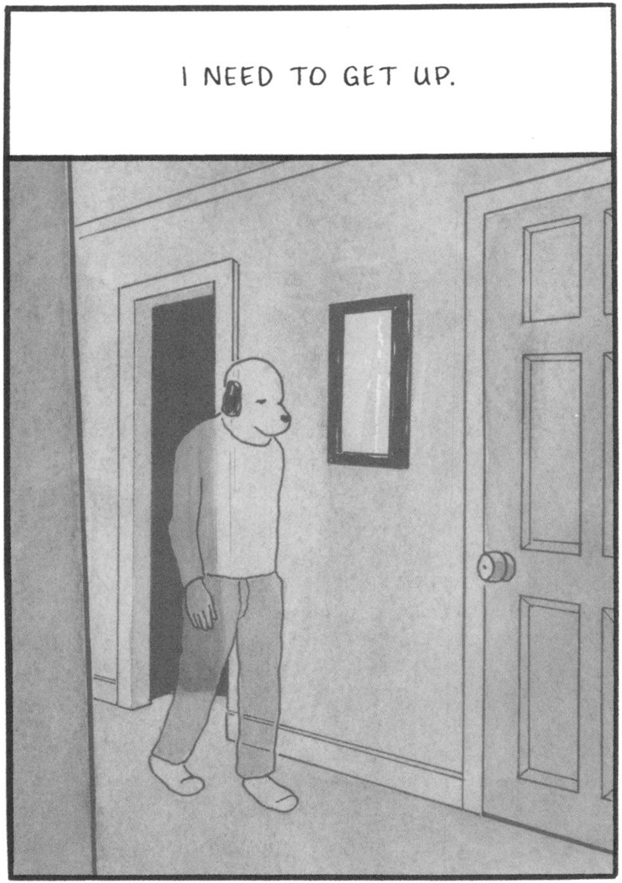
I NEED TO GET UP.

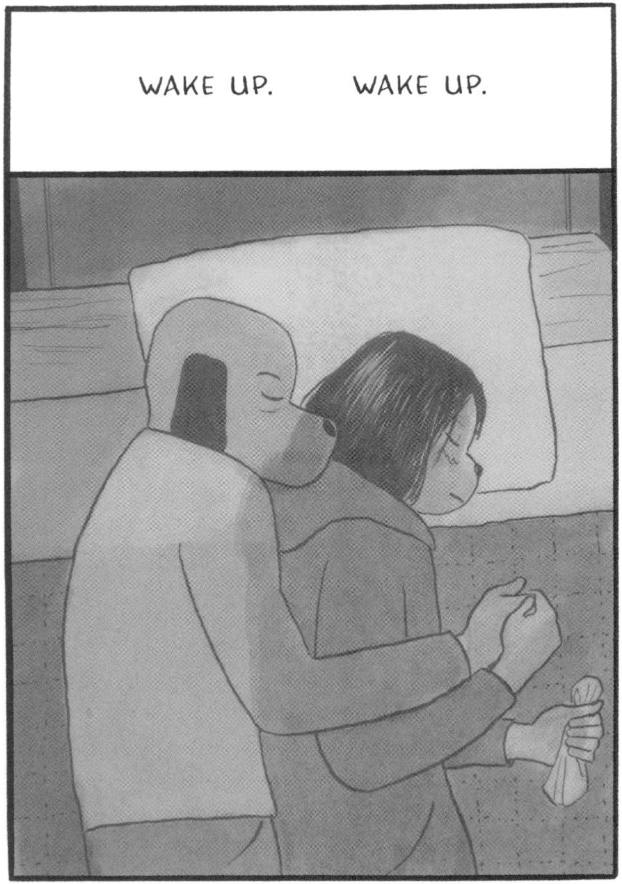
WAKE UP.
WAKE UP.

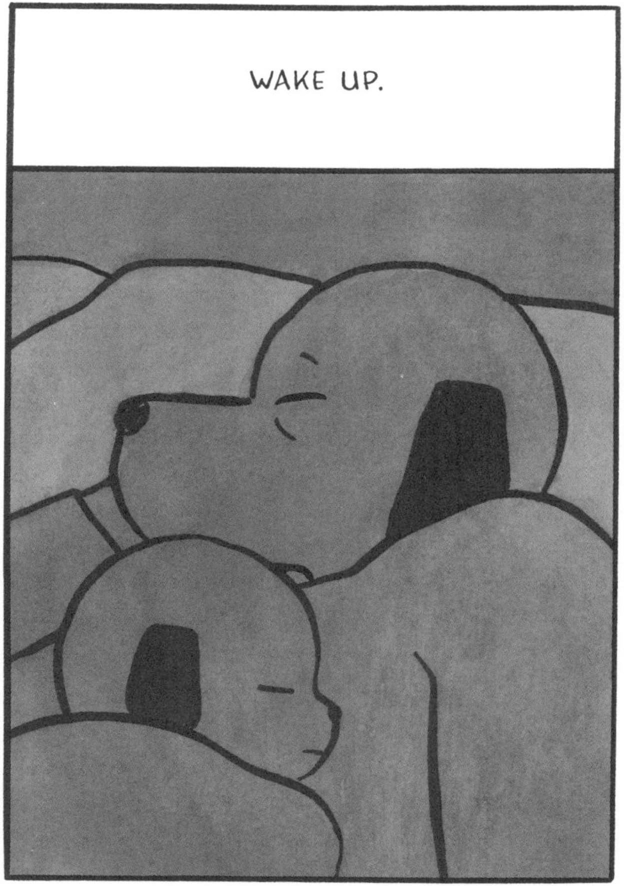
WAKE UP.

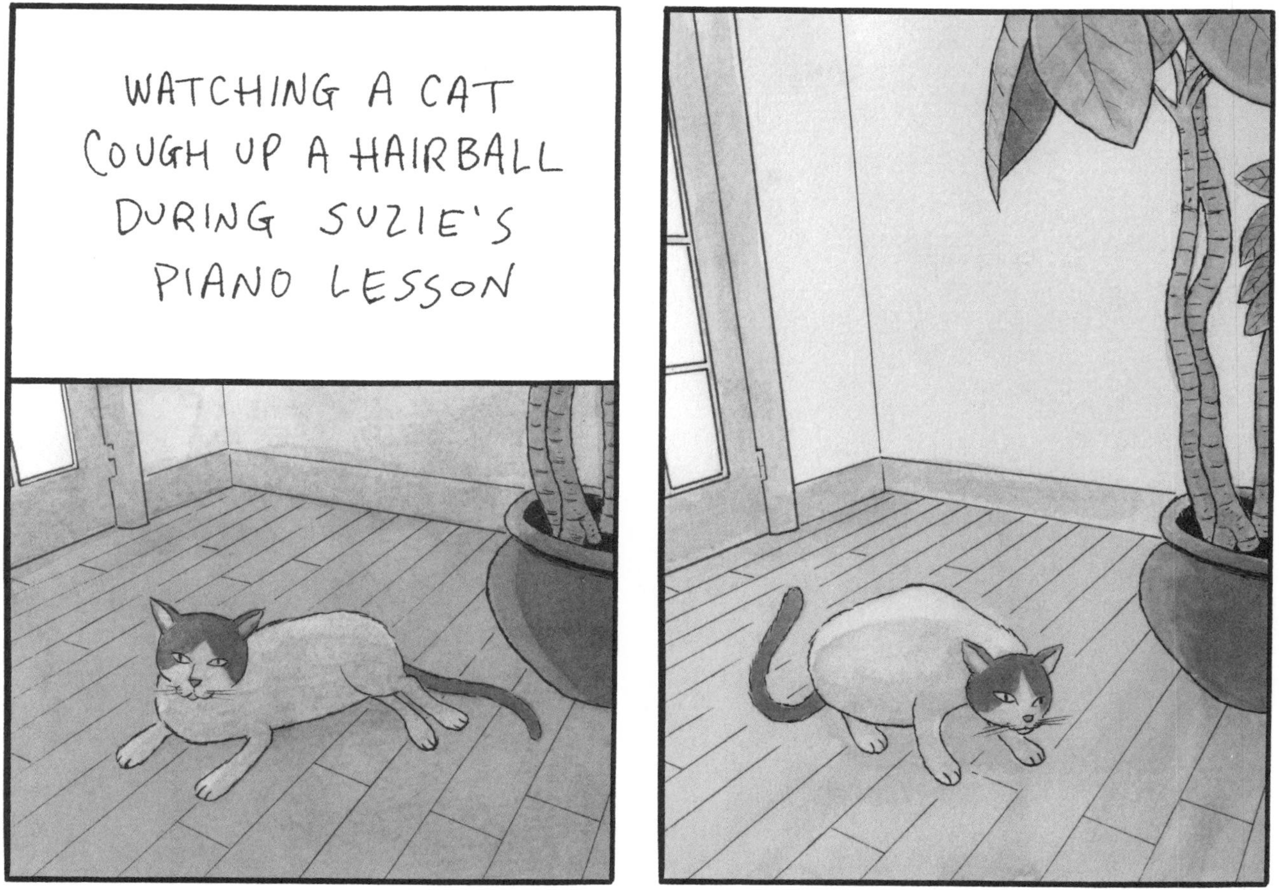
WATCHING A CAT COUGH UP A HAIRBALL DURING SUZIE'S PIANO LESSON

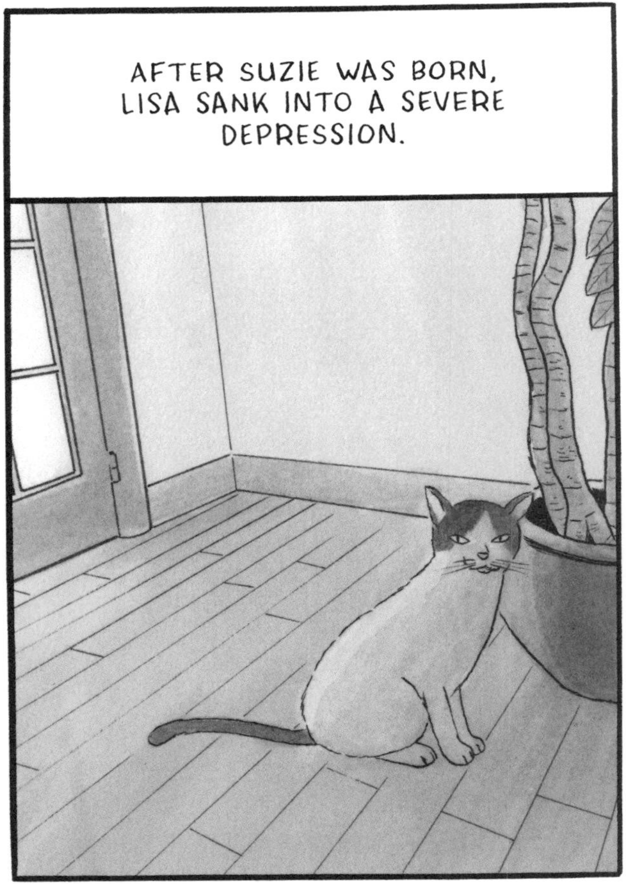
AFTER SUZIE WAS BORN, LISA SANK INTO A SEVERE DEPRESSION.

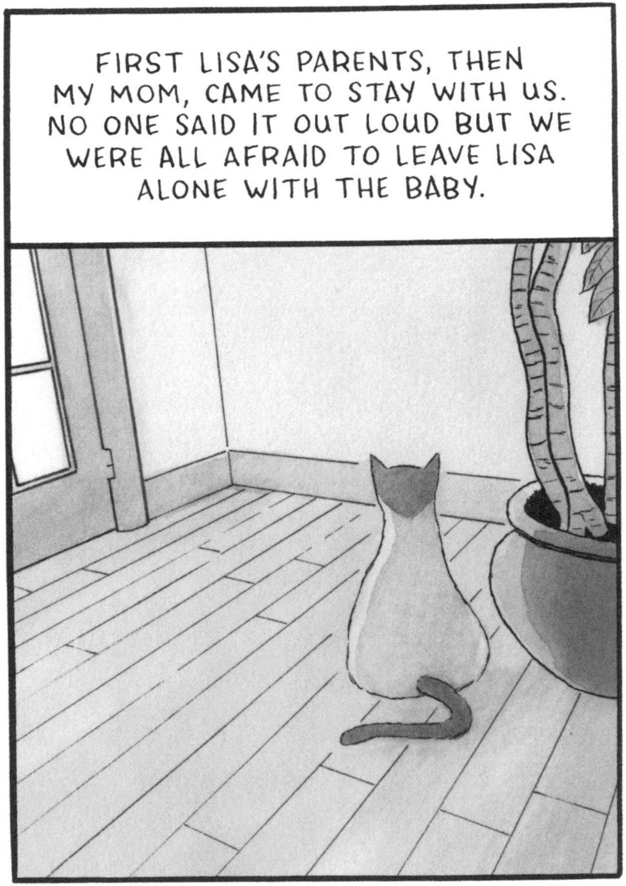
FIRST LISA'S PARENTS, THEN MY MOM, CAME TO STAY WITH US. NO ONE SAID IT OUT LOUD BUT WE WERE ALL AFRAID TO LEAVE LISA ALONE WITH THE BABY.

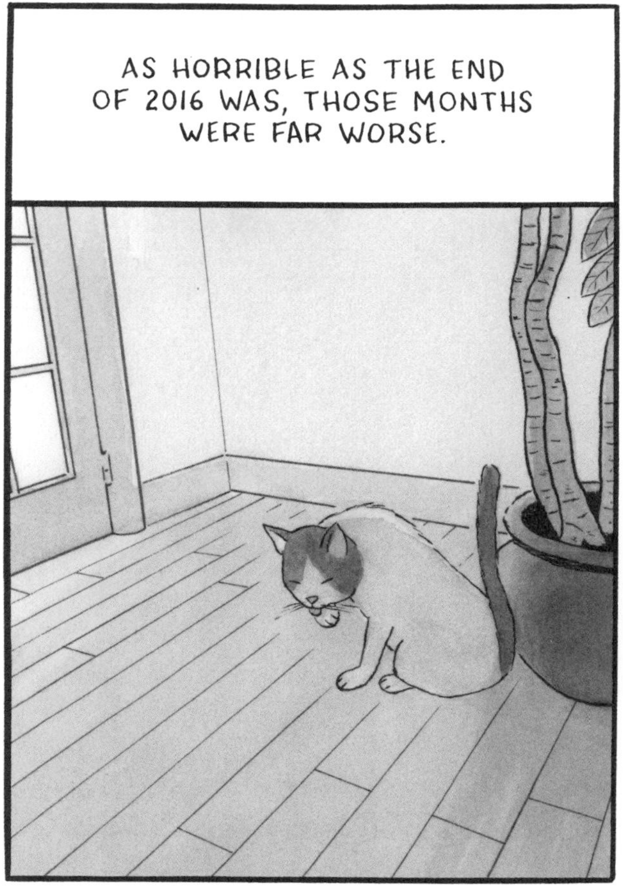
AS HORRIBLE AS THE END OF 2016 WAS, THOSE MONTHS WERE FAR WORSE.

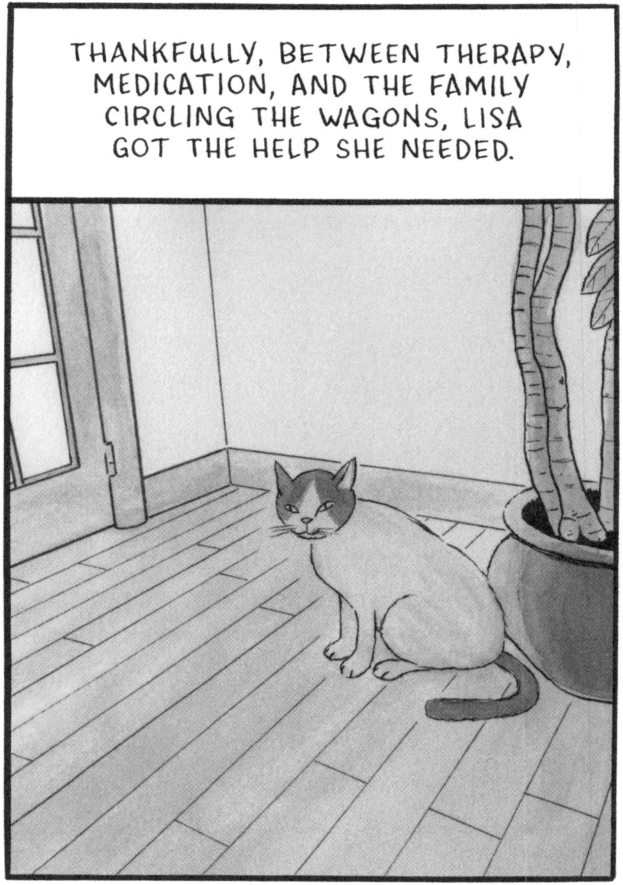
THANKFULLY, BETWEEN THERAPY, MEDICATION, AND THE FAMILY CIRCLING THE WAGONS, LISA GOT THE HELP SHE NEEDED.

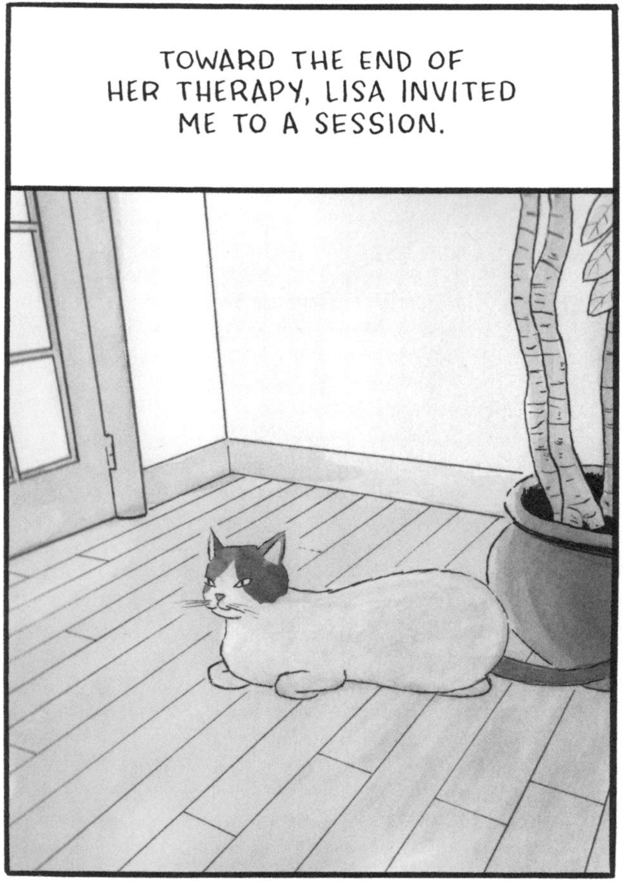
TOWARD THE END OF HER THERAPY, LISA INVITED ME TO A SESSION.

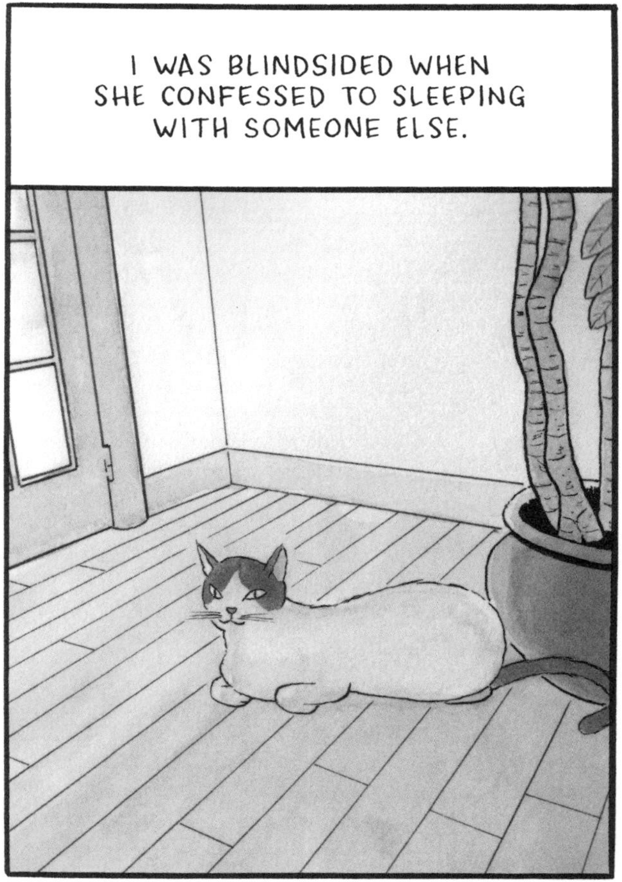
I WAS BLINDSIDED WHEN SHE CONFESSED TO SLEEPING WITH SOMEONE ELSE.

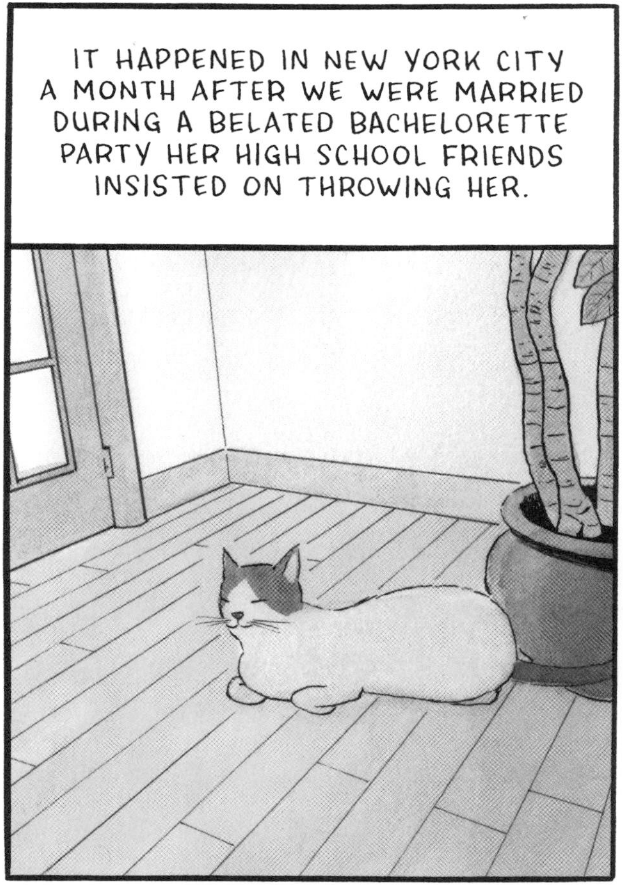
IT HAPPENED IN NEW YORK CITY A MONTH AFTER WE WERE MARRIED DURING A BELATED BACHELORETTE PARTY HER HIGH SCHOOL FRIENDS INSISTED ON THROWING HER.

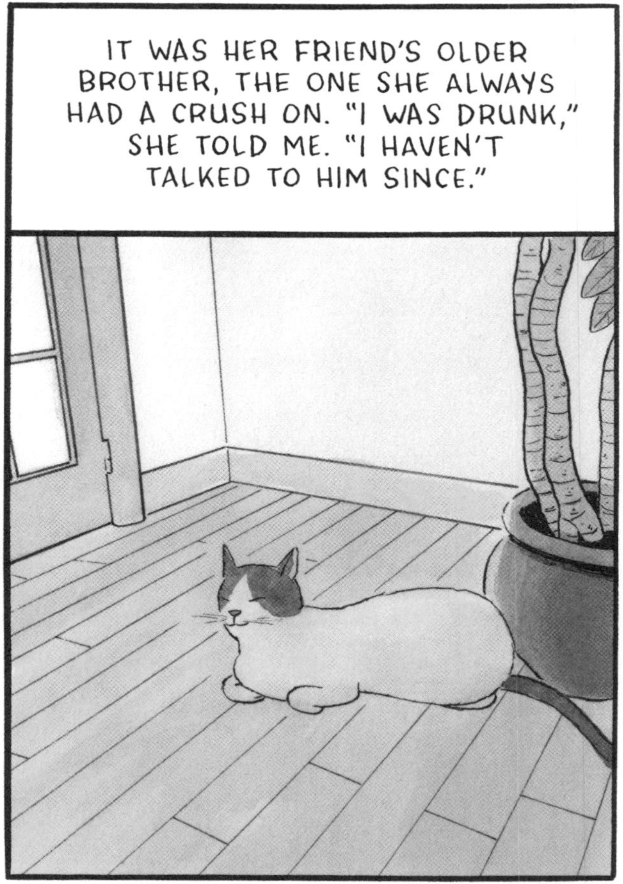
IT WAS HER FRIEND'S OLDER BROTHER, THE ONE SHE ALWAYS HAD A CRUSH ON. "I WAS DRUNK," SHE TOLD ME. "I HAVEN'T TALKED TO HIM SINCE."

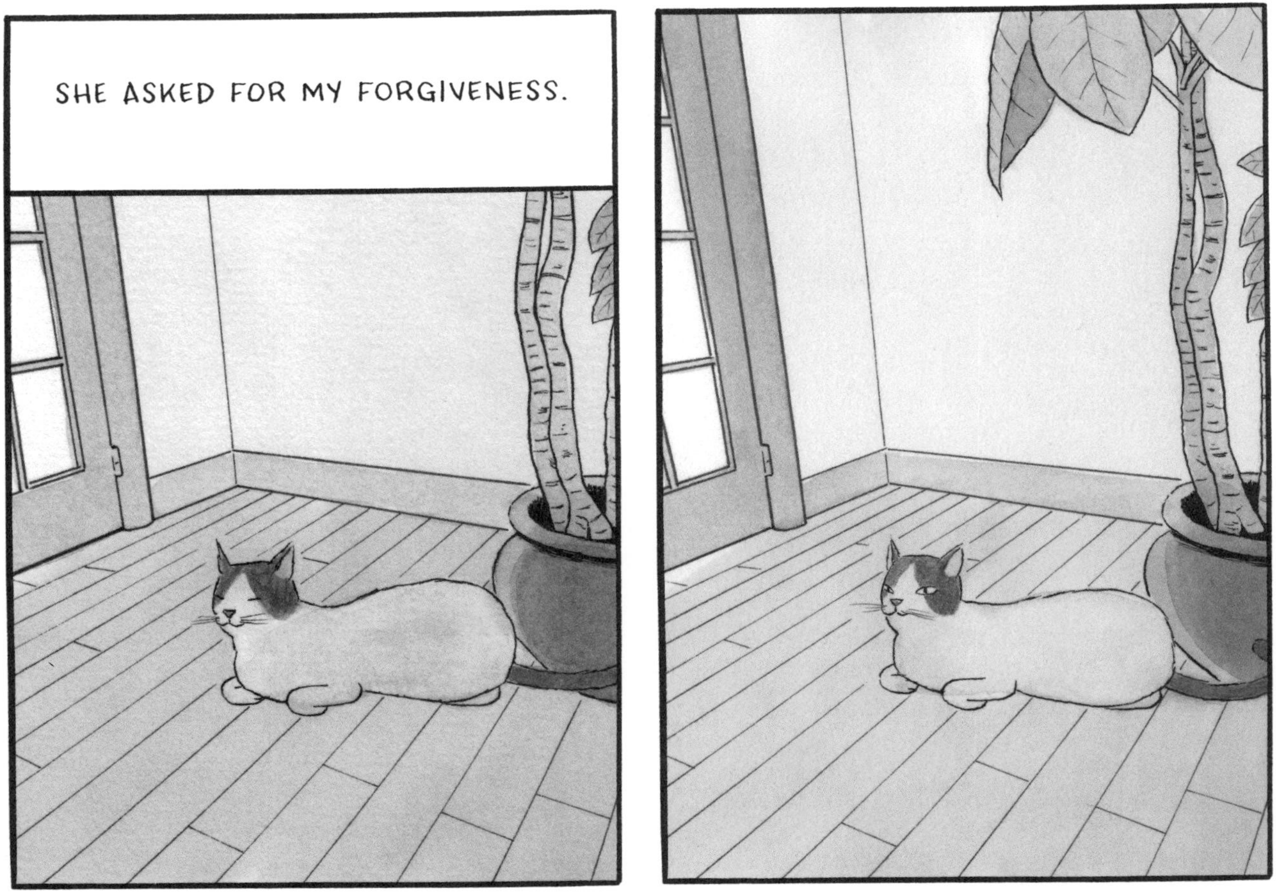
SHE ASKED FOR MY FORGIVENESS.

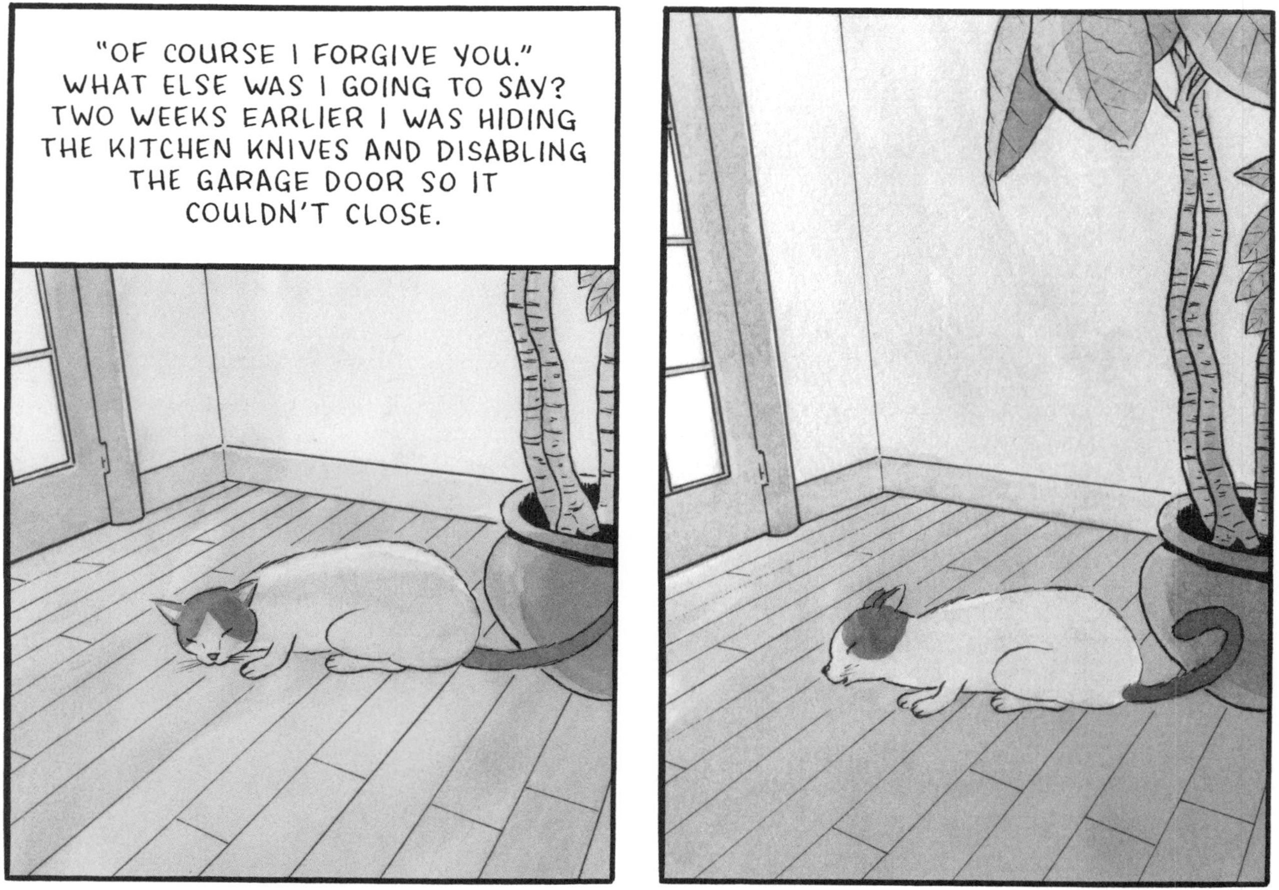
"OF COURSE I FORGIVE YOU." WHAT ELSE WAS I GOING TO SAY? TWO WEEKS EARLIER I WAS HIDING THE KITCHEN KNIVES AND DISABLING THE GARAGE DOOR SO IT COULDN'T CLOSE.

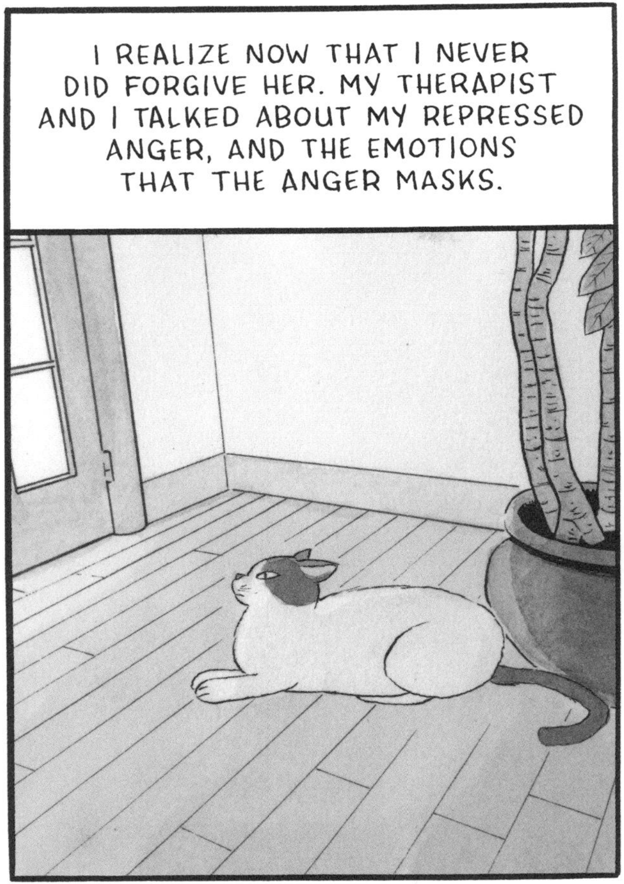
I REALIZE NOW THAT I NEVER DID FORGIVE HER. MY THERAPIST AND I TALKED ABOUT MY REPRESSED ANGER, AND THE EMOTIONS THAT THE ANGER MASKS.

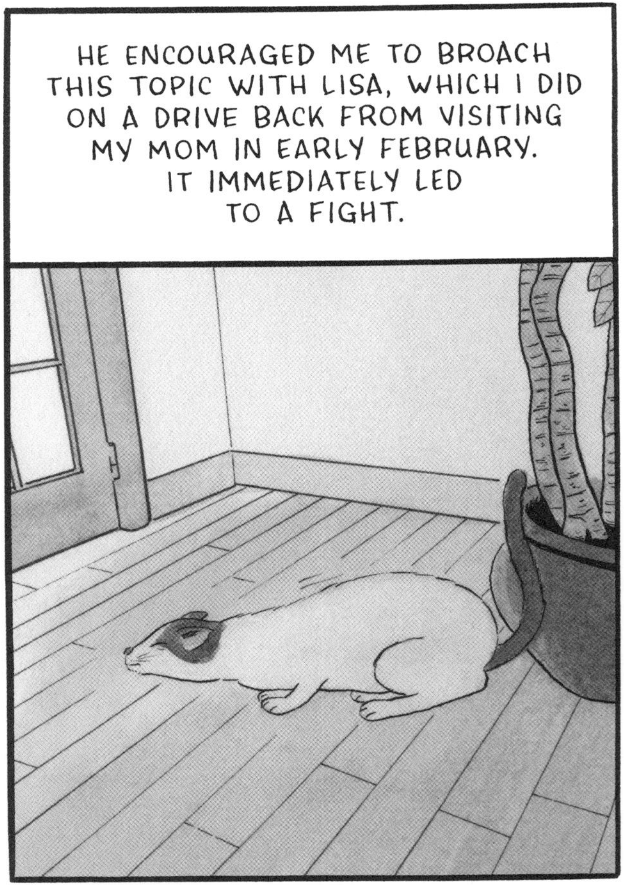
HE ENCOURAGED ME TO BROACH THIS TOPIC WITH LISA, WHICH I DID ON A DRIVE BACK FROM VISITING MY MOM IN EARLY FEBRUARY. IT IMMEDIATELY LED TO A FIGHT.

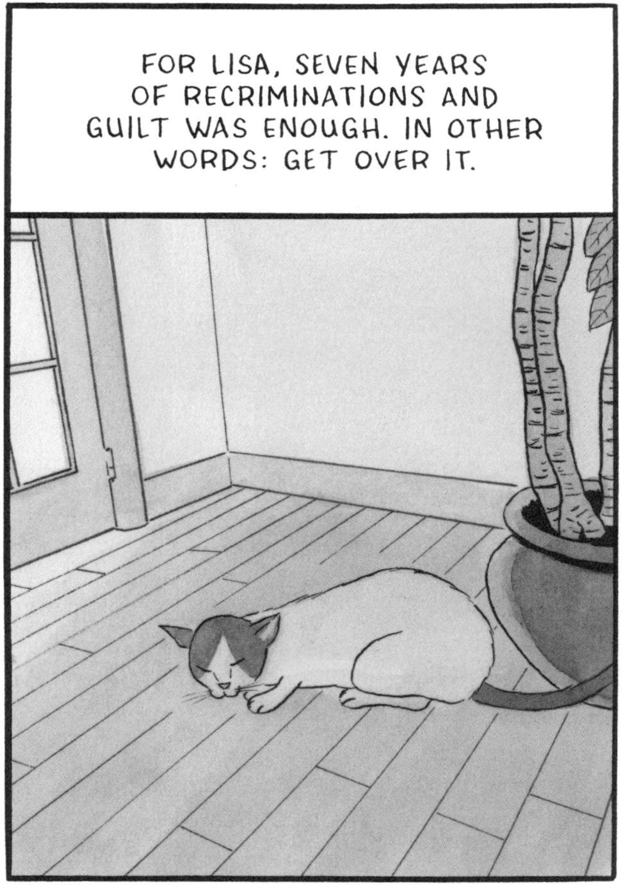
FOR LISA, SEVEN YEARS OF RECRIMINATIONS AND GUILT WAS ENOUGH. IN OTHER WORDS: GET OVER IT.

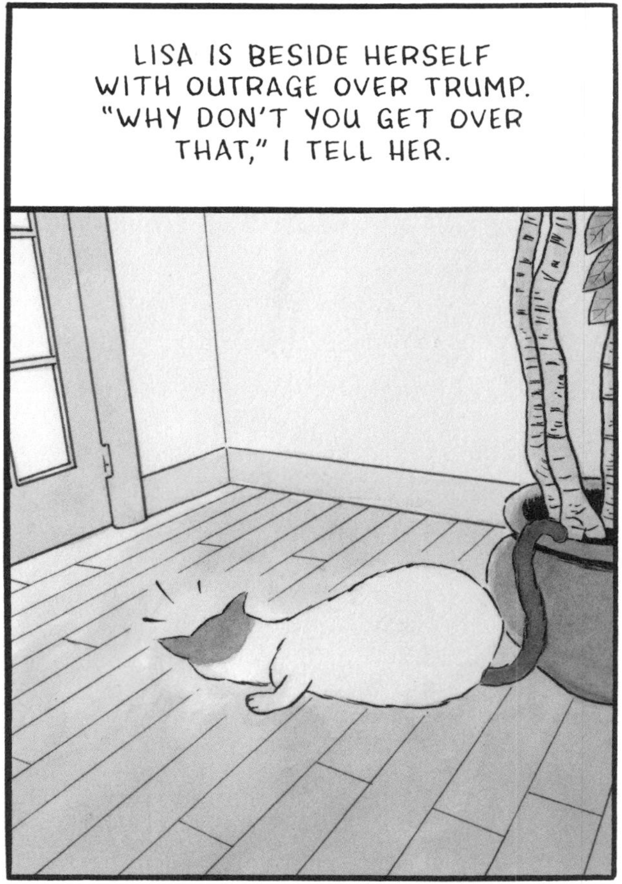
LISA IS BESIDE HERSELF WITH OUTRAGE OVER TRUMP. "WHY DON'T YOU GET OVER THAT," I TELL HER.

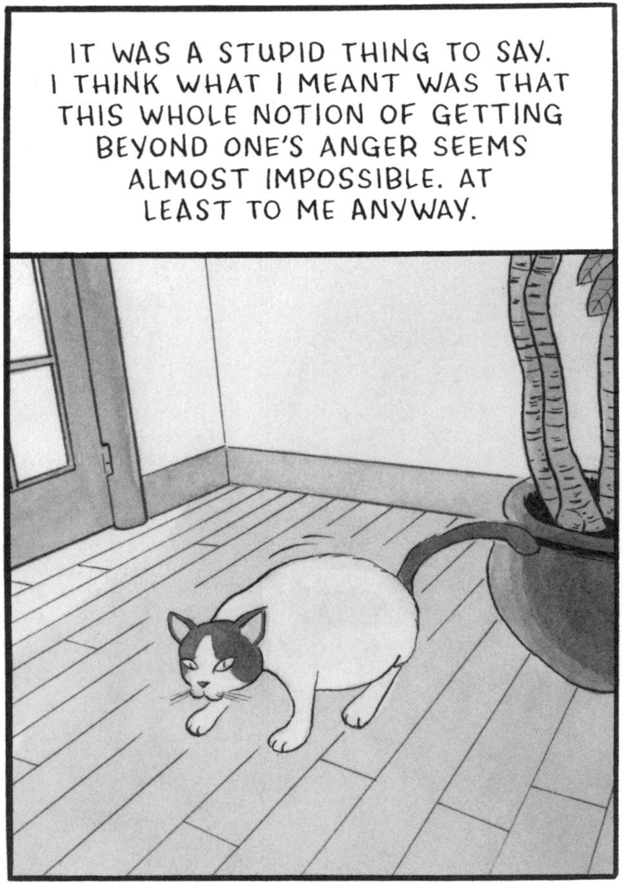
IT WAS A STUPID THING TO SAY. I THINK WHAT I MEANT WAS THAT THIS WHOLE NOTION OF GETTING BEYOND ONE'S ANGER SEEMS ALMOST IMPOSSIBLE. AT LEAST TO ME ANYWAY.

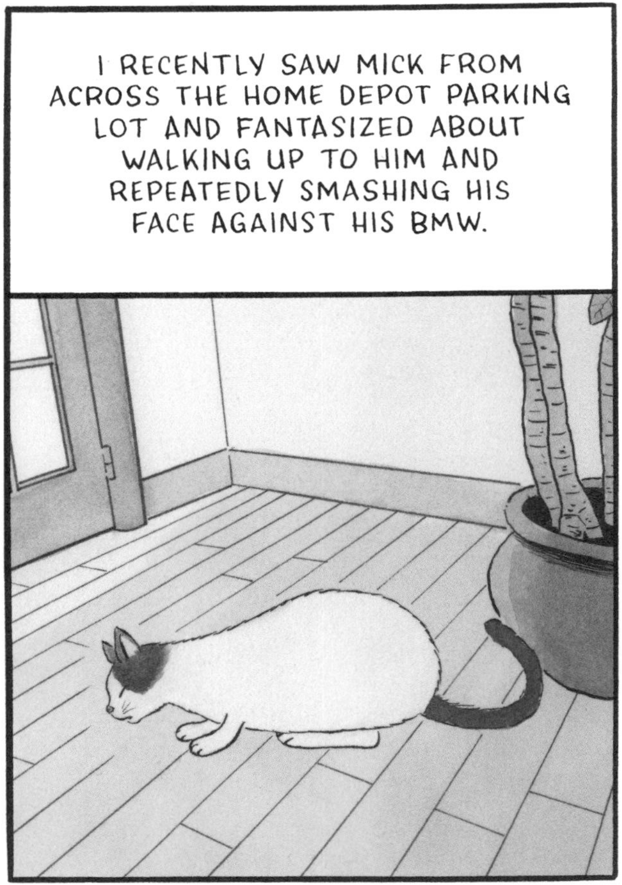
I RECENTLY SAW MICK FROM ACROSS THE HOME DEPOT PARKING LOT AND FANTASIZED ABOUT WALKING UP TO HIM AND REPEATEDLY SMASHING HIS FACE AGAINST HIS BMW.

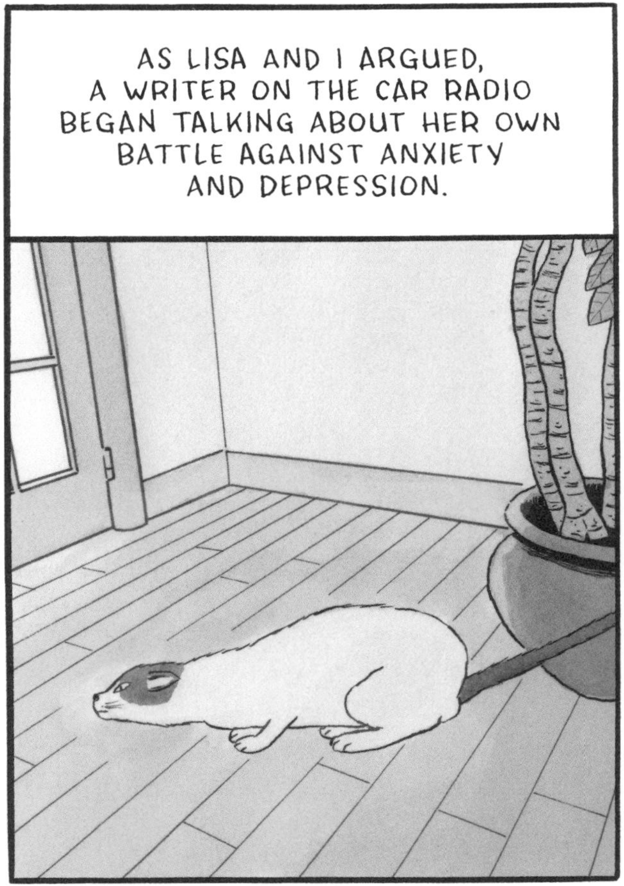
AS LISA AND I ARGUED, A WRITER ON THE CAR RADIO BEGAN TALKING ABOUT HER OWN BATTLE AGAINST ANXIETY AND DEPRESSION.

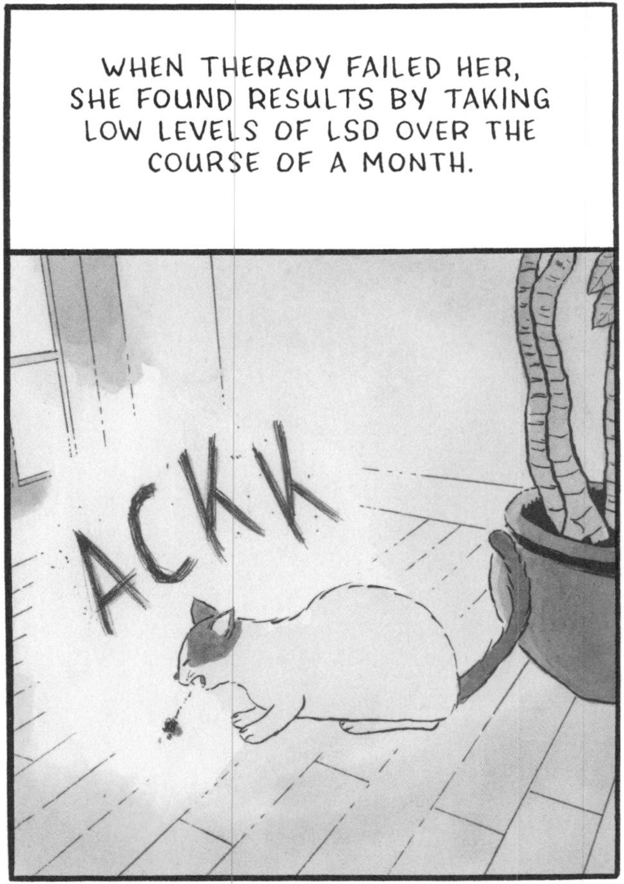
WHEN THERAPY FAILED HER, SHE FOUND RESULTS BY TAKING LOW LEVELS OF LSD OVER THE COURSE OF A MONTH.
ACKK

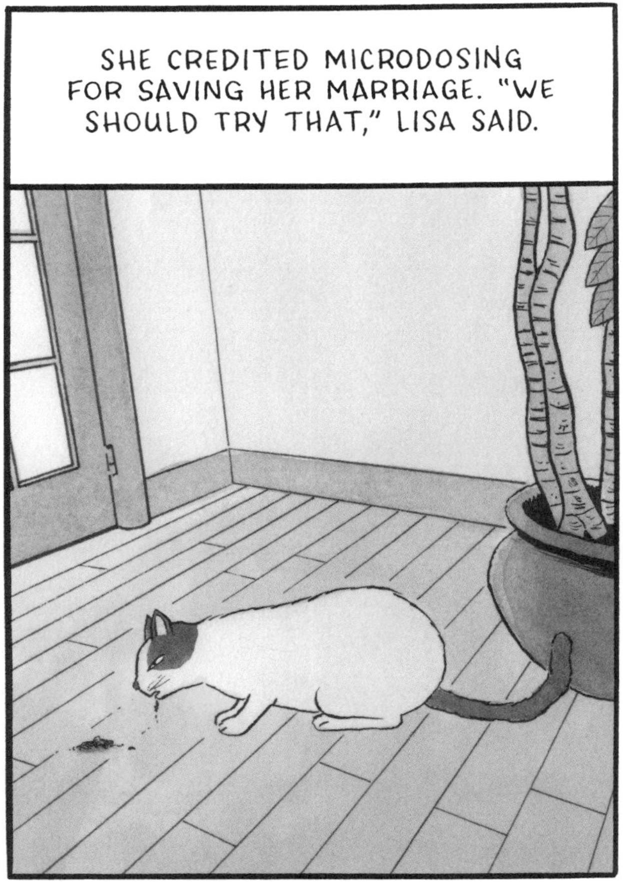
SHE CREDITED MICRODOSING FOR SAVING HER MARRIAGE. "WE SHOULD TRY THAT," LISA SAID.

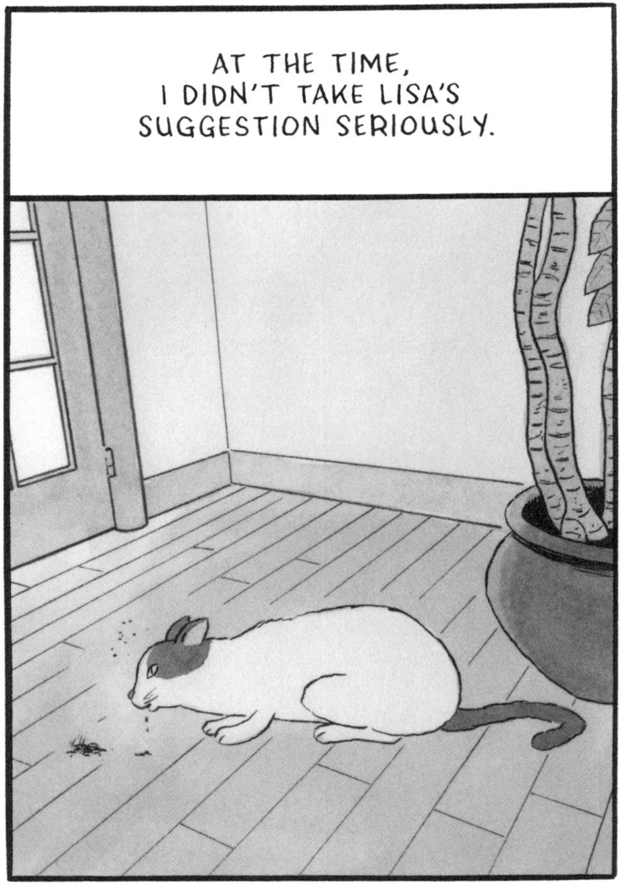
AT THE TIME, I DIDN'T TAKE LISA'S SUGGESTION SERIOUSLY.

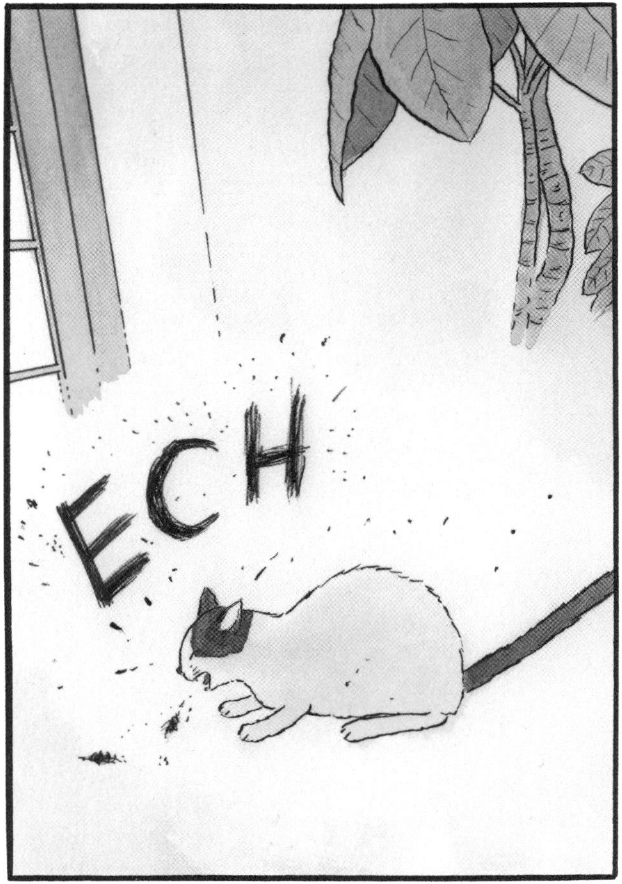
ECH

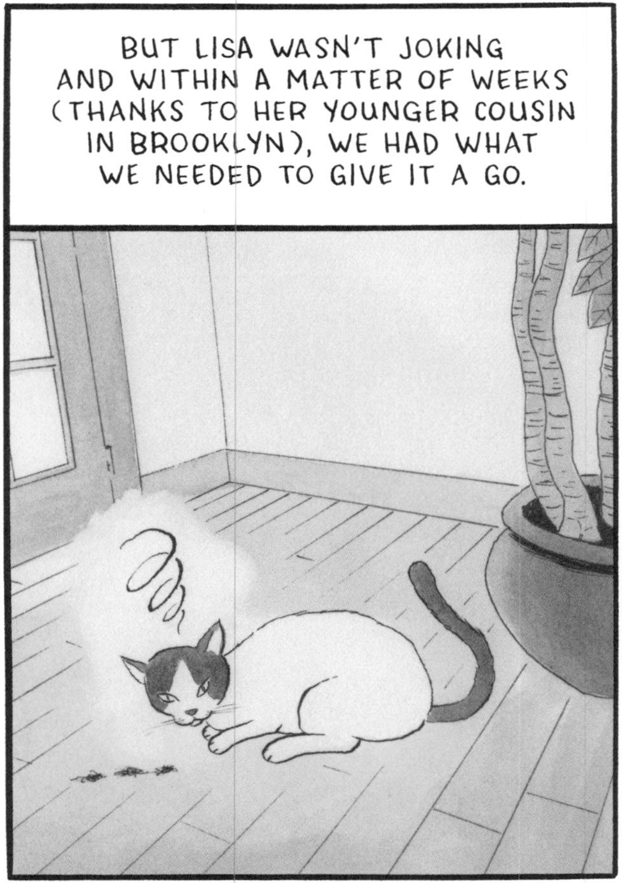
BUT LISA WASN'T JOKING AND WITHIN A MATTER OF WEEKS (THANKS TO HER YOUNGER COUSIN IN BROOKLYN), WE HAD WHAT WE NEEDED TO GIVE IT A GO.

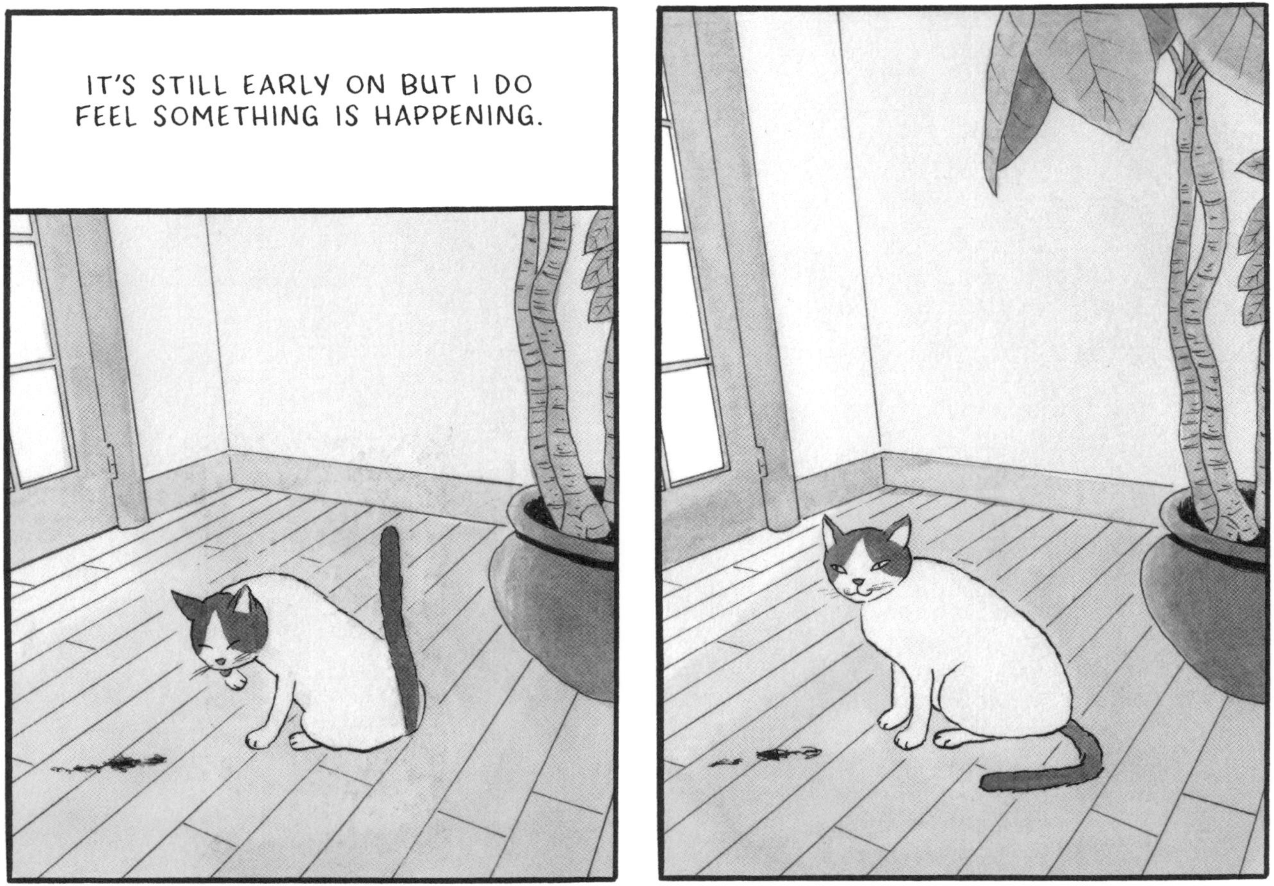
IT'S STILL EARLY ON BUT I DO FEEL SOMETHING IS HAPPENING.

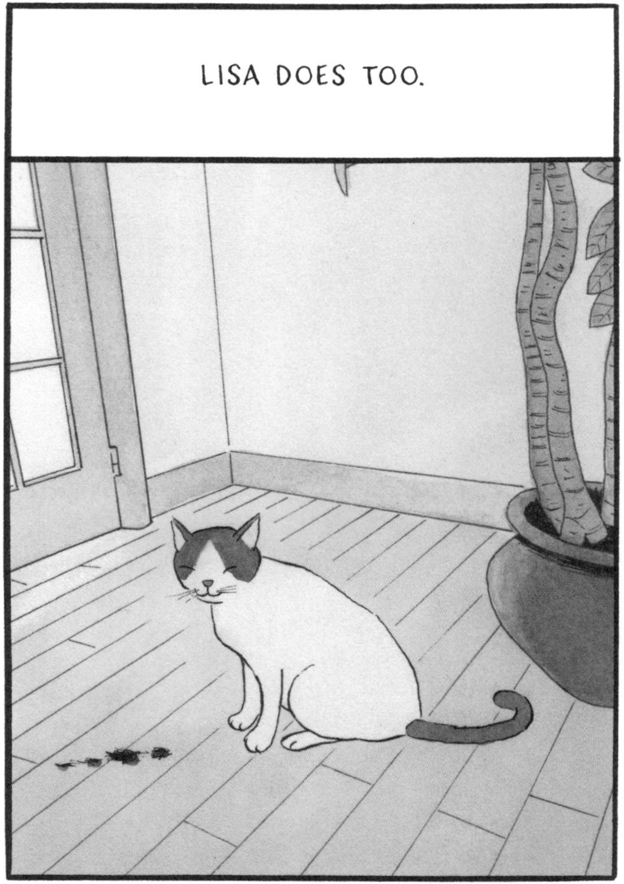
LISA DOES TOO.

Acknowledgments

During the time I worked on this book, and the year before I began it, my dear Upper Valley friends sang, cooked, and house painted me through some rough stretches. Thank you Liz, Kurt, Peter, Lucinda, Jason, Becka, Michelle, Matt, Sarah, Martin, and Julie. And thank you Jill H. for always being there. Thanks to George and Susanne for their generosity and love. Thanks Michael S. for stepping up. Thank you David Cahill and Daron Raleigh for the work you do every day. Thank you Caleb, Ricardo, and Steve for your warmth and infectious enthusiasm. Thanks to all my inspiring colleagues at The Center for Cartoon Studies. Thank you Sonny Saul for the music.

Thanks to the magical MacDowell Colony where, much to my surprise, this book took root. Thanks to the Vermont Studio Center where *Off Season* continued to grow.

I couldn't ask for a better publisher than D&Q or a better editor than Tracy Hurren. Your early enthusiasm for the book meant a lot. Special shout out to *Slate*'s Dan Kois whose early editorial input was invaluable.

Thanks to my brilliant sister, Marjorie, for her steadfast encouragement and support and helping me keep calm and carry on. Thanks you Eva and Charlotte for helping me keep things in perspective. And finally, thank you Rachel, forever and always.

drawnandquarterly.com

978-1-77046-331-8
First edition: February 2019
Printed in China
10 9 8 7 6 5 4 3 2 1

Cataloguing data fully available from Library and Archives Canada.

Published in the USA by Drawn & Quarterly, a client publisher of Farrar, Straus and Giroux. Orders: 888.330.8477. Published in Canada by Drawn & Quarterly, a client publisher of Raincoast Books. Orders: 800.663.5714. Published in the United Kingdom by Drawn & Quarterly, a client publisher of Publishers Group UK. Orders: info@pguk.co.uk

ALSO BY JAMES STURM

Graphic Novels
Market Day
The Golem's Mighty Swing
Satchel Paige: Striking Out Jim Crow
The Fantastic Four: Unstable Molecules

Children's Books
Birdsong
Adventures in Cartooning Series
Ape and Armadillo Take Over the World